Music in the Education of Children
Fourth Edition

ALSO FROM WADSWORTH . . .

A CONCISE INTRODUCTION TO SCHOOL MUSIC INSTRUCTION,
K-8, 2nd edition
by William O. Hughes

TEACHING MUSIC IN THE SECONDARY SCHOOLS, 2nd edition
by Charles Hoffer

SINGING WITH CHILDREN, 2nd edition
by Robert Nye and Vernice Nye

PERCUSSION MANUAL
by Michael Combs

PLAYING AND TEACHING THE STRINGS
by Vincent Oddo

BRASS ENSEMBLE METHODS FOR MUSIC EDUCATORS
by Jay Zorn

BASIC CONCEPTS IN MUSIC, 2nd edition
by Gary Martin

MUSICAL BEGINNINGS: FOR TEACHERS AND STUDENTS
by Gary Martin

BASIC MUSICIANSHIP FOR CLASSROOM TEACHERS:
A CREATIVE MUSICAL APPROACH
by Charles Hoffer and Marjorie Hoffer

BASIC RESOURCES FOR LEARNING MUSIC, 2nd edition
by Alice Knuth and William Knuth

Music in the Education of Children
Fourth Edition

Bessie R. Swanson

Wadsworth Publishing Company
Belmont, California
A Division of Wadsworth, Inc.

Music Editor: Sheryl Fullerton
Production Editor: Jeanne Heise
Designer: Janet Wood
Copy Editor: Genevieve Vaughn
Autography: Musica Engraving

Printed in the United States of America

1 2 3 4 5 6 7 8 9 10—85 84 83 82 81

Library of Congress Cataloging in Publication Data
Swanson, Bessie R
    Music in the education of children.

    Includes bibliographies and index.
    1. Music—Instruction and study—United States.
I. Title.
MT3.U5S92   1980   372.8′7   80–13571
ISBN 0–534–00880–1

Contents

Preface

The educational program recommended in this book focuses on the musical development of children at preschool and elementary levels. It is the position of the author that music provides another way for children and adults to know themselves, to discover their feelings, and to share beauty and the expression of feeling with others. To realize these values, music education for preschool and elementary school children must be designed to develop their ability

1. to make conscious contact with the tonal and rhythmic patterns that comprise music, and
2. to respond to music, not merely as a physical phenomenon, but as an experience with personal meaning

Music itself is the instructional material of such an educational program. The subject matter consists of information about the elements of music, principles of its composition, and its different styles and performance techniques. Musical skills grow out of a teaching method centered on many kinds of meaningful experiences with music—singing, playing instruments, listening, moving to music—that interpret or re-create musical compositions, or provide for creative music-making by children.

The opening chapter provides a brief philosophical and psychological foundation for this study, with references to resources that can be used for reading in greater depth. Chapters 2 through 6 focus on specific musical elements, together with activities that appropriately bring these elements to the attention of children. The skills of singing and listening, together with related knowledge and musical repertoire, are treated in chapters 7 and 8. Chapter 9 is designed to help the teacher implement the recommended program of music education.

In college classes consisting of prospective classroom teachers who have had limited musical experience, it may be advisable to begin the study with Chapter 2, "When Sound Becomes Music." The author has used this approach for a number of years, and has found that it immediately captures the interest of the college student. After motivation has been generated, the basic material of Chapter 1 can be drawn into study assignments and discussions.

Following introductory orientations, the material in chapters 2 through 8 is organized around three levels of maturity in children: Level I, ages three to seven; Level II, ages seven to ten; Level III, ages ten to twelve. This organization enables classroom teachers to focus their attention on the level that most applies to their teaching interests. For music specialists and administrators, it also provides an overview of the complete curriculum.

The broad objectives of the music education program recommended here are to develop favorable attitudes toward music, and to develop musical skills, musical concepts, and aesthetic sensitivity. Related instructional objectives can be considered to have been achieved when children exhibit clusters of musical behaviors consistent with those objectives. Many examples of instructional objectives are provided throughout this book. With each instructional objective, the author has provided lists of sample musical behaviors that might provide evidence that the instructional objectives have been achieved. After completing the study of this book, college students should have reviewed enough objectives to enable them to write their own for any lesson plans they might develop.

Appendix C, "Reference Material for Music Theory and Notation," along with the Glossary, will help increase their understanding of music notation and terminology. Appendix A, "Catalog of Musical Concepts," is designed as an aid in planning the learning experiences of children, and Appendix B, "Guide to Materials," includes up-to-date lists of companies supplying useful materials, many of which are cited throughout the text.

This book has grown out of the author's experience as a special music teacher and supervisor in the public schools; as an instructor in music and teacher-education classes at the University of Washington, the University of Michigan, California Polytechnic State University—San Luis Obispo, and at other colleges and universities; and as a student and performing musician. Many children, classroom teachers, musicians, school administrators, university teachers, and colleagues with whom the author has been associated, have contributed significantly to the development of this book.

1
Children and Music—
Foundations of the Study

Music has a place in every culture. It stimulates the feelings and intuitions, letting people express and understand what cannot be communicated in other ways. In interacting with the environment, young children naturally rely on their senses and intuitions. As they begin to develop cognitive abilities children should continue to refine their intuitive, creative abilities by active involvement with music and other arts that touch emotions and intuition. In its publication *Coming to Our Senses*,[1] a Special Project Panel of the American Council for the Arts in Education reiterated the need for the arts as a part of education by saying: "The arts are a function of life itself, and the process of making art—both creative and re-creative—can give insight to all other areas of learning." Three basic principles were stated:

1. The fundamental goals of American education can be realized only when the arts become central to the individual's learning experience
2. Educators at all levels must adopt the arts as a basic component of the curriculum deserving parity with all other elements
3. School programs in the arts should draw heavily upon all available resources in the community

These principles are cited here to suggest that there is a rising concern for the arts in education and to demonstrate how important the general teacher's involvement is in bringing the arts into the classroom. David Scott, a planning consultant for the National Gallery in Washington, D.C., said, "Art is a life-enhancing experience. It isn't just a craft or busywork. It's a whole way of looking at life. . . . It looks to me as if art must be placed parallel to the other disciplines. Art has the role of consolidating, of pulling together intuitively. Art is the mortar of learning."[2]

The classroom teacher, who has primary responsibility for the complete educational development of the children in a single class, must be involved if the arts are to be at the center of the children's educational experience. The artist-teacher, the musician who knows how to work with children, is also essential to the educational team. Such an individual has musical insights and skills that enhance school music experiences and acts as a link to the community's musical resources.

In this first chapter we will briefly consider the value of music and why we teach it. A second topic, learning music, provides a psychological basis for the rest of the book. This leads into a consideration of the characteristics of the children we would teach, and of how they learn. Finally, an overview of typical music instruction programs allows you to see the different ways children can be involved with music, what they can learn, and who contributes to this effort.

THE VALUE OF MUSIC—PHILOSOPHIC ORIENTATIONS

For many people, music is almost exclusively entertainment; for others it is a practical aid in worship, in promoting patriotism, or in otherwise helping the individual establish an identity and relate to others. More important, through music we can perceive and respond to meaning, feeling, and beauty, subjectively and nonverbally. Music provides another way, called the aesthetic domain, of knowing about ourselves and the world. In addition, music, like other subjects, can enhance intellectual and psychomotor development (the cognitive and psychomotor domains). It makes contributions to the individual's social and emotional adjustment as well. We will consider each of these values, and it would be useful for you to identify the ways in which music has been significant in your life.

Music as Aesthetic Education

In his introduction to aesthetics, Irwin Edman said, "Every canvas or musical composition that can awaken us more exquisitely and accurately to the infinite and various surface of our experience does that much to sharpen life and render it thereby more alive. If part of the aim of an ordered civilization is to prolong life, certainly part of its ambition is to variegate life and fill its moments with the quality of living."[3]

The American composer Aaron Copland believes that there is a basic, primitive relationship between human senses and feelings and music. "On that level, whatever the music may be, we experience basic reactions such as tension and release, density and transparency, a smooth or angry surface, the music's swellings and subsidings, its pushing forward or hanging back, its length, its speed, its thunders and whisperings—and a thousand other psychologically based reflections of our physical life of movement and gesture, and our inner, subconscious mental life. That is fundamentally the way we all hear music . . ."[4]

People who may never have gone beyond this primitive response to music have found in it lifelong therapy and enrichment. In the school curriculum, where academic rigors are often highly prized, music can keep children in healthy contact with the important world of feeling.

Susanne Langer[5] looks upon music as a symbolic form of feeling. She says, "music has all the earmarks of a true symbolism, except one: the existence of an assigned connotation." That is, it can mean different things to different people. Langer continues: ". . . what music can actually reflect is only the morphology (the features or shape) of feeling . . ." For instance, some music seems to bear a sad and a happy interpretation equally well; that is because some sad and some happy conditions may have a similar morphology.

Music can express symbolically the wide range of feelings; significant aesthetic experience in music, however, depends upon the individual's ability to hear and respond to what is expressed in music. Copland says that the higher forms of music imply a listener whose musical taste has been cultivated, and that "refinement in musical taste begins with the ability to distinguish subtle nuances of feeling. . . . The talented listener recognizes not merely the joyous quality of the piece, but also the specific shade of joyousness. . . ."[4] If music is to function most effectively as lifelong enrichment, the individual must have ever broader and deeper experiences with it.

Intellectual Development and Musical Experience

The intellectual aspect of education is seen as an active process of inquiry and problem solving. The individual acquires the knowledge of various fields and develops fluency in using it. Early cognitive development depends upon input through the senses. The experiences of art exercise the senses: visual (color and design), aural (music and poetry), tactile (textures and surface), kinesthetic (movement and dance). To assure maximum cognitive growth, each sense must have adequate development. Through experience, children learn to perceive more and to organize their perceptions for more complete understanding. Those of you concerned with early childhood education should be aware of the emphasis Maria Montessori[6] put on the early development of the senses. In dealing with sounds, the order of procedures she recommended was:

1. Recognizing identities, e.g., finding two instruments that sound the same
2. Recognizing contrasts, e.g., finding two instruments that produce different sounds
3. Discriminating among sounds produced by similar objects, e.g., ordering from low to high pitch a series of bells identical in appearance

The art of music uses sound, infinite variety and shadings of sound, for expressive purposes. Experience with musical sound offers opportunities to develop the aural discrimination that is so important to language development.

Psychomotor Development and Musical Activities

Singing and playing music require people to develop performance skills. These skills may involve using the hands, fingers, breath or total vocal mechanism, as well as the ears and eyes. Music performance contributes to physical development, for it demands precise, expressive response within a rhythmic time frame. To create the desired musical effect, the player's fingers or voice must produce the required tones in precisely the right order, at the right time, and with the necessary expressive nuance. Even handicapped children sense the need to make the music sound "right" and are thereby highly motivated to meet the physical demands of the performance.

In music education, to foster the development of rhythm and other aspects of musical expression, we borrow large body movement from dance and physical education. When musical learning, primarily thought of as aural and visual learning, is related to physical movement that involves kinesthetic (muscle-sense) learning, we tap a prime learning medium of children. Once trained to respond to music, the kinesthetic receptors, located in the joints, tendons, and muscles of the body, develop "memory" and "imagery" that can be called upon in subsequent musical encounters. Such memory and imagery are essential to expressive musical performance, but they contribute as well to the listener's subjective response to music.

Music's Contribution to Social and Emotional Maturity

Music can be an individual activity, but it also is the most social of the arts; people share feelings and enjoyment through music. Children come to preschool classes as individuals who need to learn to relate to others, to do things together; group music activities foster social interaction.

Education consists in part of helping people identify themselves as individuals and as members of various groups. Music has a part in this process because cultural identification begins in childhood and includes learning traditional lullabies, singing-games, dances, story songs, and folk songs. In almost every society children learn to associate certain patriotic music with the idea of nationality and citizenship; other music is associated with church and comes to represent religious ties and beliefs.

Identity-development is something individuals work out for themselves with the aid of music wherever they find it. All of us have songs of sentiment that remind us of special times and important persons in our lives. Young people often identify with a particular music that sets them apart from older generations. The strong percussive beat and hypnotic repetition in the music of teenage stage bands and singing groups, the social comment of the guitar-accompanied folksinger, and the contemporary protest songs have provided musical identity for some groups. The music of Bach and Handel (the early 18th century), with its rhythmic drive and clear blocks of contrasting sound, appeals to many young, contemporary intellectuals as music that is unaffected and worthy of their commitment. Members of each generation maintain a common bond in the music that helped define their experience and feeling at a particular time.

Through contact with the music of other cultures children learn that people in other parts of the world use music to enhance their ceremonies, to enliven their dance, and to underscore feelings of love, joy, and grief. Although the music itself is significantly different, simply knowing that people of other cultures use music in feeling, human ways helps children relate to them as fellow human beings. Music education makes important use of the music of this country's minority groups. By helping all children share and enjoy the musical heritage of American Indians, Afro- and Mexican-Americans, and people of other origins, we lay a foundation for great- er social understanding. Music is not an international language; but it is a universal way in which people symbolize their experience and enrich their lives.

Every individual can participate successfully in music. School music teachers have identified talent and encouraged many gifted children toward careers in music. Music can also help the handicapped child to grow. Juliette Alvin reports that for such a child, music can provide a chance for achievement and sensory development, an emotional outlet, a mental stimulus, and a means of socialization. "These many aspects of a single factor give music an integrating power because they are indissolu- bly linked with one another and they involve the mind, body, and emotion of the child in one experience."[7]

In all music-making—singing, playing, creative composition—we find oppor- tunities for involving the mind and feelings. This involvement can be therapeutic as well as recreational. Daniel A. Prescott and his Committee on the Relations of Emotions to the Educative Process[8] say: "The conscious use of aesthetic experience to maintain morale may be not only a means of social control and integration but also a mark of personal maturity. The use of aesthetic expression as a means of release, escape, or catharsis from unbearable tensions may be a mature means of

emotional reactions." For music to have value for this or any

must be able to make music or respond to it at a level

concerned with psychological considerations for learn- otivation, and readiness of the children, as well as dif- ognitive, psychomotor, aesthetic, and others—that are ng studied.

and readiness are essential to learning. Of these, attitude ecause it consists of the learner's feelings about certain ation. Individuals who view music learning as pleasurable aster than those who do not have these positive feelings. n personal experience, the family, peers, and other influen- or whom music is pleasurable and valuable and who helps periences with it can influence children's attitudes toward it. we are concerned with attitude; not only does a positive o learn music, but also, children who develop strong, favor- usic and who feel they can participate effectively in it will nusic throughout life.

(Thesis) Statement "exposure to music is an important part of a student's education."

Motivation has many of the characteristics of attitude. It goes beyond general-ized feelings, however, to a tendency to act, to participate or not participate in an activity or study. On a practical level, a certain amount of success is needed to support motivation to accomplish a goal. If they are sufficiently varied to accommo-date different abilities and interests, musical activities themselves provide opportuni-ties for success. For this reason, the musical experiences described in this book range from exploring sound to singing, listening, and moving to music.

The teacher, when planning learning activities, must take into account the child's physiological, cognitive, and social readiness to perform a given musical act. For example, in certain music skills, a given level of physical development is neces-sary for success; to play a clarinet, a child's fingers must be well-enough developed that the span of keys can be played. Readiness implies not only maturation, but also growth derived from experience. Therefore, teachers should provide preliminary activity to break complex skills into simpler components that can be mastered ear-lier. As an example, before children can play the clarinet they can be taught to play the recorder (an end-blown wooden or plastic flute). James Mursell,[9] an advocate of the concept of musical growth, said that the idea of "readiness" should not suggest that there are definite, separable stages in music growth. The concept should, howev-er, stand as a warning not to try to teach something before the learner is able to benefit from it.

The Learning Process

In teaching children music we are primarily concerned with three kinds of learning: (1) cognitive—what one knows, how one thinks and uses symbols in reference to music; (2) psychomotor—performance skills such as playing instru-ments and singing; and (3) aesthetic—having to do with feeling and awareness of "a deeper reality of the world in which we live in our ordinary experiences."[10]

Perception is central to all types of learning. This is the process by which the individual, beginning in infancy, collects information through the senses (sight, hear-ing, touch, . . .) and codes it for storage in the brain. Each of these bits of informa-tion is associated with a feeling quality or affect. When percepts—derived from experience with objects and events—are integrated and related in the brain, they become concepts—ideas and understandings about objects, self, people, and their interaction.

Cognitive Development

This brings us to the research and writings of the Swiss psychologist Jean Piaget,[11] which have helped shape current understanding of the kinds of knowledge that characterize children at different ages. The following outline shows the stages of development identified by Piaget. As with other characteristics of growth, there are no distinct dividing lines, but rather a gradual development from one kind of thinking toward the other, with some children moving into the next stage earlier than other children.

1. *Sensorimotor Stage:* Birth to age one or two

    Children progress from simple reflex action to physical experimentation, trial and error, that aids mental development.

2. *Preoperational Stage:* Age one or two to age six or seven

    a. During this period the child learns with increasing effectiveness to use spoken words to refer to objects in the world.

    b. Between age five and a half and age seven, the use of spoken language is characteristically more articulate.

    c. There is growing organization of concepts throughout the period, but this seems to be a loose collection of concepts, not representative of an operative system of thought found in the next period, hence the label "preoperational."

    d. The years between ages four and seven sometimes are characterized as the "period of intuitive thought," because the child, whose thought is not yet highly organized, cannot yet reason effectively and must leap to conclusions.

3. *The Stage of Concrete Operations:* Age six or seven to age eleven or twelve

    a. Children's cognitive resources now are well-enough organized that when they deal with new information, they can operate within patterns of thought. New data are assimilated into these cognitive structures, i.e., integrated with, rather than merely added to, what the child already knows.

    b. Children are able to use written as well as spoken language to represent perceivable, concrete events and objects of their world.

4. *The Stage of Formal Operations:* Age eleven or twelve into adulthood

    Individuals now begin to be able to use propositional or hypothetical thinking. Since they are no longer tied to concrete events and objects, they can use language to deal with abstract ideas.

Please note that, according to Piaget's outline, only in the sixth or seventh grade do children begin to be capable of using language in connection with abstract ideas. In this book, addressed to teachers of early childhood and elementary classes, musical experience is the basis for all approaches to musical learning.

Jerome Bruner, Professor of Psychology at Harvard University, has been concerned with incorporating Piaget's outline of children's thinking into a psychological description of cognitive growth. In an essay, "Patterns of Growth,"[12] he described the three ways in which he believes human beings conserve past experiences for mental storage and retrieval:

1. *Through action (the enactive mode):* Some things, like riding a bicycle or playing a violin, are learned by doing and seeing them done. This kind of learning has a place at any age; it is the principal way young children learn about their world and store knowledge for future use. As an example, body movement is incorporated into musical experience so that children can develop concepts about music (fast–slow, even–uneven, high–low, rising–falling, etc.) through their own body elevation and movement.

2. *Through summarizing images (the iconic mode):* We are concerned here with perceptual organization, using pictures and diagrams that give a visual representation of the object or event as it is. In teaching young children, pictures can be used in lieu of immediate concrete experience if there is sufficient previous experience to make the picture meaningful. The flow of notes on a music staff and a line showing the rise and fall of a melody are pictured (iconic) representations of melody. Duple meter can be diagrammed with alternate heavy and light slashes, evenly spaced:

▌ı ▌ı ▌ı ▌ı

3. *Through words or other symbols (the symbolic mode):* Words and symbols do not resemble things and events in the way that pictures do, but they are the most economical and effective way of dealing with ideas. When you wish to indicate duple meter you can use a 2 in the meter signature $(\frac{2}{4}, \frac{2}{2}, \frac{2}{8})$; this is a more precise way of dealing with the concept than that provided by the diagram shown above.

In his analysis of verbal learning, David Ausubel[13] discussed the difference between "discovery learning" and "reception learning." Discovery learning arises out of experiences with objects that have to do with a given subject. In receptive learning, what is to be learned is presented verbally in final form; the learner internalizes the information so that it is available for future use.

The adult can deal with knowledge in all three ways, but infants begin to learn and know because they have acted out the idea. For teachers of young children, "learning by doing" is an essential approach; pictures, diagrams, words, and symbols are gradually related to the phenomenon, so that at later stages the individual can deal with the ideas in these more efficient ways.

Learning Physical Skills

Musical learning in general education at the elementary level involves participating in music-making and includes developing skills related to what one knows and how one thinks about music. Since the mind controls the muscular response, participation and skills learning are referred to as the psychomotor domain. Under this heading we find the development of skills such as playing instruments, singing, and reading music.

Here again, the first step is perception, which implies awareness and a receptive attitude. James Mursell[14] saw skills development as consisting of two problems, the first being control, by which he meant mental control governing what one wished to do musically, and the second being the action-pattern needed to achieve the musical objective.

When Suzuki teachers start three-year-olds playing the violin, they first acquaint the child with the musical sound of the violin and provide musical examples on records and in the teacher's and the mother's playing. Similarly, before children begin to read music, they should have a background of musical experience, so that they are motivated to learn and so that they are acquainted aurally with the rhythmic and melodic movement they see represented on the page.

Defining Aesthetic Behaviors

During the late 1970s, significant effort was brought to defining and clarifying what is meant by aesthetic education, which includes visual art, drama, poetry, and so forth, as well as music. As with all other learning, the aesthetic encounter begins with perception. In his article "Aesthetic Behaviors in Music,"[15] Bennett Reimer discussed seven major behaviors identified with aesthetic encounters. These are grouped into three categories:

1. Perceiving and reacting are classified as "ends behaviors." The teacher's primary goal is to improve each individual's ability to perceive and to respond to music.
2. Producing, conceptualizing, analyzing, and evaluating are "means behaviors." By making music, by knowing and thinking about it, and by developing the ability to analyze and evaluate it, individuals improve their perception and response to music—the primary objectives of aesthetic education.
3. Valuing is classified as an "outcome behavior." If teachers help children to grow in their ability to perceive and respond to music, the children will find value in music.

Reimer believes that teaching objectives and strategies for each music lesson can be centered on some or all of these objectives.

THE GROWTH CHARACTERISTICS OF CHILDREN WITH IMPLICATIONS FOR MUSIC EDUCATION

If you would teach children, you must know children—how they perceive, react, feel, and learn—at whatever age you encounter them. Experience is a great teacher, of course, and one of the best ways to know children is to work with them. It is also helpful to know what characteristics to look for, and which are most important to teaching and learning.

Throughout this book, experiences that can promote many kinds of musical learning are laid out on three levels: Four-, five-, and six-year-olds are considered under Level I, which will be of most interest to those who deal with preschool, kindergarten, and first grade classes; Level II deals with children from ages seven to nine (grades two to four); and Level III includes the middle-childhood years, ages nine to eleven (grades four through six).

Since children differ markedly in rate of growth and development, and change is gradual and continuous, it is not possible to be arbitrary about the ages included in each level. These groupings are helpful, however, because they force us to categorize directions of change at three points on the continuum and to shape the musical experiences accordingly.

Level I—Ages Four through Six

Preschool children excel in creative ways of learning—they question, search, manipulate, and play as part of their creative approach to learning. Both rhythm and melody instruments should be available, so that children can explore musical sounds during this kind of creative play.

Four-year-olds are great talkers; they like to dramatize and make up new verses as they act out songs and rhymes. In their play a few key words are extended by nonsense syllables to create chants that accompany rhythmic activity. Vocal play and flexible use of the voice in chanting and crooning should be encouraged.

At ages four and five children like stories and songs with repetitive action and repetitive phrases. It seems possible that at the kindergarten level such activities may replace some of the more creative activities of younger children. Torrance[16] reports "discontinuities in creative development" at about the kindergarten level to be "one of the most persistent and recurrent findings of creativity research with children." However, Torrance believes this slump in creativity can and should be averted. The teacher must actively plan for creative opportunities and make suitable materials available to children.

Zigmond and Cicci[17] collected research data revealing the following music-related characteristics of children: At age four children can match sound-blocks by loudness, but at age four and a half they can grade sound-blocks in order from softest to loudest.

At four and a half, children can remember short sentences and imitate a melody. Six-year-olds can remember tunes and reproduce them on request, and they are able to blend isolated sounds into words. Since they imitate sounds well, they can learn easy folk songs in the original foreign language. This both expands the child's facility with word sounds and broadens cultural horizons.

Children at Level I enjoy gross motor activity, but they also have developed some skill and gracefulness in hand movements. Finger plays and action songs are appropriate for these children. Running, walking, bending, stretching, and turning can be used freely. At age four, children generally can blend a step and a hop into a gallop. The ability to skip develops about age five. When musical accompaniments are provided for such activities, they should be adapted to the child's tempo and movement style.

At this level children are able to explore their world independently—physically, with language, and with their imaginations. Young children, however, are egocentric and tend to be individualistic in their activities. Some group activities in music are possible at this level, but you should provide many opportunities for independent music-making by individuals and smaller groups.

Intellectually, the years from four through six are categorized by Piaget as the period of intuitive thought. During this period children are subject to perceptual dominance—that is, when an item has several attributes, they can take into account only one at a time. As an example, a musical tone has pitch, duration, loudness, and a particular quality of sound, but young children will notice only the one attribute that dominates their attention at a given time. As a teacher you must be satisfied to help children switch their attention from one attribute to another at different times, so that the separate concepts are developed and ready to be combined into a complete idea as the children mature.

Level II—Ages Seven to Nine

The stage of "concrete operations" (Piaget) begins around age seven. At this intellectual level children can deal more effectively with the multi-dimensional qualities of music. The study of rhythm and melody is of prime importance during this period.

The eight-year-old is beginning to be capable of sustained and coordinated group work, but opportunities for musical activities by individuals and pairs of children continue to be valuable. At this level children build habits of industry and perfect their performance skills. Since their physical dexterity and kinesthetic sense now are well developed, children of these ages can begin to learn to play the piano and standard instruments of the band and orchestra as well as the various classroom musical instruments.

Second and third graders are imaginative and creative; interest in dramatization continues during these years, but the topics begin to have different appeal for different individuals. Some seven-year-olds prefer cowboy and Indian roles, and some like to dramatize machines and vehicles, while others relate to delicate creatures and colorful but less aggressive situations. Most children are interested in animals and will readily dramatize a wide variety of them.

Torrance[16] reports a second discontinuity in creative functioning at the fourth grade level. This may be related to the child's motivation to master certain functional skills at this age, but it is a serious problem that Torrance believes should be overcome by guided, planned experiences in creative thinking. Creative music projects can be laid out for individualized experiences, and classroom singing can be handled in such a way that fourth graders find "music" to be not only facility in singing and playing the "right" notes, but a means of creative expression as well.

Level III—Ages Ten and Eleven

Language is used by ten- and eleven-year-olds to represent relationships in the physical world, and some sixth graders begin thought processes characterized as "formal operations." For most children at this level, however, you must continue to supply concrete examples of the musical phenomena you wish them to consider.

Children of these ages urgently need companionship with their peers. The peer group helps the child to move from a dependent relationship to an independent relationship with adults. These children idolize certain people they know, and this relationship may foster skills development and inspire children to set long-range goals to emulate the admired person. The study of musical instruments, individually and in groups, continues during these years.

At this age children like to sing, and many of them have sufficient control of their voices to make singing particularly satisfying. Those who have sung continually from early childhood can develop a vocal range of two octaves. They can learn to sing harmony parts and often find belonging to a school choir especially rewarding.

Boys of this age are pressed by family and society to develop "manly" characteristics; therefore you should avoid singing sentimental songs that boys are unable to reconcile with their view of social expectations. Some sixth grade boys enter the first stage of puberty with its attendant voice changes, so it is important that they have contact with a teacher who understands the changing voice and its changing range.

Eleven-year-olds begin to be interested in jazz and popular music, and they listen avidly to recorded music. At this level children enjoy gross motor activity, and folk dancing can be a favorite form of study and recreation. Work with dances of the national groups discussed in social studies is very profitable during these years.

AN OVERVIEW OF THE INSTRUCTIONAL PROGRAM IN MUSIC

We have reviewed the positive contributions music can make in the education of children, and have noted its special value as a subjective, nonverbal medium of expression and personal enrichment. To make it possible for them to get the most out of their encounters with music, now and in the future, music education for preschool and elementary children must be designed to develop children's ability:

1. To perceive, that is, to make conscious contact with the tonal and rhythmic patterns that comprise music, and
2. To respond to music, not merely as a physical phenomenon, but as an experience with personal meaning

To achieve these ends you must help children develop musical skills and build concepts that will let them interact with music at increasingly more mature levels.

Defining and Stating the Objectives of Instruction

Instruction in music consists of student interaction with the instructional material, the subject matter, and the teaching method. Instruction is viewed as a process that results in various products. These products are the objectives of instruction.

Broad objectives for education in music (products) might be stated as follows:

1. To develop a favorable attitude toward music—the basis for valuing music as an expressive experience and for assuring lifelong involvement with music
2. To develop skills enabling individuals to listen and to produce music that matches their level of maturity
3. To develop concepts of music that will help individuals to learn to analyze, evaluate, and grow in their response to music
4. To develop aesthetic sensitivity—the ability to perceive and respond to those qualities that make music expressive

Developing the first three of these objectives—attitudes, skills, and concepts—supports and makes it possible to realize the fourth objective, aesthetic sensitivity. Within these four broad headings, we can identify more specific instructional objectives that develop out of a given unit of study. Many examples of instructional objectives are provided in the following chapters of this book. With each statement of instructional objectives you will find a list of musical behaviors expected to provide evidence that the objectives have been achieved. Since these instructional objectives are related to procedures for an entire unit of study, more than one instructional objective is stated in most cases.

By the time you have completed Chapter 8 in this book, you should have reviewed enough instructional objectives that you will be able to state objectives and design evaluation procedures for lesson plans (such as the examples in Chapter 9). Although it does not center on music, *Stating Behavioral Objectives for Classroom Instruction* by Norman Gronlund[18] is recommended for its concise discussion and practical examples of instructional and behavioral objectives.

The Instructional Material

Music itself is the instructional material of music education. This can include a wide variety of folk songs, composed songs, and simple pieces children can play, and both live and recorded performances of many kinds of instrumental and vocal music. In this book you will find many songs used or referred to as musical examples. Other song material is readily available in basic series music books and their related recordings (see Appendix B-I), in other publications, and on commercial recordings. Recorded instrumental compositions serve as musical examples in the following chapters, and Appendix B-II contains lists of recorded compositions that are particularly useful in elementary music education.

The Subject Matter of Music Instruction

The elements of music, principles of musical composition, and different musical styles and performances are areas for cognitive learning in music. Broad headings for organizing this knowledge in teaching elementary music are shown below. In Appendix A you will find these headings in a "Catalog of Musical Concepts" that will be helpful as you plan learning experiences for children.

If you have had considerable experience with music you will have some idea of the scope of the following topics. Each of the major headings is dealt with in detail in one or more chapters in this book. Those of you who have little background in music will need to develop your knowledge of music as you gain experience with it in the music methods course. Appendix C, "Reference Material for Music Theory and Notation" and the Glossary at the back of this book should be helpful sources of information. The Subject Index is comprehensive and is intended to lead you to definitions and examples for any topic within the scope of this study.

Tone color. (Timbre; pronounced "tambur") Musical tone is produced in different ways, and instruments are classified according to both the medium and the method of tone production. Voices, as well as instruments, have distinctive qualities of sound. Tone color is given primary attention in Chapter 2.

Rhythm. This word comes from the Greek term meaning "measured motion"; please take special note of its spelling. Primary attention is given to rhythm in Chapters 3 and 4.

Melody. The shape and movement of melody are primary expressive factors in music. Chapter 5 provides a comprehensive review of melody in the context of singing and playing melody instruments.

Musical Texture and Harmony. Texture is the density of simultaneous sound, and harmony is the vertical relationship of simultaneously sounded tones, i.e., of chords, their characteristics, and their combination. Chapter 6 focuses on these elements.

Dynamics in Music. The relative strength of sound varies with the expressive intent of the music. Dynamic change can be gradual or sudden, and can involve one or many voices or instruments. You will find examples and discussion of dynamics in music in several chapters in this book.

Form in Music. Form has been called the intellectual aspect of music, because the mind must remember and compare how rhythmic, melodic, and harmonic elements are used at any one point with how they are developed and used throughout the composition. Form permeates the study of many other elements. It is given much attention in Chapter 8.

Style in Music. Style is the result of particular ways of using the elements of music and procedures of composition. One can learn to identify different styles of concert music, folk music, and popular music. A sampling of different styles is included in the music referred to in this book.

The Musical Skills

Four general kinds of musical skill can be developed:

1. Performance skills include expressing music through body movement and gesture, singing, and playing instruments.
2. Aural skills begin with development of the ability to hear, discriminate, and identify the elements of music, and include, at more advanced levels, the identification of harmonies, musical textures, and styles.
3. Reading and writing skills allow the individual to use music notation.
4. Creativity incorporates one or more of the other skills in the act of improvising or composing original music, but it also is present to some extent when one performs (re-creates) music.

The medium of musical expression is organized sound and silence. Notation is a visual representation of the sound of music, but it is not the art itself. Only after a person has had such extensive experience with music that seeing the notation actually promotes an inner hearing of the music can "notes" and "music" be considered analogous.

The child's introduction to music is through its sound; then gradually its notation can be used to define and support what the ear perceives. This is the normal development of any musical concept:

1. It is experienced by the ear; e.g., one may hear and sing the "amen" at the end of a hymn.
2. It is identified to the ear; one recognizes the "amen" as a common chord progression that often accompanies the word "amen."
3. Its notation is related to it; one sees the "amen" chords in notation, learns how they are formed, and understands their relationship to one another.

The discussion of the music program in this book is designed to follow this developmental pattern. While people need to be able to talk and exchange ideas about music through spoken language, they also find that music's unique symbols provide a useful visual representation of music. Although in some cultures music remains an aural tradition, those who would participate fully in music-making need to develop skill in the use of music notation.

The Teaching Method

Chapters 2 through 8 of this book are designed to show how musical learning can arise from musical experiences that can be provided in early childhood and elementary classrooms. Following is a brief description of the musical activities.

Creating Music. The first musical experiences described in this book (Chapter 2) involve the creative use of sound. In this early creative work, an open, exploratory attitude and sensitivity to tone color and rhythm are all that are needed. Later chapters describe procedures you can use to help children create melodies and provide musical settings for poems. Creative work of all kinds fills the children's need to work either alone or in small groups, thus accommodating several levels of musical development.

In a broad sense, creativity is a part of all the other musical activities. When children, through body movement, through color and design on paper, or through speaking, express what they hear, they are responding creatively; when they choose instruments to produce desired musical effects, or when they sing a particular song in a special way, they create a mood.

Adults too often impose their standards on children. They demand that children develop skills before they have a chance to discover that they can express something from within themselves through their own simple music. Watch a group of children producing rhythmic sounds with a drum or with their feet; observe a six-year-old picking out a melody on the small xylophone; or a ten-year-old improvising a melody around chords he can play on the guitar; listen to a child singing at work, and you will hear the creative music of children.

Moving to Music. In a discussion of "The Musical Impulse" the American composer Roger Sessions says that on a primitive, direct, simple level the basic ingredient of music is not so much sound as movement.[19] This statement points up the importance of body movement as a related activity in musical experience.

Beginning in infancy children express themselves directly and effectively through movement. Studies in psycholinguistics report that the infant's whimper is accompanied by actions that help define the desire or need.[20] Gesture and movement support communication throughout early childhood. In addition, children explore their world and develop concepts with the aid of body movement. Impersonation and dramatization are normal activities of children, easily related to the expressiveness of songs and instrumental music.

When using body movement as a response to music, children do more than merely run, skip, and gallop with the music; they use these natural movements to express the more elusive qualities of feeling that the music conveys. Through activities involving body movement, children develop concepts of space and time that help them when they listen to music and follow its flow through time. Music listening is more than an auditory response; it has kinesthetic implications as well.

Singing. Singing is an immediate and personal way for children to make music because each child has a singing voice, developed or undeveloped, that has the potential for personal expression. In the elementary grades the music program often is organized around singing because it has strong socializing implications, and many activities can be related to it. In this book you will find songs that appeal to children of varied ages; learn some of them, and collect others that may be useful to the children you will work with. You will have an opportunity to learn to accompany songs on the autoharp, guitar, or piano, and this will be a very useful skill.

Playing Instruments. All sorts of simple instruments have been adapted for use by children. They have an important place in the music program—for improvising, for accompanying singing, and for the practical study of music. Children often develop dynamic, rhythmic chanting patterns, using the voice and combinations of rhythm instruments. Original melodies grow out of opportunities to play simple melody instruments, and the desire to play a known melody can lead to an understanding of music notation. Children with talent and interest can be encouraged to study the piano and standard orchestral instruments. If the elementary school music program functions effectively, such specialized studies are a natural outgrowth of earlier experiences in playing classroom instruments.

Listening to Music. Listening, too, is a creative activity. Roger Sessions states it this way: "The really 'understanding' listener takes the music into his consciousness and remakes it actually or in his imagination, for his own uses."[21]

Listening is basic to all music-making. As children sing and play instruments, they listen. As they interpret music through body movement, they listen. All these activities help children in the important project of learning to listen, which is the chief musical activity of most adults. Much music listening can be shared by a group; but children should also have opportunities—and facilities—to listen and learn about music individually. Although listening experiences are discussed in the last sections of this book, they are, in a sense, first in importance in any consideration of music.

Throughout this book you will find examples of ways to plan and guide children's musical activities. Specific material is suggested and techniques are outlined that will foster the development of musical concepts and growth in musical skills. As far as possible, the age levels at which the skills and concepts can be developed are suggested; but curricular materials must accommodate individual levels of growth as well as group needs. No grading of this type can be considered valid for every group of children because musical aptitudes and experiences vary widely. With some experience, however, you will learn what can be expected of children at whatever age and musical experience you encounter them.

MUSIC EDUCATION—A JOINT RESPONSIBILITY

The education of children takes place both in the home and in the classroom. Since much significant learning occurs in the first two or three years of life, parents bear unique responsibilities for providing environment and stimulation that will lead to the child's optimum musical growth simultaneously with other kinds of growth.

Education in the preschool and elementary school develops out of a close relationship between a teacher and a group of children. One teacher may be responsible for all aspects of the education of the children in a given class. Some elementary school districts organize teaching assignments to accommodate "team teaching" and the "open classroom," where several teachers, with a variety of skills among them, work together with a larger group of children. Other school districts provide resource teachers to help the general teacher with subjects that require special skills; many schools employ music specialists who are responsible for most of the music teaching.

Decisions about teaching personnel usually are made by the principal and other school administrators. The influence of a school principal often determines the place of music in the curriculum and the role that music has in the school.

The Contribution of Parents

Research has shown that the home environment can significantly influence the musical response of first grade children. John Shelton[22] reported that the following factors show a close relationship to musical response at this age:

1. Frequent opportunities for the child to hear singing in the home
2. Frequent opportunities to sing with other members of the family
3. Frequent opportunities to hear records played in the home
4. Ability of mother and father to sing and to learn new songs

In addition, a home that has many sound-producing objects that children are allowed to experiment with in making sounds and rhythms will contribute substantially to children's development of elementary musical concepts, even before they enter kindergarten. Many of the materials and procedures suggested in this book can be adapted for home use if teachers will share the information with parents and encourage them to create a home environment that fosters musical development.

The Importance of the Classroom Teacher

The classroom teacher is in a position to see that studies in different subjects are interrelated in the child's experience. Because the potential contributions of music are great, it should be a regular part of the curriculum for every child at every level of elementary school and in early childhood classes. In considering the classroom teacher's role in music education, two points must be stressed: (1) the active interest of the classroom teacher is essential to an adequate program of music in the elementary school, and (2) music should be a daily activity because it is an integral part of life, and it should function this way in the classroom.

Actually, teachers need music in life as much as children need it. By participating in the arts they achieve self-esteem and personal satisfaction. Almost in self-defense, however, because they fear that music is only for the talented, those who have little musical experience may claim complete inability and lack of interest. Yet a few successful experiences with music can grip such self-doubters with enthusiasm, and that's what Chapters 2 through 8 of this book are all about. Here you will find descriptions of musical experiences that teachers can become involved in and later share with children. In the music-education class the instructor and more musically experienced students will model musical skills you may need to develop; in the elementary classroom the special music teacher or supervisor should provide this service.

The Roles of the Music Teacher

Elementary schools need music teachers with three different kinds of expertise: (1) general classroom music, (2) special choral groups, and (3) beginning instrumental classes and ensembles. The teaching assignments may be the responsibility of one, and sometimes two people: the music teacher trained in vocal music usually has general music classes as a major responsibility and may develop special choirs at the primary or intermediate level. The instrumental music teacher works with small groups of children electing to study orchestra or band instruments and sometimes develops an elementary band or orchestra for more advanced players. Responsibility for the general music program sometimes is part of the assignment. The teacher assigned general classroom music is concerned with the musical growth of all the children as opposed to the smaller number who join special choral groups or beginning instrumental classes and ensembles.

For many years classroom music in the elementary school was synonymous with singing; eventually, classroom instruments were introduced, and body movement and listening came to be integral to the program. The development of musical concepts, attitudes, and aesthetic responses now is equally as important as the singing and sight-reading skills that once dominated the program. Music educators now view "general music" as the core of elementary music education.

The general music specialist may serve in various capacities in the elementary school. Under one plan the music specialist is a resource person, a technical advisor, and a musical assistant to the classroom teacher and the children. How much time the specialist spends in any one classroom depends upon the skill and musical background of the classroom teacher and the generosity of the school administration in providing enough specialists. Under optimum conditions, the music specialist works in the classroom with the teacher and pupils as often as necessary to create an effective music program. In some cases the specialist may keep a regular, once or twice weekly, appointment with teacher and class. Under this plan, the musical experiences of the class utilize whatever skill and understanding the classroom teacher is able to provide. Over time the teacher's skill in guiding musical activities and learning may be strengthened, and part of the music specialist's assistance can be withdrawn. Other teachers may be so capable musically it is enough help for the music teacher to arrange special events and, in a monthly conference, to bring requested resource material and suggest new techniques.

Under another plan the music specialist may teach a class three or four times a week, and the classroom teacher may have the music period as contracted "release time" (preparation time) away from the class. When there is good communication between the teachers about the needs and progress of the children, as well as mutual respect and cooperation, this can be an excellent arrangement. The music specialist should be aware of the particular interests and areas of study in which the children are involved and should supply music that can be related to other subjects. The classroom teacher should maintain an interest in the children's musical activities, and support the work of the music teacher.

Music teachers who are well prepared as musicians and as educators, and who can work cooperatively in the best interests of the children, can find positions of respect and appreciation for their unique abilities. Such a person might be thought of both as a teacher and as the school's "musician in residence" who brings a depth of understanding and artistry to the school's musical activities. The specialist knows and can evaluate musical repertoire, materials, and equipment, and is skilled in involving amateurs in rewarding activities that will lead to greater independence and musical learning.

The Influence of the School Principal

The person ultimately responsible for the quality of the educational program of the school is the principal. This individual must see that all the educational needs of the children are met and that there is a good balance among the various subjects of the curriculum. Implementation of any program depends on the principal's approval of time and funds to be spent. The attitude of the principal is especially significant in a subject such as music, where cooperative effort and the development of aesthetic responses are so important. When the special music teacher's expertise is combined with the general teacher's broad understanding and the principal's ability to implement, it is possible to realize a program of music that will meet the varied needs of all the children.

The Community of Musicians

Every school music program can be enhanced by drawing on the talents of musical people in the community. Amateur and high school musicians can contribute by giving informal concerts and sharing enthusiasm for music with younger children. Local professional musicians can be employed for special performances, and private teachers can provide music lessons for children who might benefit from them. Teachers should reach out into the community to enrich the school's musical offerings. They should also orient children and their parents to the musical opportunities available outside the school.

CHAPTER NOTES

1. American Council for the Arts in Education, Arts Education and Americans Panel, **Coming to Our Senses** (New York: McGraw-Hill Book Co., 1977), p. 248.

2. Quoted in "Artists" by Sherwood D. Kohn, pp. 13–14 of **The National Elementary Principal,** 55, no. 3, (January/February 1976). Published by the National Association of Elementary Principals.

3. Irwin Edman, **Arts and the Man** (New York: W. W. Norton and Company, Inc., 1928, 1939), p. 46. Copyright 1928, 1939, by W. W. Norton and Company, Inc. Copyright renewed 1956 and 1967 by Meta Markel. Reprinted by permission.

4. Aaron Copland, **Music and Imagination** (Cambridge, Mass.: Harvard University Press, 1953), p. 14. Reprinted by permission.

5. Susanne Langer, **Philosophy in a New Key,** 3rd ed. (Cambridge, Mass.: Harvard University Press, 1960), pp. 238–240.

6. Maria Montessori, **Dr. Montessori's Own Handbook** (New York: Schocken Books, 1965), "Sensory Education," pp. 65–123.

7. Juliette Alvin, **Music for the Handicapped Child** (London: Oxford University Press, 1965), p. 25.

8. Daniel A. Prescott, **Emotion and the Educative Process** (Washington, D.C.: American Council on Education, 1966), pp. 93, 102, 284. Reprinted by permission.

9. James L. Mursell, **Education for Musical Growth** (Boston, Mass.: Ginn and Company, 1948), p. 62.

10. John Dewey, **Art as Experience** (New York: Capricorn Books, G. P. Putnam's Sons, 1958), p. 195.

11. Piaget's theories are clearly outlined in John A. R. Wilson, Mildred C. Robeck, and William B. Michael, **Psychological Foundations of Learning and Teaching** (New York: McGraw-Hill Book Co., 1969), Chapter 11, "Cognitive Growth."

12. Jerome S. Bruner, **Toward a Theory of Instruction** (Cambridge, Mass.: The Belknap Press of Harvard University Press, 1967), Chapter 1.

13. David P. Ausubel, **The Psychology of Meaningful Verbal Learning** (New York: Greene and Stratton, Inc., 1963), p. 16.

14. Mursell, **Musical Growth,** Chapter 10.

15. Bennett Reimer, "Aesthetic Behaviors in Music," from **Toward an Aesthetic Education** (Washington, D.C.: Music Educators National Conference, 1971), p. 65.

16. E. Paul Torrance, **Creativity,** Dimensions in Early Learning Series (Belmont, Calif.: Fearon Publishers, 1969), p. 17.

17. Naomi K. Zigmond and Regina Cicci, **Auditory Learning,** Dimensions in Early Learning Series (Belmont, Calif.: Fearon Publishers, 1968), p. 17.

18. Norman Gronlund, **Stating Behavioral Objectives for Classroom Instruction** (New York: The Macmillan Company, 1970), pp. 7–17.

19. Roger Sessions, **The Musical Experience of Composer, Performer, Listener** (Princeton, N.J.: Princeton University Press, 1950), pp. 11–16.

20. Roger Brown, **Words and Things** (New York: The Free Press of Glencoe, 1958), Chapter 6.

21. Sessions, **Musical Experience,** pp. 19, 97.

22. John Shelton, "The Influence of Home Musical Environment upon Musical Response of First-Grade Children" (Ed.D. Dissertation, George Peabody College for Teachers, 1965), Microfilm Order No. 66-4419.

2

When Sound Becomes Music

What is your idea of music? Must it have melody? Must it be beautiful? Are unconventional combinations of sound or silence "music" to your ears? In this generation "music" has come to be so broadly defined that for some, any expressive use of sound and silence can qualify; it may not involve melody or harmony. Two influences have helped make this view of music possible:

1. The mass media—radio, television and recordings—have made music of all cultures available to us. In some of this music we find that particular uses of tone color, dynamics, rhythm, and texture are more prominent than melody and harmony.
2. The experimental music of our time, while not widely accepted in the concert hall, has had great impact through the mass media. The new sounds are used extensively in television and radio commercials and the background music of movie and television drama. Much of this sound montage has little to do with the melody- and harmony-centered music studies traditionally taught in schools.

A study of the music of early childhood[1] has shown that young children attend first to sound (variety in tone color), then to rhythm in their early, spontaneous musical activities. These observations lead to a broad view of music for children—one that relates to contemporary music itself. We will therefore begin by considering music in a broad context, relatable to world music, contemporary composition, and to the spontaneous music of children.

THE COMPONENTS OF TONE

Sound is intrinsically interesting to human beings, and it captures a child's attention at a very early age. Children create sound with their own voices and with objects that they strike and manipulate to produce soft and loud sounds of different qualities. For the child, to discover tone is to perceive the sound of voices and the sound of struck or scraped objects. Jean Piaget made the following notes about his daughter's interest in the sound of her own voice: "Sometimes, for instance, the wail which precedes or prolongs the crying is kept up for its own sake because it is an interesting sound (1 month, 22 days). Sometimes the cry of rage ends in a sharp cry which distracts the child from his pain and is followed by a sort of short trill (2 months, 2 days)."[2]

Very young children also manipulate objects to create interesting sounds. Piaget observed his children, at age four to eight months, intentionally rubbing dolls and rattles against the wicker of the bassinet, for the sake of the sound they made.[3]

Although a child's concept of tone grows out of the infant's explorations of sound, there is a long period of development before children choose objects and manipulate them deliberately to create specific sounds they expect to hear. To the toddler, mother's pots, pans, mixing bowls, and other household equipment have great potential for the exploration of sound. Later, the nursery school, kindergarten, and primary teacher must provide instruments and conditions that will lead children to continue to explore sound and to develop concepts related to the materials they manipulate.

Concepts of Tone and How They Are Developed

A concept is an idea about something. In the case of musical tone you can have a concept about its quality or color (timbre); you can also think in terms of the highness or lowness of the tone (pitch), its degree of loudness (dynamics), or how long it lasts (duration).

Timbre (pronounced "tambur"), or tone color, is a property of both vocal and instrumental sound. You hear timbre of a tone when you notice the "booming" quality of a drum as contrasted with the "ringing" sound of a triangle, or the "raspy" sound of sandpaper blocks. These are descriptive words applied to different timbres; you and the children with whom you work may find other words to use in labeling these sounds. As labels these words are subjective; they have meaning in this context only when the individual has been able to sort out timbre from the other dimensions of a tone, and has compared it with the contrasting timbre of another instrument. (Some practical approaches are suggested under Experiences at Level I in this chapter.)

Pitch in musical tone is determined by the rate of vibration in the instrument, e.g., a drumhead, or a metal object such as a triangle. The faster the rate of vibration, the "higher" the pitch produced. "Higher" and "lower" are labels we attach to this phenomenon. Both the concept and the labels must be learned. To develop a concept of pitch, children must hear it change from one tone to another while all other dimensions are held constant. You can strike two tone blocks, both of the same kind of wood, the first slightly smaller than the second, and notice the "higher" pitch in the small one. You can do the same with two triangles made of the same metal.

Dynamics or degree of loudness is another variable element of tone. When a drum is struck forcefully so that the vibrations of the drumhead are intense, the resulting sound is "loud." Conversely, when the drum is struck gently, the pitch and timbre of the tone remain generally the same, but there is less intensity in the vibrations of the head, and the tone is said to be "soft." Degrees of loudness and softness in music are its "dynamics." Since loudness relates directly to the amount of energy or force needed to produce the tone, it is one of the first musical concepts that children develop.

Duration is the length of time a tone lasts. The tone is "long" or "short," depending upon how long it can be heard. When a percussion instrument is struck, the tone begins immediately to fade (decay). The tone of a triangle or a gong has much longer duration than the tone of a tone-block or a drum. If you are very quiet, you can measure the length of time some tones can be heard by counting silently; other tones fade immediately.

Duration can be much longer when the tone is produced by bowing, scraping, blowing, or restriking the instrument. This is an easy concept to develop, because the physical act of sustaining the tone shows its duration.

Children will not develop a concept of tone that includes all these factors until the intermediate years; in nursery school and kindergarten, however, they are capable of endless exploration and observation of objects that produce sound. All the small discoveries they make will eventually fit together into a composite understanding of musical tone as they mature intellectually.

Categories of Sound Sources

Many sound sources can be combined for expressive musical purposes. Among these are "raw" sounds, which include:

1. Body sounds, such as clapping, patting the knees and tapping the feet, clicking the tongue, and snapping fingers
2. Vocal sounds, which could include spoken chant, whisper, sigh, moan, repeated words, consonants, vowels, vocal siren, and yell
3. Sounds created by striking or rubbing pieces of metal, wood, or stone

Related to the "raw" sounds are the traditional musical sounds of voices and instruments. It is useful to think of these sounds in terms of their method of production (the tone-generator) and how they are changed and shaped for expressive purposes (tone modification). In electronic sound, these two processes are separate steps; but in vocal and instrumental performance they are inseparably linked.

Vocal sounds. The tone-generator for vocal sound is the breath that passes through the vocal chords, causing them to vibrate. Vocal tone is modified by the shape of the mouth, tongue, lips, and resonance cavities in the head. It is shaped and cultivated differently in different cultural traditions. As an example, the sound of Nashville country music singers (e.g., Johnny Cash) is readily distinguished from the sound of the operatic star (e.g., Luciano Pavarotti or Beverly Sills), or the blues singer (e.g., Bessie Smith or Louis Armstrong).

Instrumental sounds developed in different musical traditions through generations of experimentation, in which materials of many shapes were struck, rubbed, plucked, or blown. They fall into four main classes.

In common sound-makers such as tone-blocks, castanets, maracas, cymbals, bells, and gongs, a naturally resonant solid material such as wood or metal is struck, scraped, or shaken to produce the tone. Sound waves are created by the vibrating body of the instrument itself. Pitch is the result of the relationship among length, width, thickness, and density of the material. In resonant-solid instruments the type and size of the resonating chamber, together with the nature of the vibrating material, determine the timbre and range of loudness. A bit of experimenting with classroom percussion instruments will demonstrate these principles.

Drums produce sound when a membrane (animal skin or other material) stretched over a round frame or hollow cylinder is made to vibrate. The thickness and size of the vibrating membrane, together with the size and shape of the resonating chamber, determine the pitch and timbre of drums. The use of different kinds of mallets (hard versus soft) modifies the tone quality.

There are many types of stringed instruments. Among these are instruments such as the guitar, ukelele, dulcimer, balalaika, sitar, and koto; keyboard instruments (the piano, harpsichord, and clavichord); the harp; and the stringed instruments of the orchestra. In all of these, strings of various thickness are tuned by being stretched between two fixed points.

The string vibrates when it is plucked with the fingers or by a mechanism, struck with mallets or hammers, or bowed. A wooden soundboard or a hollow wood body amplifies the tone and shapes the timbre by adding the sound created by the vibrating wood.

Wind-blown instruments include simple folk instruments such as panpipes and other flutes, single- and double-reeds, and horns, as well as the brass and woodwind families of symphonic bands and orchestras, and the pipe organ. Tone is produced when the column of air inside the instrument is set in vibration. The length of the column of air determines the pitch, and the type of mouthpiece and shape of the instrument determine the timbre.

Electronic sound sources. A final category of sound sources consists of those having electronically produced tone. These include electronic organs and pianos and the synthesizer. Recorded sounds, modified by manipulating the tape recorder, are also considered electronic. Much commercial music uses electronic sound, and some children at the intermediate level can begin to work creatively with electronic sound if suitable equipment is available; see Experiences at Level III, later in this chapter, for a discussion of procedures and equipment.

Sources of Instruments

There are four sources of sounds and instruments that you can draw on as you begin to accumulate materials for the activity sections that follow:

1. Traditional or folk instruments that you can borrow from a friendly music teacher or community musician, or those that you own. These might include Latin-American maracas, claves, different kinds of bells, or well-constructed drums of different cultures.

2. The rhythm instruments traditionally used in the primary grades. Among these are triangles, tambourines, rhythm sticks, finger cymbals and other useful instruments of some durability and reasonably good tone quality. These can be purchased singly or in sets from local music stores and from some of the national distributors listed in Appendix B. A complete survey of primary-school instruments is made in Chapter 4.

3. Durable instruments you can make, and which sometimes may have a better tone quality than the traditional school rhythm instruments. If you or a colleague are skilled in crafts, you might produce instruments of a quality rivaling the folk instruments described above. *Drums, Tomtoms, Rattles* by Mason,[4] now out of print but possibly available in a library, gives detailed instructions for making such instruments. Directions for making a few particularly useful instruments are provided below.

4. Sound-makers that you or the children can construct from easily available materials. Although these usually are not as durable and have less interesting sounds, they nevertheless can be useful in exploring sound. Among such homemade instruments are:

   a. rattles and shakers that look alike (e.g., empty fiber or plastic soft-drink bottles or juice cans) but sound different because they contain different rattling material (sand, rice, beans, . . .)

   b. large nails, bolts, or other pieces of metal that produce ringing sounds of different pitch or tone quality

   c. simply constructed "drums" made from oatmeal boxes, coffee cans, and so forth. You will find directions for making such instruments in Mandell and Wood, *Make Your Own Musical Instruments;*[5] Romney and Watt, *The Musical Instrument Recipe Book;*[6] and an English publication, *Making Musical Instruments,* by Peter Williams [7]

Making a Drum. If you are willing to spend some time collecting materials, constructing, and decorating, you can make a drum that will last for many years. Three kinds of material are needed:

1. A wooden barrel, keg, or pail, 10 or 11 inches in diameter. This should be quite sturdy, open at one end, and having a smooth rim over which the drumhead material is stretched. (New barrels and kegs can be purchased at cooperage firms in the larger cities.) If the barrel is old and dry, soak it for several hours so that the tacks can be driven in more easily. A larger barrel makes a drum with a deeper tone.

2. Hide or gum rubber for the drumhead. Scraped rawhide can be used if it is soaked in water until it is pliable enough to be stretched over the drum. Plastic drumheads are available from music dealers (or as broken discards from the high school band director). Commercial, pure-gum sheet rubber, 1/16-inch thick, also can be used as a drumhead. Buy a square slightly larger than the diameter of the barrel; by the time it is stretched, it will have ample edge for tacking.

3. Upholstery tacks with large heads. Drive these in about an inch from the edge of the rubber or hide. Put in three tacks rather close together; then pull the drumhead across the opening and drive in three more tacks. Work on alternate sides around the drum. Putting in a group of tacks will prevent the material from tearing.

The drum will last longer if the hand or a padded drumstick is used to strike it.

Making Sandblocks. These instruments produce an uncomfortable scratching sound, with different grades of sandpaper or emery cloth (preferred for durability) producing rough or less rough sounds. The following materials are needed:

1. Two half-sheets of emery cloth (9″ x 5½″) that can be purchased at your neighborhood hardware store
2. Two pieces of plywood (3″ x 9″) that might be picked up on the scrap pile at the lumber yard
3. A 4-inch piece of ¾-inch scrap lumber for a handle

The construction is simple. Attach the handle with short nails driven through from the plywood side. Draw the emery cloth smoothly around the plywood base, and thumbtack it on the top side. Do not glue it down; it makes a better sound when it is merely drawn tight around the wood base.

Making Maracas and Guiro (gourd rasp). Both of these instruments can be made from dried gourds, if gourds are available in your vicinity. For maracas, choose a pair of dried gourds that have one long end, to provide a handle. With a fine coping saw or bandsaw, cut the top off the wide part of the gourd, horizontally; clean and shellac the inside; reseal the gourd, leaving inside a small amount of fine rattling material (e.g., rice, shot). If the gourds have been buffed on the outside, they can be painted and lacquered in colorful Mexican designs.

A guiro can be made from a large dried gourd; just file twelve or fifteen grooves in one side to give a washboard effect. Decorate and lacquer it, and when it is dry you can play it by scraping a lightweight stick (chopstick or pencil) over the grooved area.

Making Rhythm Sticks and Tone Blocks. At the hardware store or lumber yard you can find doweling of several thicknesses. Buy 36-inch pieces of ⅝″ and ¼″ doweling, and cut each into four 9-inch lengths. Smooth off the ends with sandpaper, and stain them any desirable color (do not paint them).

Two halves of a coconut make fine-sounding tone-blocks. Buy a small coconut at the grocery (they are available only in certain seasons) and drain the milk from the coconut. Using an electric bandsaw, cut it evenly in half; scrape out the meat. When the shells are dry, scrape and polish them inside and out; shellac if desired.

In other chapters in this book many kinds of musical instruments are referred to and compared in terms of the tone quality produced. This chapter focuses on the exploration and creative use of sound. At each of three levels you will find examples of materials and procedures that are both interesting and educational. You can bring many principles of sound production and modification to children's attention through the activities given here. These are written so that you will be tempted to try some of them and discover for yourself the interest and value they might have for children.

EXPERIENCES AT LEVEL I

During the preschool years, children explore sound as much as they explore any other medium, but adults in their society suppress this behavior ("Johnny, don't make so much noise!") because they find sound disturbing. In an elementary school a child can work at the art easel or table exploring color, design, and textures without impinging on others in the room, but when sound is approached in a similar manner, a problem arises because ears have no earlids! If preschool children are to use sound to develop their aural discrimination and exercise their creativity, the teacher must find ways to deal with sound-making so that it can be free and spontaneous without disturbing others.

Larger classrooms that are carpeted can absorb more sound; sometimes the area is divided into storage space and workrooms that small groups can use. The authors of *Music in Early Childhood*[8] suggest creating individual "sound-exploration carrels" from very large boxes and cans. These can be put in different places in the room, and children can crawl inside to experiment with sound-makers available there. Read Chapter 4 of that book for specific suggestions about the construction of such carrels and sound-makers. As more versatile schools are built, these buildings should include carrels and corners conditioned to absorb sound.

Individual and Group Use of Instruments

The spontaneous music of groups of children often includes several instruments played together dynamically. For the children, the motivation is direct expression of feeling, sharing sound-making for its own sake, and sometimes interacting in sound "conversations" with one another. The Pillsbury Foundation study, *Music of Young Children*,[1] describes and provides recorded examples of such spontaneous music-making by groups of young children.

Many classrooms have activity centers, and music has its center where instruments are kept. Sound-making and listening are the basis for exploration, but because noise can disturb others, acceptable times for the activity are limited. Some small groups use the instruments before school, after school, or during recesses and activity periods. During good weather, the more durable instruments may be taken to a special place outside.

In the early stages, you can guide free exploration of sound by limiting the number of available instruments. Drums are often the first instruments placed in the instrument center. As an introduction, arrange a demonstration–discussion in which you encourage the children to show and tell what they know and can do with the instruments. Some of the ideas that emerge may lead children to explore the instruments further. Later, when someone makes an interesting discovery (a new combination of instruments or a new, effective way to play an instrument), you can bring it to the attention of the entire class. In *Children Discover Music and Dance*[9] Emma Sheehy gives interesting examples and suggestions for use of the instruments. Read pages 85 to 95 in that book for a delightful description of exploring instruments.

Music in Early Childhood,[8] pages 48 to 52, provides descriptions of "Sound Play Encounters" utilizing sound carrels equipped with various sound-makers, pictures, and other sensory stimuli that children can use in creative ways.

MMCP Interaction[10] is a source of strategies for sound exploration and creative activity by young children. It describes simple games involving paper, metal, and vocal sounds. This interesting curriculum guide suggests five phases of creative activity: (1) free exploration, (2) guided exploration, (3) exploratory improvisation, (4) planned improvisation, and (5) reapplication. Each phase is laid out with an outline of Sample Encounter, Principal Ideas, Objectives, Procedures, and Evaluation. If possible, try out one of these strategies with a group of children.

Developing Aural Discrimination through Sound Games

Sound games can be devised in which children interact by identifying instruments or matching sounds. Here are some possibilities that work well with classroom instruments:

1. Two instruments are shown, sounded, and identified (e.g., drum, triangle), then both are placed out of sight while only one is sounded. Some questions follow: "Which instrument did you hear? How can you tell it was a triangle? What kind of sound does it have? How long does the sound last? Raise your hand when I play the instrument; keep your hand up as long as you hear it." In beginning experiences, the two instruments might have quite distinct and different sounds; later the two sounds should be more similar in quality, requiring finer discrimination for accurate identification, e.g., a high-pitched drum and a low-pitched drum, a small triangle and finger cymbals.

2. Once children are well acquainted with the sounds and names of the instruments, they can be asked to identify:
   a. an instrument they hear, but cannot see
   b. an instrument heard in a tape recording

Since there are not only different kinds of instruments, but also different sizes of the same type, and different ways of playing a single instrument, there are extensive possibilities for helping children develop aural discrimination and early concepts of sound production. At different times, sound games can center on different qualities of the sound itself: pitch (high or low), dynamics (loud or soft), duration (long or short), tone color (tinkle, boom, tap, . . .).

Instructional Objectives: To help children discriminate among sounds of classroom percussion instruments; to bring to their attention different attributes of the sounds; and to build a vocabulary of words that describe the sounds of instruments.

Behaviors providing evidence that these instructional objectives have been achieved: The children will

□ identify an unseen instrument used to produce a sound (first by pointing to a like instrument, and later by naming the instrument sounded)

□ identify one of two instruments sounded which produces a longer sound

□ identify one of two instruments sounded which makes a "ringing" sound

□ identify one of two instruments sounded which makes a "loud" sound

This kind of activity has implications for the development of aural discrimination as well as for musical learning *per se*. If you are a teacher of young children, read pages 43 to 51 of *Auditory Learning*[11] by Zigmond and Cicci for rationale and for other examples that can be used in the general classroom.

Using Sound Effects in Songs, Poems, and Stories

Group exploration of sound can be an outgrowth of selecting suitable instruments to use with songs and rhythmic activities. Instruments as well as hands and feet can be used to create sound effects. Several pairs of chopsticks tapped rapidly and lightly, or many fingernails clicking on desk tops or on paper, provide excellent rain-on-the-roof effects. Sandblocks make train sounds. Experiment and listen to decide what instrument produces the sound desired in a particular song. "Who's That?" suggests the use of two sounds, one that has a light "tapping" quality and another with a heavier "knocking" quality.

EXAMPLE 2.1

WHO'S THAT?

Moderately fast   *Virginia*

Reprinted by permission of the publishers from Dorothy Scarborough, *On the Trail of Negro Folk-Songs* (Cambridge, Mass.: Harvard University Press, 1925, 1953).

Alternate lyrics:

> Who's that pressing on the door chime?
> Who's that, wants to come inside?
> Tony*, pressing on the door chime!
> Tony, wants to come inside!

* Substitute child's name

After singing the song, try out several sound-makers and decide which two sounds should be used. Experiment to find out when and how the instruments should be played with the song to give a satisfying effect.

Instructional Objectives: To notice the difference in the quality of sound produced by different rhythm instruments; and to use the sounds for expressive effect.

Behaviors providing evidence that these instructional objectives have been achieved: The children will

☐ choose two instruments, one with a light, soft sound, the other with a lower, heavier sound

☐ discriminate between the two sounds chosen, and equate one with "tapping" and the other with "knocking"

☐ play each instrument rhythmically during the appropriate phrase of the song

Stories and poems offer opportunities for creative use of sound. Read "Wind Is a Cat" aloud several times; you might want to employ choral speaking techniques, in which different voices are used on different lines of the poem.

EXAMPLE 2.2

WIND IS A CAT[12]

Wind is a cat
   That prowls at night—
Now in a valley,
   Now on a height,
Pouncing on houses
   Till folks in their beds
Draw all the covers
   Over their heads.
It sings to the moon
   It scratches on doors;

It lashes its tail
   Around chimneys and roars.
It claws at the clouds
   Till it fringes their silk,
Then laps up the dawn
   Like a saucer of milk.
Then, chasing the stars
   To the tops of the firs,
Curls down for a nap
   And purrs and purrs.

There are many words and phrases in this poem that suggest added sounds. Crushing paper, rustling foil wrap, and scratching a wire screen with a nail are ways sounds might be created. Collect a few sound-makers, and have a small group create a sound-effects accompaniment for the poem. At this level you will notice that children readily find sounds to add coloristic effect to particular action words (e.g., "prowls at night," "pouncing on houses,"); but they are not able to add background effects that create the added dimensions of tension or relaxation in the composition. You can enhance the creative effort by using verse-choir techniques: (1) solo voices versus group, and (2) high-, medium-, or low-pitched voices on different lines of the poem. Mary Val Marsh provides an example and several poems in the book *Explore and Discover Music*.[13] The most important aspect of this project for children is the process—exploring sound effects and choosing those that seem appropriate. Do not be concerned if the product—the sounds selected—are different from those you might have chosen.

Record the spoken poem and the sound effects, then discuss the expressive qualities of the production: "Which is the most interesting sound created for the composition? Can you tell why? Which sounds are high? Which are low? Is any sound longer than the others? Can you think of any sound effect you would like to add? How do the voices help make the composition effective? Could the voices be used in more imaginative ways to create greater expressive effect?"

When you ask questions such as these, you begin to focus attention on the basic elements of music: timbre, pitch, and duration. At any level, the development of concepts about music deals with these elements.

Instructional Objectives: To interpret a poem imaginatively and to select and use sound in ways that will enhance the feeling and mental imagery of the poem.

Behaviors providing evidence that these instructional objectives have been achieved: The children will

- ☐ identify words and phrases with sound effects
- ☐ use high and low pitch for particular effects
- ☐ use timbre (quality of sound) for particular effects
- ☐ change the duration of sound to meet expressive needs
- ☐ change the intensity of sound to meet expressive needs

Seven-year-olds might go a step further into creativity by making a "sound-story." The theme would depend upon the kind of sound sources available, but topics such as "An autumn trip through the woods," "A train ride through the canyon," "A visit to a haunted house," or "An afternoon thunderstorm" could provide a basic idea for such creative work. Start out by creating sound effects that might be related to the topic: "What would we hear on an autumn trip through the woods? How could we make a sound of rustling leaves? (Find more than one way.) What could make the sound of a twig breaking, a squirrel scampering, a bird chirping?" Project 5, "Pictures in Music," in *Sound and Silence*[14] by Paynter and Aston, describes procedures that are useful.

Sounds used in such a composition could be vocal sounds (such as humming, clicking, speaking syllables), body sounds (clapping, clicking the fingers, rubbing hands or feet on different surfaces, and so on), or mechanical sounds (e.g., rumpling paper, or rubbing, striking, or tapping metal or wood). Work with the sounds until you discover in which order they should occur, and what amount of repetition or contrast is needed. It probably will be helpful to make a diagram showing the sequence of sound events in your soundscape. Some children might want to draw related pictures that capture the same mood.

Record the creative composition, and play it back so that the performers can hear the expressive qualities they created and evaluate them objectively. Discuss the completed work: How does the composition reflect the title or topic chosen? Are there any long sounds in the piece? Why is a long sound used? Why are some sounds repeated? Was the same number of sounds used throughout the piece? Was the sound thicker or thinner at some points? Louder or softer? Why?

A music curriculum designed for early childhood should provide opportunities for such spontaneous music-making by having a good variety of sound-makers available to children. In addition, by planning appealing group explorations of sound, you can help children develop sensitivity to different qualities in sound. When pitch, tone color, dynamics, and duration of tone are demonstrated and labeled, at the children's level of language development, they will begin to use language in thinking about the different dimensions of sound.

EXPERIENCES AT LEVEL II

The activities suggested above can also be used with children ages seven to nine. In addition, more systematic exploration of sound is possible, because at these ages children are able to take into account more than one dimension of an object or idea. Every sound has four principal qualities (pitch, timbre, loudness, and duration), and the child at this level can begin to understand how these are interrelated in a single sound. For this reason, a number of sound-discovery and sound-analysis procedures are included here.

Children of these ages are spontaneous and imaginative and should have opportunities to use musical resources creatively. They can do this in two ways: (1) by creating their own compositions from sound-makers available to them, and (2) by combining sounds with other arts, such as stories, poems, and drama.

What Can You Hear in Sound?

Following are approaches that can be taken in listening to and analyzing sound.

1. With eyes closed to mask visual distractions, be completely quiet for ten seconds; listen for any sounds in the environment. Then discuss what you heard: How many different sounds occurred? In what order? Describe the quality of each sound (buzz, thud, drip, roar, . . .). Was the sound loud or soft? Was the sound high or low in pitch? How long did it last? Was the sound constant, or did it change in some way?

2. Search in your environment for an object that can be used to create an interesting sound. A good source of such sounds might be the garage, basement, or kitchen, where you can investigate the sound potential of such things as a cookie tin, an

oven rack, or a wrench used to strike a length of pipe. In exploring the sound potential of any object, you may find that it can be sounded in more than one way, with more than one kind of striker. If you can get three interesting sounds from one object, you rank as a superior sound sleuth. These are called "found" sounds. Now try to categorize the several dimensions of each sound in the following ways:

Pitch. Two aspects can be considered:

a. is it high or low, or modified as very high, very low, or in a middle range of pitch?

b. is it definite or indefinite, that is, can it be labeled exactly or approximately as a pitch in a given octave on the piano (C, D, E, F$^\sharp$, . . .), or is it impossible to identify a specific pitch?

Timbre. This can be described in various ways:

a. ring, tinkle, click, scrape, thud, boom, and so forth

b. metallic, dry, resonant, hollow, dark, and so forth

Loudness. Two aspects should be considered:

a. the natural sound itself as soft, very loud, or moderately loud (some materials produce only one general level of sound)

b. the loudness resulting from how the material is manipulated; i.e., it may sound loud if struck or scraped with force, or it may sound very soft if tapped gently

Duration. Two aspects can be considered:

a. the decay of the sound, i.e., the natural dying away of the sound after the object has been struck or otherwise set into vibration; decay can be rapid or slow

b. the prolongation of the sound by repeated tapping or shaking; in this case, the duration would depend upon the action of the player

Affective Quality. If it is an "interesting" sound, does it arouse associative feelings? In what expressive context might it be used? In sound exploration groups, individuals often spontaneously associate events out of their experience with sounds they have created; e.g., "it sounds like walking through leaves in the forest," or "a clock ticking at night." Take note of the sound, and plan to use it later in a soundscape in that context.

In the above exercise you probably used the senses of sight and touch to aid the ear in categorizing the sound made when a given object is manipulated. Would you be able to describe a sound source and define its qualities if you depended upon hearing alone? The following exercise might demand more skill in hearing.

3. Have someone drop an unidentified object on an unidentified surface out of sight. Describe the properties of the object dropped (i.e., its size, weight, shape and physical composition); the conditions under which it was dropped (i.e., from what height onto what surface); and finally the dimensions of the resulting sound (pitch, loudness, timbre, duration, as discussed under item 2 above).

4. Other sounds with high expressive potential are vocal and body sounds. These might include hisses, hums, repeated phonemes or words, imitations of animal or bird sounds, claps, stamps, clicks, laughter, or any of childhood's vocal play. Develop an interesting sound that can be sustained or repeated for ten seconds.

Make a tape recording of a number of these sounds, and describe each of them in terms of pitch, dynamics, timbre, duration, and affect as suggested under item 2. In these sounds, did you discover any dimension significantly different from those in the "found" sounds you analyzed? Do you think vocal and body sounds are more or less varied than those you created by using other sound-makers?

5. The ability to hear, to describe its various dimensions, and to make imaginative use of sound can be carried a step further if you use a cassette tape recorder to capture sounds of familiar events (water running down a drain, a repeated door slam, verbal mumbling, a person walking on a creaky floor).

   Ask someone else to describe, in terms of loudness, duration, pitch and tone quality, the sounds heard on the tape. If the children want to describe the sounds in terms of their "feeling" qualities (the sound has a friendly, happy connotation, or there is something sinister about it), this is fine; be receptive, but do not try to evaluate these personal impressions as either appropriate or inappropriate. Finally, identify the sound source if you can.

These projects can be used with children at Level II. You will find that many children have portable cassette tape recorders that they could use for collecting sounds at home and in the neighborhood.

Instructional Objectives: To interest children in sound; to help focus their attention on different dimensions of sound; and to help them begin to realize the suggestions of feeling that sounds convey.

   Behaviors providing evidence that these instructional objectives have been achieved: The children will

   ☐ express interest by searching for sounds
   ☐ categorize a single sound in terms of at least three of its attributes (timbre, pitch, dynamics, duration)
   ☐ feel free to suggest that a particular sound conveys certain feelings

At this level, we have given much attention to the cognitive domain in the analysis of sound; but let's also be sure to notice the aesthetic impact of these sounds. They can be used in various kinds of creative composition. Children ages seven to nine who have not had previous experience in using sound effects for expressive purposes could profit from some of the experiences outlined under Level I, or they could use sound in the following ways.

What Can You Do with Sound?

Form a group with three or four fellow students, each having a simple percussion instrument or using a "found" sound. Improvise briefly, exploring the combined effects possible from these sound-makers. Gradually shape a composition about one minute long that uses single as well as group sounds in the context of a particular mood, feeling, or expressive idea. Start by having everyone explore the sound-making potential of the instruments in the group, then develop dialogue and interaction among the sounds. When you begin to get a sense of a mood the group projects (whimsical, strong and driving, gentle and delicate, . . .), develop it further so there is a sense of beginning, a climax, and an ending.

Using crayons and a piece of drawing paper, make a diagram of your composition—a visual representation of what you have created in sound. Finally, tape record the composition so you can listen to it objectively.

Play each recording and have other members of the class discuss what they hear in the composition:

1. What was its overall expressive effect? (Forceful, tranquil, humorous, . . .) Individuals will differ in their interpretation, given their different backgrounds and personal experience. Don't try to evaluate these responses as right or wrong.
2. What was the most important element in the composition? (Rhythm, dynamics, tone color, . . .)
3. Is the sound essentially the same throughout the composition, or are there moments of contrast? How is any contrast achieved?
4. In what ways does the diagram lead the observer to anticipate the composition's quality and possible events? (Sometimes it is interesting to look first at the diagram and have others suggest what qualities they expect to hear in the taped composition.)

The teacher's role in this creative work is to help individuals and groups discover the expressive qualities in their music, hearing and giving recognition to all the different compositions and being enthusiastic about these creative efforts. Compositions can be compared, not because one is better than the other, but because one can observe differences and discover new ways to create interesting effects. The composers can be asked how they created a certain effect, or if they "intended it that way."

Instructional Objectives: To provide a structure within which children can: (1) combine sound in expressive ways and be aware of the musical elements that they used; (2) have the satisfaction of creating a composition that is expressive to them, thus experiencing and appreciating the efforts of the composer; (3) realize that their choice of sounds and their ways of combining them determine their composition's expressive effect.

Behaviors providing evidence that these instructional objectives have been achieved: The children will

□ compose a piece of music, and make a tape recording and a diagram of it

□ listen to their composition and that of other groups, and point out how each composition differs in its expressive effect

□ point out the particular use of at least one aspect of tone or other musical element in their composition

□ express interest in creating another composition

Thoughtful questions and discussion through several creative encounters can guide children in developing concepts that are compatible with their musical and intellectual maturity. Throughout this questioning you, the teacher, will be guided by your knowledge of musical sound and concepts related to it; but you should help children arrive at their own observations, rather than giving them an adult analysis for which they are not ready.

Using Sound in Drama

Seven- to nine-year-olds could produce a very effective accompaniment for "The Wind Is a Cat," shown in the material for Level One of this chapter. They can also create an accompaniment of sound effects for stories they read, dramatize, or produce as puppet plays. "Daniel Boone and the Bear" is a story that provides opportunities for the creative use of sound.

EXAMPLE 2.3

DANIEL BOONE AND THE BEAR[15]

Of all the bear-and-Indian fighters from the early days of our country, most people thought Daniel Boone was the smartest. Here is one reason they thought so.

Daniel Boone had been in the woods for many weeks when he came on a stretch that seemed quite unfamiliar to him and made him a little unsure about where he was. To get rid of his uncertainty Daniel climbed a tall tree and looked around until he knew where he was. Then he started to climb down. He had almost reached the main crotch of the tree when a rotten limb broke and he fell. There was a hole just at the main crotch, and Daniel fell plumb into it.

He was not hurt, but he was annoyed when he found out what had happened to him. The trunk of the tree was hollow and he had landed on the inside at the bottom. The sides were so smooth he could not climb them and so high he could not reach up and pull himself out. He was a prisoner with no way of escape. All the rest of the day he stood there looking up through the hole at the top to the blue sky, listening to the sounds of the woods all around him.

About an hour after it was completely dark, Daniel heard a strange noise. There was a scratching and a grunting on the outside of his prison. Some kind of animal was climbing the tree, for the noise was getting higher and higher. Suddenly he knew that the hole above him was filled up, because he could no longer see the star that had been shining down on him. Then the scratching and grunting started again, but this time it was coming down toward him. Daniel could tell from the scratching, which was nearer to him, and from the grunts, that the animal was coming down backwards. Instantly, he realized that he had fallen into the hollow-tree home of a big bear.

Slowly the bear backed down toward him. Foot by foot, the hindquarters of the fierce beast got closer to Daniel. All of a sudden Daniel jumped up and grabbed the bear by his stubby tail. "Aiooup!" he yelled at the top of his voice.

The bear was so frightened at this unexpected attack that he gave one big grunt and dashed up out of the hole just about a hundred times as fast as he had come down into it. Daniel kept hold of the tail and went along with him. Down the tree trunk went the bear and off into the woods. Daniel turned a complete somersault when he finally let go. Well, that is how Daniel Boone outsmarted a bear.

Get acquainted with the story, and determine which moods and ideas lend themselves to amplification by added sound; find the best way to create the desired effect. "Found sounds," body and vocal sounds, or classroom instruments could be used. Remember that:

1. The type of instrument (material, composition, and shape) determines the quality of sound produced.
2. Individual instruments can be manipulated in different ways to produce different sounds.

One or more individuals can be assigned to read or tell the story. As many others as seems appropriate can contribute the creative background, drawing on whatever sound sources are available. You may need to appoint a director for this production, to signal the readers and players so that the story and sound effects are effectively integrated. When the masterpiece has been recorded, listen to it to decide:

1. How pitch and timbre were used to enhance the story's ideas
2. Whether the added accompaniment amplified the story's mood changes appropriately
3. How silence as well as sound, duration of sound, and intensity were used for expressive effect
4. What changes in pace in voices and instruments were used, and whether the pace was appropriate to the expressive ideas highlighted
5. Whether the accompaniment did indeed make the story more expressive

Instructional Objectives: To give children incentive to interpret a story imaginatively; and to select and use sounds in ways that enhance the story's feeling and imagery. In doing this, they will listen to sounds with more interest, analyze their component parts, and become aware of some of the musical elements that shape a composition into an expressive whole.

Behaviors providing evidence that these instructional objectives have been achieved: The children will

☐ discuss their reactions to the story and how their arrangement of sounds improves it

☐ try out different sounds and ways of using them as they create the musical arrangement

☐ listen to the completed work and observe its overall shape, beginning, climax, and ending, in terms of how dynamics, timbre, texture, and other elements were used

Creative use of sound is given considerable attention in current basic series music books for this level. You may want to study some of these resources (see Appendix B for book titles):

CM Z3A-207T   NDinM II-146
ExM II-35, 104   NDinM III-81
ExM III-100   NDinM IV-51
ExM IV-18, 109, 123   SBM IV-20, 62, 94, 109, 147, 190

EXPERIENCES AT LEVEL III

If ten- and eleven-year-olds have not had opportunities to explore and use sound in some of the creative ways described earlier in this chapter, you should arrange such encounters. Once they have had experience exploring sound, you can use Level III experiences to give more attention to compositional techniques. Music by contemporary composers can also be studied for a broader perspective on how musical materials are used. In addition, children can have experience altering sounds electronically. Many children have their own cassette recorders, which they could use to gather sounds from many sources. Using these means, you might help children who are especially interested in musical composition and tape recorders to work out their own creative compositions.

What Makes a Musical Composition?

After you have had some experiences creating small compositions, diagramming, and discussing them, you should notice that in creative work musical elements other than those identified as components of sound are being considered. The opposite of sound, silence, is potently expressive, and dynamic contrasts help shape the work. Repetition and contrast of musical elements are basic components of musical form; and variety in texture (the simultaneous sounding of few or many instruments) can be a controlling feature.

To explore these principles, you might set up additional criteria for compositions using "found sounds," percussion instruments, or vocal and body sounds:

1. Create a composition that makes significant use of silence.
2. Create a composition that uses repetition and contrast.
3. Create a composition in which all the sound sources have a similar timbre, but in which you achieve significant contrast through change in texture (thin sound, one or two instruments, contrasted with thick sound having many simultaneous lines).

A publication by participants in the *Manhattanville Music Curriculum Program*[16] (MMCP) contains sample strategies for music learning based on such a creative approach. The program encompasses sixteen learning cycles applicable to third grade and above. Each cycle begins with an analysis of the particular aspects of the musical elements (timbre, dynamics, pitch, form, and rhythm) to be dealt with, and includes a catalog of musical skills and vocabulary to be developed. The sample strategies in Cycles 1 and 2 are particularly useful for early creative work.

Small ensembles of four or five player-composers make comfortable working groups. With colored crayons, chart the instrumentation and form of the composition, using lines and other graphic symbols. This exercise gives the musicians more tangible evidence of their work and forces them to hear and analyze the music that has been created. Quite simple diagrams will meet the needs of younger children, but ten- and eleven-year-olds will be able to show the detail of the composition more completely.

Children's natural approach to such creativity will be through improvisation, searching for the sound combination that meets their needs, in contrast to the cerebral, "thinking-out" approach adults might take. Until children have a background of experience that provides some governing principles, the exploratory approach is the right one; but they should then stop to make a diagram or score, so that they can analyze what they have done. Children who have reached the stage of "formal operations," as well as adults, can benefit from reading descriptions of these kinds of activities.

R. Murray Schafer, a Canadian composer-teacher, has led groups to explore sounds and put them together in expressive ways. He wrote five booklets describing his nonconventional approach to teaching music and dealing creatively with sound. These recently have been combined in one unified book.[17] Any one of his topics, "Ear Cleaning," "The New Soundscape," "When Words Sing," is highly recommended as resource material.

In developing their creative compositions, children find out about many musical effects by playing, listening, analyzing, and evaluating their work. In some instances this may include listening to music of an established composer. If you can find a composed work that has some parallel characteristics to the children's ensemble, they will listen with great interest.

Toccata for Percussion, Third Movement, (ExM III R8 or Urania URLP 7144), by Carlos Chávez, is useful. Consider some ways the composer used his material:

☐ *Timbre*—variety, contrast . . .

☐ *Dynamics*—level, change, silence . . .

☐ *Texture*—thick, thin, changing . . .

☐ *Rhythm*—repetition, variety, metric, nonmetric . . .

☐ *Form*—repetition, contrast, variation . . .

Listen to the music, and think about each of the points listed above. How has the composer used these musical elements and compositional principles? Replay parts of the music so you can focus on particular effects; compare what was done at different points in the composition. These are some techniques that should be identified when you think about the composition of this music:

1. The timpani is the initial tone color heard in the composition, and it is important throughout the piece.
2. Contrast of timbre is an important principle in this composition.

3. The successive addition of different tone colors thickens the texture at certain points.
4. Rhythmic drive and change of intensity influence the music's expressive effect.
5. Repetition of the timpani motif is an organizing principle in the composition's form.

After studying such a composition, the player-composers are very likely to return to their own creative work with new perspective on the performance capabilities of their instruments and on possible compositional techniques. Other recorded percussion ensembles that might be studied are: Golden Crest Records, Inc., CR4016—*Variations on a Handmade Theme,* by Warren Benson; *Afro-Fuga,* by John Alling; and others. Time Recording 58000—*Amores* and *Double Music,* by John Cage; *Ostiato Pianissimo,* by Henry Cowell; and others.

Instructional Objectives: To provide an opportunity for children to work creatively with sound, to develop positive attitudes toward their own potential for creative use of sound, and to gain a basis for more rewarding listening and for understanding the principles of musical composition.

Behaviors providing evidence that these instructional objectives have been achieved: The children will

□ complete an original composition, record it, and diagram it

□ speak enthusiastically about the experience, and plan for another composing project

□ request to study recordings of other percussion compositions

□ diagram and discuss simple principles of musical structure in connection with their composition

Exploring Sound through Electronic Alteration

With a portable tape recorder at hand, search for three interesting sounds. It is a good idea to find sounds that have different qualities: one might have variation in pitch (high and low), another might have variety in dynamics (loud and soft), and another might feature a definite rhythm. Because each original recorded sound should last for a full minute, it may be necessary to repeat the sound several times.

After the sounds have been collected on tape, listen and compare them in terms of pitch, loudness, duration, rhythmic elements, and the mood or expressive effect each conveys. Which seem to have the most intrinsic interest? Have you any idea how they might sound when speeded up or slowed down? What happens to pitch when the tape is played at a faster speed? If you have one minute of the sound on the original recording, how long will that segment be when played half as fast? Let's move to the next step to find out.

Dub the most interesting sounds from the cassette player to a three-speed machine, recording them first at the slow speed of 1⅞ inches per second (ips), and then again at the fast speed of 7½ ips. When the slow dub is played successively at

3¾ ips and 7½ ips, the original sounds will be heard twice as fast and then four times as fast. When the fast dub is played successively at 3¾ and 1⅞ ips, the original sounds will be heard twice as slow and then four times as slow. Listen to the result and describe how each altered sound differs from the original recorded sound. Consider changes in pitch and duration and the way these affect the sound's expressive quality. Now, which do you find most interesting? If possible, find words to describe the changed sounds as compared with the original sounds.

If you wish to keep these sounds, dub them again to a tape moving at 7¾ ips. Alter the speed of the tape from which you take the sounds, and do not record more than one minute of each sound you wish to preserve.

Make a list of the sounds you have on your tape. State the original sound source and how it was altered in each instance. Then describe the expressive properties of each sound in terms of its

pitch and variation of pitch	tempo and variation in speed
loudness or softness	rhythmic qualities
timbre (quality, color)	mood projected

You probably will find that you have a few very interesting sounds that you spontaneously hear in a descriptive context. Some of them might provide sound support for a story or drama. Why not plan to use them in that way!

One further, long-range creative project is suggested if you or the children you teach have the equipment and the interest to carry it out. For this activity you will need:

1. two tape recorders, at least one of them stereophonic
2. the tape of electronically altered sounds that you created earlier by speeding up and slowing down the recording of environmental, or "concrete," sounds
3. a tape splicer, leader tape, and splicing tape
4. patch cords to connect the tape recorders, and two empty reels

Get well acquainted with the expressive quality of the sounds you have recorded on tape; then decide:

1. which appeal to you most
2. which might be used as the main element in your composition
3. which would serve as contrasts to the main element
4. which might support and amplify the main element

The objective is to create a composition that has some interest and quality of feeling; it may or may not have literal meaning such as a story conveys. By using the stereophonic capabilities of one machine, you can combine two or more sounds by simultaneously recording the sounds of two tracks onto one track, or by using the sound-on-sound capability if your machine provides that option.

If you have some material you would like to use repeatedly as one motif or an underlying accompaniment (an ostinato) in the composition, you can make a tape loop. This piece of tape can be from 18 inches to several feet in length, depending upon the length of the musical idea to be used. Splice the end of the tape to the beginning of the tape segment so the sound you want to use can be played repeatedly without a pause. Arrange the loop over the playback head of the tape recorder between two empty reels, and let it hang loosely or even run across the floor at the back of the machine. When arranged properly in relation to the reel that turns, and with slight tension or weight applied, the loop can be made to move smoothly across the receiving head of the machine so that it plays continuously. You can re-record this continuous sound on one channel of the stereo machine as one element of your creative composition.

A tape loop is useful in elementary tape-recorder composition because it presents an easy way to create repetition in building form and texture. More than one ostinato can be used. Some machines have a reverberation (echo) capability that can add interest to a composition. Various publications suggest other techniques to use in such a project.[18] A sound filmstrip, *Creating Music Through Use of the Tape Recorder*[19] provides eighteen lessons on different aspects of the subject.

You probably have discovered that a composition of any kind needs a beginning and an ending, with some kind of growth, development, and contrast in between. If the composition has two sections, the second different from the first, the form would be two-part, or binary (A B). The form might be a basic repetition after contrast (A B A), or you might have enough interesting sounds to create a rondo (A B A C A). Let your own sense of feeling for sound and shape guide your splicing and editing. This project may take you many hours, but if your final product is interesting and expressive to you, your work is successful. Make a diagrammatic score, showing how the sounds in your composition are successive and simultaneous.

This type of composition has the formal name of *musique còncrète*, that is, music created through the electronic alteration of recorded natural sounds. "Electronic music" uses sounds generated by electronic means, but altered and combined using some of the same techniques developed for *musique còncrète*. Sounds of instruments and voices can be treated in similar ways.

Instructional Objectives: To give children an opportunity to work creatively with contemporary sound resources and techniques, to develop understanding of the work and creative product of contemporary composers, and to expand children's understanding of basic principles of musical form and composition.

Behaviors providing evidence that these instructional objectives have been achieved: The children will

☐ complete an original composition and provide a diagrammatic score for it

☐ seek out and study recordings of *musique còncrète* and electronic music compositions

Sounds of New Music (Folkways Records FX6160) contains good examples of these kinds of music. Current basic series music books provide suggestions and materials for creative work with both concrete and electronic sounds. These are some possible resources:

CM Z3B-18, 23 NDinM V-209 to 211
CM Z3C-279 NDinM VI-212 to 218
ExM V-13, 188 SBM V-221 (satellite)
ExM VI-32, 193 SBM VI-223 (satellite)

CHAPTER NOTES

1. Gladys Moorhead and Donald Pond, **Music of Young Children,** 4 vols. (Santa Barbara, Calif.: The Pillsbury Foundation for the Advancement of Music Education [P.O. Drawer A, 93102], 1941–51; 5th printing, 1978).

2. Jean Piaget, **The Origins of Intelligence in Children,** translated by Margaret Cook (New York: International Universities Press, 1952), p. 78.

3. **Ibid.,** pp. 168–169.

4. Bernard S. Mason, **Drums, Tomtoms, Rattles** (New York: A. S. Barnes and Co., Inc., 1938).

5. Muriel Mandell and Robert E. Wood, **Make Your Own Musical Instruments** (New York: Sterling Publishing Co., Inc., 1968).

6. Emily Romney and Dan Watt, **The Musical Instrument Recipe Book** (Newton, Mass.: Elementary Science Study of Education Development Center, Inc., 1968).

7. Peter Williams, **Lively Craft Cards, Set 2: Making Musical Instruments** (London, England: Mills and Boon, 1971).

8. Barbara L. Andress et al., **Music in Early Childhood** (Washington, D.C., Music Educators National Conference, 1973), Chapter 4.

9. Emma D. Sheehy, **Children Discover Music and Dance** (New York: Teachers College Press, 1968).

10. Americole Biasini, Ronald Thomas, and Lenore Pognowski, **MMCP Interaction,** Early Childhood Music Curriculum (Bardonia, New York: Media Materials, Inc., n.d.).

11. Naomi K. Zigmond and Regina Cicci, **Auditory Learning,** Dimensions in Early Learning series (Belmont, Calif.: Fearon Publishers, 1968).

12. Ethel Romig Fuller, "Wind Is a Cat," **White Peaks and Green** (New York: Harper & Row, 1928). Used by permission.

13. Mary Val Marsh, **Explore and Discover Music** (New York: The Macmillan Company, 1970), pp. 13–17.

14. John Paynter and Peter Aston, **Sound and Silence, Classroom Projects in Creative Music** (New York: Cambridge University Press, 1970).

15. From **America Sings Stories and Songs of Our Country's Growing** by Carl Carmer. Copyright 1942, and renewed 1970 by Carl Carmer. Reprinted by permission of Alfred A. Knopf, Inc.

16. Ronald B. Thomas, **MMPC Synthesis,** USOE V-008 and USOE 6-1999 (Bardonia, New York: Media Materials, Inc., 1970).

17. R. Murray Schafer, **Creative Music Education** (New York: Schirmer Books, A Division of Macmillan Publishing Company, Inc., 1976).

18. Merrill Ellis, "Musique Concrète at Home," **Music Educators Journal** (Nov. 1968), p. 95; David Ernest, "So You Can't Afford an Electronic Studio?" **Music Educators Journal** (Feb. 1973), p. 45; Terence Dwyer, **Composing Music with Tape Recorders:** *Musique Còncrète* **for Beginners** (London: Oxford University Press, 1971); Brian Denis, **Experimental Music in the School** (London: Oxford University Press, 1970).

19. Anne D. Madugna, **Creating Music Through Use of the Tape Recorder.** Multimedia Kit KTR-6 (New Haven, Conn.: Keyboard Publications, n.d.).

3

Body Movement, Rhythm, and Musicality

Rhythm in music is the expressive organization of sound in time. It is shaped around points of tension and release in a manner that reflects our human existence: We experience rhythm in the beating of the heart, in breathing, in walking, in the alternation of night and day, summer and winter, youth and age. The qualities of tension-relaxation, expectation-fulfillment are basic to all of these, as they are basic to music.

The rhythm of music is heard, it is felt kinesthetically, and it is seen in physical movement. Emile Jacques-Dalcroze, the eminent music educator of Geneva, Switzerland, during the 1920s created a system of interpreting musical rhythm through body movement. This physical response to rhythm he considered essential to the development of musical expression. Influences of that system remain strong, and body movement is an important means of developing rhythmic perception and rhythmic response in the study of music.

Movement can reflect musical qualities other than rhythm. In the experiences of this chapter, therefore, you will find your attention drawn to musical phrasing and form, melody, dynamics, tone color of instruments, as well as mood and characterization.

Expressive movement, as a musical activity, has a relationship with school programs in physical education and creative dramatics. In all of these, skills in movement and freedom for expression are necessary. In physical education, expressive movement is used to promote physical development, health, and poise; music assists by helping to make the movement rhythmic. In creative dramatics, movement expresses what the individual feels; music is selected or composed to support ideas already present.

When body movement and creative dramatics are used to support music education, the objectives are:

1. To identify music as an expression of physical movement and feeling
2. To provide musical experiences that unify the physical sense of self with the mind and feelings
3. To provide experiences that will give added dimension to music listening
4. To develop concepts of music that, in turn, permit keener musical perception

Whether the activity is creative movement, folk dancing, or conducting a song, these objectives for the music program remain the same. But children's experience in physical education and creative drama is also valuable and contributes toward a richer musical experience; the more flexibility and physical control children have, the more they are able to express what they feel in music. The imaginative approach to movement that is developed in creative dramatics gives children the necessary feeling of freedom to express confidently what they hear in music.

THE COMPONENTS OF RHYTHM

Rhythm has many dimensions. In this chapter, discussion and examples are limited to the aspects of rhythm that are most readily expressed in body movement. Chapter 4, featuring percussion instruments, will consider rhythm in greater detail and will include the study of notation for rhythm. For reference material on this topic, see the Catalog of Musical Concepts, Appendix A, and Reference Material for Music Theory and Notation, Appendix C.

Early Concepts of Rhythm

Young children's use of movement in locomotor activities, games, and creative dramatics can contribute to an early understanding of rhythm. Rhythmic activities are part of children's whole-life experience and they cannot be limited to any one period during the day. The classroom teacher provides the link between the children's spontaneous activities and their application in music education. Classroom experiences during early childhood can help develop the following concepts:

Movement has rhythm. As children move with walks, runs, and gallops, the teacher can help them notice the characteristics of the movement and that each movement is a "rhythm." Singing games and dances provide a musical structure for unified rhythmic movement of different kinds.

Different movements make different rhythms. Comparing two different movements, such as run and gallop, help children realize that different kinds of movement produce different rhythms. They should compare the muscular feeling of the different movements, and they should hear the difference in the sound of the movements and in the rhythm of the music that accompanies each type of movement.

One basic rhythm can have different qualities. One fundamental rhythm might be executed in a variety of ways, e.g., with different levels of weight and dynamic impact, or with greater or lesser use of space. All locomotor movements can be done with larger or smaller movements, louder or softer sound, and faster or slower steps, for different expressive effects.

Rhythms have different patterns. There are three general types of rhythm patterns readily related to movement:

1. Short, even movement or sounds, e.g., run, walk, jump, hop, tip-toe
2. Long, smooth, even movement or sounds, e.g., swing, sway, turn, twist, skate, if the movements are regular
3. Uneven movement or sounds, e.g., gallop, skip, peg-leg walk, irregular hop, jump

These elemental concepts of rhythm arise when we direct children's attention to their own movement and relate it to music. Gradually, however, children should be asked to adjust their movements to music they hear, so that they can then develop awareness of other aspects of rhythm.

The Elements of Rhythm Related to Movement

The concepts outlined in this chapter can be developed by means of the experiences described in this chapter and in Chapter 4. It is expected that those discussions of music and procedures will be brought to life in the music methods class, so that readers with no background in music will have practical examples of these elements.

Rhythm. As a broad concept, rhythm can be defined as "measured motion"; it includes all the following concepts, which pertain to the movement of music through time.

The beat. The beat is a regular, recurring pulse that provides a frame of reference for musical rhythm. Sometimes it is clearly heard and felt, but often it is unobtrusive. Although most rhythm is related to beat, rhythm is the expressive factor, and the two should not be confused. Beat is easily represented by body movement.

Tempo. The idea of a faster or a slower pace in music (tempo) gives yet another dimension to the concept of rhythm. A single composition can be played or sung faster or slower without otherwise changing the rhythm. Tempo is identified in terms of the speed of the beat underlying the rhythm, and even in preschool classes, when children use body movement to dramatize various kinds of action, their attention can be directed so that they are aware of "faster" and "slower" pace.

Accent. Several different conditions in music are thought of as accent. Cooper and Meyer[1] define accent as "a stimulus (in a series of stimuli) which is marked for consciousness in some way." In a group of long and short tones, one tone can be central because of its length or its position in the group; in a series of regular, recurring beats, every second or third is felt as a point of renewal or accent.

Accent is also created when one tone is given prominence by increasing its dynamic level, e.g., by greater energy in the production of the tone or by the addition of another instrument. Children can understand accent in this context fairly early, because it can be associated with a demonstrable act; they create accents in their independent use of movement.

The motif (or "motive"). The smallest expressive unit of rhythm is the motif, defined as a group of one or more unaccented tones related to an accented tone. The word "pattern" conveys a similar concept, and this is the term used with children. In this book, motif and pattern will be used interchangeably, although in some instances a child's rhythm pattern may consist of more than one motif. Since rhythm patterns are spontaneously created as children chant and play percussion instruments, this element, together with its composite, melody rhythm, will be given primary attention in Chapter 4.

Meter. The concept of meter has two dimensions, beat and accent, that are organized into simple duple and triple groupings with the accent on the first beat in each group. These basic groups can in turn be combined to produce meters of four, five, six, seven, or more beats.

Much music of other cultures and of the 20th century is not confined rhythmically to meter. Although a great deal of music that is used with children—rhythmic games, dances, and marches—is closely tied to meter, children's concepts of rhythm should not be limited to rhythm that is metrically oriented in this sense. In addition, they should not be left with the idea that meter is an ever-present thump-thump, or thump-thump-thump in music. It is useful to think of meter as a structure underlying the rhythm, but not necessarily intruding itself into the music.

Although much rhythm is organized around meter, rhythm is not necessarily confined within measure bars. Rhythm flows across bar lines; upbeats lead to more important tones of the pattern, which have the accent position in the measure. Examples of this concept follow in this chapter.

Duration. The concept of duration has to do with the relative length of tones or silences. Although young children spontaneously stamp or clap rhythm patterns with a series of rapid or less rapid blows, they have no realization of duration as a variable factor in the sounds they produce.

In Chapter 2, duration was mentioned as a supporting concept in observing the tone produced on different instruments; that more limited context, however, did not involve the ongoing relationships of long and short within a given span of time. In a rhythm pattern or a musical phrase the duration of tones must be considered in relation to movement through time. As a frame of reference, duration is usually measured against the beat, at a particular tempo. Children at Level II can begin to understand duration in this context by using body movement related to music.

Ritard, accelerando, and hold. These three artistic variables of rhythm (gradually getting slower, gradually getting faster, and coming to a temporary stop) are concepts that children can begin to acquire in the primary grades. They experience the effects in dramatic play and other movement and can learn the concepts, if not the particular terminology.

MANAGEMENT OF SPACE FOR MOVEMENT

To have enough freedom in movement related to music, considerable space is needed. Skipping, galloping, and twirling require more space than walking and marching. A fruitful classroom program of rhythmic movements often requires readjustment of furniture so that there are two or three wide aisles, or space at the front of the room. Whereas the classroom has the advantage of being available at any hour, a multi-purpose room or a gymnasium has more space. In a very large room, however, there may be so much space that movement seems to have no limitations. When free creative movement is the goal, this is ideal; but when the objective is the interpretation of music, the children may not relate well to music that is too far away or difficult to hear.

When the space is limited, fewer individuals are able to respond at any one time. Those who do not participate in full body movement can use arm and trunk movements as they sit in chairs or on the floor. This permits response in a limited way and orients participants to the rhythm so that when it is their turn to move with the full pattern, they will be more successful. In each lesson there should be some music for large free movement, and other music for more limited movements, such as swaying, stepping, or rocking, so that the entire class can respond as a group.

Experiment with movement, having individuals go in different directions to develop freedom and originality. Even in marching, the group should not always follow in a line, but should learn to "go different ways" for more freedom of ideas and movement. You will notice that some individuals are very creative and imaginative, and a few prefer to follow the lead of others. To get the timid child started, suggest that "Tommy, go with Joe," or "Sue, follow Amy." Since those who feel insecure in this activity generally will be happier moving in a group rather than individually, it may be advisable to plan space and activity for large-group participation during much of the first two or three lessons that use movement.

Children who have never participated in expressive movement as a classroom activity may have difficulty adjusting to the need for thoughtful response. In their own spontaneous play they use a wide variety of movement for its own sake, but the use of movement for interpretive and expressive purposes demands that attention be given both to the movement and to the ideas represented, or to movement and to the music it interprets.

A certain amount of structure may be needed to help children learn the limitations that must be placed on expressive movement when it is used in the classroom. Plan to use some of the following techniques to maintain a constructive approach to movement:

1. Have the children spread out around the room so their outstretched hands don't touch anyone (colored decals on the floor can provide predetermined spacing). Many kinds of movement can be done in place . . . without going anywhere.

2. When the music or other accompaniment stops, the children should "freeze" in whatever position they are in. Make a game of this at first, so they will remain alert for possible stops. Later, if movement becomes uncontrolled or unproductive, you will have a management technique to use.

3. Discuss with the children the idea of "personal space." As each of us moves, we carry our personal space with us; we do not violate the personal space of others by touching them when we are engaged in movement activities. The children will be interested in this idea and can practice moving about, going close to others, but without touching. Bumping and touching are unproductive and can be minimized with this technique. If intentional contact does occur, stop the music or activity immediately.

4. Help the children focus their attention on the different quality that can be brought to different movements:

   □ Walk like a crippled old man, or as though you were big and fat and weighed 300 pounds.

   □ Walk like a relative, your mother or father.

   □ Gallop like a pony; like a big work horse.

   Later you can help them understand that these differences in quality are the result of a particular use of space (smaller or larger steps), time (fast or slow movement), weight (heavy or light movement), and flow (smooth or jerky movement).

5. Young children tend to become inattentive to the movement and the accompaniment if the activity is carried on too long. Limit the activity to the length of time that attention can be directed to the music and movement.

6. In early movement experiences, recorded music that is used should be short and have a clearly defined rhythm, so that the children have no difficulty finding a movement pattern that will fit the music.

7. Use two consecutive pieces of music that require markedly different movement, so the children will understand the need to adapt the movement to the music.

8. Children who have had no experience with expressive movement as a classroom activity may need the support of structured ideas to get them started (as in item 4 above).

9. Occasionally it may be necessary to have a few children move at a time, with small groups taking turns, as when skipping, running, or galloping is desired; other children can sit and participate with movement of the arms and trunk.

10. One or two individuals may be very well coordinated, imaginative, bursting with ideas, and eager to "perform." If this represents a sincerity of purpose, and creativity rather than craving attention for its own sake, these children can sometimes initiate ideas; but be careful not to promote a "star." Such an individual can discourage others from participating.

In planning early experience with rhythmic movement, you should start with music in which the beat moves at about the rate of the child's heartbeat (72–80 beats per minute), because children coordinate their movement with music most readily at this tempo. After they have had some experience at this optimal pace, they will develop physical control that will permit them to respond accurately, first at faster and then at slower tempi (more control is needed for slow movement). You should note also, that music based on duple meter is easier to respond to than triple meter when you use bilateral movement such as walking or marching. Both $\frac{2}{4}$ and $\frac{6}{8}$ $(\frac{2}{\bullet})$ are appropriate, as are other meters that contain an even number of beats in a measure.

At Level II children usually are quite receptive to rhythmic movement, providing the teacher can manage the social dynamics of the situation. As with any group enterprise where there is interaction and movement, there must be agreement about procedures before the encounter begins. If individuals are to hear the music as they move, there should be no talking, and feet should move quietly on the floor (bare or slippered feet are recommended). Responding to music through body movement is also a listening experience. In music of all styles you will find compositions that can be expressed in movement. Musical games and dances from different cultures should be found, and music of the 20th century should be used, as well as that of more traditional styles.

Activities in physical education develop coordination and skill in movement, and a program in creative dramatics encourages freedom of expression. You will find Chapters 5 and 6 of *Creative Rhythmic Movement for Children*[2] by Gladys Andrews particularly helpful in establishing freedom of movement. *Creative Dance in the Primary School,*[3] *Music, Movement and Mime for Children,*[4] and *Music and Movement Improvisations*[5] are valuable resources for teachers of young children who wish to study approaches to movement in greater depth.

An application of Dalcroze eurhythmics is found in *Rhythm and Movement*[6] by Elsa Findlay. Each chapter in the book is centered on a different musical element that can be reflected in music. Beth Landis and Polly Carder provide useful procedures and suggest musical compositions to be used in "Realization in Movement as a Way of Comprehending Music."[7]

EXPERIENCES AT LEVEL I

Tactile and kinesthetic experiences are important ways in which young children learn. These modes of learning, in turn, facilitate early verbal and visual learning. Although the verbal and visual modes become more efficient ways of learning at later stages, the development of complex motor skills at any level involves kinesthetic memory and imagery that have their roots in early experience.

Child-Created Movement

Children have lively imaginations and energized, growing bodies. This combination results in spontaneous creative movement of all kinds that can be categorized under two general headings:

1. Axial movement—turning, twisting, bending, and other movement of the body on its axis
2. Locomotor movement—walking, running, galloping, skipping, hopping, and other ways of moving from one point to another

There are, of course, innumerable combinations of these two types used by children in their spontaneous movement and in pantomime and dramatization of their world.

You should approach rhythmic movement at the children's point of understanding, foster their ability and freedom to move in expressive ways, and then relate this movement to music. You will find many useful procedures for helping children discover movement and related sound in *Book One, Seeds of Movement* by Genevieve Jones[8] and *Creative Movement for the Developing Child* by Clare Cherry.[9]

The early steps can be taken in several classroom or playground situations. The general teacher is the logical person to make this connection between music and everyday activities of children. During "sharing time," when children tell of their experiences, you might say in response to a child's narration, "Yes, Allison, show us how you walked to the store. Did you feel happy? Were you in a hurry?" And perhaps Allison will be able to reconstruct her mood and movement so the whole class will know how she felt, and realize that movement reveals feeling. This is creative dramatics, but it can be related to music if a rhythmic accompaniment (drum or piano) can be provided for the walking. You might guide the rhythmic experience a step further by suggesting that other children "go with Allison to the store just as she did." The experience becomes an impersonation when the other children follow the pattern set by Allison, and interpretive movement if they listen and follow a musical setting for the movement.

Stephen may one day give his physical interpretation of the way the bear moved in a story. A deep-sounding drum or sandblocks might be played in the rhythm Stephen establishes; other children may join in or take turns being the bear. At a later time the children might find reasons why the bear would move at another speed. "He is tired and is looking for a place to hibernate" or "He is charging a hiker who has invaded his territory." A change in the accompaniment could be provided to support the change of mood and movement.

There are a number of qualities of movement that can be explored and later will be reflected in the children's interpretations of music. In their impersonations, you should lead children first to enact and then to verbalize these contrasting qualities.

smooth—bumpy	loud—soft
curved—with corners	fast—slow
heavy—light	getting faster—getting slower
strong—weak	even—uneven

Since they are more readily caught up in movement that has dramatic content or purpose, help children relate these qualities to creative situations, for example:

☐ Move like a heavy elephant going through the woods.

☐ Walk as though you had your leg in a cast.

☐ Walk like a relative.

In these early stages of rhythmic development, a rhythm instrument or the piano provides the best accompaniment for movement, because the tempo can be adjusted to give the child optimum freedom in movement. Try the following pattern with rhythm sticks or two halves of a coconut shell struck together to suggest running:

The same pattern played more slowly may suggest walking. Try a heavy-light-light pattern for skating or sliding:

You can accompany galloping and skipping by playing a steady beat:

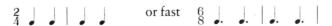

A more exciting accompaniment can be created by playing the characteristic recurring pattern on coconut shells or a drum, alternately sounded in the middle and tapped on the rim:

The rhythm patterns for skipping and galloping are interchangeable. However, the $\frac{6}{8}$ pattern shown above gives a feeling of flow and roundness to skipping. For galloping, which is a more sharply defined movement, the following $\frac{2}{4}$ pattern is more suitable:

Play this pattern slowly and heavily as an accompaniment for leaping or jumping.

Any of the above rhythms can be sounded using piano, guitar, or Autoharp chordings. Play a tonic chord (e.g., C major) in the rhythm needed to support the movement; change to a dominant-seventh chord (e.g., G^7) for development and action in the movement; return to the tonic chord at the end. (Instructions for playing these chords and instruments are provided in Chapter 6.)

If you cannot play the piano in the traditional manner, use it as a percussion instrument to create a rhythmic accompaniment. You can play a single three-tone chord with one or both hands, either high or low, in a running, walking, or galloping rhythm. By sounding simultaneously several adjacent black keys or white keys, create what are called "tone clusters." These can be played at different pitch levels in any desired rhythm and with variety in dynamics. The best approach is to go to a piano and begin experimenting with its sound-making potential. Don't think of "playing" it in the traditional sense. There are no "notes"—just interesting, rhythmic combinations of pitch.

Simple approaches to improvisation at the piano are shown in kindergarten and first grade books of the basic music series. Easy accompaniments for rhythmic movement are also shown in these books, and one composition, played faster or slower, louder or softer, or in a higher or a lower register, can provide a suitable accompaniment for several kinds of movement (see NEW DIMENSIONS IN MUSIC, *Kindergarten*, pp. 156–83, or EXPLORING MUSIC, *Book I,* pp. 2 and 3, 48, 91–92, 134).

In the college class, use the above ideas or your own experience as a basis for creative movement and its accompaniment. If possible, divide into teams with some "movers" and some accompanists. Create a sequence of expressive movement involving an animal, imaginary characters, or people that you can share with the class.

By associating children's natural movements with accompaniments of various kinds, you can help them begin to hear and respond to rhythm, tempo, and dynamics in music. The following points summarize the procedures that can be used to achieve this goal:

1. Work from the child's fundamental movements, such as walking, running, crawling, galloping.
2. Help the child find freedom of movement within limits of the classroom.
3. Show children in what respect their movements are rhythmic.
4. Relate movement to rhythmic sounds.
5. Provide opportunities for individuals to move in a rhythm established by another child.
6. Help children learn to move in any of the fundamental rhythmic patterns at will.
7. Help the children arrive at the point of being able to adjust their movement to music in a predetermined tempo.

The individual children, the group, the situations that arise, and your own way of working, all help to determine how the steps are accomplished.

Early Interpretive Movement

In progressing from child-created movement to the interpretation of music, children are asked to adjust their movements to what they hear, rather than having the accompaniment pick up their rhythm. It will be a gradual transition, in which you accommodate a wide variety of individual aptitudes for movement. The interpretation of songs with dramatic interest provides an avenue for this development.

In many songs, both the text and the rhythm of the music suggest the activity. In some of these, rhythmic movements can be combined with pantomime. "The Wind Blow East" is a song that inspires a mood. The use of colorful scarves would help children get a realistic sense of wind movement and at the same time would enable them to enact the holds on "east" and "west."

EXAMPLE 3.1

THE WIND BLOW EAST
Nassau, Bahamas

From the Library of Congress Archive of Folk Song, AFS 485A.

You can sing and accompany this song with guitar or Autoharp chords, playing the verse slowly with arpeggiated (harp-like) chords. The refrain can move at a more lively pace. Feel free to adjust the tempo of the music to the general speed of the children's movement. After the song is familiar to the children, you might change the tempo and ask them to move as fast or as slow as the music. An objective is to have the children become aware of the music as they move and to learn to coordinate the two.

Pantomiming the rhythmic movements of a heavy piece of machinery such as a wrecking machine in "Old House" (see next page) provides a different type of expressive, rhythmic experience. The musical contrast between this song and "The Wind Blow East" will demonstrate that each song requires a different quality of movement.

EXAMPLE 3.2

OLD HOUSE

American Folk-Game Song
Collected by John W. Work

Resolutely

Old house.   Tear it   down! Who's going to help me? Tear it   down!

Bring me a ham-mer.   Tear it   down! Bring me a   saw.   Tear it   down!

Next thing you bring me,   tear it   down! Is a   wreck-ing   ma-chine. Tear it   down!

Used by permission of John W. Work.

What kind of wrecking machines could be used to tear down a house? What kinds of movements does your wrecking machine make? How heavy is it? Show us. How fast does it move? Sing the song thinking about the movement, and see if you can get the music going at a good speed for these wrecking machines to operate. Experiment with heavy minor chords on guitar, Autoharp or piano to find a suitable accompaniment for this song and related movement. Some percussion instruments might be used to provide added weight and sound that reflect the "wrecking machines."

Rhythmic movement should reflect both the text of the song and the musical

setting. The rhythm of this song swings in twos ♩ ♩ | ♩ ♩ | and some of the
1   2   1   2

"machines" might move with this beat. Other heavier equipment may be panto-mimed as moving slowly, starting on the accented beat of each measure:

♩ | ♩ |, which is half as fast. The song also has an uneven rhythm pattern:
1   2   1   2

♫ ♩. ♩ · This is a good pattern to chant and clap, so that this uneven quality is
"Tear it down"

noticed. To give contrast to the sequence of movement used with this composition, individuals might move and sound instruments whenever this pattern occurs.

Try some of these ideas for expressive movement, and add some of your own. Look for songs that children in your class might enjoy interpreting through movement. Here are some titles:

"Little White Duck" **ExM I-128**
"The North Wind and the Sun"
(a story) **SBM I-60**
"Six Little Ducks" **SpM I-31**

"The Three Bears" **ExM I-95**
"Train is A-Coming" **NDinM K-104**
"Way, Hey, and Up She Rises"
DMT ECh-117

Instructional Objectives: To enable children to perceive the expressive qualities of both the text and the music and to respond with movement that reflects those qualities.

Behaviors providing evidence that these instructional objectives have been achieved:

Tempo. The children will

☐ move at a pace corresponding to the tempo of the music

☐ acknowledge that a fast pace, as well as one that is twice as slow, can fit the music

Rhythm. The children will

☐ echo-clap or sound on an instrument the repeated rhythm pattern heard in the music

Dynamics. The children will

☐ reflect the mood and feeling of each song by responding with appropriate strong, loud, or gentle, soft movements

☐ use words or identify pictures that reflect the feeling qualities of each song

Musical values can be derived from dramatization that involves two or more characters in related action. In this context, actual rhythmic movement may be less important than the sincere portrayal of an idea. "The Old Gray Cat" is an excellent example of a song that can be used in creative dramatic play leading to musical learning.

EXAMPLE 3.3

THE OLD GRAY CAT
Alabama Folk Song

Dramatically

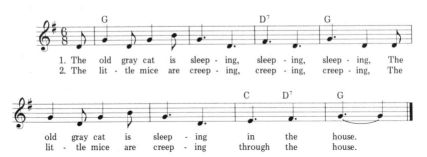

1. The old gray cat is sleep - ing, sleep - ing, sleep - ing, The
2. The lit - tle mice are creep - ing, creep - ing, creep - ing, The

old gray cat is sleep - ing in the house.
lit - tle mice are creep - ing through the house.

3. The little mice are nibbling in the house.   5. The old gray cat comes creeping through the house.
4. The little mice are sleeping in the house.   6. The little mice all scamper through the house.

Used by permission of Dr. Byron Arnold, from whose collection of Alabama folk songs it is taken.

Some individuals can pantomime the mice who creep and nibble around the house, always slightly fearful and watching as the old gray cat sleeps; but watch how they scamper when the cat wakes up!

The musical interpretation of this song should be adjusted to fit the ideas in the text. (You can use a guitar, Autoharp or a piano to play the chords shown above the music.) Notice how the dramatic effect can be changed by varying the tempo and the dynamics at different points: Sing the first stanza moderately softly and very smoothly, so that the cat will continue to sleep. The second stanza will be quiet, but with a little more movement; the fifth stanza might be changed to minor mode (play G minor, using B♭ instead of B in both the melody and the tonic chord) to suggest the danger of the cat; the final stanza must move rapidly and with excitement as the mice scamper away.

As the teacher, you must serve as a guide, helping participants develop, evaluate, and refine their responses. The words of the song contain the ideas upon which to build an impersonation. If the music and text are well mated, the rhythmic characteristics for the movement can be heard in the music. Look for two or three other songs that would be useful for dramatization. You will find that some songs describe an animal or other character, but in a manner that is objective and serves as a commentary rather than suggesting movement. Evaluate the rhythmic possibilities of songs, and use movement only when it is convincing.

Instructional Objectives: To provide children with an opportunity to respond through movement to a dramatic plot accompanied by music that supports the plot development, and thereby to expand their understanding of possibilities for musical expression.

Behaviors providing evidence that the instructional objectives have been achieved:

Rhythm. The children will

- □ move to a faster or a slower tempo when they hear it
- □ verbally identify a tempo as fast or slow

Dynamics. The children will

- □ reflect in their movement the dynamic level of the music
- □ verbally identify music as loud or soft

Mode. The children will

- □ recognize the minor mode as "different" and respond with a different quality of movement

Singing and Clapping Games Children Play

Chanting, singing, and movement are companion activities in the lives of children. The related action involves various combinations of axial and locomotor movement. As a preliminary to games and dances, have the children explore the movement of various joints and hinging points in their bodies. Play some moderately paced rhythmic accompaniment and move your attention from one child to another as they demonstrate the operation of these joints and hinges. When an interesting movement is identified, have others copy that movement. At another time, use a singing game such as "Did You Ever See a Lassie" so that movements the children initiate can be utilized in the context of the game.

EXAMPLE 3.4

DID YOU EVER SEE A LASSIE
Germany

In countries around the world, young children spontaneously sing and play ring games such as "Ring Around a Rosy," which utilize locomotor movements of walking or skipping. The children set their own tempo for such a game, learn to keep the movement going at a steady pace throughout, and begin to realize that movement can be related to rhythmic sound.

The English singing game "Looby Loo" has been used by many generations of children in this country. It has the practical purpose of helping children identify the right and left hand or foot. Black children of Alabama call it "Loop De Loo."

EXAMPLE 3.5

LOOBY LOO (Loop de Loo)
Singing Game

Brightly

Refrain

Here we dance Loo - by Loo, Here we dance Loo - by Light,

Here we dance Loo - by Loo, All on a Sat - ur - day night.

1. I put my right hand in, I put my right hand out,

I give my right hand a shake, shake, shake, and turn my - self a - bout.

2. I put my left hand in, . . .
3. I put my right foot in, . . .
4. I put my left foot in, . . .
5. I put my head right in, . . .
6. I put my whole self in, . . .

Dance directions: Children form a circle and move counterclockwise, singing and clapping the beat during each refrain. At each stanza the children face the center of the circle and enact the words sung. Repeat the refrain and the related movement after each stanza.

A sense of phrase is developed as the children follow the movements described in the song. Skill in moving at a different pace, and a concept of tempo can be developed if the children sing and dance at different speeds, e.g., slower, "as though you were very tired."

There are many singing games that can be joint physical education and music activities. The following singing games and dances would be appropriate for children at Level I:

"All Around the Kitchen" SBM 184   "Kagome" DMT I-27T
"Bluebird, Bluebird" GwM K-105   "Old Brass Wagon" NDinM K-37
"Clapping Land" ExM I-2

Instructional Objectives: To promote musical development by helping children learn to move with a steady beat and to make their interpretive movements relate both to the words and to the music.

Behaviors providing evidence that these instructional objectives have been achieved:

Rhythm. The children will
   ☐ clap or move rhythmically with the beat in the music

Tempo. The children will
   ☐ be able to establish a fast and a slow tempo for the game
   ☐ verbally identify the fast or slow tempo

Phrasing. The children will
   ☐ change movements in the game as governed by the words and the phrase structure

The Fundamental Movements and Musical Interpretation

When children have discovered that their fundamental ways of moving, running, and walking can express different purposes and moods, they can begin to use movement to learn musical concepts and skills. They learn that music has tempo in that it moves fast or slow; that a musical phrase has shape that is governed by its movement; that rhythm can be regular and in a continuous pattern; or that it can alternate in long and short tones to suggest other kinds of movement. In the children's song "Rig-a-Jig-Jig," the words and rhythm of verse suggest walking, but the refrain, with its repeated short–long patterns, strongly suggests skipping or galloping.

EXAMPLE 3.6

RIG-A-JIG-JIG
Singing Game

Play and sing this song at a lively tempo, and then at a slower tempo to change the mood and feeling of the song.

Every kindergarten and first grade basic music series book provides music for fundamental movement such as walking, running, marching, skipping, and galloping. One composition may suggest several movements. "Gigue" from *Suite No. 3* by Corelli is suitable for skipping, galloping, walking, bending, swaying, or "rowing boats."

EXAMPLE 3.7

GIGUE
Arcangelo Corelli

From *The Kindergarten Book* of Our Singing World Series, enlarged edition. Used by permission of Ginn and Company, owner of the copyright.

There is nothing boisterous or heavy about this composition. Whatever movements are adopted should be carried out in a gay dancing spirit with a sense of freedom and flow. Movement in response to music must be conceived in terms of its melodic flow and textural qualities as well as its rhythm, and therefore the ideas expressed will go beyond thinking merely that "this is music for skipping" or "this music sounds like running."

Plan for variety in the music you use during one lesson. When the children hear obvious differences in rhythm, tempo, and dynamics, they understand the need to move in different ways. *First Book of Creative Rhythms* by Rosanna Saffran,[10] and *Music for Active Children* by Elsie Braun[11] are good sources of easy piano accompaniments for movement. In addition, you will find a number of such compositions in these basic series music books: **NDinM K-156 to 185, DMT ECh-84 and 87.** Although simple, all these compositions should be played in an appropriate musical style, with dynamic contrast and articulation (smooth or staccato) that are compatible with the music.

After the children have learned to relate to the musical elements found in songs and piano pieces, recorded music can be used. This music should be selected carefully, and in the earlier experiences of primary children, it is important that it be:

1. In a tempo that children can easily adjust their movements to. Music suitable for the free rhythmic activities of young children is somewhat faster than that appropriate for adults.
2. Steady in rhythm, without breaks or ritards to interrupt the basic movement.
3. Interesting, appealing music—rhythmic, rich in tone color, and conveying mood and feeling as well as rhythm.

Quality is important because the value of the musical experience depends heavily on the music used. In the early stages of rhythmic movement, the music must be simple; but there is a difference between simple, uncomplicated music and music that is dull and lacking in character.

Some instrumental recordings include narration or singing, and others feature the piano or small instrumental ensembles. "A Visit to My Little Friend," "My Playful Scarf," and others can be found under the *Children's Record Guild* label.[12]

Among useful titles on *Young People's Records*[12] are "When the Sun Shines," "A Rainy Day," and "Whoa! Little Horses, Lie Down." Hap Palmer provides a guitar accompaniment for "The Elephant" and other songs in his album series, *Learning Basic Skills Through Music*.[13] *Rhythm Time* and other Bowmar Records albums[14] and *Rhythms of Childhood* and *Dance Along* by Ella Jenkins[15] are some good recordings created especially for rhythmic response in early childhood. The current basic music series books for kindergarten and first grade have related recordings that contain good selections for expressive movement. Listen to and move to some of these compositions. Discuss the possibilities each offers for expressive movement, and collect information about other recorded music especially designed for use by groups of children.

The RCA ADVENTURES IN MUSIC Series and the BOWMAR ORCHESTRAL LIBRARY are available in many schools and are useful because they contain the music of composers representative of several periods of musical styles. (See Appendix B-II for a complete listing of the musical contents of these two recorded series.) In these collections you will find a number of marches that children will enjoy, together with many other short, attractive instrumental compositions. Following are the titles of two compositions from each collection. Listen to the music of either pair and then create movement that reflects the musical qualities of each piece.

"Pantomime" from *The Comedians* by Kabalevsky AinM I-1	"Circus Polka" by Stravinsky BOL #51
"Air Gai" from *Iphigeniein Aulis* by Gluck AinM I-1	"Badinerie" by Corelli BOL #56

When you are preparing to use a composition with children, you should know the music well. It is a good idea to make a chart of each piece, showing on a time-line the musical events in each. Following are sketches of the more important characteristics and musical events in two of these compositions. Could you make a similar sketch of the other two named above?

"Pantomime" by Kabalevsky
$\frac{4}{4}$ meter, slow, heavy
minor mode, cello and bass
Section A: four phrases, four
  measures each
  brass accents in second phrase
  timpani in third phrase
Section A: exact repetition
Section A: one phrase, four measures

"Air Gai" by Gluck
$\frac{4}{4}$ meter, lively, playful
Introduction: six measures
  bustling strings with
  loud brass chords
Section A: twelve measures
  full string sound
  trumpets in transition measure
Section B: twelve measures
  flute and horn
  oboe and horn
  strings
Section A: four measures
  full string sound
Coda: seven measures
  full orchestra
  timpani accents, ritard

Instructional Objectives: To lead children to discover that they can move (run, walk, skip, . . .) in different ways to express different feelings and moods; to help them understand that tempo, rhythm, and dynamics of movement have an effect on the feeling conveyed, and that musical compositions can express similar qualities.

Behaviors providing evidence that these instructional objectives have been achieved and can be related to the following musical elements:

Tempo. The children will

☐ demonstrate and correctly label movement as fast, moderate, or slow

☐ adjust their movement to reflect the tempo of music they hear

Dynamics. The children will

☐ demonstrate and correctly label loudness or softness in movement and sound

☐ reflect in the quality of their movement the loudness or softness heard in music

Rhythm. The children will

☐ enact different rhythm patterns and label each as even (walk and run) or uneven (skip, gallop, or hop)

☐ reflect in movement the even or uneven rhythm patterns heard in music

In addition to the special educational recordings cited above, look for suitable music in your own record collection. Excerpts from many compositions are useful, especially suites of dances, incidental music from opera and ballet, and dance music from other cultures as well as folk dances.

EXPERIENCES AT LEVEL II

Children ages seven to nine are capable of more highly organized group activities. At this level you will be able to expand experiences with folk dancing and challenge them to reflect in movement more musical details that begin to come within their conceptual grasp.

Children learn the components of rhythm by internalizing them through repeated use of movement, games, and dances. If their attention is directed to the repetitions and contrasts in the music, they will develop expectations of musical form that will serve them in many other encounters with music. Games and dances of different cultures bring variety to the experience because the musical characteristics (rhythm, form, melody, and so on) differ somewhat from one culture to another. If you help the children notice these differences, their understanding of music will expand within the playful context of the game or dance.

Rhythmic Games and Dances

For seven- to nine-year-olds, singing games are replaced by games and dances that are more sophisticated in music and text. "Hokey Pokey" has a delightful syncopated rhythm. There is opportunity for creative movement in this dance, and the dancers should try to invent interesting, "jazzy" movements to fit the music.

EXAMPLE 3.8

HOKEY POKEY
Children's Game Song

Robustly

1. You put your right foot in, you put your right foot out, you put your right foot in and you shake it all a - bout; you do the Ho - key Po - key, and you turn your-self a - round, That's what it's all a - bout!

2. You put your left foot in . . .
3. You put your right arm in . . .
4. You put your left arm in . . .
5. You put your whole self in . . .

Notice that the rhythm makes consistent use of an upbeat (three notes) leading to a downbeat on the word "right." As you do this dance, lift your foot on the upbeat and bring it down firmly on the accent. Experiment with an accompaniment (Autoharp, guitar, piano, or drum), trying different speeds for the beat to see which tempo is most appropriate in terms of the character of the dance. Should "Hokey Pokey" be fast or slow? How fast?

Singing, dancing, and hand-clapping games can be found all over the world. Undoubtedly you remember some from your childhood; you will find these and others still alive among the children of your class. A recent book, *Step It Down,*[16] by Bessie Jones and Bess Lomax Hawes, provides a fascinating view of games, plays, and songs from the Afro-American heritage. Bring the various cultural heritages of the children to school by inviting them to share their games and dances with the class.

Although singing games are the first group dances used in the classroom, children soon learn to enjoy folk dances that may or may not have words to tell what to do. The words may be incidental, and unlike in the singing game, singing is not expected to be the only accompaniment. It is not until the children are able to enjoy a rhythmic, patterned movement that they use the folk dance rather than the singing game. Participation in folk dances often begins in the second or third grade.

"Shoo, Fly" is a folk dance in three-part sectional form (A B A); that is, it begins with a refrain (A), has a verse (B) that has different lyrics and music, and ends with the refrain (A).

EXAMPLE 3.9

SHOO, FLY
Singing Game

There are two essential parts to a folk dance; the foot pattern is the response to the basic recurring rhythm of the music. The easiest foot patterns are skipping, marching, a bouncy walk, or a step-slide to the side. For many dances more than one type of foot pattern is suitable; the selection of a particular one is determined by the tempo of the music and the dancer's skill in movement.

Phrasing and sectional form in the music determine the floor pattern and the directional movement that the dancers take. "Shoo, Fly" can be done as a circle dance, using a bouncy walk while holding hands; to facilitate movement, each circle should be limited to eight to twelve dancers.

The refrain of "Shoo, Fly" consists of four two-measure phrases. Listen for the repetition, and move into and out of the circle on each double phrase to create the floor pattern. In following the four-measure phrases of the verse, move clockwise in a circle on the first phrase, and counterclockwise on the second phrase. Notice the fermata (hold) on the note preceding the return to the refrain; enact this by raising hands high above your head, and enjoy the feeling of anticipation it brings for a return to the beginning.

American square dancers follow the directions of a "caller"; in other dances the participants learn the sequence of movement and follow the phrasing and sectional changes in the music. The most beautiful folk dancing is that in which the dancers keep precise rhythm and execute the various directional patterns in perfect coordination with the changing phrases and sections of the music.

Instructional Objectives: To provide children with pleasurable experiences in relating movement to music; and to demonstrate that musical elements such as beat, accent, upbeat (anacrusis), tempo, syncopation, hold, phrase, and cadence help shape the dance into a unique musical form.

Behaviors providing evidence that these instructional objectives have been achieved: The children will

- □ dance with obvious pleasure and total involvement
- □ clap or move accurately with the beat in the music
- □ reflect the upbeat and the syncopation through appropriate movement
- □ clap or move at a slower or faster tempo
- □ hear the phrase changes, accelerando, and hold; and adjust their movements to them in following the dance

Here are titles of games and dances that are included in recent basic music series books at this level:

"Bomfalleralla" SBM IV-47   "Hula P¡ū'ili" CM Z3A-230 and 231
"Buffalo Gals" SpM V-150   "The Needle's Eye" ExM III-42
"Hato Popo" SBM III-101   "Seven Steps" DMT IV-119

Using any resources available to you, find two additional games or dances that would be appropriate for use at the level of your teaching interest. These might have a relationship to cultures of the neighborhood or those considered in social studies or language arts. Try to find two that differ musically from each other in some way. Learn the music, analyze it in terms of its most obvious musical features, then learn the dance and teach it to a group. State the primary instructional objective you would have in using each dance, and list the behaviors of the children that would provide evidence of such learning.

Clapping and Patschen in Accompaniments

Patschen is a German word meaning "to pat the knees." Since no simple equivalent is available in English, the term has been adopted by American music teachers who use the Orff method in music education. Stamping, patschen, clapping, and snapping the fingers are body sounds that can be used as rhythmic accompaniments for songs, and as the basis for creative experiences in rhythm.

Accompaniments of this kind can be simple or complex, depending upon the rhythmic sophistication and skill of the group. Adapt one of the following accompaniments to these rhymes in duple meter:

Rain on the green grass,   Lift the nozzle

Rain on the tree,   To your muzzle;

Rain on the house top,   Let it swizzle

But not on me.   Down your guzzle.

Try other variations of these basic movements, maintaining the steady beat as the basis for the sounds. Notice the characteristics of these rhymes:

1. The quality and mood is distinctive in each and would appeal to different individuals.
2. With the exception of the last line, each phrase in "Rain" begins on the strong beat.

More advanced accompaniments can be devised using the steady beat and divided beats in various ways, e.g.:

The Orff method of music education makes extensive use of rhythm and speech exercises. Echo clapping, rhythm canons (imitation of one part by another), and persistently repeated patterns (ostinati) in accompaniments are basic techniques. See *Music for Children I—Pentatonic*,[17] for a variety of exercises and examples of this type.

Songs can be accompanied in a similar manner. The easiest songs to use are children's chants, such as "It's Raining, It's Pouring," because more attention can be focused on the accompaniment when the melody is simple.

EXAMPLE 3.10

IT'S RAINING, IT'S POURING
Traditional Nursery Rhyme

With Energy

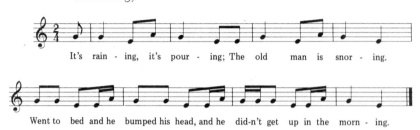

It's rain - ing, it's pour - ing; The old   man is snor - ing.

Went to   bed and he   bumped his head, and he   did-n't get   up in the   morn - ing.

Have the group sing the chant as they use one of the accompaniments shown above, or their own creative version. As the accompaniment is sounded, have another group clap the rhythm of the melody for the first four measures. Repeat this several times so the melody rhythm is very familiar. Now you can create a rhythmic rondo. This is a term for a musical form consisting of a principal musical idea alternated with successive new ideas, usually of the same length. We can label a rondo as A B A C A, which shows two (or more) contrasting sections sandwiched between the original musical idea and repetitions of it. The new sections can be improvised, that is, made up in the course of the performance. The group providing the accompaniment should continue in a steady tempo as a different individual improvises rhythm patterns that: (1) contrast to those of the melody rhythm in "It's Raining," but (2) are the same length (four measures in this case). As many contrasting sections as desired may be created, but the composition should end with the original melody-rhythm (A).

Instructional Objectives: To develop skill in rhythmic response and the ability to improvise rhythm within a metric structure; and to develop the concept of the rondo as a musical form.

Behaviors providing evidence that these instructional objectives have been achieved: The children will

□ accurately sound a rhythm pattern within the established accompaniment

□ improvise a four-measure rhythmic phrase that fits with the duple meter established by the accompaniment

□ correctly describe rondo form and label it as A B A C A

When coordination and skill have been developed in using these body sounds in various rhythmic combinations, folk songs with greater melodic interest can be provided with accompaniments. Try "Shoo, Fly" (Example 3.9) using any of the above patterns, or others of your own creation.

"Hokey Pokey" (Example 3.8) could have this kind of an accompaniment too, but the upbeats that this song begins with make it more difficult to coordinate the singing with the accompaniment. Children at Level II can do this if the teacher is able to provide a correct model for them.

Portraying Musical Detail through Movement

Both songs and recorded instrumental compositions provide opportunities for children at Level II to get involved with music by using body movement and thereby to notice its details. In this section you will find two songs and two instrumental compositions in which movement can be related to musical detail. Because the number of examples included here is limited, you will make more extensive use of the musical details found in each piece than you should attempt in a classroom.

"A Ram Sam Sam" is an energetic folk song from Morocco. As you sing it the first time, tap or clap the steady beat. The words are delightful, repetitious nonsense as far as Western ears are concerned, and they are easy to learn.

EXAMPLE 3.11

A RAM SAM SAM

Moroccan Folk Song

From *Sing It Again*. Copyright © 1958, World Around Songs, Inc. Used by permission.

Continue working with the song in these ways:

1. Sing, clap, and march to the steady beat.
2. Sing, march to the steady beat, and clap the melody rhythm.
3. Repeat item 2, but step more heavily on the first beat in each measure to show the accent. This should help you notice that each phrase in this song begins on an upbeat.
4. Sing and let your feet dance the melody rhythm.
5. Sing, move in a line around the room, marching to the steady beat, clapping the melody rhythm and changing the direction of movement at the end of each two-measure phrase.

6. Divide the class in two groups, repeat exercise 5 above, but sing "A Ram Sam Sam" as a two-part round (twice through) with the second group beginning the song when the first group gets to the star (*).

Now you might put more imaginative action into the rhythm of the words. Create your own movement if possible, or do the following:

□ Bend the arms at the elbow, making a fist, waist high.

□ Pull backward on beat 4 (which is the upbeat) and push forward on the first beat of the measure; repeat, forward and back on each beat while the pattern lasts.

□ Open the fingers and shake the hands rhythmically in a horizontal movement about waist high while singing this pattern.

□ Make a fist, pull the arm down on beat 4, and raise it strongly, high above the head, on the accented high pitch (at "ra").

As a final participation, march in two circles, singing the round and doing the agreed-upon arm movements. Notice how the arm movements dramatize the different parts of the round being sung simultaneously.

Now, make a list of the various musical elements of this song that were shown through bodily movement. (You should count at least seven musical elements.)

"When the Saints Go Marching In" has rhythmic vigor and simplicity combined with a very singable melody and is easily accompanied by three basic chords (D, A^7, G). Clap the steady beat as you sing it the first time.

EXAMPLE 3.12

WHEN THE SAINTS GO MARCHING IN
Negro Spiritual

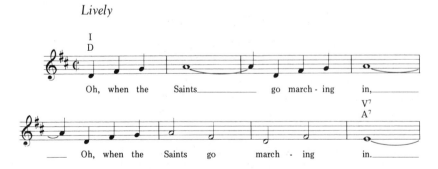

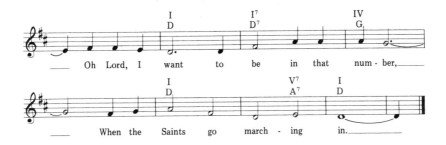

How many times did you clap in each measure? This song is in cut-time (¢), and clapping half notes (♩), two for each measure, gives the most comfortable speed for the beat.

As the music is repeated, use body movement to participate in these ways:

1. March to the steady beat.
2. March and reverse the direction of march at the end of each musical phrase (there are two eight-measure phrases in the song).
3. March to the beat, but make the first beat of each measure (the accent) noticeably heavier; clap as you step on that beat:

LEFT, right	LEFT, right
1 2	1 2
clap	clap

Did you notice that the song does not start on the first beat of the measure? The group of three quarter-notes at the beginning is an upbeat leading to the down-beat at the beginning of the first full measure. This effect occurs five times in this song.

4. March at half speed, so you are stepping only on the accent as another group marches with every beat:

5. Sing and clap the rhythm of the melody.
6. Sing, clap the rhythm of the melody, step the rhythm of the melody simultaneous-ly, and notice the long tones.
7. Sing, clap the rhythm of the melody, and march to the steady beat, trying to relate the melody's long tones to the beat.
8. Sing, clap the steady beat, and step the melody rhythm.

The last activities suggested here require considerable coordination and rhythmic skills. It is usually best to start with a single element, the beat or the melody rhythm, and add responses to other elements as skills develop.

Instructional Objectives: To involve the children physically, mentally, and musically with a piece of music, so that they perceive musical effects clearly and refine their ability to respond to rhythm and phrase structure within the music's time-frame.

Behaviors providing evidence that these instructional objectives have been achieved: The children will

☐ accurately march and clap to the beat and accent in the music

☐ demonstrate the relationship between the beat and the melody rhythm (including the upbeat and the long duration of some tones) by performing both simultaneously

☐ demonstrate their awareness of phrase groupings by changing direction of movement at the end of each phrase

"March" from *King David* by Honegger is found in a record collection, LEARNING TO LISTEN TO MUSIC.[18] This is a 20th-century composition that is programmatic in that it suggests the Biblical march of the Philistines in David's encounter with Goliath. (When this music is used in the classroom, the descriptive details should be withheld and discovered by the children as they listen to the music and decide who is marching.) As you first hear the music, pat the beat on your knees. As the music is played a second time, march to the music, pantomiming the attitude and movement of the characters who might be marching.

Discuss the characterization suggested by the music. How did members of the class show who was marching? Those who moved heavily or swaggered might demonstrate as the music is played again. How does the music suggest the marching of military giants? (It is loud, low in pitch, has strong accents, and is quite slow.) Play the music again as several individuals demonstrate the marching of Goliath's soldiers, showing through body movement the heaviness and strong accents in the music, but at the same time moving to the steady beat.

In a study such as this, individuals center their attention on the music in order to respond to it with movement; they identify the elements in the music that combine to convey the feeling characteristic of the music as a whole. You will have an opportunity to use this composition in later chapters with other activities that can be used to point up its musical characteristics.

A 19th-century composition by the French composer Georges Bizet provides an opportunity to respond to other elements prominent in music. "Carillon" (**BOL #78**) is from *L'Arlesienne Suite No. 1* by Bizet, and suggests the ringing of bells, although no bells are used in the orchestration.

Listen to the music and begin to find ways in which you could respond to the music through movement. Would the same movement fit the music all the way through? Is more than one kind of movement appropriate at any one time?

The room should be large enough so the entire class can move freely, "feeling out" the music without bumping into one another. When the music is stopped (perhaps at the end of the first part), all should sit down on the floor where they find themselves. Discuss the music (listen again to parts of it as necessary): What is the first and most obvious suggestion for movement in this music? (A repeated pattern in threes, ♩ ♩ ♩ | ♩ ♩ ♩ played by horns.) Does the music begin high or low in pitch? loud or soft? smooth or staccato? Does it remain the same throughout this part of the composition? How does it change? A few individuals or the whole group could move to the horn motif, showing its loud and soft moments through body carriage and weight.

Another musical line moves along with the horns' repeated pattern in threes. Have a few individuals continue moving to the horn pattern, in a circle around the edge of the space, as others in the middle enact the smooth-flowing line of the stringed instruments. Notice the rising, falling, circling movement of the melody; it may suggest turns, circles, and dips in movement.

The group might then sit and discuss the musical qualities, which include obvious dynamic changes as well as other qualities previously mentioned. At this, or a later session, movement possibilities for the composition's middle or contrasting part can be worked out.

One obvious feature about this music is its three-part form (A B A), with a break between the first two parts and a "sneaky" return from B to A at the end of the second part. Hear the middle section and work with foot and body movements until you develop satisfactory movement for it. Notice the repeated, smooth-flowing, gently rocking rhythm and the long rising and falling melody lines. A few individuals who capture the feeling of this gentle music could move to that part and others might volunteer to enact the more vigorous triple meter at the beginning and the end. Those showing the triple meter should listen carefully and show exactly when and how their music resumes at the end of the B section.

At the beginning of a study such as this, you should attempt to hear, enact, and discuss only the more obvious features of the music. The movement should be original and spontaneous, but should represent an honest effort to reflect the qualities in the music. By discussion and exploration of movement within the group, all can begin to improve and refine their ways of moving. No set steps or preconceived movements should be taught.

Instructional Objectives: To help children perceive expressive detail in the music and to understand how those musical details are combined to create a significant musical composition.

Behaviors providing evidence that these instructional objectives have been achieved: The children will

□ move accurately to the steady beat in the music, and change movement when the music changes from one meter to the next

□ use arm movements and change in body elevation to show rising and falling melody lines

□ reflect the form of the music by changing the character of movement when the music changes

□ reflect change in dynamics by changing the quality and energy of their movement

□ reflect changes in timbre (tone color, instrumentation) by moving only when a particular instrument is sounded

Characterization and Drama in Music

Movement described in the previous section was centered on enacting various elements in the music, rather than upon developing a character or a story line. There are some programmatic compositions that can be studied at Level II and developed into dance-dramas based on story elements as well as on the music's expressive qualities. As far as possible, focus attention on the musical elements—rhythm, dynamics, melody, form, instrumentation, and so forth—as they are used to create a dramatic situation.

The Nutcracker Suite by Tchaikovsky (**BOL #58**) is a group of eight short compositions based on a fairy tale. Many people know the story from the annual television productions seen during the Christmas season, but in classroom work, try to create your own dances and drama for the music. For many classes, it would be sufficient to use three or four contrasting sections. Here is an outline of the eight movements:

☐ "Overture Miniature"—This sets the stage for the "once-upon-a-time" drama. There are two main themes here, and they suggest movement by contrasting groups.

☐ "March"—Marie has a Christmas party and this march announces the guests' arrivals and excitement of the affair. A crisp, precise main theme, played by horns and trumpets, is heard several times, alternating with contrasting themes played by strings and woodwinds.

After the party Marie falls asleep and dreams all of the following scenes of dancing toys and dolls, presumably previously seen on the Christmas tree.

☐ "Dance of the Sugar-Plum Fairy"—a delicately graceful dance featuring a celeste and stringed instruments played pizzicato.

☐ "Trepak"—a fast vigorous dance traditionally done by Russian men; it features short repeated phrases that move faster as the dance progresses.

☐ "Arabian Dance"—a langorous dance in which scarves can be used to help portray the long, smooth melody lines. Woodwinds are featured, supported by strings and a touch of tambourine.

☐ "Chinese Dance"—music that features flutes and piccolos and suggests a structured dance of tiny steps.

☐ "Dance of the Mirlitons" (toy flutes)—There are three sections in this music, with flutes at the beginning and end, and brass instruments playing the middle section.

☐ "Waltz of the Flowers"—Here a long introduction, featuring the harp, French horns, and numerous other instruments, leads to the waltz melody played by the violins.

The musical movements of *The Nutcracker Suite* are short and varied. They should provide an opportunity for everyone in the class to participate with movement in some way. The first two movements and the final one could be interpreted by large groups, and the five middle episodes might be worked out by individuals or small groups. All participants should listen to the music and develop dances that reflect what they hear. Additional details of the story, and notation of some musical themes, can be found in *The Music Box Book*,[19] EXPLORING MUSIC, *Book II*,[20] or MUSIC FOR YOUNG LISTENERS, *The Crimson Book*.[21]

You would need to use several lessons if you wished to depict the whole of this suite in movement. Each lesson would result in different behaviors, depending upon the musical content. As an example, a lesson centered on "Dance of the Sugar Plum Fairy" and "Trepak" might have objectives stated as follows:

Instructional Objectives: To direct the children's attention to differences in the expressive qualities of these two musical compositions; to have them analyze and explore the music through movement, so that they recognize the chief musical features that contribute to these differences.

Behaviors providing evidence that these instructional objectives have been achieved: The children will

- □ respond to "Dance of the Sugar Plum Fairy" with graceful, delicate movements, some smooth and flowing and others pointed and sharp, to reflect the contrast between legato, pizzicato, and staccato
- □ take turns dancing to the music of the celeste and strings, showing how these instruments are related within the orchestration
- □ verbalize qualities they hear in the music by describing the different phrases as smooth, flowing, or pointed, staccato, and so on
- □ respond to "Trepak" with brisk vigorous movements that are rhythmically compatible with the music's rhythm and increasing speed
- □ reflect phrase structure by movement that suggests cadence and renewed beginnings

In *Peter and the Wolf* by Prokofiev, the narration of the story is integrated with the music and offers interesting opportunities for character portrayal. In the introduction, the narration informs the listener of the instruments (musical timbre) assigned to each character. Equally important are the other musical elements used to create the characters and their interaction. Notice the free swinging rhythm and happy melody of Peter's theme. These qualities contrast markedly with the angular rhythms and minor tonality of Grandfather's theme. Use the introduction to help the children work out the basic movements for these characters. As time permits, gradually work through the rest of the composition, encouraging the children to respond to changing details in the music. The body movement should show not only the characterizations, but also their interaction in the drama. Alternate short periods of listening with periods of movement, so that the musical details can be heard.

Among recordings useful at this level is *Listen, Move and Dance* by Vera Gray and Daphne Oram (**Capitol Records H-21006**). This pair of recordings features instrumental and electronic sounds in compositions for creative movement. Volume I, Side 2, *Electronic Sound Pictures,* stimulates interesting pantomime and dramatic interaction. "Notes for Teachers" in the ADVENTURES IN MUSIC Series and the BOWMAR ORCHESTRAL LIBRARY (see Appendix B-II) will be helpful in identifying music in those series that is especially adapted to creative movement.

Dancers should "live" the character they portray; facial expression, body weight, and posture as well as rhythm should be representative. To do this, there must be a seriousness of purpose. Part of this work should be directed, so that participants expand their understanding of what can be heard in music and of the varied ways of expressing these ideas through movement. Balancing this directed work, there should be ample opportunity for individuals to listen carefully and develop their own interpretations.

EXPERIENCES AT LEVEL III

Ten- and eleven-year-olds have the physical dexterity and the intellectual ability to do very creative work with music and expressive movement. In many schools, however, the use of movement and dance is not a continuous program, and children who have not "grown up" with such activities may not be automatically receptive at this level. In spite of the problem, there are some approaches that can be taken.

A World of Folk Dance

In the intermediate grades, American square as well as circle dances are popular, and a wide variety of dances from different countries can be used. It is not necessary to perfect all the intricacies and variations the native dancers put into their art, but you should work with each dance enough to begin to acquire a feel and appreciation for its rhythm and unique style. The general procedures in developing dances within the music program are these:

1. Promote a feeling for the basic rhythm of the song and learn to move with the characteristic foot pattern of the dance. Some individuals can play rhythm instruments and sing while others do the pattern individually or in a line around the room.
2. Determine how the appropriate foot pattern is related to the metric beat and accent of the music.
3. When partners are needed, learn to do the foot patterns by working with another person.
4. When a floor pattern is required, develop one that follows the phrase structure of the music. Use a circle or a line formation, and basic floor patterns such as:

   a. Reverse direction on alternating long phrases.

   b. Move into and back out from the center of the circle on shorter phrases.

   c. Turn around a partner on shorter phrases, and so forth.

Songs and dances used in a program correlated with social studies include American circle and square dances. "Shoo, Fly" (Example 3.9) can be used as a couple dance and as a "mixer" at this level. The musical objectives are simply to respond to the steady beat and follow the phrase structure of the song as partners change in the dance. You will find easy dance directions in EXPLORING MUSIC, *Book V.*

The polka is a couple dance in lively $\frac{2}{4}$ meter. It originated in Bohemia (western Czechoslovakia), but is found in the folk tradition of many north-European countries. The schottische is similar to the polka, but slower, and is often in $\frac{4}{4}$ meter.

Adaptations of both can be used in the intermediate grades. The foot pattern for the schottische is smooth and even:

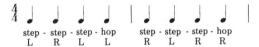

The polka is a combination of slide, step, and hop; its pattern varies, depending on which beat the music begins on. This pattern can be used for the polka:

"Holla Hi! Holla Ho!" is a good song for practicing the schottische, taking one step on each quarter-note value in $\frac{4}{4}$ meter.

EXAMPLE 3.13

HOLLA HI! HOLLA HO!
German Folk Song
English by Peter Kunkel

From *Work and Sing*, Copyright 1948, Cooperative Recreation Service, Inc., Delaware, Ohio. Used by permission.

Observe the rhythmic difference between the first and last parts of this song. The evenly divided beats of the first two phrases give a greater sense of speed than the slower notes in the last two phrases.

Some of the body-sound accompaniments recommended at Level II can be adapted to dance songs such as this. Try some variation of the following as an accompaniment for "Holla Hi! Holla Ho!" with one group doing the patschen and clapping and another group stamping and snapping fingers.

Songs and dances of a number of Latin American and Near East countries can be useful studies in rhythm and phrasing. The Israeli *hora* is a simple circle dance featuring an exhilarating *accelerando* that leaves the dancers moving at a breathless pace at the end. The popular song "Havah Nagilah" works well as an accompaniment for this dance, which is executed as follows: the dancers stand in a circle with arms on each other's shoulders; the dancing circle moves continuously counterclockwise. Taking two steps to each measure in the following song, everyone uses this foot pattern:

1. Make a step with the left foot.
2. Bring the right foot up behind the left foot and shift weight to it.
3. Make another step with the left foot.
4. Hop on the left foot and swing the right leg forward.
5. Step on the right foot.
6. Hop on the right foot and swing the left leg forward.

(Repeat this sequence throughout the dance.)

EXAMPLE 3.14

HAVAH NAGILAH
Israeli Folk Song
Words Adapted

Moderately, with increasing speed

Ha - vah   na - gi - lah,   ha - vah   na - gi - lah,   ha - vah

na - gi - lah,   Come, cir - cle a - bout!   Come, mer - ri - ly   shout!

Ha - vah   n' - ra - ne - nah,   ha - vah   n' - rah - ne - nah,   ha - vah   n' -

ra - ne - nah,   See how it   is   done!   Come, dance with your   friends!

Out   in   fine green mead - ows,   Mu - sic is play - ing fast - er, fast - er,

Peo - ple are danc - ing fast - er,   fast - er,   Hear how the beat   is

loud - er,   loud - er,   Hear how the tune   is   high - er,   high - er,

See how it's done!   En - ter the fun!   Dance the ho - ra joy - ful - ly!

There are several interesting details in this song. From the middle of the song to the end there should be a gradual but relentless speeding up of the beat. Notice what happens to the melody as the song gets faster—it seems to be natural for voices to rise when people get excited, and in this song the melody accommodates this human tendency. Clapping and strong rhythmic strumming of guitars, autoharps, balalaikas, or whatever, is needed to support the dance. The *accelerando* to the end not only adds to the excitement but makes the ending seem very abrupt.

Folk music of every culture has certain unique features. Certainly the differences between this and the previous well-balanced German folk song used as a polka or schottische are easy to hear. You don't need to be able to verbalize all of the differences, but continued exposure to a good variety of folk music will enable you, and the children you teach, to savor the unique flavor of each style.

Instructional Objectives: To enable children to recognize general stylistic differences in the music and dance of various cultures; to develop skill in responding accurately to the beat; and to recognize how the floor pattern of the dance is related to the musical structure.

Behaviors providing evidence that these instructional objectives have been achieved: The children will

□ dance to the music, keeping with the established beat

□ respond to expressive changes in the rhythm (*accelerando*, ritard, hold, and so on)

□ follow the phrase structure of the music in beginning and ending the various parts of the dance

□ identify verse and refrain as sections in a song or dance

□ recognize the ongoing developmental form of the *hora* as different from the sectional form of other dances

Many good folk dances are available on commercial folk recordings, and examples for all levels are also found in these collections, which are widely available in schools.

Bowmar Records
Folk Dances
Singing Square Dances
Folkways Records
American Square Dance Music

RCA Victor Corporation
Festival of Folk Dances
The World of Folk Dances

Basic music series books for intermediate grades contain dance songs from various countries; the series book, COMPREHENSIVE MUSICIANSHIP THROUGH CLASSROOM MUSIC, *Zone III-A,* has excellent material relative to Hawaiian dances. The SILVER BURDETT MUSIC SERIES has a "Satellite" section, "Responding Through Movement," near the end of the 5th- and 6th-level books that includes ideas for movement with a very contemporary flavor as well as dances from other cultures.

The March as an Approach to Expressive Movement

The social orientation and rhythmic appeal of marches make them a natural musical study for intermediate grades. For those who have not had previous experience in moving to music, the march can open the way to expressive movement. Marching can first be done in the multi-purpose room or gymnasium, where interesting two- or four-abreast formations can be worked out. Given a rousing Sousa march such as "Stars and Stripes Forever" (**BOL #54** or **AinM IV-2**), individuals will participate eagerly because they can identify with a marching band. Such marching, however, is only a beginning, a means to an end and not the musical objective.

When marching has produced an enthusiasm for participation and an appreciation for moving in rhythm with the music, begin to look for variety in marches. Good sources are the BOWMAR ORCHESTRAL LIBRARY Album #54, *Marches*, as well as other albums throughout the Bowmar series and the ADVENTURES IN MUSIC Series. To begin, have the children discuss the different uses for marches; military or school-band marches, wedding and other ceremonial marches may be suggested. "How do these differ and why?" Excerpts from two marches might be played and discussed. "March" from *Aida* by Verdi (**BOL #61**) may be compared with "March" from *The Love of Three Oranges* by Prokofiev (**BOL #54**). The former has strong, regular accents, a majestic long-lined melody featuring brass instruments; the latter is a caricature with strong, irregular accents and dissonant harmonies. The length of stride, general carriage, and body weight convey the expression of musical character. One can move to the march from *Aida* with a slow regal stride, or with a more brisk step, twice as fast. The pace and movement for the Prokofiev march can be regular, but the sudden changes in dynamics, disjunct melody lines, and unusual rhythmic accents suggest body movement reflecting these qualities.

Assign a group to each of these marches. Individuals in each group should experiment with different styles of movement to find what best reflects the music. They should listen to the music and discuss the use of musical elements (rhythm, melody, dynamics, texture, harmony, and instrumentation) to determine how the composer created that particular quality and style in the march. Work out a routine of marching that will reflect some of these musical events—if the texture is thin, have few individuals marching; if the texture becomes thick, add marchers. If there is more than one theme, let some individuals march to one musical idea and others take over when the melody changes.

Instructional Objectives: To enable children to accept body movement as an effective way to respond to music; to listen carefully to the musical details of rhythm, melody, timbre, and form; and to come to know certain compositions well as a result of this involvement.

Behaviors providing evidence that these instructional objectives have been achieved: The children will

☐ request opportunities to march to the compositions used in the study and will seek other music to treat in a similar manner

☐ move rhythmically, using whatever stride and body carriage seems appropriate to the music

☐ reflect the music's form and instrumentation by changing direction at the ends of phrases and sections, and by moving in response to a single instrument or group of instruments

☐ reflect melodic shape and dynamic changes by changes in body elevation and intensity of movement

Other marches can be used in the same manner, and when the group has learned to enjoy movement as an expression of different kinds of marches, they may be ready to move on to interpretive movement in response to other music.

Musical Analysis through Movement

At all educational levels, movement can be used to study the component parts of rhythm in different compositions. Ten- and eleven-year-olds can work with a greater variety of meters and successfully deal simultaneously with more aspects of rhythm. Having a longer acquaintance with musical instruments and perhaps beginning to learn to play orchestral and band instruments, they might be expected to more readily identify the sounds of instruments heard on recordings. Orchestration is another element of musical composition that can be reflected in body movement.

Two compositions have been selected to show the use of movement with 20th-century compositions having less conventional rhythms and instrumental combinations. Dave Brubeck is a performer and recording artist whose compositions have been popular for some time. "Take Five" features the Brubeck trio (piano, clarinet, and percussion), and lends itself well to the exploration of several aspects of rhythm.

Listen to the music and tap the steady beat; the beat you should be feeling is fairly rapid and is evenly spaced. Pat your knees and count the beat to find the accent that reveals how the beats are grouped into a meter. You may hear two accents, but one is secondary to the other:

Stand up and begin to move with this meter in these ways:

1. Move around the room stepping each beat; notice the lopsided effect of the $\frac{5}{4}$ meter.
2. Show the accents by stepping more heavily on beats 1 and 4 and by snapping your fingers or shrugging your shoulders.
3. Now, step only on the accents and snap fingers or shrug shoulders on the beats in between.

This is the metric framework over which the music develops. Now, listen to the music and find another rhythmic element which continues throughout the piece. You should be listening for a rhythmic ostinato, a persistently repeated pattern sounded by the low tones of the piano. When you hear the ostinato, pat it on your knees or dance it. You can also count it like this:

In a group situation form three concentric circles and move around the room enacting these rhythmic components as you listen to the music:

- ☐ Group A—step every beat and shrug shoulders on primary and secondary accents
- ☐ Group B—step primary and secondary accents and snap on the in-between beats
- ☐ Group C—dance the ostinato rhythm and clap the accents

As you move, try to make the rhythmic response automatic so you can listen to the improvised solos played at different times by the three instruments.

By doing all of this, with the help of someone who can label the various musical components correctly, participants can develop skills and concepts related to these qualities of rhythm:

beat (in fives here)   meter ($\frac{5}{4}$ here)
accent   rhythmic ostinato
secondary accent

We can also hope that the experience was enjoyable and that the dancers became acquainted with an interesting contemporary musical composition.

Now let's work with another 20th-century composition, the third movement of *Toccata for Percussion* by Carlos Chávez.[22] This music uses seven different percussion instruments. Although some of the instruments play alone at times, the piece is interesting because the texture changes. As you listen to the music, select one instrumental timbre to follow and enact, first by patting your hands rhythmically on your knees, and later with free dancing movements. Dance only when your instrument sounds, and move with its tempo, rhythm, and dynamics as much as you can. When several instruments play together there should be one person moving to each part.

After you have become acquainted with the music, try to follow the events as labeled on the following time-line:

1. timpani alone

2. snare drum added

3. tom-toms added

4. claves added

5. timpani alone

6. snare drum added, with tom-toms, chime

7. maracas leads, with timpani, snare drum

8. chimes, with maracas, timpani, snare drum

9. timpani leads, with tom-toms, claves, snare drum

10. cymbals, with timpani, tom-toms, snare drum

11. timpani alone; (recapitulation)

12. snare drum added

13. tom-toms added

14. claves added

15. timpani ending

If you are to follow the part of an instrument accurately, you will have to listen to the music several times, until you are able to anticipate when that instrument will begin to play. In effect, the group will be dancing the orchestration of the music, and at the same time, showing the rhythm, dynamics, and texture when several parts sound at once.

At Level III there is considerable variety in the compositions suggested for interpretation through movement. Children vary in their experience with music and with movement, and in their receptivity to this activity. These experiences may have given you some idea of the value of movement as an approach to music, but your attitude toward it will have a great deal to do with your success in implementing such activities in the classroom. You will need to decide whether to begin with a structured situation (folk dances or straightforward marches) to get the class started; or whether they could adapt exploratory creative movement to musical compositions having clear, obvious rhythm and form. Seek out music of any genre that would appeal to the class and would lend itself to body movement. Analyze it in terms of the most obvious characteristics that could be expressed in movement, then try it out with a group.

Learning to Conduct Songs

Within the framework of traditional gestures available, the conductor of a symphony orchestra conveys to the orchestra all the feeling of musical rhythm, melody, dynamics, and other expressive factors that make possible the interpretation of any musical work. Conducting is a highly developed use of movement and gesture that untrained individuals can only approximate in simple ways. But nine- or ten-year-old children can begin to apply gesture and arm movement to the interpretation of music by learning to conduct their own songs. Rhythmic arm movements of a general nature should be an early kind of participation. When rhythmic response is well established, children can learn the conductor's patterns for the common meters of $\frac{2}{4}$, $\frac{3}{4}$, $\frac{4}{4}$, and $\frac{6}{8}$. The conductor's pattern can be of great help to a singer in analyzing and singing the rhythm of a song. When children can keep the proper metric beat, they will automatically hold long notes and provide time for rests.

In conducting, extend your hand forward, palm down, with a supple rather than a rigid or flabby feeling, the elbow slightly away from your body. Only when directing large groups should you raise your arm high. It takes practice to develop an expressive conductor's beat, but the initial objective is to establish the rhythmic movements in the proper direction. The patterns shown below are for the right-handed person; when the left hand is used, the opposite left and right directions are taken (see below). When you are learning the hand movements, practice conducting well-known songs that begin on the first beat of the measure. Songs meeting these requirements are shown below in conjunction with each basic conducting pattern.

In conducting $\frac{2}{4}$ meter, the movement is essentially down and up with a slight movement to the right preceding the upward stroke. Every conductor must give a preparatory beat to let the singers know when to start; this takes the form of a slight upward movement preceding the downward stroke on which the singing begins.

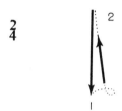

"Merrily We Roll Along":

For $\frac{3}{4}$ meter, the conductor's pattern is in effect a triangle moving to the right. The $\frac{4}{4}$ pattern moves first to the left across the body and then to the right.

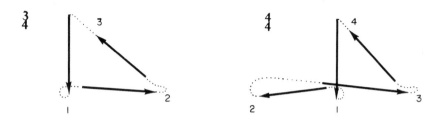

Other than the preparatory beat, which comes only at the beginning of the composition, the dotted lines indicate the slight rebound of the hand between beats, which gives the conductor's pattern the necessary fluid rhythmic movement.

"America":

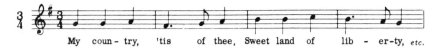

"Lovely Evening":

"Are You Sleeping?":

A two-beat pattern is usually used with $\frac{6}{8}$ meter, so that there is a subdivision of three on each beat (in contrast to the "1-and-2-and" two-part subdivision in $\frac{2}{4}$ meter). If a song is sung in slow $\frac{6}{8}$ meter, each beat is indicated.

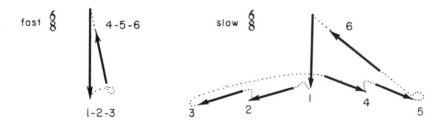

"Row, Row, Row Your Boat":

Row, row, row your boat Gent - ly down the stream, *etc.*

SWEET AND LOW :

Sweet and low, sweet and low, Wind of the west - ern sea,_____ *etc.*

A song in $\frac{9}{8}$ meter (e.g., "Down in the Valley," Example 6.2) would be conducted using a three-beat pattern.

In learning to direct songs, first establish an automatic rhythmic movement of the hand in the pattern for each meter. Although a conductor does not outline the beat pattern with both hands, in the early stages both hands should be used so that (1) left-handed persons will not be confused in direction, and (2) the teacher can face the group and not confuse the students by a reverse movement. The $\frac{3}{4}$ pattern when done with both hands is:

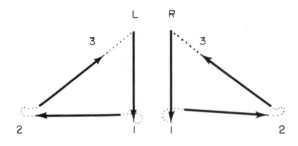

Many songs begin on other than the first beat of the measure. In such cases the preparatory beat will be the one that precedes the beat the song begins on. "The

Star-Spangled Banner," in $\frac{3}{4}$ meter, begins on the third beat; therefore the preparatory beat will take the form of a short movement in the direction of the second beat in $\frac{3}{4}$ meter:

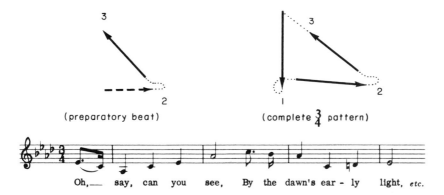

Other well-known songs beginning on upbeats are:

"America the Beautiful" in $\frac{4}{4}$ meter
TMT V-206
"Shalom Chaverim" in $\frac{4}{4}$ meter
SpM V-90

"Streets of Laredo" in $\frac{3}{4}$
meter (Example 6.27)
"Down in the Valley" in $\frac{9}{8}$
meter (Example 6.2)

Inexperienced song leaders sometimes count out the entire measure when a song begins on a fragment of a measure. Songs such as "Oh! Susanna" pose special problems, because they begin on the last half of the second beat. In this song establish the tempo by saying as you conduct:

"Home on the Range" is in $\frac{6}{8}$ meter but has two beats to the measure. Conduct the whole measure in duple pattern and say:

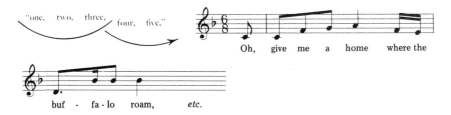

All intermediate children should have an introduction to the accepted conductor's patterns. Those who develop the necessary skill can be encouraged to serve as song leaders. Fifth and sixth grade groups may elect a song leader for a one- or two-week period. Often children who are especially interested and have richer musical backgrounds become natural musical leaders and are so recognized by the class.

Instructional Objectives: To teach the traditional conducting patterns for common meters, so that the children will have a concrete frame of reference for each meter, which will aid them in hearing and seeing music on the printed page; to develop in students an appreciation of the role of the conductor as a musical performer—the need for an accurate sense of tempo, precise cues of entrance, and expressive interpretation of the music.

Behaviors providing evidence that these instructional objectives have been achieved: The children will

- ☐ identify gestures associated with duple, triple, and quadruple meter
- ☐ keep a steady beat, using the conducting patterns for duple, triple, and quadruple meter
- ☐ use one of these conducting patterns to lead classmates in singing a song
- ☐ report that they have seen a conductor in action and comment on the conducting technique

CHAPTER NOTES

1. Grosvenor Cooper and Leonard B. Meyer, **The Rhythmic Structure of Music** (Chicago: The University of Chicago Press, 1960), p. 8.
2. Gladys Andrews, **Creative Rhythmic Movement for Children** (Englewood Cliffs, N.J.: Prentice-Hall, Inc., 1954).
3. Joan Russell, **Creative Dance in the Primary School** (New York: Frederick A. Praeger, Publishers, 1968).
4. Vera Gray and Rachel Percival, **Music, Movement and Mime for Children** (London: Oxford University Press, 1962).
5. Miriam B. Stecher, Hugh McElheny, and Marion Greenwood, **Music and Movement Improvisations,** Threshold Early Learning Library, vol. 4 (New York: The Macmillan Co., 1972).
6. Elsa Findlay, **Rhythm and Movement, Applications of Dalcroze Eurhythmics** (Evanston, Ill.: Summy-Birchard Company, 1971).
7. Beth Landis and Polly Carder, **The Eclectic Curriculum in Music Education: Contributions of Dalcroze, Kodály, and Orff** (Washington, D.C.: Music Educators National Conference, 1972), pp. 178–190.
8. Genevieve Jones, **Book One, Seeds of Movement** (Pittsburgh, Pa.: Volkwein Brothers, Inc., 1971).
9. Clare Cherry, **Creative Movement for the Developing Child,** rev. ed. (Belmont, Calif.: Lear Siegler, Inc., Fearon Publishers, 1971).
10. Rosanna B. Saffran, **First Book of Creative Rhythms** (New York: Holt, Rinehart and Winston, Inc., 1963).

11. Elsie Braun, **Music for Active Children** (New York: Stephen Daye Press, Inc., 1957).

12. The Franson Corporation (see Appendix B-III).

13. Educational Activities, Inc. (see Appendix B-III).

14. Bowmar Records (see Appendix B-III).

15. Ella Jenkins, Folkways Records (see Appendix B-III).

16. Bessie Jones and Bess Lomax Hawes, **Step It Down** (New York: Harper & Row, Publishers, 1972).

17. Carl Orff and Gunild Keetman, **Music for Children, I—Pentatonic,** English adaptation by Doreen Hall and Arnold Walter (Mainz, Ger.: B. Schott's Söhne, 1956, Edition 4470; New York: Associated Music Publishers, Inc.) pp. 66–84. English version adapted by Margaret Murray (Mainz, Ger.: B. Schott's Söhne, Edition 4865), pp. 50–78.

18. LEARNING TO LISTEN TO MUSIC, record album and pamphlet (Morristown, N.J.: Silver Burdett Co., 1969), or Vanguard VR 6 1090.

19. Syd Skolsky, **The Music Box Book** (New York: E. P. Dutton and Co., Inc., 1946).

20. Eunice Boardman and Beth Landis, EXPLORING MUSIC, **Book II** (New York: Holt, Rinehart and Winston, Inc., 1971).

21. Lillian Baldwin, **The Crimson Book,** MUSIC FOR YOUNG LISTENERS (Morristown, N.J.: Silver Burdett Co., 1951).

22. Carlos Chávez, *Toccata for Percussion,* Third Movement, found in Exploring Music, Grade III, Record 8, or Urania recording URLP 7144.

4

Musical Participation and Study Using Percussion Instruments

From the earliest times people have used percussion instruments in music-making, and almost all ethnic groups use them to accompany chanting, singing, and dancing. This chapter gives primary attention to the way these instruments can be used to stimulate children's interest in rhythm and build their skills in responding to it, playing and understanding it.

Appendix A-II lists concepts children can develop through the experiences described in this chapter. A survey of that material can be helpful both before you study this chapter and as you develop lesson plans using the procedures recommended here. Appendix C-1 supplies reference material on meter and rhythm.

THE SEQUENTIAL DEVELOPMENT OF CONCEPTS AND SKILLS IN RHYTHM

The Pillsbury Foundation Study, *Music of Young Children,*[1] reported that in their spontaneous music-making, children are inclined to sound rhythmic motifs rather than a steady beat. The pervading rhythm pattern heard is that found in children's chant:

Its accent, determined by the verbal structure of the words used, may fall on the first tone of the first or the second measure, or both may be accented, thus making it a compound motif.

It was also noted that the rhythm most often played on drums by children as they march has the same motif: ♩ ♫   . The researchers described the following as "the rhythmic germs which seem to be most characteristic of the young child's instrumental music":   ♫♩   and   ♪| ♩. ♫   and   ♪| ♩ ♪. Observe that in all of these patterns one or two unaccented tones lead to the accent on the longer tone. Since the spontaneous rhythmic motifs shown here are native to children's early music-making, it seems reasonable to use rhythm patterns to help children develop concepts of rhythm as a whole.

Working with Rhythm Patterns

The attention of young children should first be directed to rhythm patterns—simple groupings of long and short sounds—that they can clap or play on rhythm instruments. Here are some examples; they incorporate a simple way of labeling the long and short values of the notes:

ta	ta	ti ti	ta	ta	ti ti	ta		ti ti	ti ti	ti ta

These techniques are used in early childhood classes:

1. Identify and clap rhythm patterns, as found in the rhythm of the words in rhymes, chants and songs.
2. Play echo games with rhythm patterns.
3. Identify patterns with rhythm syllables, discovering that some words have one syllable, others two or more syllables.
4. Relate the patterns to visual diagrams.

At Level I, these verbal labels and the stick notation shown above are two ways children identify patterns that they have first learned by rote. After the pattern has been used in a song and in practice materials, the children can be responsible for identifying it when they hear or see it in this simplified notation. However, rhythmic experience cannot be limited to these simple patterns; children should have experience singing and playing more complicated patterns than the ones used in building a vocabulary of basic patterns they can identify.

The Melody Rhythm

When children know a song well, they can tap the rhythm of the words. Because most songs children sing are syllabic (one syllable to each musical tone), they then are tapping the melody rhythm. Four- and five-year-olds can learn to tap the melody rhythm for familiar songs.

In responding to the melody rhythm and the beat (discussed below), children are dealing with two dimensions of rhythm; but each itself is also a continuing whole. The whole that is "melody rhythm" contains motifs or patterns, which are labeled and dealt with individually, as described above.

The Beat

Many five-year-olds can learn to tap the steady beat of a familiar song; as shown in Chapter 3, the beat is the basis for much body movement related to music. Young children can focus their attention on only one musical element at a time. When they are clapping the beat, they are not able to take the melody rhythm into account. At Level I, therefore, it is important to provide experiences "designed to shift the perceptual focus from one aspect of a musical stimulus to another for clarification of the total stimulus."[2] To focus attention on the beat, you can diagram it with evenly spaced vertical lines; then verbalize the beat by saying:

This should be identified as the "steady beat." When both the concept and the skill to sound the beat are developed through encounters in many kinds of songs, a child should be able to respond independently to the beat of an unfamiliar piece that resembles one used in previous experiences.

Accent and Meter

People tend to perceive any series of continuous beats in groups; a strong beat followed by a weak beat is called "duple" meter. Triple meter consists of a strong beat followed by two weaker beats. Labels have been developed for beats in different positions in the group and for divisions and subdivisions of the beat.

Counting, a universal means of labeling, has been applied to rhythm as it relates to the music's underlying metrical organization. Here you see sets of two beats and sets of three beats, with even divisions of the beat designated "and":

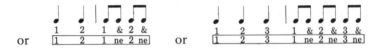

Going beyond this simple division of the beat, other syllables can be used to label the rhythms of different subdivisions of the beat:

Fast ⁶⁄₈ meter is duple meter with three divisions of each beat. It is very common in nursery rhymes and in children's songs of Western Europe and the United States. Unfortunately, the meter signature does not clearly show this duple characteristic, unless the symbol ²⁄♩. is used, as in some educational music books. This meter should be considered to be in six beats to a measure only when taken so slowly that each of the six beats has its own prominence—a condition found in some folk songs used at the intermediate level. Rhythm patterns related to this meter can be counted using the following syllables:

Fast ⁶⁄₈ (²⁄♩.)   ♩ ♪ ♪ ♩ ♪ ♪   (e.g., "Pop, Goes the Weasel," Ex. 4.11)
                    1 lah lay 2 lah lay

Slow ⁶⁄₈   ♫ ♫ ♫ ♫ ♫ ♫   (e.g., "Night Herding Song," Ex. 4.17)
           1 & 2 & 3 & 4 & 5 & 6 &

To make children aware of the underlying metric organization, we begin by having children count and play the steady beat, and clap or play the accent (the "ones"); the goal, however, is to have them learn to sense the position of the accent and to respond to it intuitively rather than having to count each beat. To make this possible, it is necessary to develop both physical response and an understanding of metric organization.

The Time Value of Notes

The terms "quarter-note," "eighth-note," "half-note," and so on, are labels applied to notes of various lengths (see Appendix C-I). These terms are derived from the concept of a whole note as a "full measure" of time, which we find only in ⁴⁄₄ meter ("common time"). Many children's songs and folk songs are in duple meter, rarely using a whole-note; a "quarter-note," therefore, is a symbol indicating a relative length of time, but not actually a "quarter" of anything. In ²⁄₄, ³⁄₄, ⁶⁄₈, and other meters, full measures are not equated to the whole note, and so we must take care that the labels used for notes do not suggest false concepts that will require correction.

In directing children's attention to long and short tones in music, we should:

1. Begin with rhythm patterns that incorporate tones having the length of a beat (♩ or ♩.) or the divided beat (♫ or ♫♪).

2. Use some notes longer than the beat (♩ or ♩.).

3. Occasionally use rests that are equal in time to the beat or divisions of it.

At Level I children should respond to rhythm notation by using rhythm syllables; at Levels II and III, rhythm syllables can be used, and symbols can be used ("quarter-notes" and "eighth-notes," and so forth), when necessary; but they should not be described as being a quarter or an eighth of a whole.

Patterns with Upbeats

Meter in music leads us to expect to give prominence to tones that fall on certain beats of the measure. Music motifs are created so that they make use of such expectations. Although some motifs begin on the strong beat of the measure, many do not. (Review the rhythmic motifs found in the spontaneous music of young children, discussed earlier in this chapter.) Patterns with upbeats should be examined and compared with other patterns so that children understand the music function of the upbeat. An upbeat or anacrusis is an unaccented tone leading to a point of weight and repose. There are very good physical prototypes for this—lift your foot and prepare to make a step; pull your arm back in preparation for striking something. The preparation is an important part of the action, but the point of arrival is the objective of that act, just as it is in the musical motif that has an upbeat.

Bar lines are convenient markers to show where we might normally expect an accent in a metrical grouping, but they do not determine rhythmic groupings; music flows across bar lines. As noted earlier, young children create rhythm patterns that demonstrate their early ability to use upbeats. All you need to do is bring all kinds of patterns to the attention of children and help them notice the relationship between the accented and unaccented sounds.

The Effect of Articulation and Rests

The effect of a musical pattern or phrase can be markedly changed by the way the note is sung or played. A dot **under** a note, to indicate a short stopped sound, can result in an effect similar to that of a short note followed by a rest:

$$\text{♩}\quad\text{♩}\quad\text{♩}\quad\text{♩}\qquad\text{♪}\text{?}\;\text{♪}\text{?}\;\text{♪}\text{?}\;\text{♪}\text{?}$$

Rhythm and expressive musical effect are influenced by the length of the sound and the way it is attacked and released. Part of an individual's preparation for being an informed, perceptive listener, as well as for having potential capability to perform, is having experience with music concepts of this kind.

Silence shown by rests is an important factor of rhythm. Try to bring to the children's attention the rests that make a musical difference, e.g.:

Although they have something to do with meter, rests tacked on at the end of a phrase, to fill up the measure, do not provide a convincing demonstration of the musical function of a rest, e.g.:

THE INSTRUMENTS

All instruments, of course, play rhythm, but among "percussion" instruments—those in which the tone is produced when the instrument is struck, rubbed, or shaken—we find a large group that can produce only one or two levels of pitch, and so are incapable of playing a melody line. In the percussion section of the symphony orchestra, such instruments are standard equipment: drums of various kinds, cymbals, gong, tambourine, and so on. Small copies of symphonic percussion instruments have been adapted for young children and are widely used in kindergarten and primary classes. A number of folk instruments, such as bongo and conga drums, maracas, and others, are added to collections used by older children.

Any musical instrument planned for active use in a classroom must be durable enough to last for a long time, and parts that wear out should be replaceable. A drum, to be more than a decorator's item, must have a head that is sturdy enough to be struck repeatedly with a padded mallet. After two or three years of active use, it may be necessary to replace the drumhead, but at a small part of the original cost.

The quality of sound in the instruments is also important. If there is anything that will put such an instrumental program in the "toy" classification, it is the use of instruments with poor, indistinct sound.

A Basic Group of Instruments

As you begin to obtain percussion instruments for your classroom bear in mind that (1) if a complete set of instruments is not available immediately, you can gather a basic group first and then accumulate the rest later; (2) some homemade instruments are more durable and have better tone than those which are bought.

Drums. Every classroom should have at least one drum and, where possible, two or more of contrasting size. A tunable, 14-inch modern dance drum is a lightweight, versatile instrument that can be used to produce interesting, varied tonal and rhythmic effects. Drums from other musical cultures usually have skin heads and are available in many sizes, from small hand drums to the large ceremonial drums that rest on the floor. These are durable and have a splendid tone, but they are quite expensive and therefore may not be available to the average classroom. A less expensive drum with a reasonably good sound can be constructed as described in Chapter 2.

Rhythm sticks. In the symphony orchestra or in a Latin-American orchestra the claves are a pair of thick, resonant wooden sticks that are struck together. Rhythm sticks are their counterpart among rhythm instruments for children, and three or more pairs should be available. The most resonant tone is made when the sticks are held loosely in the hands as they are tapped together. Rhythm sticks can be purchased, but the homemade version is just as satisfactory.

Chopsticks. For a lighter, contrasting sound that is especially appropriate for faster rhythm patterns, obtain several pairs of inexpensive chopsticks.

EXAMPLE 4.1

PLAYING POSITIONS FOR RHYTHM INSTRUMENTS

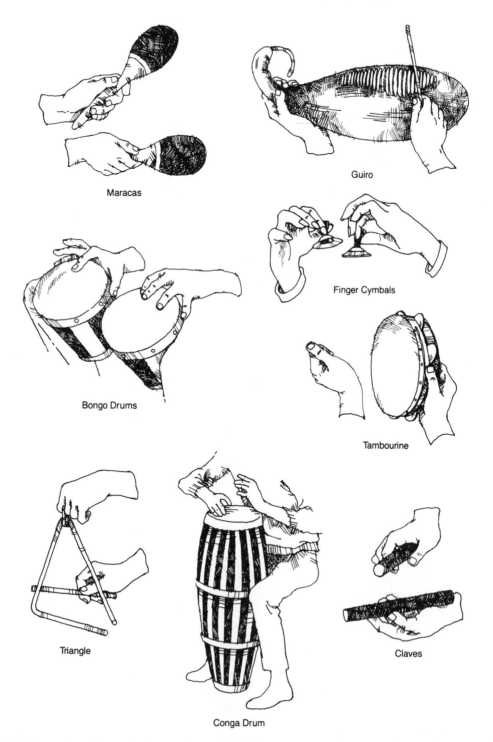

Maracas

Guiro

Bongo Drums

Finger Cymbals

Tambourine

Triangle

Conga Drum

Claves

Triangle. The 5-inch triangle with striker is adequate. For quality in sound, the commercially made triangle is best, but a large nail struck with another nail will produce a similar tone. The triangle or nail must be suspended by a short piece of twine so that the tone will ring freely. Two or three triangles are necessary for bell and other tinkling effects.

Sandblocks. Two or three pairs of sandblocks are useful, so it is advisable to make your own as described in Chapter 2.

Coconut shells. Nothing makes a better sound for galloping and trotting horses than hollow halves of coconut shells tapped together. Two pairs are recommended.

Sleigh bells. It is best to buy medium-size bells that are attached to a handle. Three or four of two different sizes are enough.

With the group of instruments described above, you will have variety and will be able to promote very worthwhile instrumental activities. It is desirable, of course, to have a greater selection of instruments available at times. The following instruments should be stocked by every school, to be loaned to teachers as the need arises.

Tambourine. Homemade tambourines are rarely adequate in quality of sound. It is worth the money to buy a good-quality instrument. Two or three 7-inch tambourines are sufficient.

Tone-blocks. Two sizes of these are very useful for clock sounds. The tone-block is tapped with a small wooden mallet. Commercial tone-blocks are recommended.

Cymbals. One pair of small 7-inch cymbals is enough. Many commercially made small cymbals leave something to be desired as far as tone quality is concerned, so it is worthwhile to get the best quality available.

Gong. This is a more expensive item, but one that is important because it can be used to enhance climaxes and dramatic effects. It should be suspended, struck with a padded mallet, and allowed to vibrate freely. Sometimes large pieces of scrap metal can be found that will produce a reasonably good gong-sound.

Maracas. One or two pairs of commercial resonant wood maracas are recommended. It is worthwhile to buy a better quality instrument, for the handles of the cheaply made kind come off. Teachers have made good-sounding maracas from dried gourds that have been cut open, cleaned and shellacked inside, and resealed with a small amount of rice, shot, or other fine rattling material inside. If the gourds have been buffed on the outside, they can be painted and lacquered in colorful Mexican designs.

Guiro (pronounced wēr′ō). This Latin-American instrument consists of a hollow gourd with a serrated surface. It is played by rhythmically stroking a light stick over the notched area. One of these will serve special purposes from time to time.

Handcastas. These are the childhood counterpart of castanets. They are less expensive and easier to play.

Finger cymbals. Two pairs will provide special effects as needed.

Bells. Any small bells are useful. You can make wrist and ankle bells, for children to wear while dancing, by sewing small jingle bells to a circlet of elastic. Small brass bells can be found in import shops. Try to get a variety of pitches among the bells, and use them individually for their distinctive tone color.

Folk Instruments at the Intermediate Level

Although authentic rhythm instruments from different countries are useful in the primary classroom, they play a more important role at the intermediate level. Prestige is given this work when such instruments are used. Instead of rhythm sticks, use claves, the authentic Cuban instrument, consisting of a pair of thick rosewood or mahogany sticks that are struck together. It is necessary to buy these instruments in order to get the desired tone quality. Tambourines should be larger than those used in the primary grades. Maracas, castanets, and guiros or other types of rasps (notched sticks or other sound-makers that are scraped), are especially valuable with Latin-American songs.

Triangles, cymbals, or a gong may be used occasionally for special effects and, when possible, should be of the standard orchestral size. If orchestral instruments are not available, pupils can explore the potential of different metal objects that, when suspended and struck, make sounds of acceptable quality.

Drums may be of several kinds, as previously described; the bongo and conga drums are of particular interest to children in the intermediate grades. Bongo drums are a pair of small drums, one higher in pitch than the other, bound together so that one player can hold them between the knees and sound them with both hands. Very intricate rhythms can be played on the bongos. A conga drum is much lower in pitch because it is longer. It can stand on the floor, tilted at an angle so that the sound is free; or it can be held between the legs as the player sits on the floor and plays it with both hands. Because Latin-American and West Indian songs are included in the basic series music books, there is a reason for having authentic native instruments. Homemade substitutes for bongo and conga drums can be made of heavy cardboard tubing or fiber waste pipe. The application of goatskin drumheads and tuning procedures are described in *Make Your Own Musical Instruments* by Mandell and Wood.[3]

As pupils become acquainted with people of other cultures they become interested in the typical instruments, such as drums and rattles of the American Indian, the steel drums of the West Indies, the assorted drums, rattles and bells of Africa, Chinese woodblocks and gongs, the Hawaiian *uli-uli* (a small pair of smooth stones that are clicked together), *ipu* (a large hollow gourd), *pū `ili* sticks (fringed bamboo sticks that are struck together), and drums. **CMP Z3-A,** p. 245, shows drawings of these instruments. Often authentic instruments of these types are available in the community and can be obtained for display or limited use.

A Classification of Sound

The use of percussion instruments to provide musical experience must take into account the sound produced by each instrument. We are not concerned here with the detailed study of sound, as in Chapter 2; nevertheless, tone color and duration should be given some attention. The following classification will help you select instruments of contrasting sound to play in studying the different musical elements discussed in the next section of this chapter.

1. Short, dry sounds can be produced by:
   rhythm sticks   *skinhead drum*
   tone-blocks   *coconut shells*
   sandblocks—short, quick stroke   *tambourine*—tapped
   guiro—quick stroke   *castanets*

2. Sustained, dry sounds are produced by:
   maracas—shaken   *guiro*—stroked slowly
   sandblocks—rubbed slowly together

3. Sustained tones with greater resonance are produced by:
   larger drum with skin head   *tambourine*—shaken
   drum with rubber head

4. Tinkling sounds, higher in pitch, are produced by:
   triangle—tapped   *finger cymbals*
   cymbal—tapped lightly with hard stick

5. Ringing sounds of longer duration are produced by:
   triangle—struck repeatedly and   *cymbals*—crashed together or struck
      rapidly at one corner (for a   with a padded mallet and allowed
      louder tone, the striker can be   to vibrate freely
      rung repeatedly around the entire   *bells*—allowed to vibrate freely
      inside of the triangle)   *gong*—struck with a padded
   sleigh bells—shaken for the   mallet while hanging, and
      desired duration   allowed to vibrate freely

EXPERIENCES AT LEVEL I

Five- to seven-year-old children have experience with rhythm, both in the rhymes and chants of childhood and in their natural rhythmic activities. As you study the examples in this section, try to think of other rhymes, chants, and songs that you and the children know and enjoy; then apply these techniques to that repertoire. From such musical experiences children gain the ability to deal with the steady beat and rhythm patterns found in the melodies of numerous easy songs.

From Word Rhythms to the Melody Rhythm

Children begin to explore sound at a very early age, through verbal babbling and by manipulating sound-makers. Up through the preschool years, children continue rhythmic play with words, and they use instrumental sounds to accompany their activities. The Pillsbury Foundation report[4] gives numerous examples of verbal sounds, reiterated phrases, and rhyme heard during the creative play of young children. Children verbalize such phrases as:

"Dance on your ear,   "Red, red, gingerbread;
Dance on your eye."   Red, red, go to bed."

Undoubtedly they feel and enjoy the rhythm as well as the sound of the words they speak. Say each of these rhymes several times, and simultaneously tap or clap the rhythm of the words. Both are spontaneous chants of children, but there is a fundamental difference in the rhythm of each.

You can encourage continued verbal play of this kind. Emma Sheehy[5] says, "It is fun to surprise the child and play with him . . . catching his pitch and rhythm." Music-making in the preschool and kindergarten years is an informal affair; it can go on at any time of day. A classroom teacher should encourage this kind of musical play.

Playing with speech patterns can help children understand rhythm. Start by finding familiar rhymes and chants. Then sound the syllabic rhythm of the words on rhythm instruments and develop an accompaniment. Here are some procedures to use with jump-rope chants and counting rhymes:

1. Say the rhyme several times to feel its rhythm:

    "Red, red gin-ger-bread;   or   "Mic-key Mouse bought a house!
    Red, red, got to bed."   How did he paint it?
                                              Slow strokes, broad strokes,
                                              Spat-ter, spat-ter, spat-ter!"

2. Tap the syllabic rhythm of the words as you say the rhyme. "The rhythm of the words" is an important concept to develop, and it will be used extensively in song rhythms. It is especially important to notice that some words (e.g., "gingerbread") are made up of several syllables.

3. Tap the rhythm of the words on chopsticks and just think the words. Did you notice that the sticks seem to "say" the rhythm of the words? At this point the rhythm has been extracted from the words in which it previously was embedded. The fact that children can recognize a pattern when disassociated from the words is a significant musical development for them.

Say interesting single words repeatedly and use chopsticks to tap the syllabic rhythm:

gin-ger-bread, gin-ger-bread
spa-ghet-ti, spa-ghet-ti
ma-ca-ro-ni, ma-ca-ro-ni

Try to hear the qualities in the rhythm itself. How many sounds are in the word? Where is the heavy syllable in relation to the light or unstressed syllable? You can investigate the rhythm of names. How many different rhythms can be found in the names of members of the class? Here are some examples:

☐ *One syllable*—J̄ohn, Ānn, P̄aul

☐ *Two syllables*

(heavy-light) B̄et-ty, P̄er-ry, T̄om-my

(light-heavy) J̆o-anne, Ĕu-gene, K̆ath-leen

☐ *Three syllables*

(heavy-light-light) C̄hris-to-pher, J̄on-a-thon, J̄en-ni-fer

(light-heavy-light) R̆e-bec-ca, Y̆o-lan-da, N̆a-tha-niel

You could investigate the names of foods (ham-bur-ger, cher-ry pie, "Big Mac"), birds, flowers, cars, or other things, and put them together in combinations that have an interesting rhythm. Listen to examples of this kind of rhythmic expression; you will find some on the Orff and Keetman *Schulwerk* recording *Music for Children.*[6]

Talking and rhythms can be incorporated into creative stories. A fine motivational record for this is *Little Indian Drum,*[7] in which a boy named Red Fox learns to communicate by drum with his father. All the suggestions made above are as much a part of the language arts program as of music and should be utilized as a part of general classroom work.

For further experience with rhythm, sound the rhythm of the words in songs. The clearly defined, light sound of chopsticks tapped together is good for this activity. "Chickama Craney Crow" or any strongly rhythmic song having one syllable for each note is suitable for this use.

EXAMPLE 4.2

CHICKAMA CRANEY CROW
Southern Folk Song

Whimsically

Chick-a-ma, Chick-a-ma, Crane-y Crow, I
went to the well just to wash my toe; When I got home, one
chick-en was gone! Chick-a-ma, Chick-a-ma Crane-y Crow!

From Berg, Burns, Hooley, Pace, and Wolverton, *Music For Young Americans,* Kindergarten Book. American Book Company. Used by permission.

As you sing the song, tap the syllables of the words (as shown by the X-marks above the words) so that the sticks "say the rhythm of the words."

Make a game of tapping the rhythm of the words of an unnamed, but very familiar song and asking someone to identify the song. There is good rhythmic contrast between "Row, Row, Row Your Boat" and "London Bridge"; can you discriminate one from the other when hearing only the rhythm of the melody?

EXAMPLE 4.3

ROW, ROW, ROW YOUR BOAT
Traditional Round

With spirit

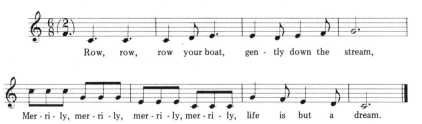

LONDON BRIDGE
Children's Game

Lively

Most children's songs and many folk songs have one note for each syllable in the text; in these songs, the rhythm of the words is also the "melody rhythm." Sounding the melody rhythm of familiar songs should be a frequent activity at Level I. The playful echoing of repetitive patterns in the melody will lead to the identification of rhythm patterns. This subject will be discussed after the other general approach to rhythm: sounding the steady beat.

Instructional Objectives: To get children playfully involved with rhythm; to help them perceive long and short sounds; to help them respond accurately in playing the melody rhythm.

Behaviors providing evidence that these instructional objectives have been achieved: The children will

☐ identify a familiar song when its melody rhythm is tapped on a rhythm instrument

☐ identify as melody rhythm that element when heard extracted from the song

☐ tap the melody rhythm of a familiar song so that others can identify it

Developing a Concept of the Steady Beat

As you march and walk rhythmically to music, you can highlight the beat by adding a rhythm instrument (drum, rhythm sticks or tone-block). Rhythm instruments can be used to sound the beat in marches, walks, runs, skips, and gallops as outlined in Chapter 3. March, sing, and clap the beat of "Yankee Doodle"; notice that the beat (shown by the X-marks above the notation) is steady and goes right along with the regular movement of marching or walking.

EXAMPLE 4.4

YANKEE DOODLE
Traditional

As you march and sound the beat, say "tah, tah, tah, tah" to identify the beat; make a visual representation of it by drawing evenly spaced vertical lines as shown here:

| | | |

Any songs or instrumental compositions with two strong beats to a measure can be accompanied by a percussion instrument played on the beat. The marches and other strongly rhythmic music suggested in Chapter 3 would also be useful in this activity. (Do not treat gentle, quiet songs in this way, for it would be out of character with the mood of those songs.) Here are titles of children's songs that work well for this purpose:

"Clap Your Hands" SBM I-37   "The Farmer in the Dell" NDinM K-89
"If You're Happy" DMT ECh-15   "Mister Rabbit" SBM I-35
"Johnny Schmoker" TMT III-61   "Jimmy Crack Corn" ExM I-49

Young children can learn to sound the steady beat or the melody rhythm in many familiar songs, but these two skills should be kept separate. Do not ask young children to respond to both elements in the same song; instead, give them much experience responding to each element in different songs.

Instructional Objectives: To get the children pleasurably involved with rhythm, and to help them perceive and respond to the steady beat in songs and other strongly rhythmic music that has regular meters.

    Behaviors providing evidence that these instructional objectives have been achieved: The children will

    ☐ identify as "steady beat" a regular tapping that matches the underlying metric organization of songs and other strongly rhythmic music

    ☐ accurately play on rhythm instruments the steady beat of strongly rhythmic music

Working with Rhythm Patterns

    You can make a game of tapping and verbalizing rhythm patterns found in the melody rhythm of familiar songs when the patterns in the song are simple and regular. "Bell Horses" (Example 5.8) and "Hey, Betty Martin" are good examples of songs in simple duple meter ($\frac{2}{4}$) that have easily identified rhythm patterns.

EXAMPLE 4.5

HEY, BETTY MARTIN
Early American

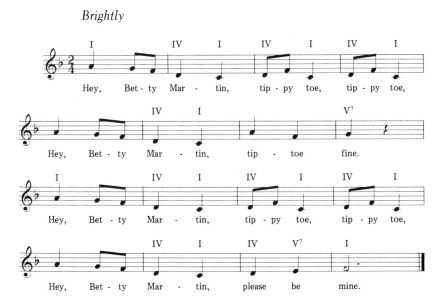

Come, let's go walk-ing, walk-ing, walk-ing;
Come, let's go walk-ing, far a-way.
Come, let's go walk-ing, walk-ing, walk-ing;
Come, let's go walk-ing, on our way.

This song consists of rhythm patterns that can be verbalized as follows:

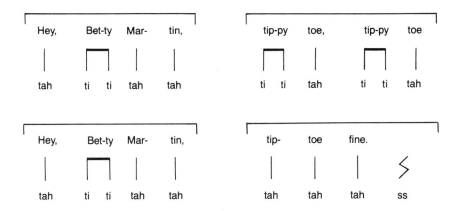

Tap or clap each pattern and have someone echo it back. Make a game of it by sounding the patterns in a different order; then say the rhythm syllables as you clap or tap each pattern. On a rest, hands are moved apart and a quiet "ss" sound can be made. Individuals or the group should be able to respond in copy-cat fashion, tapping and verbalizing each pattern.

When the above procedures have been used with a number of patterns, show the stick-rhythm notation on cards; identify the pattern by clapping and using rhythm syllables. The group or individuals should then learn to tap or clap the familiar patterns when they see them in notation.

Some songs are in compound duple meter ($\frac{6}{8}$ or $\frac{2}{8}$.), in which each beat is divided into three equal parts. Such songs also have long–short patterns, and when they are simple and regular as in "Jack Be Nimble," they are easy to tap and verbalize.

EXAMPLE 4.6

JACK BE NIMBLE
Traditional Children's Rhyme

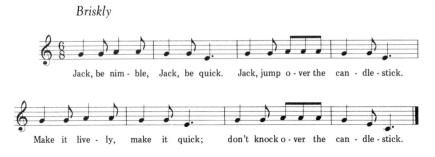

This song has two patterns, which would be verbalized and diagrammed like this:

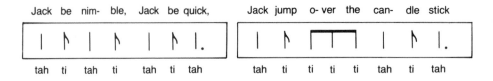

The rhythm syllables are verbalized and learned by rote; the stick notation is the only visual representation used in this work. To build an adequate repertoire of rhythm patterns, you will need to deal with a variety of songs. Here are some traditional songs with good rhythm patterns:

$\frac{2}{4}$ "Bingo" ExM I-135

"Hop, Old Squirrel" DMT ECh-52

"Bow, Belinda" NDinM K-34

$\frac{6}{8}$ "Rig-a-Jig-Jig" (Example 3.6)

"Fiddle-dee-dee" SpM III-147

"Row, Row, Row Your Boat" (Example 4.3)

Look for simple, regular patterns in songs you would like the children to sing. Make rhythm charts for the patterns they are able to tap easily.

You can play echo games using rhythm patterns that you have identified. Up to seven or eight tones can be used in echo clapping or tapping rhythm instruments. It is important that the "echo" begin on the beat immediately after the initial example is given. The patterns in Example 4.7 are from "This Old Man" ($\frac{2}{\bullet}$) and "Rig-a-Jig-Jig" ($\frac{2}{\bullet}$.):

EXAMPLE 4.7

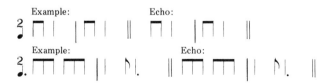

Practice clapping or tapping patterns that are to be echoed by a partner or a group. You will have to give a signal to start the children clapping at the right time. Do not clap with them, however, if you want to know whether they can respond to the aural memory of the pattern itself, which is an important musical skill. When a pattern has been accurately "echoed," attach rhythm syllables to it and repeat the echo procedure. What rhythm syllables would you use with the two patterns shown in Example 4.7?

Some teachers use echo clapping as drill, unassociated with any musical composition, or as an attention-getting, control procedure. When the patterns are used in this way, they lack the expressive musical meaning they have when associated with a musical composition. The most fruitful use of these techniques comes when you begin by tapping the melody rhythm of a song, and then identify patterns within that melody.

Instructional Objectives: To sensitize children to rhythmic motifs in the songs they sing and the music they hear, and to help them recognize particular long–short combinations of sound.

Behaviors providing evidence that these instructional objectives have been achieved: The children will

- □ accurately echo clap or tap rhythmic motifs consisting of quarter-notes and eighth-notes
- □ attach accepted verbal labels to those patterns
- □ chant rhythm syllables and tap simple rhythm patterns they see in stick notation

Rhythm Ensembles

At Level I children should play rhythm instruments to highlight one musical element at a time. Kindergarten or first grade is too early for mass use of the instruments to be beneficial. The traditional "rhythm band," promoted at this early age, had practices that directly opposed the approach to instruments recommended in this chapter.

1. Young children are individualists who have not yet learned to work together. To put a rhythm instrument into the hands of every child is to promote indiscriminate sound-making rather than to develop sensitivity to the tone quality of the various instruments.

2. In a "rhythm band" at Level I, the children are required to learn how to play the instruments, and at the same time, learn when to play them in the orchestration.

3. When an orchestration is predetermined by the teacher, as it must be at Level I, the children must learn the various parts by rote. Their response is not prompted by an understanding of the elements of rhythm and musical form.

4. While the project may strengthen the children's automatic response to certain elements of rhythm, body movement is a much more effective way to develop such response.

5. At this age, only a few especially talented children are ready to participate in the rhythm band. Their talents are exploited and "stars" are developed; the majority of the children, however, have little opportunity to grow in their ability either to play rhythmically or to understand the interrelationships of the various elements of rhythm.

There is a place for an organized percussion ensemble, beginning at Level II and in Level III, as described in the learning experiences in this chapter.

EXPERIENCES AT LEVEL II

The basic rhythmic experiences initiated at Level I can be expanded with seven- to nine-year-olds. Children at this level can learn to play in a group in which two or three elements of rhythm are sounded simultaneously on percussion instruments, and they can learn to read notation for simple rhythm patterns. They will also exercise musical taste and judgment as they select specific instruments to play particular musical elements.

Playing the Melody Rhythm and the Steady Beat

If seven-year-olds have had considerable experience playing the melody rhythm with some songs and the steady beat with others, they will be able to combine these, some children playing one, other children the other, simultaneously in one song. Try it with "Train is A-Comin'."

EXAMPLE 4.8

TRAIN IS A-COMIN'
Spiritual

Energetically

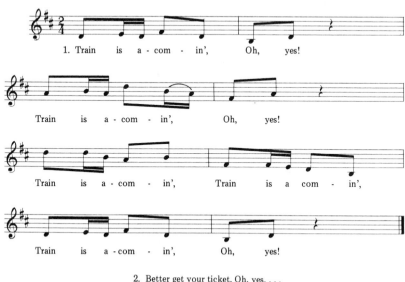

1. Train is a-com-in', Oh, yes!
Train is a-com-in', Oh, yes!
Train is a-com-in', Train is a com-in',
Train is a-com-in', Oh, yes!

2. Better get your ticket, Oh, yes, . . .
3. Room for many more, Oh, yes, . . .
4. Train is a-leavin', Oh, yes, . . .

Two or three players can sound the beat on sandblocks to suggest the "choo, choo" sound of the train. When that is going well, two or three others can play the melody rhythm on claves or rhythm sticks while the class sings. This provides a two-part rhythmic accompaniment for the song:

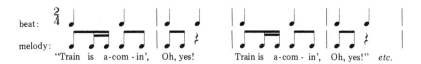

The objective of this experience is to learn to play either the steady beat or the melody rhythm at will. Players must keep their attention on the element they are playing or they may inadvertently get on the other part. Similar two-part accompaniments might also be created for the following songs:

$\frac{2}{4}$ "Paw-Paw Patch" (Example 6.19) $\frac{4}{4}$ "Sarasponda" DMT III-124
"Get On Board" SBM I-40   "The Magic Penny" (Example 4.13)
"Old Joe Clark" SBM III-8   "Turn the Glasses Over"
ExM IV-30

Make sure that the steady beat and the melody rhythm are played on instruments of contrasting timbre. Chopsticks are good for a rapid melody, and they can be combined with a drum or rhythm sticks that sound the beat. Two or three players on each part usually provide a good balance for the singing. Sometimes the players should stand in front of the class as they accompany the singers. The others then can listen and watch first one rhythm part and then the other, and finally hear both parts together along with the singing. Developing the awareness of individual parts within a composite sound has implications for listening at all levels. Combining watching with listening gives visual support to what is heard.

Playing the Accent and Knowing Meter

Another experience appropriate at Level II is sounding the accent in the underlying meter of the song. This technique should be developed after individuals have learned to respond easily to the steady beat and melody rhythm. Playing a rhythm instrument on the accent is appropriate with "Sandy Land."

EXAMPLE 4.9

SANDY LAND
American Singing Game

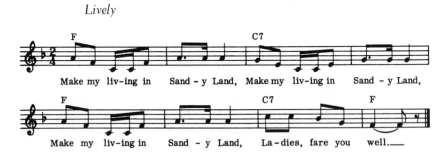

To develop an understanding of accent, work from the steady beat. Play the beat on the rhythm sticks, counting "one-two, one-two" while the class sings the song. Following this, a drummer should play only the "ones." Counting can help you find the accent; if you have no difficulty, counting aloud may be dispensed with. When you clap or play the accent, move your hand or drumstick rhythmically in the opposite direction on the unsounded beat, so that your total response is rhythmic and follows the meter. The goal in this work is to sense the position of the strong beat (the accent) and respond to it intuitively rather than having to count each beat. To make this possible, both physical response and understanding of metric organization must be developed.

These techniques should be used with strongly rhythmic songs in both duple and triple meters. Play a tambourine on the accent and chopsticks on the steady beat in "Sing Your Way Home." If necessary, count "one-two-three, one-two-three," to learn to feel the position of the accent on "one" in this triple meter.

EXAMPLE 4.10

SING YOUR WAY HOME

Camp Song

Leisurely

Sing your way home at the close of the day,

Sing your way home, drive the shad - ows a - way.

Smile ev - 'ry mile, for wher - ev - er you

roam, It will bright - en your road,

It will light - en your load If you sing your way home.

At this level you can speak of rhythms that swing in "twos" or "threes." The goal is to listen, sense, and respond to meter as duple or triple. When this has been achieved you can take note that when the music "swings in twos," the meter signature is $\frac{2}{4}$. The point of observation is only that the upper number in $\frac{2}{4}$, $\frac{3}{4}$, or $\frac{4}{4}$ shows how the music "swings" and how often the accent occurs.

Another duple meter that "swings in twos" is fast $\frac{6}{8}$ meter. The beat is verbalized ♩. ♩. | ♩. ♩. |. Sing "Pop, Goes the Weasel" and play the steady beat
1 2   1 2
on rhythm sticks.

EXAMPLE 4.11

POP, GOES THE WEASEL
American Singing Game

Lively

All a-round the cob - bler's bench, Mon - key chased the wea - sel, Mon-key thought 'twas all in fun, Pop, goes the wea - sel.

Pen - ny for a spool of thread, Pen - ny for a nee - dle,

That's the way the mon - ey goes, Pop, goes the wea - sel.

In this meter there are three divisions to each beat, rather than two as in simple duple meter ($\frac{2}{4}$). The song still has two beats to every measure and you can find the accent by counting as shown above, and sounding a heavier instrument (possibly a drum) every time you say "one." These are titles of other songs in fast $\frac{6}{8}$ ($\frac{2}{\bullet\cdot}$) meter:

"The Animal Fair" SpM II-128   "Rig-a-Jig-Jig" (Example 3.6)
"Down the River" ExM III-118   "Lemons" SBM III-186

The earliest experiences in rhythm should be kinesthetic and aural rather than visual. First feel, hear, and learn to respond to each element of rhythm; then listen for a combination of two or three of the elements and learn to play any of them at will. Most seven- or eight-year-olds readily learn to play in a group that combines the melody rhythm, steady beat, and accent, if they have had experience using instruments to play one and then two of these elements at a time.

As soon as you can comfortably do so, play any one of the three elements of rhythm (steady beat, accent, melody rhythm) while the class sings the song. Then, with a group, try the following routine with "This Old Man" or any of the preceding songs. Each instrument should keep playing after it has started. Use one or two players on each part.

EXAMPLE 4.12

THIS OLD MAN

English Folk Song

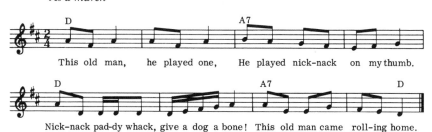

As a march

This old man,   he played one,   He played nick-nack   on my thumb.

Nick-nack pad-dy whack, give a dog a bone! This old man came   roll-ing home.

1. Establish the steady beat using one kind of instrument.
2. Play the accent on a heavier-sounding instrument.
3. Sing and play the melody rhythm using a lighter-sounding instrument.

As the three parts are played, try to achieve a balance of sound between instruments and voices.

Instructional Objectives: To help children develop concepts of the steady beat, the accent, and the melody rhythm; to build skill in playing each element at will, and learn to play in an ensemble with other parts sounded simultaneously.

Behaviors providing evidence that these instructional objectives have been achieved: The children will

☐ play accurately the steady beat, the melody rhythm, or the accent, alone or in an ensemble of three parts accompanying a known song, in duple or in triple meter

☐ identify the meter and accurately play the steady beat or the accent of a new song in duple or triple meter

☐ indicate which of the three elements is being played as accompaniment to an unfamiliar piece in duple or triple meter

☐ be eager to play the parts with which they feel comfortable

Playing Repeated Rhythm Patterns

Working with the melody rhythm of a song can lead to discovering rhythm patterns that can be pointed up by being played on an instrument of a different tone color. "The Magic Penny" is a lively song in $\frac{4}{4}$ meter that accommodates a percussion accompaniment very well. Because it has two different sections, you can highlight the change by using different instruments for the second section. Notice that this song has a three-part form (A B A)—after the contrasting section is sung, the first section is repeated.

EXAMPLE 4.13

THE MAGIC PENNY

Words and Music by Malvina Reynolds

The Magic Penny. Words and music by Malvina Reynolds. © Copyright 1955, 1958, by Northern Music Company, New York, N.Y. Used by permission. All rights reserved.

What instruments do you think would work well with this song? Select one instrument to play the steady beat throughout, then choose two different light sounds for the melody rhythm, using one for each section. Sing the song and try out your choices of instruments. Did you notice the repeated motif "Give it away"? In this song that, of course, is the key to the magic! Let's give that magic motif a special sound by playing its rhythm on finger cymbals each time it happens. Now sing and play the song again and enjoy the instrumental contrasts that have been developed for the song. Pass the instruments around and let different individuals have a chance to play the accompaniment.

"San Sereni" can be sung with a simple rhythm accompaniment consisting of chopsticks playing the steady beat and finger cymbals playing the accent.

EXAMPLE 4.14

SAN SERENÍ
Spanish Folk Song

San Se - re - ní, la bue - na, bue - na vi - da,

Ha - cen a - sí, ha - cen los za - pa - te - ros, A -

sí, a - sí, a - sí, a - sí, a - sí, a - sí.

1. *los zapateros*—the shoemakers
2. *los carpinteros*—the carpenters
3. *los vaqueros*—the cowboys

Notice that the melody of "San Sereni" contains these two rhythmic motifs:

Sing the song again as two or more players sound the first pattern on claves and the second pattern on maracas whenever they occur in the song.

If the players are sufficiently secure in playing such patterns, either of the two can be played as a persistently repeated pattern (an ostinato) in the rhythm ensemble accompanying the singing. Playing two or three parts of the following rhythm accompaniment would be a good activity at Level II. Try different combinations of the parts, but do not feel obliged to use more parts at once than the group can hear or feel comfortable playing.

Often a single specialized rhythm pattern provides a very suitable accompaniment for a song. Such a pattern is not selected arbitrarily, but is integral to the rhythmic scheme of the song. For example, with "Pop, Goes the Weasel" (Example 4.11) or with "Rig-a-Jig-Jig" (Example 3.6), two tone-blocks can play an ostinato throughout the song in this galloping rhythm, which is found in the melody:

"Farewell to the Old Year" is a song in $\frac{6}{4}$ meter (two groups of three beats in each measure) that can be accompanied by rhythm instruments sounding some of the rhythm patterns in the song. This kind of activity is important preliminary experience leading to the use of tuned instruments (to be considered in Chapter 6).

EXAMPLE 4.15

FAREWELL TO THE OLD YEAR (CANON)

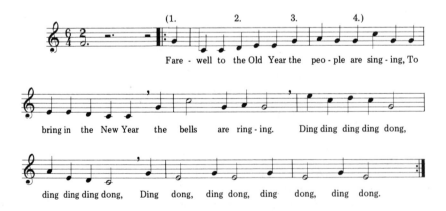

In the following songs you will find rhythm patterns that can be used as ostinato patterns:

$\frac{2}{4}$ "Jingle Bells" TMT IV-181 $\frac{6}{8}$ "Down the River" ExM III-118
   "Skip to My Lou" DMT III-9   "Noah's Ark" TMT IV-126

Sounding an ostinato is a more advanced use of the instruments, for you must sometimes respond independently of the melody rhythm. To establish a security that will permit you to continue it successfully throughout the song, play the ostinato as an introduction for two measures before the singing begins. Some children may need time to develop the concentration and independence to play an ostinato successfully. Playing along with a more accomplished performer may help them to do this sooner.

Labeling and Reading Rhythm

Jingles and short poems can be explored to determine how the rhythm of the words is related to the beat. "Diddle, Diddle Dumpling" begins on the beat and has a few evenly divided beats:

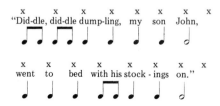

Clap the steady beat and chant the rhyme until you discover that some of the words move right along with the beat and others move twice as fast. Use some system of verbalizing the rhythm. At Level I the system shown here was recommended to help define simple relationships of the melody rhythm and the steady beat:

As the children begin to understand the function and meaning of measured rhythm you can verbalize rhythm patterns by speaking the numbers used in defining a meter:

This system defines the position of the note in the measure and is useful in verbalizing more intricate rhythms. Throughout this book verbalization is recommended in the analysis of rhythm, so that performers learn to say or think the underlying metric framework for the rhythms they play.

As soon as children can identify rhythm patterns aurally, the patterns can be represented visually. Use a felt marking pen to chart patterns such as those shown for "San Sereni" (Example 4.14); put only the rhythm notation (not the syllables) on the chart.

Chant the rhythm syllables as you point to the charted rhythm notation; afterwards, sing the words as you point to the notation. Because using rhythm syllables involves one less element than using the words, it is easier to focus on the rhythm when the rhythm syllables are used.

Many familiar rhymes fall in compound duple meter ($\frac{6}{8}$), in which there are three parts to each beat. Such rhymes can be verbalized as shown here with the charted patterns from "Rig-a-Jig-Jig":

1 lah lay 2 lah lay 1   lay 2   lay 1   lay 2   lay 1   lay 2

"Rig - a - jig - jig and a - way   we go,   a - way   we go,   a - way   we go."

In this meter there are two beats to a measure, but each has an underlying division of threes. These divided beats are typically grouped as seen in the patterns of this song. Use a variety of rhythm patterns, verbally and in chart notation, but relate them to the songs from which they are taken; in this way, the study will not lose its expressive purpose.

Children can respond by playing percussion instruments to melody rhythms that are more complex than they can analyze and read. Plan to provide both levels of experience; have the children work aurally with melody rhythms in a variety of meters even as they study in detail simple patterns in $\frac{2}{4}$, $\frac{4}{4}$, or $\frac{6}{8}$ meter.

Developing an Orchestration

Rhythm instrument accompaniments have been previously suggested with several activities. At Level II, children can learn to play in a group in which three or more rhythmic components are heard simultaneously: the beat, the accent, the melody rhythm, or repeated patterns. Many songs can be accompanied in this way. In addition, some recorded instrumental compositions can be used as a basis for rhythm orchestrations.

The first pieces treated in this way could be compositions that have been used for interpretation through body movement. One or two parts could be played, depending upon what concepts of rhythm the children have developed. In a march or dance the steady beat could be played; the instruments used should have a timbre compatible with the orchestration heard. "Dagger Dance" from *Natoma* by Victor Herbert (**AinM III-1**) is a stylized American Indian dance with a very regular drum beat in fours. Two or three drums could be played throughout, sounding that regular pattern of fours, with a strong accent on the first beat:

After the children have played the steady beat and accents, at the speed and dynamic level of the recorded music, other instruments might be added. If the music has special effects like a drum roll or a cymbal crash, these might be matched by playing an appropriate rhythm instrument. In "Tarantella," from the *Fantastic Toy Shop* by Rossini (**AinM III-2**), the fast, steady, duple beat could be played throughout on a crisp, dry-sounding instrument. The featured instrument is the tambourine, which is rapped on accents and sometimes is shaken on long notes. At the ends of some phrases, the drum responds with accents. Obtain this record and try some of these instrumental effects. For a good total musical effect, you will find that a balance of sound between the recording and the accompanying percussion instruments is essential.

When you add rhythm parts other than regular beats and accents, you will need to hear a composition often enough to anticipate where the special effects should be added. The first section of "Tambourin," from the ballet music for *Céphale et Procris* by Grétry (**AinM III-1**), is fairly easy to orchestrate with two light beats to a measure. At several points in the music, the triangle can be heard. The triangle player should listen to the music enough to be able to anticipate where the triangle occurs and to sound the instrument at those points.

Each eight-measure phrase in the first section of "Tambourin" is announced with three loud chords, which can be played on drums or cymbals. The music is in three sections (A B A), with the middle or contrasting section having a more flowing character. In the middle section, select and play only one or two instruments that sound compatible with the music.

The development of rhythm orchestrations should grow out of a study of instrumental timbre and out of skill in responding to the music's rhythmic components.

Instructional Objectives: To use rhythm instruments in ways that provide challenging, pleasurable musical participation and enable the children to build skills in responding to rhythmic details; and to develop concepts of rhythm, musical form, and instrumental timbre.

Behaviors providing evidence that these instructional objectives have been achieved: The children will

☐ be eager to participate in each ensemble performance

☐ accurately play the music element selected for their instrument

☐ choose, with discrimination, instruments to be used for different parts in the orchestration

□ identify sections of a musical composition as being the same or different when working out an orchestration

To experience the pleasure and musical learning that can arise from this use of percussion instruments, try some of the pieces mentioned above, or others that have comparable rhythmic and formal clarity.

EXPERIENCES AT LEVEL III

Boys and girls in the intermediate grades should have well-developed concepts of the steady beat, melody rhythm, and accent, and should be able to play any of these rhythmic components at will. If this is not the case, they will learn readily if, using music appealing to older children, you apply some of the techniques described in the previous section. Here are titles of songs that these children will enjoy, but that will give them experience with basic rhythm elements in a simple musical piece:

"The Galway Piper" $\frac{4}{4}$ DMT VI-47   "Night Herding Song" $\frac{6}{8}$ NDinM V-130

"La Cucaracha" $\frac{3}{4}$ DMT VI-69   "Oh, Susanna!" $\frac{4}{4}$ DMT V-55

"Mama Don't 'Low" $\frac{2}{4}$ SBM V-4   "Riding Song" $\frac{3}{4}$ ExM VI-104

"Minka" $\frac{2}{4}$ ExM VI-96   "When Johnny Comes Marching Home" $\frac{6}{8}$ ExM V-6

Relating Beat, Accent, and Meter

When you can deal comfortably with the beat, accent, and melody rhythm of songs in simple meters, begin work with other metric organizations. The beat in duple meter can be represented by a quarter note ($\frac{2}{4} = \frac{2}{}$), by a half note ($\frac{2}{2} = \frac{2}{}$), or by an eighth note ($\frac{2}{8} = \frac{2}{}$). The determining factor is the speed of the beat; it should be comfortable for clapping, tapping, stepping, or conducting. Music written in $\frac{2}{2}$ meter tends to look slower, more leisurely or majestic.

Sometimes there are four quarter beats in a measure, but the meter signature shows ₵ ("cut time") because the song needs to move rapidly, and it would not be comfortable to tap or conduct in four beats. In this case, the measure has two beats, with every half note ($\frac{2}{}$) getting one beat. "This Land is Your Land" is an example of a song in cut time.

EXAMPLE 4.16

THIS LAND IS YOUR LAND

Words and Music by Woody Guthrie

This Land Is Your Land. Words and music by Woody Guthrie.
TRO—© Copyright 1956, 1958, and 1970, Ludlow Music, Inc.,
New York, N.Y. Used by permission.

Sing and accompany the song with a three-part orchestration consisting of steady beat, accent, and melody rhythm. This orchestration will point up the unique rhythmic characteristics of the song. It is very repetitious, consisting of one rhythmic motif repeated several times:

Notice that the rhythmic motif consists of a three-note upbeat (anacrusis), leading to the accent. This occurs six times, creating a bit of expectation that is resolved when, after a long note, the final phrase begins squarely on the downbeat. The text in the last line, by its positive statement, "This land was made for you and me," supports this musical feeling of arrival and climax.

This is essentially a simple song, but it is well constructed to convey the strong positive feelings Americans have about their country. Playing such a rhythmic accompaniment may help children notice the way the rhythmic structure contributes toward that feeling.

The first experience with different meters should be aural: The children should first play the appropriate beat, accent, and melody rhythm of whatever song is used; then, you can refer to the rhythm notated on the printed page. When meters such as $\frac{4}{4}$, slow $\frac{6}{8}$, and $\frac{5}{4}$ are encountered, they can play both the primary and the secondary accents in the meter.

EXAMPLE 4.17

NIGHT HERDING SONG
Cowboy Song

Quietly

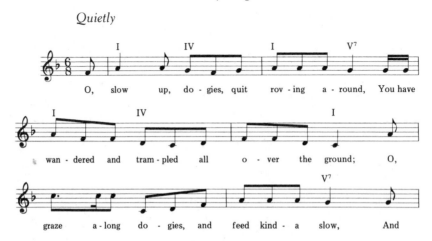

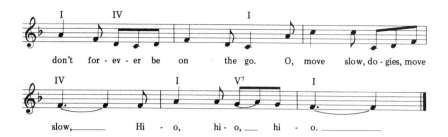

don't for - ev - er be on the go. O, move slow, do - gies, move

slow,_____ Hi - o, hi - o, ___ hi - o. _____

"Night Herding Song" is a cowboy's lullaby to his cattle. It is set in a slow $\frac{6}{8}$ meter, and the rhythmic organization can be pointed up by developing an accompaniment of rhythm instruments:

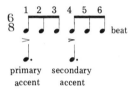

The steady six beats to a measure could be sounded on muffled sleighbells (held in the hand); the accent and secondary accent (beats one and four) might be played softly on a gourd rasp (guiro), to suggest some of the sounds of the saddle and bridle or spurs as the cowboy rides around his herd in the quiet of the night. This song moves slowly enough so that all six beats are felt. Notice how often the upbeat occurs in these rhythm patterns, which can be counted like this:

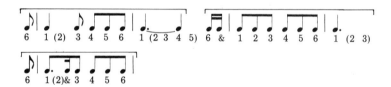

Instructional Objectives: To give the children an opportunity to choose instrumental timbres appropriate for a particular composition, and to give them experience playing the beat, accent, and melody rhythm in an ensemble accompanying songs in different meters.

Behaviors providing evidence that these instructional objectives have been achieved: The children will

□ give a rationale for the instruments they select to accompany a particular piece

□ be able to verbalize correctly the rhythm of the melody

□ accurately play in the accompaniment the steady beat, accent, and secondary accent in $\frac{4}{4}$ or $\frac{6}{8}$ meter

□ play with appropriate dynamics and articulation, producing a well-balanced accompaniment

In Chapter 3, clapping and body movement were recommended as responses to "Take Five" by Dave Brubeck. The organization of rhythmic elements in that music looks like this:

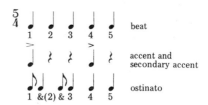

Sound these components of the rhythm on different percussion instruments while the record is played. Try to select sounds that relate well to the music, and play them in a way that makes a well-balanced ensemble.

Although the secondary accent in this piece falls on beat 4, other music having a meter of fives may be organized so that the secondary accent falls on beat 3:

Compare the effect of this organization with that of "Take Five" by playing first one placement of the secondary accent and then the other.

The following compositions in unusual meters are equally useful for experience and study at this level:

"Gerakina" $\frac{7}{8}$ (Greek)   "Softly Calls the Cuckoo" $\frac{5}{4}$
 SBM VI-113   (Bulgarian) **ExM VI-102**
"Sim Sababin" $\frac{5}{4}$ (Danish)   "Unsquare Dance" $\frac{7}{4}$ (Brubeck)
 DMT VI-128   Columbia S9284

Some music is unique in that it has changing meters. "The Twelve Days of Christmas" is a delightful English folk song, and part of the musical interest lies in the meter's changes from $\frac{4}{4}$ to $\frac{3}{4}$ at several points.

EXAMPLE 4.18

THE TWELVE DAYS OF CHRISTMAS
English Folk Song

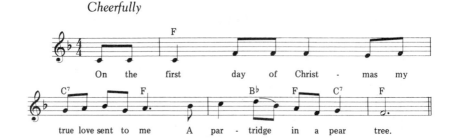

2. On the second day of Christ - mas my true love sent to me
3. On the third day of Christ - mas my true love sent to me
4. On the fourth day of Christ - mas my true love sent to me

Two tur - tle doves And a par - tridge in a pear tree.
Three French hens;
Four call - ing birds;

5. On the fifth day of Christ - mas my true love sent to me

Five gold rings; Four call - ing birds; Three French hens;

Two tur - tle doves and a par - tridge in a pear tree.

6. On the sixth day of Christ - mas my true love sent to me
7. On the seventh day of Christ - mas my true love sent to me
8.-12.

Six geese a - lay - ing; Five gold rings; Four call - ing birds;
Seven swans a - swim-ing;

Three French hens; Two tur - tle doves and a par - tridge in a pear tree.

8. On the eighth day . . .   10. On the tenth day . . .
Eight maids a-milking; . . .   Ten lords a-leaping; . . .

9. On the ninth day . . .   11. On the eleventh day . . .
Nine ladies dancing; . . .   Eleven pipers piping; . . .

12. On the twelfth day . . .
Twelve drummers drumming; . . .

The changes in meter are necessary to accommodate the lyrics where short phrases lack the syllables to fill out $\frac{4}{4}$ meter. These shifts in meter also keep a long, reptitious song from becoming dull and tiresome. Point up the changes in meter by using chopsticks to sound the beat and finger cymbals to sound the primary accent in each measure as you sing the song. To get ready for the changing meters, practice this exercise and find finger cymbal players who can shift from $\frac{4}{4}$ to $\frac{3}{4}$ meter with some skill:

These songs in basic series music books also feature changing meters:

"Come, Come, Ye Saints" NDinM V-66   "El barco chiquitito" ExM V-156
"Look Out" SBM V-43   "Shenandoah" DMT V-116

Instructional Objectives: To give children experience playing accompaniments with compositions of unusual meters or changing meters, and to develop an understanding of the organization of those meters and the musical effect they achieve.

Behaviors providing evidence that these instructional objectives have been achieved: The children will

☐ accurately play a percussion instrument accompaniment involving the beat and accent in an unusual or changing meter

☐ arrange a similar accompaniment for another song with an unusual meter or changing meters, and perform it accurately

☐ write rhythm notation showing the position of the accent and secondary accent in a meter based on five or seven

You should also work with music of other cultures in which the underlying beats or pulses are not organized into metric groupings. The music of American Indians, and some musics from Africa and Asia provide examples of rhythm that does not conform to metric schemes. In some musical styles rhythmic ideas may extend over twelve or fifteen beats without being related to smaller groups of beats. "Sara," from *Music in Honor of the Dead Kings of the Hausa People of Nigeria,*[8] is a good example, for it features twelve-beat rhythmic ostinati for drum and cowbell. Play the recording and tap the recurring rhythm of the drum. Then tap the rhythm of the cowbell. Finally, sound a drum and a bell along with the patterns you hear in the music. This is the way the patterns relate to the twelve underlying pulses and to each other:

Besides these repetitive percussion parts, this music includes a part for a type of brass horn, and a chanting narrator who recites the history and virtues of the dead kings. This is ceremonial music in Nigeria.

Authors of the various basic music series books provide recordings and explain the system of rhythm underlying different musical styles in other cultures. Related rhythmic activities with appropriate percussion instruments can be used with the music. Although a metric organization of rhythm is basic to music influenced by Western European music practices, not all music has or needs such an organization. *Source Book of African and Afro-American Materials for Music Educators*[9] gives many musical examples and teaching strategies that can be used at this level.

Instructional Objectives: To give children experience with music of another culture; to help them understand that such music can be unique and interesting in rhythm as well as in other ways, and to have the children listen and participate in order to understand those differences.

    Behaviors providing evidence that these instructional objectives have been achieved: The children will

    □ play two repetitive percussion parts so that they are compatible with the recorded music

    □ describe the contribution of the vocalist and the "ceremonial" function of the music

    □ request to hear other examples of music from this and other African cultures

Off-Beats and Syncopation

    After you have had much experience with basic rhythmic responses, you can begin to clap and play the off-beats, a common form of rhythmic participation in reels and dance songs. In order to play the off-beat successfully, you must hear and feel the downbeat. Often the spectators at a square dance tap a foot on the downbeat and clap on the off-beat:

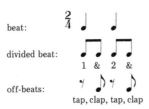

If necessary, count the divided beat as shown above and have someone tap both parts of the divided beat as others clap just the off-beat.

    In fast $\frac{4}{4}$ meter the beats might not be divided, but the off-beats would be related to the meter in a similar way:

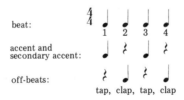

"Polly Wolly Doodle" is a lively song in $\frac{4}{4}$ meter that could be used as a circle dance, with an accompaniment that has different instruments playing the accents and off-beats:

EXAMPLE 4.19

POLLY WOLLY DOODLE
American Folk Song

Instead of sounding six beats in "Night Herding Song" (Example 4.17), children could play the off-beats on the bells, in combination with the guiro playing the accent and secondary accent:

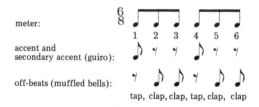

Learning to play any of these rhythmic elements at will prepares the children to play more complicated syncopated patterns of the type shown in the next example.

Folk songs from Italy, Spain, and central Europe make interesting uses of rhythm. Latin-American songs are filled with the uneven dotted rhythm patterns of the habanera and the syncopated patterns of the tango:

At first, such special rhythm patterns are experienced as they are found in the melody of the song. The words of a song such as "Tinga Layo" support the pattern and make it easy to play.

EXAMPLE 4.20

TINGA LAYO
Calypso Song from the West Indies

With an easy swing

From *Calypso Songs of the West Indies* by Patterson and Belasco.
Copyright 1943 by M. Baron Company. Used by permission.

As you learn this song, accompany it with bongo and conga drums, claves, and maracas. At first the claves might be played on the steady beat, and the conga drum on the accent. As the melody becomes familiar, bongos and maracas may be used to play the melody rhythm, and a shake of the maracas can sustain the half notes. After this is successfully carried out, look for typical rhythm patterns. The particular characteristics of the rhythm patterns can be brought out by playing them against the steady beat, which is sounded on another instrument. Notice that the pattern played on the bongo drums is "syncopated"—the longer note begins after the beat.

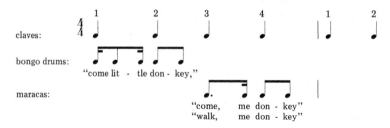

These patterns may then be chanted with rhythm syllables and played continuously over and over, one on the bongo drums and the other on the maracas, while the song is sung. A conga drum may be added on the accents or played continuously in the pattern shown below.

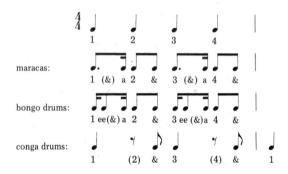

Instructional Objectives: To develop a percussion accompaniment that will enhance the singing of "Tinga Layo," and give the children opportunities to (1) play more than one accompanying part simultaneously, (2) understand the principle of an ostinato accompaniment, (3) respond accurately in playing a syncopated ostinato pattern, and (4) play in a way that will provide a well-balanced ensemble.

Behaviors providing evidence that these instructional objectives have been achieved: The children will

☐ play one or more ostinati appropriate to this song accurately and at a good dynamic level

☐ use the same principles to develop an orchestration for another Latin-American song

☐ identify a "syncopated" rhythm pattern among other patterns used

To develop readiness to play continuous complex patterns, many simple experiences must be provided. Playing one pattern at a time will suffice in the early stages. Ten- and eleven-year-olds should learn to identify and play syncopated patterns found in songs such as the following:

"In Bahia" ExM VI-14   "La Raspe" DMT V-136

"La Conga" NDinM V-128   "Water Come A Me Eye" SBM V-76

Rhythm instruments can provide introductions and codas as well as accompaniments. Combinations of the accent, beat, afterbeats, or specialized rhythm patterns from the melody can be used.

Percussion Accompaniments with Recorded Compositions

 In some music, composers use rhythmic motifs as prime organizing factors. At other times a particular use of instruments is featured. Both these factors can provide the basis for use of percussion instruments that will require careful listening and musical judgment in the selection of instruments to be played. See if you can play the Spanish rhythms in one or two of the following compositions.

 "Spanish Dance No. 1" from *La Vida Breve* by Falla (**AinM VI-1**) features castanets as an outstanding percussion instrument. Play these rhythm patterns throughout the composition:

If castanets are not available or if your playing technique is not sufficiently developed, play the pattern on claves, with alternating hands on your knees, or on dry-sounding drums.

 "Bolero" by Ravel has the following easily heard rhythm patterns:

The upper pattern can be played on high and low drums. Since the lower pattern moves very rapidly, practice it first by tapping fingertips of alternate left and right hands on a table top; then play maracas or bongo drums, so that both hands are used alternately.

 Throughout the "Habanera" from *Carmen* by Bizet, "Jamaican Rumba" by Benjamin (**BOL #56**), and "Grand Walkaround" from *Cakewalk Ballet Suite* by Gottschalk-Kay (**AinM V-1**), the habanera rhythm pattern can be played almost continuously:

To be successful, you must be able to play the repeated pattern at the tempo heard in the recording. You should listen to the music as you play and conform to the dynamics and any rhythmic changes that occur.

If you find this use of percussion instruments interesting, look for other suitable music. A number of compositions in the record collections listed in Appendix B-2 could be used this way.

CHAPTER NOTES

1. Gladys Moorhead and Donald Pond, **Music of Young Children**, 4 vols. (Santa Barbara, Calif.: The Pillsbury Foundation for the Advancement of Music Education [P.O. Drawer A, 93102], 1941–51; 5th printing, 1978), vol. 2, **General Observations** (1942), p. 15.

2. Marilyn P. Zimmerman, **Musical Characteristics of Children**, From Research to the Music Classroom, NO. 1 (Washington, D.C.: Music Educators National Conference, 1971), p. 20.

3. Muriel Mandell and Robert E. Wood, **Make Your Own Musical Instruments** (New York: Sterling Publishing Co., Inc., 1957).

4. Moorhead and Pond, **Music of Young Children**, Vol. 1, Chant (1941), pp. 9–10.

5. Emma Sheehy, **Children Discover Music and Dance** (New York: Holt, Rinehart and Winston, Inc., 1959), p. 43.

6. Carl Orff and Gunild Keetman, **Music for Children**, Angel 3582B.

7. The Franson Corporation, Young People's Record 15006.

8. From **Niger—La Musique des Groits**, Ocora, OCR 20. An excerpt is found in Sidney Fox, Barbara Reeder Lundquist, and James A. Standifer, THE WORLD OF POPULAR MUSIC, **Afro-American** (Chicago: Follett Publishing Co., 1974), album XL-11, side 2, band 1–d.

9. James A. Standifer and Barbara Reeder, **Source Book of African and Afro-American Materials for Music Educators** (Contemporary Music Project, Music Educators National Conference, 1972).

5

Learning Melody through Singing and Playing Instruments

In its broad outlines, melody is an expressive flowing curve of sound, but as we listen more closely we find interesting details of construction that give added insight into the music. As teachers we must nurture children's response to the total expressive quality of melody, and at the same time help them develop awareness of detail within melodic movement.

Some of our composers have tried to describe melody. Aaron Copland[1] said, "A beautiful melody, like a piece of music in its entirety, should be of satisfying proportions. It must give us a sense of completion and inevitability." To meet the conditions of his definition, Copland said, "the melodic line will generally be long and flowing, with low and high points of interest and a climactic moment near the end." Boys and girls can become sensitive, not only to the general shape of a melody, but also to the feeling of building toward a melodic climax, sometimes rising through a series of secondary high points, and falling to resting points (cadences) with different degrees of finality. In teaching, it is useful to list concepts relating to melodic shape in this way:

- ☐ Direction : upward—downward
  : abrupt rise—gradual rise
- ☐ Register: general highness or lowness
- ☐ Range: the spread of pitches
- ☐ Climax : earlier—later
  : strong—less strong
- ☐ Cadence: strong—less strong

In Appendix A-III you will find sample listings of concepts about melody that children can acquire, and which will amplify this discussion for those who have limited experience with music.

A succession of tones alone does not, of course, create a melody. In general we can say that melody is comprised of both longer and shorter tones, and that a change in rhythm changes the character of the melody. There are two common types of melodic–rhythmic movement: (1) melody in which the tones move in a single long sweep, and (2) melody that is made up of shorter groups of tones called motifs. Even though the two types may have some characteristics in common, it is worthwhile to distinguish between them.

Children can learn to respond to and think of melodic movement in terms of:

1. *Intervals*—the tonal distance between two different pitches. A melody can move by small intervals (half-steps or whole steps), large intervals (leaps), or repeated tones

2. *Motif* (pattern)—the shortest expressive melodic unit (two, three or four tones), and the basis for the most comprehensive work with melody at Level I and Level II

3. *Line*—a series of intervals that result in melodic movement in an upward or downward direction, either by half-steps or whole steps (scalewise), or by larger intervals or by leaps

4. *Phrase*—a division of the melodic line into longer units, comparable to a simple sentence in speech

Melodies go up and down, and move through time with various rhythmic characteristics. Most melodies also are oriented to tonal points of reference that are essential to the melody line's expressive quality. Children can understand that the various tones of a melody relate to a central tone as a kind of home base. All of us have a home that we leave in the morning and return to at the end of the day, with an office, school, shopping center, or a friend's home as secondary stopping places. So a melody has a "tonal center" that it leaves and returns to. One tone is acknowledged as central to the group of tones used; other preferential relationships among tones govern the melodic structure. "Tonal" melodies (i.e., melodies featuring a tonal center) include those classified as being in the major mode ("mode" meaning a way of organizing the tones), and those classified as being in the minor mode.

For analysis, we can rearrange the tones of a melody to create a ladder of rising pitches (called a scale). The "key note" is the particular pitch that serves as the tonal center for a melody; it is the first tone of the scale in which the melody is written.

Although exceptions occur in music of the 20th century, most composed music, as well as music utilized in daily life by Americans of all social classes, is "tonal" music. Although children who grow up in this country are exposed to tonally oriented music and begin to acquire a sense of tonality around the age of seven,[2] they can become aware of a broad spectrum of melodic organization:

☐ *Tonal—Atonal* (no tonal center)

☐ *Major—Minor—Modes* (utilizing seven basic pitches in different configurations of whole and half steps)

☐ *Pentatonic* (utilizing five different pitches, usually with no half-steps)

☐ *Whole-Tone Scale* (utilizing six pitches at whole-step intervals)

☐ *Twelve-Tone Row* (utilizing twelve pitches at half-step intervals)

As you help children develop concepts about melody, try to relate it to concrete representations, such as (1) gestures, (2) the relationship of keys and fingers when a melody is played on an instrument, or (3) notation for pitch. Later, in discussing sequence in activities and materials, we will continually relate what is heard to what children can do or see.

USING SYMBOLS AND ICONIC REPRESENTATIONS OF MELODY

The most specific method we have for showing melody in the Western European tradition is the five-line staff, expanded into the grand staff using two or more clefs and leger lines. (Definitions and examples of these musical terms can be found in Appendix C-III and C-IV and in the Glossary.) Supporting the music staff, various systems exist for labeling pitch and showing the relationships among tones. These useful procedures are summarized below and then applied in the experiences recommended for children.

Staff Notation

The lines and spaces of the music staff represent half-steps and whole steps. These steps belong to one particular system of dividing up the tonal distance between one pitch and its repetition an octave higher or lower. The system used accommodates what, since about 1700, has been known as the "tempered" scale, having twelve half-steps of equal size. Modern keyboard instruments are tuned to the tempered scale, and individuals learn to discriminate pitch on this basis.

In the early stages of music teaching, we use the music staff to direct attention to, and to make more concrete, the concepts of high and low, up and down, large intervals and small intervals. Even though they can't interpret notation precisely, children can follow the notation and relate some of these general features to the music they are singing. We also use it to show tonal patterns with which we build a tonal vocabulary of intervals and motifs. In both of these uses, we begin with a meaningful musical experience, isolate the features we are concerned with, and show how they appear in notation.

Letters and Numbers Designating Pitch

The first seven letters of the alphabet label seven basic pitches in the octave (see Appendix C-III). In the elementary general music program, these are learned when children begin to play tuned instruments, because the pitch names are related directly to a particular tone bar or playing position on the instrument.

Scale numbers serve a uniquely different purpose, because they refer specifically to the seven different tones of a major or a minor scale. The tonal center in both major and minor keys is the first step *(1)* of the scale. When we wish to define the position and function of a pitch in a scale, we use scale numbers, *1* through *8* (or *sol-fa* syllables, which will be discussed in the next section). Scale numbers are helpful because they are a tool children know how to use.

The Sol-Fa Syllables

The term *solmization* derives from the two syllables *sol* and *mi* used in a system of labeling the tones of the scale: *do   re   mi fa   sol   la   ti do*. The origins of this system date back to the 11th century, when a monk-choirmaster, Guido of Arezzo, created the syllables to aid his choristers in sight-singing. These were refined into the "movable *do*" system developed in England and widely used for sight-singing, as well as the notation of choral music, during the 19th century. At this time, hand signs were developed to represent each syllable of the scale, so that melodies could be silently dictated (see Appendix C-IV).

In major keys, *do* always represents the first step of the major scale (the tonic), *re* the second scale step, *mi* the third scale step, and so on, regardless of the actual letter name of the notes. In applying the *sol-fa* syllables to minor mode, the same order of syllables is used, but the tonal center is shifted to *la*. The following illustrates this relationship, which provides a simple procedure for slipping from the major scale to the relative minor having the same key signature. (Modern systems simplify the spelling of *sol* as *so*.)

EXAMPLE 5.1

Note: The "movable do" system of syllables shown here can be applied to any major key and its related minor key.

Music Reading and Sol-Fa Syllables

The *sol-fa* syllables have been used in the United States since the early 18th-century New England singing schools. Early in the 20th century, comprehensive courses in elementary school sight-singing that incorporated the *sol-fa* syllables were widely used in the midwestern states. Many children learned to sight-read music, but their musical education was limited, because of mediocrity in the musical materials and the narrowness of the program.

In Hungary, music education was revitalized after World War II through the efforts of the Hungarian composer, Zoltán Kodály. Kodály was obsessed with the idea of teaching and preserving the "musical mother tongue" of Hungary (the rich tradition of folk music). In seeking a means for doing so, he adapted the *sol-fa* syllables and related hand signs, which he discovered in England, to the needs of

Hungarian music education. Great dedication and high musical standards were brought to this work.

Kodály and his assistants screened an immense collection of folk music to find exemplar melodies for every level of musical development and sight-singing. Wherever necessary, Kodály created exercises and new choral works to complete the method. The result has been a choral method that music educators from many countries admire, but which they are not able to use in its entirety because the Hungarian musical mother tongue is not the musical mother tongue of any other country.

Books by Helga Szabo[3] and J. Ribiére-Raverlat[4] describing the Hungarian system are available in translation. These books should be of interest to those wishing to make a careful study of the Kodály method. Musical materials composed by Kodály and used in the course of study for choral music were translated and edited by Percy A. Young and published by Boosey & Hawkes.[5]

An early adaptation of the Kodály approach in America resulted in the *Threshold to Music* (a teacher's manual with classroom charts) created by Mary Helen Richards.[6] A more broadly based program called *Education Through Music* (ETM) has now been developed by the Richards Institute.[7] Recent American publications featuring the Kodály principles include *The Kodály Method* by Lois Choksy,[8] and a variety of new material made available by the Kodály Musical Training Institute.[9] Music sight-reading and choral singing are central to these programs.

To be effective, music education with a prime objective of sight-singing must begin training the ears and voices of the children from three to five years of age, using the chants and nursery rhymes that appeal to such young children. (The Hungarian system of music education is carefully structured and controlled, and therefore effective for the children enrolled in the program.) Since between the ages of six and eight, children are oriented to learning symbols for language and numbers, they also can be readily involved in discovering the function of musical notation; they find the *sol-fa* syllables an acceptable way of verbalizing melodic relationships. For these reasons, the *sol-fa* syllables are used in this chapter. Although this must not be the only early childhood musical study, it can be utilized along with many other activities recommended for musical development during these years. One great concern, at this or any other age, is that music is an aural art; the ear should be trained to hear, and the voice or fingers to produce music. Any use of notation should support these normal human musical activities and not supplant them.

In the United States few schools offer consistent, high-quality music instruction from preschool through the sixth grade. Consequently, sight-singing studies based on essential early childhood experiences are rarely possible.

Boys and girls in the middle grades need to develop musical skills that will serve them in social relationships with others. They should have opportunities to play accompaniments, to improvise on social instruments, and to be involved in small-group creative musical ventures, using a variety of sound media. Music notation can be approached through music writing as well as through music reading; music education approaches such as the Manhattanville Music Curriculum Project[10] and authors cited in Chapter 2 take this as an essential point of view.

This text does not recommend developing an intermediate general music program that is focused on music reading. It is quite reasonable, nevertheless, to expect that groups organized for the main purpose of choral singing can be motivated to develop music reading skills. In such instances, some regular, systematic use of *sol-fa* syllables and parts of the Kodály Choral Method are in order.

THE MELODY INSTRUMENTS

A very good way for children to develop elementary concepts about melody is by playing tuned instruments. These may range from tuned glasses and bell instruments of various kinds to the piano and standard orchestral instruments. In early playing experiences, it is important that the instruments be simply constructed and demand little skill in playing. Then the freedom that children develop in playing rhythm on percussion instruments (described in Chapter 4) will carry over into the playing of tuned instruments.

Children should do much of their playing in conjunction with the singing program. Instruments can help enrich the singing activities, develop the ability to listen and to discriminate different combinations of pitch. They can also promote interest and skill in interpreting simple melodies and tonal patterns that are seen in musical notation.

The xylophone and glockenspiel are classed as percussion instruments because they are struck with mallets. They are also called keyboard instruments because the tone bars are arranged in the same order as the piano keyboard. Some of them may be simplified so that only a few tones are used.

Instruments of the xylophone type have wooden tone bars and those of the glockenspiel type are made of metal. The larger sizes are chromatic; that is, they have tone bars representing both black and white keys on the piano, providing a tone for every half-step. They therefore can be played in any key. Smaller instruments that have only eight or ten tones of the diatonic scale (utilizing specific combinations of whole and half-steps) are used in many primary classrooms.

The instruments with metal bars have a bell-like quality. They are most useful in early singing and instrumental work. Sets of diatonic "bells" with fixed tone bars in the key of C have been used in primary classrooms for many years. They consist of eight or ten tone bars sounding an octave above:

A diatonic, eight-tone set of bells is inexpensive, but it is limited in the melodies that it can be used to play. Some companies offer an additional unit that makes it possible to attach $B^\flat$ and $F^\sharp$ tone bars to the frame of the key of C song bells, and thus also to play in the keys of F and G. To provide children concrete experience with the upward–downward movement of melodies, bell instruments in staircase configurations have been developed (sometimes called "step-bells"). If samples are not available, write to firms listed in Appendix B-V for catalogues showing pictures of these useful instruments.

Other types of diatonic glockenspiels have tone bars that are removable. When desired, F and B or other tones may be omitted so that a pentatonic scale or other limited group of tones is obtained. Alternate $B^\flat$ and $F^\sharp$ tone bars are supplied with the diatonic instrument, so that the keys of F and G major may be used.

Chromatic glockenspiels, Song Bells or Melody Bells, are used extensively in the intermediate grades. When the children have sufficient knowledge and skill to play easily, these are good instruments to use.

Resonator bells are tuned metal bars, each of which is mounted on a separate block of wood. These form the chromatic scale when properly arranged, or they may be rearranged to form any single scale, chord, or selected group of tones. They are more expensive than some other bell types but they are also more versatile. Resonator bells are available in both higher and lower registers. The lower, which corresponds in range to the singing voice, is generally preferred.

Very good-sounding school xylophones are available in both chromatic and diatonic models with adjustable tone bars. The distinctive tone quality of the wooden instrument is valuable in ensemble playing. Various sizes of xylophones and glockenspiels are available. (Write for catalogues from firms listed in Appendix B-V.)

The recorder (a flute with a whistle-type mouthpiece, also known as the "blockflöte" or "fipple" flute) is a classic among wind instruments. Originally made of wood but now also available in plastic, it has a two-octave range and a pleasing tone. Much music was played on recorders during the Renaissance, and its use in ensemble playing has been revived. Of the several sizes, the soprano recorder is most often used in the elementary music program.

The Song Flute, Tonette, and similar plastic instruments have been used in the schools for many years. The construction of these instruments does not permit individual tuning of the pitches as they are being played; the tone is less interesting; and the range is limited to a ninth, as shown below. The soprano recorder also sounds these tones, but can be "overblown" to play an additional octave above the range shown here.

The recorder, like the keyboard instruments, is useful because it specifically defines tonal relationships. When the melody moves along the scale, the fingers move consecutively; when the melody skips a third, two fingers are raised, and so on. Keyboard instruments are generally preferred because children can sing as they play. However, many benefits can be derived from recorders if they are used wisely in conjunction with the singing program.

All melody instruments should be correctly tuned because children must become accustomed to the correct sound relationships among the tones in the scale. Cheap, carelessly tuned toy instruments do not serve the purposes of music education. Instruments played in combination must be tuned to the same standard of pitch.

When other melody instruments are not available, tuned water glasses can be used. If the glasses ring well and are accurately tuned, their quality is pleasing, quite mellow, and easy to match with the voice. Eight-ounce glasses may be tuned in the key of C; to get the complete scale, smaller glasses should be used for the higher tones. If the glasses are to be played regularly, the water line and correct scale number should be permanently marked on each glass so that the children can keep them in order and fill them correctly. The F and B tuned glasses can have the water line for F$^\sharp$ *and* B$^\flat$ marked for alternate tuning when needed. You will need to experiment a bit to determine how much water is needed in each glass; the more water in the glass, the lower the pitch.

Various kinds of bottles can be partially filled with water to make a tuned scale. Those with screw-on tops have an advantage in that the water does not evaporate, as in glasses, and they can be suspended from a rack with cord or wire. The tone quality of such bottles is not as bright and clear as that of tuned glasses. A series of suspended clay garden pots in different sizes is another possibility, but it takes considerable experimenting and careful listening to find six or eight that will produce a tuned scale.

EXPERIENCES AT LEVEL I

In early childhood classes, diatonic song bells, xylophone, and resonator bells should be available so that the children can have concrete experience with pitch and melody. They should have opportunities to explore the tone quality and range of these instruments, and to improvise with them, as suggested with other sound-makers in Chapter 2.

During "music time," the children should use these instruments to enrich their singing activities and to develop concepts basic to perception of melody. In early childhood classes, you can use *sol-fa* syllables and the hand signs for scale degrees to identify the scale tones that make up basic melodic patterns.

Playing Special Effects, Introductions, and Codas

A simple example of the use of bell instruments in early singing experiences is provided in "Hickory, Dickory, Dock." Sing the song and play the instruments in the ways suggested; find other ways to use them, so that you will have an idea of a very easy approach to the use of bell instruments.

EXAMPLE 5.2

HICKORY, DICKORY, DOCK
J. W. Elliott
from Mother Goose

Lively

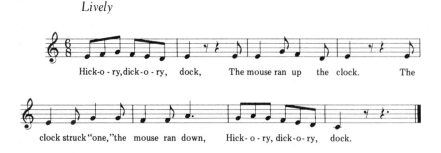

Hick-o-ry, dick-o-ry, dock, The mouse ran up the clock. The clock struck "one," the mouse ran down, Hick-o-ry, dick-o-ry, dock.

As you sing the song, play a glissando up the bells after "the mouse ran up the clock" and a downward glissando at the end of the song. This embellishment will provide a concrete example of up and down in pitch. When the instrument is held vertically, the action and visual perception of "high" support the concept of high pitch as you play toward the top of the bells.

Fragments of melody can be played as introductions or codas (endings) that add interest to the song. These provide experience in playing the instruments and in working with specific combinations of tones. As an introduction to "Are You Sleeping?" sound the key-note (F) on the bells a specified number of times to represent the hour that "Brother John" should arise. The same tone might be struck several times as an ending to the song. The concept of a repeated tone is one that can be developed by such a simple activity.

EXAMPLE 5.3

ARE YOU SLEEPING?
(Frère Jacques)
French Round

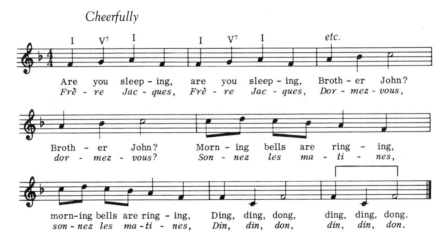

You can also create an introduction or a coda for the song by playing *F(1)* and *C(5)* in the pattern found in the last phrase of the song (bracketed in Example 5.3). The "pattern" in this instance consists of two different pitches sung or played in a rhythm. The children will learn the pattern by rote, and will recognize when it is played correctly. Unity of melodic material is provided when the introduction or coda utilizes a melodic idea found in the song itself. The children should notice that a pattern heard or played at one point is the same as that heard or played at another point. To help the singers get started on the correct pitch, have the introduction end on the note on which the song begins.

Playing Repeated Patterns

Look for songs that have easy repeated melodic patterns that the children can play. Both "Hot Cross Buns" and "Three Blind Mice" (Example 8.5) have a repeated three-tone pattern, E–D–C (downward), at the beginning and at the end. One child can play this pattern either on the piano, resonator bells, or the adjustable glockenspiel while the others sing. The children should be aware that the melody of the middle part of the song is different from the pattern played and sung at the beginning and the end of the song.

EXAMPLE 5.4

HOT CROSS BUNS
English Street Cry

Use different hand levels to show the downward movement of pitches as you sing; if the tone bars are mounted vertically, observe how naturally this shows the relationships between low and high on the instrument.

Be sure to include some experience playing fragments of songs in minor mode. "Simple Simon" has both an ascending and a descending melody line (see brackets in Example 5.5) that a child can easily play on bell instruments while others sing the song.

EXAMPLE 5.5

SIMPLE SIMON
J. W. Elliott
from Mother Goose

Other minor songs that you might use in this way include:

"Boatman's Chanty" DMT III-28   "The Wind Blow East" (Example 3.1)
"The North Wind" MMYO K-110

When the adjustable resonator bells or glockenspiel is available, place only the necessary tone bars on it and play one of the three bracketed patterns that occur in "Bye'm Bye."

EXAMPLE 5.6

BYE'M BYE
Texas Folk Song

Early song enrichments of this kind should be confined to simple, easily remembered patterns that are played rhythmically when the song is well known. In order to play a melody accurately and rhythmically, one needs some awareness of the syllabic rhythm of the words the melody is based on. When you play "number one, number two . . ." in "Bye'm Bye," you play two different tones on one word. The experience of playing the melody rhythm with chopsticks (see Chapter 4) provides a background for playing the melody rhythm on tuned instruments. Other attractive songs that have good repeated patterns include:

"All Night, All Day" NDinM I-173   "Jingle Bells" TMT II-175
"The Angel Band" SpM I-145   "Love Somebody" (Example 7.9)

When the larger chromatic bells or the piano is used, you can mark the tone bars or keys to be played for a particular pattern; or you can make a keyboard diagram to show the position of the tones. The first pattern in "Bye'm Bye" would be shown:

The following considerations are important in regard to group singing with these tuned instruments:

1. The singers should take their pitch from the instruments they are going to sing with.
2. Very rarely are the bells so tuned that they may be played with a recorded song.
3. Bells are easily covered by the voices. When the entire class participates everyone must sing lightly and listen carefully so that all voices stay in tune.
4. The rhythm of the singers should not be broken by halting performance on the instrument. You can assure rhythmic playing by carefully selecting the tone calls and phrases to be played and by using adjustable tone bars, resonator bells, or an appropriately marked keyboard.

As the children sing the song and play the melodic fragment, they should notice how often the pattern occurs. Add verbal labels ("up-down," "the melody moves by steps," "it moves by skips") so that the children become more aware of these melodic characteristics.

Instructional Objectives: To offer children musical participation that is enjoyable and stimulating, and to provide opportunities for children to play melodic fragments on tuned instruments so that they will notice melodic details and develop useful concepts about melody.

Behaviors providing evidence that these instructional objectives have been achieved: The children will

☐ play appropriate examples on the vertically mounted tone bars, to demonstrate their understanding of (1) upward and downward melodic movement, and (2) high and low pitch

☐ play on adjustable, vertically held tone bars a three-tone pattern from one familiar song

☐ be eager to participate individually by playing the tone bars

Identifying Pitch in Chants and Tonal Patterns

Throughout the world, young children engaged in rhythmic play employ chants centered on two or three tones. "Ring Around a Rosy" is a well-known example of this "universal children's chant," but many other chanting songs can be identified:

"Bye, Baby Bunting"	"It's Raining, It's Pouring" (Example 3.10)
"Jack Be Nimble" (Example 4.6)	"Rain, Rain, Go Away" DMT I-101

These chanting tones are the first melodic fragments identified and labeled in the process of building a tonal vocabulary in music. Learn to recognize the sound of this pattern, to identify it with *sol-fa* syllables, and to enact the pattern with hand signs:

Sing a name, "hello," "goodbye," or any simple nursery rhyme, using just these two tones. Play the pattern on tuned instruments. If the tone bars are held vertically with just the two necessary bars on the frame, you will have a direct transfer from the high and low of the hand signs to the high and low positions on the melody instrument.

EXAMPLE 5.7

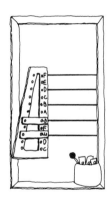

Chants incorporating the third tone *(la)* include "Bell Horses."

EXAMPLE 5.8

BELL HORSES

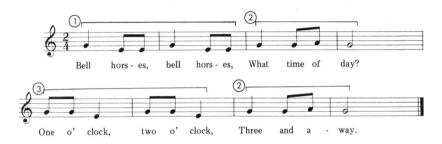

Learn the song and then sing each two-measure pattern with *sol-fa* syllables, enacted with hand signs. Each pattern can also be played on bell instruments. These procedures will make the children aware of the specific pitches in the tonal pattern and their relationship to each other.

 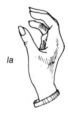

so   so   la   so   la

The fourth tone *(do)* is identified in chants where it appears, e.g., "Jack be Nimble" (Example 4.6) and "Ring Around a Rosy" (Example 5.9), and is shown with its hand sign. *Do* is the tonal center ("home tone") and has qualities of stability and finality. These qualities are suggested by the hand sign and should be felt by the children who sing and enact this tone in the pattern.

so   so   do
"all   fall   down"   do

EXAMPLE 5.9

RING AROUND A ROSY
Children's Singing Game

Steadily

Ring a-round a ros - y, A poc-ket full of po - sies, Ash - es, Ash - es, All fall down!

All these are the playful songs of early childhood. Learn them and practice singing the syllables and forming the hand signs so that you can do it fluently. You will find that the children will happily copy you in enacting the hand signs for these musical pitches. At the same time, they will be impressing on their minds, ears, and muscles the relationships of the pitches in the tonal pattern.

Although songs children sing should not be limited to these easy chants, you can continue with the identification of basic patterns by using fragments from longer songs. As an example, when the first four tones of the melodic vocabulary *(so, mi, la, do)* are well known and have been sung in various patterns in familiar songs, the fifth tone *(re)* can be identified. We find it in the context of the *mi re do* pattern in "Mary Had a Little Lamb" (**TMT II-86**), "Bought Me a Cat" (**DMT K-92**), "Old Mac-Donald," (**DMT III-40**), and "Chatter with the Angels."

EXAMPLE 5.10

CHATTER WITH THE ANGELS
Afro-American Folk Song

As the entire group sings the song, let one or two individuals have the special responsibility of singing or playing the pattern B A G *(mi re do)* when it occurs on the words "in that land" and "join that band." Over a period of time, everybody can have a chance to sing or play this special part, but no attempt need be made to have the children play or apply the syllables and hand signs to the other parts of the song.

Notice that *do* gives a sense of stability and arrival, but *re* is an active tone that can move to a more stable tone on either side of it. The hand sign for *re* suggests this quality.

At this level, the experiences with specific tonal patterns include singing, hearing the patterns, seeing the tone bars played, and associating the hand signs with each pattern. After the children know the song and the related syllables and hand signs for *mi re do,* you can vary the procedures, so that they identify the pattern by its sound, attach the proper syllables to it, play it on bells, or enact the pattern with hand signs.

Instructional Objectives: To identify basic tonal patterns within the musical context of a song, and to help children hear and correctly label the scale tones in each pattern.

Behaviors providing evidence that these instructional objectives have been achieved: The children will

☐ sing a song containing a known tonal pattern, and identify the pattern by singing syllable names or showing appropriate hand signs for that pattern

☐ recognize and identify the same tonal pattern when it is isolated and brought to their attention in a new song

Playing Melodies

Children as well as adults enjoy playing familiar melodies on bell or keyboard instruments. It is best to begin with songs that have a limited number of tones. When the song consists of tonal patterns that have previously been sung, enacted with hand signs, and played on an instrument, it is relatively easy to put them together in a melody.

"Bell Horses" (Example 5.8) is a three-tone nursery song that you will find easy to sing and play. Sing the song first; then sing and tap the rhythm of the melody on chopsticks. Finally, show the pitch level of the tones with "hand levels" (hold your hand open and parallel with the floor, and move it up and down in conformity with the pitches as you sing); or show the syllable hand signs as you sing. The task here is to identify a tone as higher or lower or the same as the previous tone. After that, you will be able to play the melody from memory, starting on the tone bar G as shown here. A 3-in. by 5-in. card placed next to the vertically mounted bells can list the pitches in order, as shown on the left in Example 5.11. If you have resonator bells, use some tagboard and draw a diagram the size of each tone block as shown on the right below in Example 5.11. When a tone bar is not used in the song, leave comparable space on the tagboard, so the player will see that the interval between tones is larger.

EXAMPLE 5.11

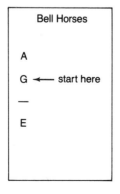

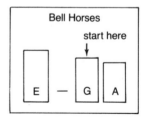

Instructional Objectives: To provide a musical activity in which children will learn to play a song on melody bells, and in doing so, internalize the melodic concepts of up–down, high–low, and repeated tones.

Behaviors providing evidence that these instructional objectives have been achieved: The children will

- □ independently play the melody
- □ demonstrate a high tone and a low tone when asked to do so
- □ demonstrate a melody moving up, moving down, or staying the same when asked to do so

Here are configurations of tones that can be set up on adjustable tone bars in preparation for playing the three- and four-tone songs listed. The letter after the song title shows the starting pitch.

<table>
<tr><td align="center">A
G
F
"Hot Cross Buns" (A)
(Example 5.4)
and
"Hop, Old Squirrel" (A)
(SBM II-65)</td><td align="center">A
G
—
E
"Bell Horses" (G)
(Example 5.7)
and
"It's Raining, It's Pouring" (G)
(Example 3.10)</td></tr>
<tr><td align="center"><u>C</u>
A
G
F
"Mary Had a Little Lamb" (A)
(TMT II-8b)
and
"Bought Me a Cat" (F)
(DMT K-92)</td><td align="center">A
G
—
E
<u>C</u>
"Jack Be Nimble" (G)
(Example 4.6)
and
"Ring Around a Rosy" (G)
(Example 5.9)</td></tr>
</table>

The bell instruments and necessary charts should be located in an isolated music center in the room, so that children can practice the melodies in their free time. Some will be more motivated toward playing melodies than others; do not be concerned if all do not participate with equal interest in this individual work. It is important, however, that the opportunity to play melodies on adjustable bell instruments be made available to those who do have the interest.

EXPERIENCES AT LEVEL II

Activities suggested for Level I—creating introductions and codas for songs, playing tonal patterns in songs, as well as playing complete melodies from memory—are equally appropriate at Level II. You will find numerous songs in the basic series music books for grades two, three, and four that incorporate suggestions for the use of melody instruments. In addition, these children can create and write original melodies for chants and rhymes. Continue to use the *sol-fa* syllables and related hand signs at this level, so that children learn the sound and relationship of the tones of the scale.

Establishing a Basic Tonal Vocabulary

While the singing repertoire will change somewhat at Level II, the basic tonal vocabulary outlined for Level I can either be introduced or reinforced with seven- to nine-year-olds. In the songs that follow, all the tonal patterns fall within these pentatonic scale tones: *mi, – so, la, – do re me – so la.* The subscript *(mi,)* indicates a scale tone below *do.*

The two Afro-American songs "Chatter with the Angels" (Example 5.10) and "Mary Had a Baby" have in common the descending tonal pattern *mi re do* (bracket 1 in Example 5.12). "Mary Had a Baby" uses the same tones in an ascending pattern, *do re mi* (bracket 2), which is repeated three times. The songs are set in two different keys; that is, the home tone, *do,* is on a different pitch in each song.

EXAMPLE 5.12

MARY HAD A BABY
Spiritual

Tenderly

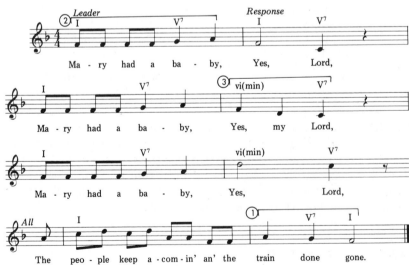

2. What did she name him . . .
3. Named him King Jesus . . .

4. Where did she lay him . . .
5. Laid him in a manger . . .

When these two songs are used consecutively, the *mi re do* patterns can be compared; notice that the notes fall on line–space–line in "Chatter with the Angels" and space–line–space in "Mary Had a Baby."

Key of G: *mi   re   do*   Key of F: *mi   re   do*

In developing concepts about music notation, children need to learn that both the lines and the spaces between lines are locations for pitches. We say that a note is drawn *in* a space or *around* a line (to differentiate from the concept in handwriting, where symbols are on—i.e., above—the line). In these two songs, *do* is the tonal center, but in the second song, *do* is located in a space instead of around a line. The children should understand that the whole "family" of tones moves when *do* moves.

Both these songs use the pattern *do la,   so,* (bracket 3 in Example 5.12). Although *la,* and *so,* are below *do* in position (note the subscript by the syllable), they still have the hand signs originally given for those scale tones; but when you make these hand signs, they should be physically placed below *do*.

Instructional Objectives: To add to the musical repertoire and tonal vocabulary by teaching two songs in two different keys, and to help children begin to understand the function of staff notation in different keys.

Behaviors providing evidence that these instructional objectives have been achieved: The children will

□ sing both songs accurately and expressively

□ hear, recognize, and label with *sol-fa* syllables the two tonal patterns (*mi re do* and *do la, so,*)

□ see the two tonal patterns in staff notation in the key of F and in the key of G; recognize and label the patterns in both keys with *sol-fa* syllables

The Ojibway Indian song "Muje Mukesin" (Example 5.13) uses some tones from the octave below *do*, but the tonal center is *la,* , giving it the color of a minor song.

EXAMPLE 5.13

MUJE MUKESIN
Ojibway Indian Tune

Moderately

From Silver Burdett Music, *Book 4*, © 1974 by the General Learning Corporation. Used by permission.

The basic pattern, *mi re do – la,* with *la* as the tonal center, can be found in other songs such as "Boatman's Chanty" (**SpM II-180, DMT III-28**) and "Canoe Song" (Example 5.26).

As a child, you may remember riding in a bus, singing one of those long cumulative songs to pass away the time. Most songs of that type have a simple humor, often boring to adults, but this is music of yet another culture—childhood. "Roll Over" can start out with ten in a bed, if you have that much time!

EXAMPLE 5.14

ROLL OVER
Old Camp Song

Playfully

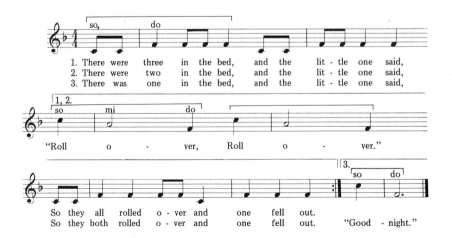

There are two repeated tonal patterns in this song: *so, do* and *so mi do*. Notice that the first pattern uses *so,* in the lower octave. You will find low *so,* in "Mister Rabbit" (**SBM I-35**), "Scotland's Burning" (**NDinM IV-155**), and "Goodbye, Old Paint" (**CM Z1B-88**). You probably won't spoil the fun of the song by showing the children how to enact the hand signs for the pitch levels as they sing "Roll Over." Chances are the motions will become a routine the children associate with the song, even when they sing it on the bus.

Extending the Tonal Vocabulary

Each step of the major scale has its own tonal characteristic in relation to other pitches, and the hand signs help express these different qualities. *Do* is shown with a closed fist, indicating stability and arrival; it is called the tonic or "home" tone. The gesture for *so,* the open hand in a vertical position, reflects the open but stable quality of that scale degree. *Mi* is calm and somewhat stable, and *la* is a bit passive. The others, *re, fa,* and *ti,* are active tones that have a tendency to move in the direction indicated by the hand sign. *Ti,* called the "leading tone," is the most restless in its need to move to the tonic. As you work with the scale tones, using the *sol-fa* syllables and hand signs, develop your own feeling for these "tonal tendencies" among the pitches of the scale.

The last two tones to be learned in the diatonic scale are the fourth *(fa)* and the seventh *(ti)*. These can be dealt with in the phrases of songs where they are prominent. The last phrase of the spiritual "I'm Gonna Sing" (**TMT II-17**) uses *fa* in a significant way, and "Bye'm Bye" (Example 5.6) uses it in a rising scale line. In the English round "Oh, How Lovely Is the Evening" (**SpM III-136**), *fa* is very prominent throughout the song. The hand signs for *fa* and *ti* are as follows:

fa

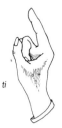
ti

The Danish round adapted below as "Quarters and Dimes" uses both these scale steps within the major mode. Sing it slowly, one phrase at a time, and form the hand signs for each degree of the scale. By doing this, you may find that you become more sensitized to the particular quality of these scale degrees.

EXAMPLE 5.15

QUARTERS AND DIMES
Danish Round
Adapted

Smoothly

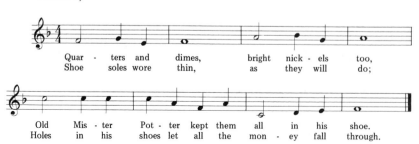

Quar - ters and dimes,   bright nick - els too,
Shoe   soles wore thin,   as   they will do;

Old Mis - ter Pot - ter kept them all   in his   shoe.
Holes in his   shoes let all the mon - ey fall through.

Each two-measure phrase in "Quarters and Dimes" is a good tonal pattern. Sing the first phrase; notice how the melody rises through the two turning motifs, revealing the restless tones to be *re, ti,* and *fa,* and the restful tones to be *do* and *mi.* The final motif is a rising scale line, *so, la, ti, do,* in which the need for movement from *ti,* to *do* is strongly felt.

Instructional Objectives: To teach an attractive song, "Quarters and Dimes," in which the active scale tones *re, fa,* and *ti,* are encountered, and to help children hear and feel how the active tones move to the more restful scale tones.
    Behaviors providing evidence that these instructional objectives have been achieved: The children will

☐ sing the song accurately and expressively

☐ when asked to sing the first three tones of the two patterns in the first phrase, express the need to move to the fourth tone *(do or mi)* as a point of arrival

☐ upon hearing the tonal pattern *so, la, ti, ,* provide the concluding pitch, *do,* which brings the pattern to rest

All the scale tones experienced in the previous songs in the major mode are also used in the minor mode, but they are used in a way that makes *la* the tonal center. Some pentatonic songs center on *la,* but do not use the active tones of *fa* and *ti,* e.g., "Canoe Song" (Example 5.26) and "Land of the Silver Birch" (Example 6.22). Many folk songs that incorporate all the scale tones are in the minor mode. When these are used, play on tone bars only the predominant repeated melodic phrase in each song; show the *sol-fa* syllables with hand signs to point up this minor quality. Songs that might be used in this way are:

"All the Pretty Little Horses" (Ex. 5.16)   "Posheen, Posheen, Posho (ExM II-70)
"The Frog and the Mouse" (ExM III-72)   "Zum Gali, Gali" (NDinM III-125)

EXAMPLE 5.16

ALL THE PRETTY LITTLE HORSES
*Collected, Adapted,
and Arranged by John A. Lomax
and Alan Lomax*

Quietly

Copyright 1934 by John A. and Alan Lomax in the book *American Ballads and Folk Songs*. Copyright assigned 1958 to Ludlow Music, Inc., New York, N.Y. Used by permission.

The last two measures in each phrase of "All the Pretty Little Horses" have an excellent yet easy pattern to sing and play.

Since one key signature can apply to either a major or a minor melody, you will need to know how to distinguish one mode from the other. Any one or all three of the following clues can be used to identify a song in minor mode:

1. The song ends on *la* ("All the Pretty Little Horses" does). This is a reliable clue, because a major song will not end on *la*. A song in minor, however, may end on *do* or *mi*.

2. The "core of tonality" in the song as a whole is *la, do mi* (the minor tonic chord). The tones of the song center around this minor chord more than they do around the major tonic chord, *do mi so*. (Notice how the melody of "All the Pretty Little Horses" begins with a leap from *la*, to *mi*)

3. *So,* and sometimes *fa,* may be raised by a sharp or a natural sign. The tones are then called *si* ("see") and *fi* ("fee"). This tonal alteration indicates the harmonic or melodic form of the minor mode (see Appendix C-IV for analysis) and is a very good clue on which to base a decision about mode. "All the Pretty Little Horses" is in the natural minor mode, so these alterations do not occur.

The first step in getting oriented to a minor key is to determine the position of *do(1)*, assuming the song to be in a major key: with one sharp, *do(1)* is on the second line (G).

In "All the Pretty Little Horses," *do* remains on the second line regardless of the mode determined. If the piece is in the major mode, the key will be G and the tonic chord that establishes this key in the ear will be G B C *(do mi so)*. If it is in the minor mode, the ear should be oriented to the minor tonic chord, E G B *(la, do mi)*, of E minor by hearing:

The singing should stop on the chord tone the song begins on (in this case, *la,*). If you need to know the name of the key, remember that *la,* is the home tone in a minor song and, therefore, this particular example is in the key of E minor.

Melodic Improvisation

In early creative uses of the melody instruments, begin by working with the three tones, E, G, A, that provide the basic intervals in chanting songs. Chant and clap short jingles and then play the same rhythm on the selected tone bars, experimenting with different combinations of the available tones.

In using a short jingle as the basis for rhythmic improvising (1) chant the words and clap the metric beat, (2) chant the words and tap the syllabic rhythm of the words:

Who   wants some pop - corn,   crun-chy crun-chy pop - corn?

Then (3) tap the syllabic rhythm on the selected tone bars. The freedom to improvise, to hear and to enjoy what one has created, is of great value to anyone. In this work children have an opportunity to combine words and tones creatively and on a level suited to them.

Easy rhymes to use as a basis for early improvisation are:

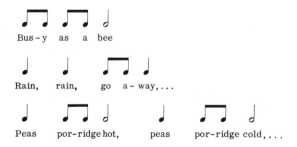

Bus - y   as   a   bee

Rain,   rain,   go a - way, . . .

Peas   por - ridge hot,   peas   por - ridge cold, . . .

As a part of this creative work, you can help children develop skills in using the ear, the voice, and tonal memory. When one child creates a five- or six-tone melody, the class can sing back and show with hand levels the pattern that was sounded on the melody instrument. When the vertical adjustable tone bars are used, there is a direct relationship between the placement of the tone bars and the hand levels used. This enables other children to replay the melody that has been created.

Early Use of Staff Notation

When seven- and eight-year-olds can play several three- and four-tone songs on melody instruments as described in the activities for Level I, you can use a flannel board with adjustable tone bars to help them work independently with staff notation for pitch. The words of a tonal pattern or phrase from a song they know can be written on a strip of chart paper and pinned to the bottom of the flannel board. Flannel notes then can be placed on the proper line or space above each syllable, and the children can play the pattern and see that the note represents the tone bar struck and that it is also related to the word below it. The Afro-American folk song "Chatter with the Angels" (Example 5.10) starts with a six-tone motif that occurs four times. This is the way that pattern would look on the flannel board.

EXAMPLE 5.17

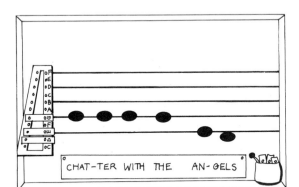

Notice how the tone bars on the instrument are directly related to the lines and spaces of the staff, and that only the tone bars needed for this fragment are placed on the instrument. Most children in the class could successfully play this pattern whenever it occurred in the song.

It is relatively easy to make this audio-visual aid. These are the materials needed:

☐ 1 light colored flannel board, 24 in. by 36 in.

☐ 1 adjustable diatonic glockenspiel (Sonor Kinderglockenspiel or Soprano Glockenspiel, G1-1, available from Hohner distributors)

☐ 1 stove bolt, ⅜-in. diameter, 2½-in. long, to hold the glockenspiel on the flannel board

☐ 1 plastic soap bottle, cut off to hold tone bars and attached to the flannel board with long brass paper fasteners.

Using a black marking pen, draw the bottom line of the staff seven inches above the bottom of the flannel board. Place the glockenspiel vertically on the flannel board so that this staff line passes directly under the middle of the tone bar marked E. Measure carefully and mark the position of staff lines that will pass directly under the middle of the tone bars G, B, high D, and high F. Use a black marking pen to draw these exactly parallel with the first line.

Pierce the flannel board with a sharp object and use the stove bolt to attach the glockenspiel so it is correctly related to the staff lines you have drawn. Pierce the back of the cut-off soap bottle and the flannel board in two places and put the paper fasteners through both, so that a pocket is provided for unused tone bars and the mallet.

Paste a piece of black construction paper on the back side of a piece of black flocked paper. When it is dry, cut out egg-shaped notes about 2½ in. long. The flocked side will readily adhere to the flannel board.

A fundamental idea resulting from research by Jean Piaget on the development of children's thinking is that sensorimotor skills and the intellect are not separated. If this is the case, we should help children develop concepts of musical pitch, tonal relationships, and flow of melody by using tuned instruments and audio-visual aids such as the flannel board, which permit children to deal with these elements in a concrete, manipulative way.

Placing notes on a music staff is similar to using a graph: both the vertical (pitch level) and the horizontal (flow through time) need to be considered. Take into account both the intellectual and the visual difficulties in this activity, and give the children many simple patterns in these early experiences with notation. When the flannel board with attached tone bars is available in the general classroom, many children can have a chance to use it during their free time.

It is desirable that all children become aurally aware of tonal patterns, and the early music training should be designed to promote this development. A few individuals may have limited talent in pitch recognition and tonal memory; the exclusive use of the aural approach can result in continual insecurity and frustration for these children. Consequently, it is important at this level to begin to use visual representation for the tonal patterns and phrases that are sung and played. Notation can be used in three ways:

1. placing notes on the staff to represent tonal patterns and melodies that have already been played and sung (reinforcing an aural experience of pitch with its visual representation)
2. placing notes on the staff and learning a tonal pattern or melody from the notes (a music-reading activity)
3. placing notes on the staff to represent a newly created melody (a music-writing activity)

Although in the early study of notating musical pitch, it is not necessary to include rhythm notation (quarter-notes, half-notes, stems, bar lines, and so on), it is important that phrases and tonal patterns be sung and played rhythmically. The early study of rhythmic notation was described in Chapter 4. After some understanding of the notation of each has been developed separately, representation of melody and pitch can be brought together with rhythm in staff notation.

First Steps in Melody Writing

With the use of the flannel board and the staff-related tone bars, the writing of melodies poses no problems beyond those described in connection with playing tonal patterns and phrases from songs. When children have had experience improvising on three tones, one child can create a melody and repeat it as often as necessary while another child places the notes on the proper lines or spaces.

EXAMPLE 5.18

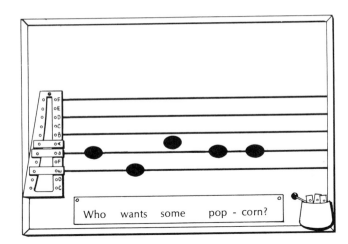

As the children mature in tonal memory, singing skill, and rhythmic response, this work can be expanded in three directions:

1. Have the children write melodies using E, G, and A, but choose longer chants such as the traditional "Diddle, diddle dumpling, my son John . . . ," the children's own jump-rope chants, "Lollypop, lollypop red and green . . . ," and others. Many examples are given in *Music for Children, I—Pentatonic*,[11] and *Music with Children*.[12]
2. Add a fourth tone (C) and later a fifth tone (D), which completes the pentatonic scale. When more tones are needed, add others of the pentatonic scale in a higher octave.

3. Add accompaniments with other instruments: one child may use the pentatonic scale to play a free improvisation (not repeated or necessarily remembered) based on the syllabic rhythm of a longer nursery rhyme. Other children provide an accompaniment by playing selected rhythm instruments on the metric beat and accent. Later they can use other tuned instruments as accompaniment.

The first stage of independent melody writing should deal only with rhymes in simple duple meter ($\frac{2}{4}$). Several months before the first melody writing (found by this author to be most successful in the last half of second grade) children should have had much rhythmic training of the type described in Chapter 4. Such training will enable them to deal independently with easy rhythms of this kind. After they have succeeded in getting notation for the melody on the flannel board, they can copy it onto staff-lined paper and add the necessary notation for the rhythm of the rhyme that was used. Children readily see the need for writing notation for the melody lines they create, but it takes longer for them to appreciate the value of notation for rhythm.

The next step in creative melody writing with the staff-related tone bars is to learn the placement and sound of other tones in the diatonic scale, and finally to write melodies using a complete scale. In moving toward this objective, continue to sing and play songs having six notes in configurations as shown here:

B♭		C		C	
A	as in "Hush,	B	as in "This Land	—	as in "Bye'm Bye"
G	Little Baby"	A	is Your Land"	—	(Example 5.6)
F	(Example 6.4)	G	(Example 4.16)	G	
—		F♯		F	
—		—		E	
C		D		D	
				C	

Example 5.19 shows photographic reproductions of two examples of melody writing from a collection of 85 two-lined tunes that second graders did completely unaided, by using the flannel board with staff-related tone bars.[2]

The composition suggests that the child who composed the setting for "Starlight, Star Bright" had developed a sense of tonality and consistency in musical form, and was quite sensitive to the word rhythms. The child who created the setting for "Crawdad Hole" took a bolder approach to melody, one influenced by the wide span of tones available. Notice the rising line that is basic to the first phrase and the wide leaps of the second phrase. This setting has an aggressive, contemporary sound with little sensitivity to the word rhythms.

When working with melody instruments, children should have opportunities to play individually. Learning to play an instrument is a personal thing; one cannot comfortably experiment and learn by doing as the entire class waits and watches. Provide opportunities for children to practice and improvise on melody instruments privately in the music center. If the rubber eraser of a lead pencil is used instead of the wooden mallet, the tone will be so soft that it will not disturb the other members of the class. Children who compose new melodies should have a chance to play them for the class and to record them on tape.

EXAMPLE 5.19

Star-light, star bright, First star I've seen to-night;

Wish I may, wish I might Have this wish I wish to-night.

You get a line, and I'll get a pole;

We'll go fish-ing in the craw-dad hole.

Playing the Recorder

Children in the middle grades can learn to play melodies on the recorder. Considerable finger coordination is needed to successfully cover the finger holes under both hands, and thus obtain a good-sounding middle C, which is the lowest available tone on the recorder. First experiences with the recorder, therefore, use music in different keys than the music first used for keyboard instruments.

For initial group work, the soprano recorder is used. There are two systems of boring the finger holes on the recorder: the "baroque" (sometimes called "English") and the "German" system. The German system provides a slightly simpler fingering, but the baroque is more widely accepted. (Fingering charts are provided with each instrument.)

The first melodies played on the recorder should be familiar, so that the player can first sing the song and then play from memory, giving maximum attention to manipulating the instrument. This will include:

1. learning to feel the tone holes and to cover each completely with the fleshy pad of the assigned finger
2. learning to initiate a good tone by tonguing: the tongue moves forward and back to sound the syllable "tu" (or "doo") as the tone is begun
3. learning to listen to the group and to play accurately in unison

Example 5.20 is a chart of baroque fingerings for the recorder.

EXAMPLE 5.20

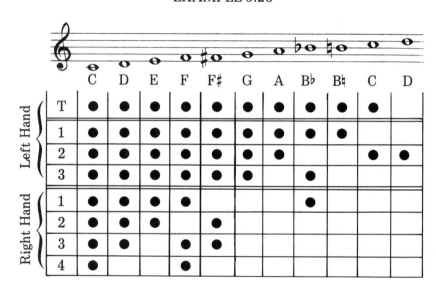

When the first three pitches are learned (G, A, B), you can play the following tunes in the key of G, starting on the pitch and scale step shown after the title:

□ "Hot Cross Buns" B *(3)* (Example 5.4)
□ "Hop, Old Squirrel" B *(3)* (SMB II-65)

By learning high C and D, you will be able to play:

□ "Mary Had a Little Lamb" B *(3)* (TMT II-86)
□ "Fiddle-dee-dee" B *(3)* (ExM II-8)
□ "When the Saints Go Marching In" G *(1)* (Example 3.12)
□ "Merrily We Roll Along" B *(3)* (CM Z2A-180)
□ "Jingle Bells" (refrain only) B *(3)* (TMT II-175)

By learning low D and E, you will be able to play:

- ☐ "Old MacDonald" G*(1)* **(SpM II-167)**
- ☐ "Chatter with the Angels" G(1) (Example 5.10)
- ☐ "Toodala" D*(5)* **(DMT K-12)**
- ☐ "Old Mister Rabbit" G*(1)* **(NDinM K-146)**

The last four songs are pentatonic. When you can play them comfortably, the same pitches can be used to improvise your own tunes. As an example, begin by playing D E—G A B in any order that pleases you, but make G (or alternatively, D) the tonal center by beginning and ending your tune on that pitch. When you feel comfortable with the freedom of choosing your own series of pitches, experiment with different rhythmic groupings until you find a combination of rhythm and melody that you like.

To test your hearing of pitches, choose a partner and echo-play improvised melodies involving the four tones E—G A B. Play by ear; do not watch the fingers of the player initiating the tune.

Learning to play F, F♯, B♭, and finally low C will make it possible for you to play many songs in the keys of G, F, D, and C. Refer to the chart of keys, Example 6.5, as an aid in transposing songs to these keys.

After you have learned the basic technique for playing the recorder, learn some new songs by following the notation. "Duérmete, mi Niño" ("Sleep, My Little One") is a four-tone Spanish lullaby that should not be difficult to read in the key of G as shown here.

EXAMPLE 5.21

DUÉRMETE, MI NIÑO
Spanish Folk Song

Instructional Objectives: To teach children basic techniques for playing the recorder, reading notation on the treble staff, and playing melodies by ear.

Behaviors providing evidence that these instructional objectives have been achieved: The children will

☐ use the recorder to play the melody of "Duérmete, mi Niño," reading from the notation and not previously having heard it

☐ hear and accurately echo-play on the recorder a new melody of eight tones, utilizing the pitches E—G A B

In an elementary class, some children will be more interested in playing the recorder than others. Those who become more proficient can add to the musical ensemble by playing added parts for songs found in their music books. You will find examples of easy part-singing and playing in the discussion of harmony in the next chapter.

Success in playing an instrument depends on practicing the skills. In a singing–playing program, all children in the class should have a chance to learn to play simple melodies; but a major portion of the classroom music time should never be given over to drill on technique. Pupils should be so motivated and the work so set up that they will practice and improvise in their free time. An instruction book[13] is helpful in organizing a classroom approach and will facilitate individual practice outside of class. Some children will develop greater skill than others and will become the natural leaders in this activity.

In combining different instruments, one of the chief problems is that of tuning. Both teacher and pupils must constantly be aware that *sound* is the important consideration. Children must learn to adjust breath pressure to correct the pitch. This skill requires maturity in listening and experience in playing.

Facility in playing the recorder can lead directly to the study of the clarinet, flute, or other woodwind instruments, because the basic techniques are similar. However, it is of greater concern to the classroom teacher that, through the use of these instruments, pupils learn to play and sing, to listen, to develop valid musical concepts, to evaluate, and to progress steadily in the ability to enjoy their own music-making as their musical judgment matures.

EXPERIENCES AT LEVEL III

The music abilities and activities of ten- and eleven-year-olds make it possible for the children to sing more varied songs and improvise and shape melody into compositions of considerable interest. When children are learning to play instruments, the melodic material should be relatively easy, limited in range and in the key signatures used. While children between the ages of nine and eleven have more sophisticated taste in songs, they often are very willing to practice quite simple melodies for the sake of mastering the instrument. You will find that some of the songs and procedures recommended for Level II will be useful in getting older children started playing tuned instruments such as melody bells and recorders.

All the tuned instruments used at this level should be chromatic (capable of sounding all twelve half-steps in an octave); it will also be helpful for them to be adjustable, so that selected tone bars can be set apart to simplify the playing of a particular melody. Resonator bells are very useful because they can be rearranged in groupings that will aid melody-writing. But the distinctive tone color of the wooden tone bars of xylophones, in contrast to the bell-type instruments, is also a feature to be considered.

Playing Melodies

As with younger children, boys and girls at Level III can learn to play melody instruments by playing easy repeated phrases in longer songs, or by playing songs with a limited range. When they play pentatonic songs, the tone bars that are not needed should be removed from the instrument, so that it will be easier to play the melody rhythmically and accurately. In most of this playing, children should play from the music score. The arrangement of the classroom or other space should make it possible for a child to practice independently.

An individual who plays a melody on an instrument must give conscious attention to details of the melody. Work with the Austrian tune "Sing *Gemütlichkeit!*" will demonstrate this need. This song has four phrases, and the first, second and fourth phrases use only four different tones: E F G A. These three phrases are almost the same, but none is exactly like the other, so the form of the song is:

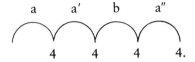

The first theme (a) returns after the contrasting theme (b), so there is a certain balance in the song as a whole.

EXAMPLE 5.22

SING *GEMÜTLICHKEIT!**
Austrian Folk Tune

* "Gemütlichkeit" is a German word meaning good nature, kindliness or geniality.

In spite of these differences, you will not find it difficult to learn to play the first, second, and fourth phrases after the tune is familiar. Use any instrument you wish, and work it out individually so you feel comfortable with the pitches and rhythm; prepare to play along when the class sings the song.

In addition to providing experience playing an instrument, work with the three phrases of this melody will show how a melody can be essentially the same, but have small, significant differences. The first phrase goes one step higher and has two more notes than the other phrases; it makes a closer connection with the beginning of the next phrase. The second phrase ends on *mi* (the third degree of the scale), which is a stronger cadence (stopping point) than the first, but not as strong as that found at the end of the song, where the last note is *do*, the home tone.

The third phrase of this song is an octave in range and would be somewhat more difficult to play, unless the player has some previous instrumental experience. However, the three easier phrases are sufficiently interesting to make this project a useful beginning for melody playing.

"The Birch Tree" is a very famous Russian folk song, so well loved that the Russian composer Tchaikovsky incorporated it as a theme in his *Symphony No. 4.* This minor tune uses only five different notes and it moves downward along a scale line (A G F E D), so it is easy to play, either on resonator bells or on the recorder.

EXAMPLE 5.23

THE BIRCH TREE
Russian Folk Song

Moderately with pensive spirit

1. Во по - ле бе - ре - за сто - я - ла, во по - ле куд-
Vo po - le be - ryo - za sto - ya - la, Vo po - le ku -

-ря - ва - я сто - я - ла. Лю - ли, лю - ли, сто-
dria - va - ya sto - ya - la. Lyu - li, lyu - li, sto -

-я - ла, лю - ли, лю - ли, сто - я - ла.
ya - la, Lyu - li, lyu - li, sto - ya - la.

The meaning of the first verse, shown above:

> In the field stands a birch tree,
> In the field it stands with crisp foliage,
> Luli, luli, it stands there.

Additional verses pay tribute to the birch tree:

> No one may break the birch tree, no one may uproot it.
> Were I to walk in the woods and find the birch tree broken,
> I would take three rods from the birch tree and I would
>   make three musical pipes;
> Then, better than four balalaikas, I would entertain the old people.

Although this is a five-tone melody, it is part of a seven-tone scale (D natural minor), not a pentatonic scale.

Like the Austrian melody just discussed, "The Birch Tree" has two contrasting phrases, but here there is no change in either theme, and they are equally balanced to create a binary (two-part) form:

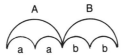

This is another way to combine different themes within a song. The form is a bit unusual in that each phrase is three measures long; it is more common to encounter phrases of two, four, or eight measures. Notice the shape of the themes; the first is a simple, stepwise movement down, and the second moves first up and then down. The special feeling conveyed by this melody results from the fact that it is in the minor mode and has predominantly descending lines. The text shown here is one used in a Russian school music book. The phonetic pronunciation of the words is given below the Russian text. Although the general meaning of the poem is shown, the experience of singing the song would be enhanced if the phonetic pronunciation could be learned.

A pentatonic scale is one that consists of five different tones, rather than seven, within the tonal distance of an octave. You could think of it as a major or a minor scale with two tones missing (usually the fourth and the seventh of the major scale). "Don't Let Your Watch Run Down" is a pentatonic melody, and if adjustable instruments like resonator bells or the Orff instruments are available, it is quite easy to play.

EXAMPLE 5.24

DON'T LET YOUR WATCH RUN DOWN
Texas Folk Song

Lively

Don't let your watch run down,   Cap - tain,

Don't let your watch run down,_____ *Fine*

Work - in' on the lev - ee,   dollar 'n a half a day,

Work - in' for my Lu - lu,   draw - in' my pay.   *D. C. al Fine*

From *South Texas Negro Work Songs* by Gates Thomas, in *Rainbow in the Morning*, PTFS Vol. 5, J. Frank Dobee, ed., 1926. Used by permission.

Set up the tone bars like this, with gaps where no tones occur in the pentatonic scale on F. When comparing this particular pentatonic scale to the major scale, you will find that the fourth scale step, B♭, and the seventh scale step, E, are not used. If you think pitch in terms of the *sol-fa* syllables, you would use *do re mi – so la,* with *do* (F) as the tonal center.

EXAMPLE 5.25

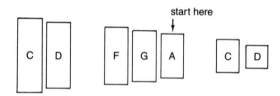

Try playing the song with the arrangement of the tone bars shown in Example 5.25; you will find it considerably easier than using the full scale of F major. The gaps in the tone bar arrangement will help you remember how the tune moves, and of course eliminate the possibility of sounding a tone that is not needed in the song. If this key seems too high for comfortable singing, play the song in the key of D or the key of C; this is the low-to-high arrangement of tone bars for those keys:

Key of D: A B–D E F♯–A B
Key of C: G A–C D E–G A

By making charts of the tones needed for different keys, you can help the children select the range best suited to their voices.

This is a song of the American frontier when the work was hard, the pay was low, and quitting time was determined by the boss's watch. The song has a good strong rhythm, and it probably was sung as the singers or listeners worked. As you learn to sing it, tap the steady beat and notice the three measures that have a syncopated rhythm in the melody.

The song is made up of short motifs that shape themselves into four-measure phrases, and when the *D.C. al Fine* is observed, the result is a three-part form:

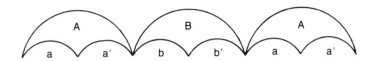

There are only two different phrases here. Each *a* phrase and each *b* phrase begins the same, but in each pair of phrases, when the phrase is repeated, it has a change that you must be aware of to play it readily. In the A section, notice that the high note, D, is sounded only once—in phrase *a;* the bottom note, C, is sounded only once—in phrase *a'*. Most of the time, then, you will be using the middle bars of the five-tone series.

Melodies in the major, minor, and pentatonic modes have a tonal center. This is determined by two factors:

1. the organization of whole steps and half-steps in the scale
2. the way the tones are used within a song based on that scale

In the pentatonic scale, the way the tones are used is most significant because most pentatonic scales do not have half-steps. The tonal center for "Don't Let Your Watch Run Down" is F, or *do* in terms of the *sol-fa* syllables. Other songs that use the pentatonic scale this way are:

"Flower Drum Song" $\frac{4}{4}$ ExM VI-120   "Night Herding Song" $\frac{6}{8}$ (Example 4.17)
"Milking Croon" $\frac{3}{4}$ SBM VI-85   DMT VI-26
                                                     "Sourwood Mountain" $\frac{2}{4}$ ExM V-72

You could, however, use the same tone bars and have another key center, because of the shape and centering of the melody among those tones. Play the "Canoe Song" (Example 5.26) on the same set of tone bars and notice that its tonal center seems to be D, or *la* in terms of the *sol-fa* syllables.

EXAMPLE 5.26

CANOE SONG
American Indian

Other songs that use the pentatonic scale this way are:

"Arirang" $\frac{3}{4}$ (Example 7.13)   "Hsiao" (Bamboo Flute")$\frac{2}{4}$
"Chimes At Night" $\frac{4}{4}$ DMT VI-25   NDinM VI-118
"Wayfaring Stranger" $\frac{3}{2}$ NDinM V-49   "Land of the Silver Birch"$\frac{2}{4}$
                                                (Example 6.22)

Songs of many cultures use pentatonic scales. "Sakura" (**SBM V-8**), a pentatonic song that can be found in many basic series music books, is an example of a song using a pentatonic scale that includes half-steps. As you will see in Chapter 7, the tuning of an oriental scale can differ from the tuning of pianos and bell instruments in this country.

Instructional Objectives: To select phrases and easy melodies that many children will be able to learn to play on tuned instruments, and to develop listening skills, tonal memory, and understanding of melody-related details. These details include melodic movement by steps and skips; melodic shape having upward and downward movement; climax and cadence; and phrase and sectional form in which repetition, contrast, and similarity are recognized.

Behaviors providing evidence that these instructional objectives have been achieved: The children will

☐ play phrases and songs accurately from memory or using notation

☐ make comments on and answer questions about melodic movement, shape, and form that reveal their understanding of music details related to those topics

Improvising Melodies

At the intermediate level children can get involved in musical improvisation in a way that will help sharpen their awareness of melody in different contexts. Using the seven pitches (C D — F G A — C D) and the $\frac{2}{4}$ meter of "Don't Let Your Watch Run Down," create your own tune. Begin by tapping the tone bars successively up and down the instrument in time with the steady beat:

When you feel comfortable about this, change one or two dimensions of your performance:

1. Divide the beat to make a more interesting rhythm; find some combinations of long and short notes:

2. Use some lower and some higher tones and find groups of tones that sound good to you.
3. If you wish to make F the tonal center of your melody, come back to it frequently and end on it. If you prefer D as the tonal center, make it prominent in the melody.

While improvising, you may not remember exactly what you have played, but try to keep improving the melody and concentrate on the details as well as the general effect. If you find a tune you like, you will need to be able to remember it, replay it, and then make a record of what you have played. Do this with a tape recorder or with staff notation, or just write down the letter names of the pitches in the order in which you played them, along with some indication of the rhythm patterns used.

If you wish, use a short jingle or a rhyme to set the rhythm of your melody. You will find all sorts of rhymes in *The Annotated Mother Goose*.[14] These procedures may help you create a melody for this verse:

1. Read the rhyme aloud until you find a satisfactory rhythm for it.
2. Chant the rhyme and tap the rhythm of the words at a moderate pace.
3. Repeat, but tap the rhythm of the words on the tone bars in any sequence that seems to you to produce a satisfying melody.
4. Listen to the melodic motifs you play and use them to organize the melody as a whole.

A different mood might be created by using a haiku poem as a basis for the improvised melody. Haiku is a Japanese form of verse that consists of seventeen syllables organized into three lines of five, seven, and five syllables each. This one by Roka Shonin is translated in *The Four Seasons.*

> Hanging sadly down
> Amid the merrymakers . . .
> Green weeping willow.[15]

Use the arrangement of tone bars and the procedures suggested for the previous verse. You probably will find that this poem has a more relaxed rhythm and may require some pauses for the best effect. Emma Lou Diemer composed melodies called "Two Haiku" (**NDinM VI-121**) that you might like to see and hear. Although they are not in a pentatonic scale, they use rhythm in an interesting way. The most important thing now is to create a melody that pleases you, whether you can put it into notation or not.

You can find a ready-made pentatonic scale by playing the black keys of the piano: F$^\sharp$ G$^\sharp$ A$^\sharp$—C$^\sharp$ D$^\sharp$. To get that same sound on white keys, leave out the fourth and seventh steps of a major scale:

$$C \quad D \quad E—G \quad A—C$$
$$G \quad A \quad B—D \quad E—G$$
$$do \ re \ mi—so \ la—do$$

You used the pentatonic scale based on F in the previous exercise, and you can have a pentatonic scale at any point on the keyboard by using this formula.

Another scale that is easy for a beginner to use is the "whole tone" scale. There are two whole tone scales possible among the twelve tones of the chromatic scale. Using a set of chromatic resonator bells, start with C or C$^\sharp$ and select pitches a whole tone apart:

$$C \quad D \quad E \quad F^\sharp \quad G^\sharp \quad A^\sharp \quad C$$
or
$$C^\sharp \quad D^\sharp \quad F \quad G \quad A \quad B \quad C^\sharp$$

Since there are no half-steps in this scale, there is no established tonal center, unless you create one by giving one tone more prominence than other tones in the melody. Play the tones of this scale several times in succession and then begin to group them into a melody. You can begin and end a melody wherever it seems pleasing to you. If you use one of the verses suggested earlier, you will get a melody in duple or quadruple meter. The whole tone scale should provide a very appropriate melody for the haiku poem; approach it in the way that was suggested when you used the pentatonic scale.

There are twelve tones in a chromatic scale, and these have been used in a special way by 20th-century composers. All twelve tones are arranged in the order the composer selects as a theme ("row") for the composition. Here is the "tone row" that the Austrian composer Anton Webern used for his *Symphony for Small Orchestra*.[16]

You will find that he used all of the black and white keys, with E as the low pitch and E$^\flat$ above that as the high pitch.

Use resonator bells and set up this series of tones in this order from left to right. Play them slowly so you can hear the kind of tonal relationships Webern chose for his composition. Now, use these tones as a basis of a melody for the haiku poem. Chant the poem softly, or sing along as you play the bells. You will need to add rhythm to fit the poem, but you must use the tones in this order. When you run out of tones, go back to the beginning of the row; you may not repeat any of the tones until all have been sounded. This is an unusual melody for a song, but it does have potential as the theme in an instrumental composition. The rhythm you use will have a great deal to do with the effectiveness of the melody you create.

Tonal variety in composing with a twelve-tone row is achieved by manipulating the tones in these ways: (1) retrograde, or playing the row backwards, (2) inversion, or turning the intervals upside down, and (3) retrograde-inversion. These principles and useful procedures are discussed in *Explore and Discover Music*[17] and in "Twelve-Tone Activities for the General Music Class."[18]

Create your own twelve-tone row by having each of twelve individuals take a tone bar from the resonator bell set; use the tone bars between middle C and the B above, so that the range will be convenient for singing. Have these twelve people stand in a line but in a random order, so that the tones are mixed up and not in scale formation. Play the series of tones slowly from left to right to hear the tone row you have created. You can rearrange the pitches to improve the sound of your "row" if you wish. Play this tone row as the melody for the haiku poem. Which of the two tone rows used do you think has the best potential as melodic material for this particular poem, yours or Webern's? Can you identify any specific reason why you prefer one to the other?

Instructional Objectives: To provide opportunities for children to manipulate melodic material in creative ways; to help them discover that melody writing utilizes both pitch and rhythm, and that choices are made on the basis of taste and the expressive intent of the composer, and to increase their skill in responding rhythmically and utilizing tonal memory.

Behaviors providing evidence that these instructional objectives have been achieved: The children will

- ☐ improvise creative melodies and play them for the class
- ☐ discuss the components of pitch and rhythm that they dealt with in the creative process
- ☐ express aesthetic judgments about the music created

Shaping a Composition

Improvisation, spontaneously playing and searching out rhythms and melody, is the first step in musical creation. If you give more time to the process, you can apply to your composition the melodic development discussed earlier; you can include repeated, contrasting, and altered phrases that are shaped into a satisfying musical form together with the use of a tonal center, climax, and cadence points. It is useful to set a goal of writing down a creative musical composition so that it will be in a tangible form; in doing so, you can develop some music writing skills. At this point, you may need the help of a special music teacher to complete the project.

Let us assume that you succeeded in creating a pentatonic melody for a haiku poem. Since it is very short, you may want to expand the form of the piece in one of these ways:

1. Create a "frame" for your melody—an introduction that will attract the listener's attention, and a coda to make an appropriate close.
2. Create a contrasting middle section for the instrument alone, and then play and sing the melody again. This would give a form of A B A.
3. Repeat one or more words in any line of the poem to extend the song and give added emphasis to that idea or feeling.

Play your melody on instruments with different timbres to hear which sound gives the best effect—bells, piano, xylophone, zither, and so on. In Chapter 6 we will consider some ways to create an accompaniment for such a pentatonic melody.

Learning to Play Orchestral Instruments

Beginning at the fourth or fifth grade, in many schools children may elect instruction on band and orchestral instruments. Special instrumental teachers usually carry on this instruction, but the classroom teacher should be involved in the program in these ways:

1. Promote interest and help to discover students who have special aptitudes, interests, or needs that would make participation in the program valuable to them.
2. Cooperate in scheduling such special classes so that they are carried on with greatest effectiveness, yet do not unduly disturb the working of the classroom.
3. Promote an outlet for the skills and interests developed in the special instrumental classes.

The attitude of the classroom teacher can greatly influence the opinions and interests of the students. If the special instrumental program is worth having, it deserves the interest and support of the classroom teacher, who should look upon it as an expanded opportunity for children. Some children have innate musical talent that should be developed; others are superior intellectually, and the challenge of learning to play an instrument may enrich their educational experience. It is not wise, however, to limit this experience to those who are the better scholars, for occasionally a child who has not found satisfaction in academic studies may find a badly needed area of success in such a music activity.

The special teacher must work during the school day, taking pupils from their classrooms. Instruction is most effective in small classes of homogeneous instruments (strings, brasses, and woodwinds separately). But since a child's preference in an instrument must also be considered, a classroom teacher may have pupils in each group absent from the room at different times. When the special teacher can teach different groups on different days, the classroom teacher can set up a study or activity period so that the absent pupils do not miss any vital subject presentation. Often, however, a specialist must teach all of the instrumental classes in one school on one day of the week. In such schools, the classroom teacher is hard pressed to find enough hours in that day to accomplish the classroom presentations with all students present. In this situation the children can be of help, because those studying instruments usually are highly motivated and compensate for classroom absences by being more efficient in their learning. When the school principal appreciates the value of special music studies, and when the teachers understand each other's responsibilities, mutually agreeable solutions can be found.

As students acquire skill in playing their instruments (whether studied in school classes or in private lessons), they should be given opportunities to play in the classroom. The players will not only acquaint the other children with the standard instruments, but will have an early, sociable use for their skills. Many music books show simple instrumental parts that instrumentalists can play to accompany classroom singing.

CHAPTER NOTES

1. Aaron Copland, **What to Listen for In Music** (New York: McGraw-Hill Book Company, Inc., 1957), p. 50.

2. Bessie R. Swanson, **An Analysis and Evaluation of Individual Melody Writing by Seven-Year-Old Children in Public School Classes** (Doctor of Musical Arts Research Study, Music Department, Stanford University, 1967), p. 74.

3. Helga Szabo, **The Kodály Concept of Music Education** (New York: Boosey & Hawkes, Inc., 1969).

4. J. Ribiére-Raverlat, **Musical Education in Hungary** (Paris: Alphonse Leduc Cie., 1968).

5. Zoltán Kodály, **Choral Method,** ed. Percy A. Young (New York: Boosey & Hawkes, Inc.).

6. Mary Helen Richards, **Threshold to Music** (Belmont, Calif.: Fearon Publishers, 1964).

7. Richards Institute of Music Education and Research, 149 Corte Madera, Portola Valley, Calif. 94025.

8. Lois Choksy, **The Kodály Method** (Englewood Cliffs, N.J.: Prentice-Hall, Inc., 1974).

9. The Kodály Musical Training Institute, Inc., 23 Main Street, Watertown, Mass. 02172.

10. Ronald B. Thomas, **MMCP Synthesis,** USOE V-008 and USOE 6-1999 (Bardonia, N.Y.: Media Materials, Inc., 1970).

11. Carl Orff and Gunild Keetman, **Music for Children, I—Pentatonic,** English adaptation by Doreen Hall and Arnold Walter (Mainz, Ger.: B. Schott's Söhne, 1956, Edition 4470; New York: Associated Music Publishers, Inc.), pp. 66–78.

12. Grace Nash, **Music with Children,** Series I, II, III, Recorder Book (Scottsdale, Ariz.: G. C. Nash, 1965).

13. **Hargail Music Press,** 157 West 57th St., New York, N.Y. 10019. Specialists in recorders as well as music for recorders and other instruments. One instruction book they publish is **The Elementary Method for the Soprano Recorder,** 1967, by Gerald Burakoff.

14. William S. Baring-Gould and Ceil Baring-Gould, **The Annotated Mother Goose** (New York: The World Publishing Company, 1967), p. 204.

15. **The Four Seasons,** Japanese haiku, trans Peter Beilenson (New York, N.Y.: The Peter Pauper Press, 1958), p. 21. © 1958 by The Peter Pauper Press. Used by permission.

16. Anton Webern, **Symphony for Small Orchestra,** Opus 21.

17. Mary Val Marsh, **Explore and Discover Music** (New York: The Macmillan Company, 1970), pp. 131–138.

18. Brian Busch, "Twelve-Tone Activities for the General Music Class," **Music Educators Journal** 65 (March 1979), pp. 42–46.

6

Study of Harmony and Texture
through Singing and Playing Instruments

Previous chapters of this book gave primary attention to the musical elements of timbre, rhythm, and melody. Music, however, is an art in which one element can scarcely be considered without referring to other elements. Thus, some organizing principles of form as well as aspects of harmony and texture were also mentioned. The main features of this chapter are musical texture and harmony; but along the way you will see interrelationships with other musical elements.

AN OVERVIEW OF TEXTURE AND HARMONY

In organizing material for teaching, it is useful to consider texture and harmony under three general headings:

1. types of texture
2. chords and their relationships
3. the structure of chords

This organization moves from general concepts accessible to primary children, to more specific details and relationships that ten- or eleven-year-olds can work out in group playing and singing. Appendix A-IV lists sample concepts that children can acquire about texture and harmony; Appendix C-IV shows the construction and notation of various chords.

Kinds of Texture

Texture is a quality of music resulting from the relationships among instrumental or vocal parts that sound together. In simple terms, musical texture can be "thick" or "thin," "bumpy" or "smooth," and so on. Children can relate textures they hear to texture they can feel in textiles or see in painting. There are three basic kinds of musical texture:

1. a single, unaccompanied melody line ("monophonic")
2. a principal melody that is supported and enriched by other tones ("homophonic")
3. two or more separate musical lines that sound simultaneously ("polyphonic")

Different textures can be created by combined rhythms as well as melodic lines, and by groups of tones at different pitch levels sounded by several instruments or voices. Children can build up musical textures by combining sounds and by simultaneously playing short melodic fragments on a variety of simple instruments.

A chord in music is the simultaneous sounding of three or more tones; "harmony" refers to successions of chords and relations among them, as well as to the relationship of the chords to a melody. The harmony created by a melody and its accompaniment can have different textural qualities, e.g., slow-moving chords that are held throughout several tones of the melody; chords that move along with the melody or faster than the melody; or chords that are broken and played in flowing accompaniment figures. The texture is thinner when there are three tones in the chord, as opposed to the thicker texture of music in which the chord tones are sounded by many instruments or voices at several different pitch levels.

When two or more melodies of equal importance are sounded at the same time, "counterpoint" is created. The round, an identical melody sung by two or more voices beginning at different times, is a simple example of counterpoint. A rhythmic–melodic pattern that is persistently repeated is called an ostinato. These are techniques of combining sounds in the type of texture called polyphony. The separate parts can move in parallel motion or in contrary motion; in rounds and certain other forms, one voice or musical line imitates another. All these concepts can be understood by children if they have musical experiences involving these aspects of texture.

Chords and Their Relationships

The simple harmonies of hymns and folk music feature three primary chords that children can learn to recognize and play on the Autoharp, guitar or other instruments. These consist of the tonic chord (I), which gives a sense of restfulness and arrival; the dominant chord (V), which is active and restless; and the subdominant chord (IV). At the beginning of a piece of music, the tonic chord defines the key in which the music is set. A cadence, or point of arrival at the end of a musical phrase or composition as a whole, is defined by the harmony. It can be temporary (a "half cadence," ending on the dominant chord), or final (a "full cadence," in which the harmony moves from dominant to tonic).

The Structure of Chords

Boys and girls in the intermediate grades can use resonator bells to build chords. They learn that the simplest chord, a triad, consists of three tones built up in thirds from any step of a scale, and that chords are labeled in three ways: with a Roman numeral, with a capital letter, or by a name indicating the harmonic function of the chord, e.g., tonic or dominant. Chords having the same letter name and formation are found in different keys; the function and effect of the chord, however, depend upon its relationship to the tonal center of the key in which it is used. In a major key the primary chords are "major," and in minor keys I, IV, and sometimes V are "minor." A dominant-seventh chord (V^7) is always "major."

The dominant-seventh chord is particularly important in the folk music of this country. Six- or seven-year-olds can recognize the difference in sound between the tonic and dominant-seventh chords; but it is usually at Level III that children build chords and use their understanding of melody as the basis for learning some of the specifics of the system of harmony. They can also investigate the musical effects of chords that are comprised of other intervals, such as the fourth, and can create more contemporary sounds by using "tone clusters" (the simultaneous sounding of several adjacent pitches).

THE INSTRUMENTS

At Level I it will be very useful if you can provide accompaniments for children's singing, using the Autoharp, guitar or piano. Children can learn to play the Autoharp at Level II and thereby begin to provide accompaniments for some of the folk songs they sing. At Level III some children can learn to play the guitar, and at all levels keyboard instruments can be combined with singing to create harmony.

Playing the Autoharp

The Autoharp is an adaptation of an older instrument, the zither, and has thirty to forty strings. By depressing a bar on the Autoharp you can set up a chord. As you strum over the entire range of strings, those strings not needed in the chord are muted by felt pads beneath the bar, but the strings needed for that particular chord vibrate freely. Twelve-, fifteen-, and eighteen-bar Autoharps are available. The fifteen-bar Autoharp, designed for school use, offers an adequate number of keys and chords and is the instrument referred to in the following discussion.

When learning to play, sit with the Autoharp lying flat on your lap, or stand with it before you on a table so you can see the chord markings. The bars that define the chords are pressed down one at a time by the fingers of the left hand.

Three different kinds of chords are present on the Autoharp: major, minor, and seventh chords. You must differentiate among them. As an example, look for three different kinds of G chord. Press successively the bar labeled G major, that labeled G-seven, and that labeled G minor. In reading chord markings for songs, you will find it common practice to print only a capital G for the major chord; the letter for minor chords will be followed by a lower case *m* (Gm), and the seventh chord will have a 7 after the chord letter (G^7). Look on the instrument, or on the diagram in Example 6.1, to see which chords appear in more than one form.

EXAMPLE 6.1

DIAGRAM OF CHORD MECHANISM OF THE AUTOHARP*

Press the buttons down with the left hand, using the pointer finger on the tonic chord. Strum with the right hand either to the right or to the left of the chord mechanism.

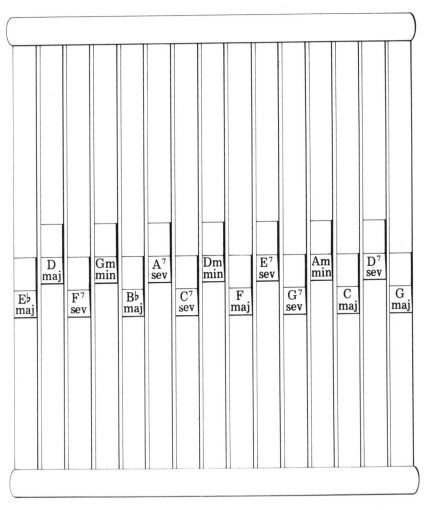

* Autoharp is the registered trademark of Oscar Schmidt-International, Inc.

The Autoharp is strummed with a pick held in the right hand. A plastic pick makes a loud, sharp tone; a felt or leather pick produces a softer tone. When learning, stroke the strings just to the right of the chord bars; later you can cross your right hand over the left and stroke nearer the center of the strings, just to the left of the bars, to produce a more resonant tone. When you no longer need to look at the labels to find the necessary chords, you can set the wide end of the Autoharp in your lap and hold the instrument against your chest so you can strum in banjo style. A shoulder strap attached to both ends of the instrument will enable you to hold the Autoharp in this position when you stand.

To coordinate strumming with tuning up and singing a song, try a few one-chord songs. Any of the following rounds and pentatonic songs can serve this purpose:

Rounds	*Pentatonic Songs*
"Are You Sleeping" (Example 5.3) F major chord; starts on F	"Bell Horses" (Example 5.8) C major chord; starts on G (5)
"Row, Row, Row Your Boat" (Example 4.3) C major chord; starts on C	"Chatter with the Angels" (Example 5.10) G major chord; starts on G
"The Ghost of John" (Example 7.6) D minor chord; starts on D	"Roll Over" (Example 5.14) G major chord; starts on D (5)

With the index finger of your left hand, hold down the chord bar needed in the song and strum (from the bottom to the top of the instrument), using a pick or the fingernails of your right hand. Press the chord bar firmly, so that a clear chord sound is heard; but strum lightly with the right hand. Stop and pluck the starting note, in the middle octave of the Autoharp, and sing the first word on that pitch. Then make two strums to a measure as you sing the song. Try several of these one-chord songs until you feel comfortable starting in different keys.

"Down in the Valley" (Example 6.2) is a well-known song using two chords. It can serve as an example for several principles in starting and accompanying songs.

EXAMPLE 6.2

DOWN IN THE VALLEY

Kentucky Folk Song

Leisurely

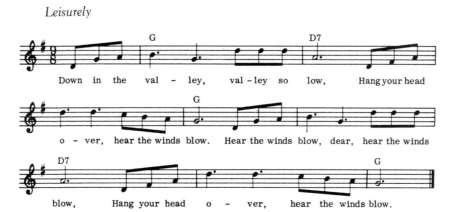

To sing with any chording instrument, you must first orient your ear to the key and to the first tone of the song by some variation of the following procedures:

1. Determine the key and the scale degree on which the song begins (see Appendix C-IV for key signatures, if necessary).
2. Sound on the instrument the tonic chord in that key, or better, play the chord progression I V^7 I to establish the key in your ear. (Play G D^7 G to tune up for "Down in the Valley.")
3. While playing the tonic chord, recognize and sing the tonic tone; then sing from the tonic to the scale tone on which the song begins.

"Down in the Valley" begins on D (*sol,* or *5* below the tonic note, *do*). If necessary, sound G and then D in the middle register of the instrument, then sing the first word of the song on the correct pitch, like this:

Keep that starting pitch in mind as you take the second step in providing an accompaniment: Establish the meter and tempo by playing a short introduction. Since "Down in the Valley" is in a triple meter ($^9_8$), instruments such as the guitar and Autoharp might sound heavy and light strums on the tonic chord as follows, with the singing beginning on the third beat:

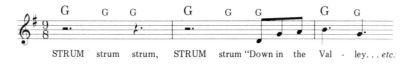

This tuning-up process should be accurate and quick; as you prepare to sing, take into account the key-note as well as the first note of the song. Most songs are key-centered. The tuning process described here not only gives you the first tone of the song, but it also accustoms the ear to the key in which you will sing.

Use the same procedures to tune up "Hey, Lollee!" (Example 6.3), which is in the key of C and starts on G (*so* or scale step *5* above the home tone, *do*). When you have the starting pitch in mind, establish the meter and tempo by strumming a short introduction.

EXAMPLE 6.3

HEY, LOLLEE!

James Leisy
Based on a Bahamian Folk Tune

2. Calypso singers sing this song, Hey, lol-lee, lol-lee lo!
   It sometimes lasts the whole night long! Hey, lol-lee, lol-lee lo!

3. First you invent a simple line, *etc.*
   Then add another to make it rhyme, *etc.*

4. While you catch on I'll sing a verse, *etc.*
   Then you do one that's even worse, *etc.*

5. We sing "Hey, lol-lee" day and night, *etc.*
   But it just don't seem to come out right, *etc.*

6. Let's put this song back on the shelf, *etc.*
   If you want more you can sing it yourself, *etc.*

Since "Hey, Lollee!" is in a fairly brisk $\frac{4}{4}$ meter, strum alternately heavy and light on the first and third beats of the measure:

STRUM		strum		STRUM		strum	
1	2	3	4	1	2	3	4

Strum continually as you sing the song, but change chords as shown above the music.

The fifteen-bar Autoharp will allow you to play such a two-chord song in other keys. Try "Hey, Lollee!" one step higher, in the key of D, then one step lower, in the key of B^b, using these chords:

	I	V^7
Key of D:	D	A^7
Key of B^b:	B^b	F^7

In each instance, the song begins on the fifth step of the scale; but you will have to adjust to the new key, following the instructions given above. In which key do you find it most comfortable to sing this song? Since it uses only five tones, it is quite possible that any of these keys is comfortable. In a song with a wider range, the difference made by a change of key would be more noticeable.

Other two-chord songs you will find easy to sing and play include the following. (The number after the name of the key shows the scale step on which the song begins.)

"Polly Wolly Doodle" (Example 4.19) C–5   "Shoo, Fly" (Example 3.9) F–3

"San Serení" (Example 4.14) C–5   "This Old Man" (Example 4.12) D–5

"Hush, Little Baby" (see Example 6.4) is a very simple lullaby that rocks back and forth between two chords, F and C^7. This song is in $\frac{4}{4}$ meter, so you have some choice in strumming. Make one or two strums to each measure, depending upon the tempo and character in which you wish to interpret the song.

	1	2	3	4
Moderate tempo:	STRUM		strum	
Fast tempo:	STRUM			

EXAMPLE 6.4

HUSH, LITTLE BABY

American Folk Song

Whimsically

1. Hush, lit - tle ba - by,   don't   say a   word,
2. If   that___ mock - ing   bird   don't___   sing,

Pa - pa's gon - na buy   you a   mock - ing bird.
Pa - pa's gon - na buy   you a   dia - mond ring.

3. If that diamond ring turns brass,
   Daddy's gonna buy you a looking glass,

4. If that looking glass gets broke,
   Daddy's gonna buy you a billy goat.

5. If that billy goat won't pull,
   Daddy's gonna buy you a cart and bull;

6. If that cart and bull turn over,
   Daddy's gonna buy you a dog named Rover.

7. If that dog named Rover won't bark,
   Daddy's gonna buy you a horse and cart;

8. If that horse and cart fall down,
   You'll still be the sweetest baby in town.

Since no chord markings appear above "Hush, Little Baby," it will be necessary for you to chord "by ear." One flat in the key signature indicates the key of F, so
F major will be the tonic chord. Be sure you get started singing on the correct pitch,
which is C or *so*, (*5*,) below the tonic note of F. Strum the F chord (I) as you sing,
and listen to determine when the C[7] chord is needed to supply a compatible harmony
with the melody. Change back to the F chord when the C[7] chord no longer fits the
melody, and so on through the song. Chording "by ear" is a valuable skill to
develop. With familiar two-chord songs it is reasonably easy to do, once you are
singing in the key established by the chording instrument.

During early experiences, when accompanying is limited to two chords, listen
for the distinctive qualities of the tonic and dominant-seventh chords. The tonic
chord is built on the key-note of a scale, and it has qualities of arrival and stability; it
is commonly called the "home" chord. In contrast, the dominant-seventh chord has
qualities of restlessness and instability, so that movement from it to the tonic chord is
desired.

When you play in different keys and make transpositions, you will find it
helpful to know that these chords are named in three different ways: in *any* key the

tonic chord is built on the first step of the scale and can be labeled with a Roman numeral I or with the name "tonic." In a *specific* key it has a letter name. Notice the relationship of chord numbers to chord letters in the four keys shown in Example 6.5. (Roman numerals for major chords are shown as uppercase; for minor chords they are shown as lowercase.)

EXAMPLE 6.5

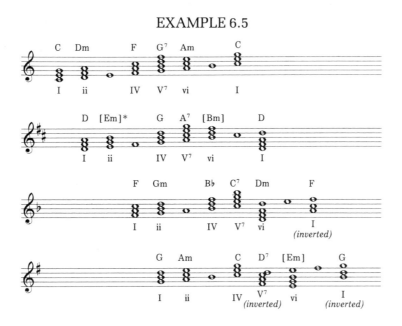

* Chords in brackets are not available on the Autoharp.

The dominant chord is built on the fifth step of the scale and is labeled V. On the Autoharp the form of the dominant chord is the dominant-seventh (V^7). This four-tone chord is used because the added tone gives a special color and dynamic quality. The chart in Example 6.6 shows the relationships of chords in the five major keys and three minor keys that are found on the Autoharp.

Chords for eight different keys can be played on the fifteen-bar Autoharp. You will encounter many songs that require a standard harmonizing scheme of three chords: the tonic (I), the subdominant (IV), and the dominant-seventh (V^7). For several keys, the chord bars are arranged so that these three chords are adjacent. When you place your left index finger on the tonic chord of a given key, the middle finger falls on the dominant-seventh chord and the ring finger on the subdominant chord of that key.

EXAMPLE 6.6

KEYS AND CHORDS ON THE FIFTEEN-BAR AUTOHARP

You have this choice of chords:

vi	6 4 ii(2) Supertonic	1 6 IV(4) Subdominant	4 2 7 V^7(5) Dominant Seventh	5 3 I(1) Tonic	*If you play in these keys:*
A minor	D minor	F major	G^7	C major ←	C major
	A minor	C major	D^7	G major ←	G major
D minor	G minor	B♭ major	C^7	F major ←	F major
G minor	—	E♭ major	F^7	B♭ major←	B♭ major
	—	G major	A^7	D major ←	D major
	—	G minor	A^7	D minor ←	D minor
	—	D minor	E^7	A minor ←	A minor
	—	—	D^7	G minor ←	G minor

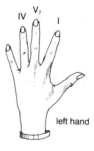

left hand

Play some three-chord songs and begin exploring the sound of the subdominant chord (IV). The chord progression IV–I has the familiar sound of the "Amen" at the end of a hymn. Compare this sound with that of the V^7–I progression, which is the most common harmonic ending (cadence) in a song. To follow chord indications in a score, it is essential that the fingering pattern for the Autoharp become automatic. With the fingers moving by touch, you can keep your eyes on the notation. Practice the finger pattern for three-chord songs with "Silent Night" (Example 6.7) and other songs in these different keys:

"Night Herding Song" F–*1*
(Example 4.17)

"Sing Gemütlichkeit!" C–*3*
(Example 5.22)

"Sing Your Way Home" F–*3*
(Example 4.10)

"This Land is Your Land" G–*1*
(Example 4.16)

"Tinga Layo" D–*3*
(Example 4.20)

"When the Saints Go Marching In"
G–*1* (Example 3.12)

EXAMPLE 6.7

SILENT NIGHT
(Stille Nacht)

Franz Gruber
Joseph Mohr

Peacefully

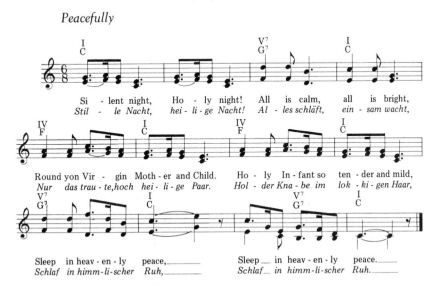

Si - lent night, Ho - ly night! All is calm, all is bright,
Stil - le Nacht, hei - li - ge Nacht! Al - les schläft, ein - sam wacht,

Round yon Vir - gin Moth - er and Child. Ho - ly In - fant so ten - der and mild,
Nur das trau - te, hoch hei - li - ge Paar. Hol - der Kna - be im lok - ki - gen Haar,

Sleep in heav - en - ly peace,_____ Sleep__ in heav - en - ly peace.____
Schlaf in himm - li - scher Ruh,_____ Schlaf__ in himm - li - scher Ruh.__

It is a bit more difficult to accompany three-chord songs by ear, but you might like to try some of the following well-known songs. Each song will begin and end with the tonic chord (I). Be sure you tune up to the right key and starting note. Change chords during the song, so that throughout, you get a harmonizing chord that is compatible with the melody. The key and starting pitch are shown, followed by the meter signature. Since some melodies begin with one or more upbeats, it is a good idea to start a strum that suits the meter signature before you begin to sing.

"Auld Lang Syne" C–5, $\frac{4}{4}$ "This Old Man" C–5, $\frac{2}{4}$

"Kum Ba Yah" C–1, $\frac{3}{4}$ "Twinkle, Twinkle, Little Star" C–1, $\frac{4}{4}$

"On Top of Old Smokey" C–1, $\frac{3}{4}$ "Yankee Doodle" F–1, $\frac{2}{4}$

The fifteen-bar Autoharp has three minor chords. The following songs in this book are in the key of D minor and use the chords shown below:

"The Birch Tree" (Example 5.23)   "Simple Simon" (Example 5.5)
Dm and A⁷   Dm and A⁷

"Old House" (Example 3.2)
Dm and Gm

Orient your ear to the minor key by strumming the chords needed in the song. Then strum the tonic chord; pluck the tonic note, followed by the first pitch of the song.

You will find songs in major keys that use an occasional minor chord; "Streets of Laredo" (Example 6.27) is an example. A song that is predominantly in the minor mode, such as "All the Pretty Little Horses" (Example 5.16), may incorporate some phrases that need to be harmonized by major chords. Try to have variety in the songs you use, and learn to recognize and enjoy the different sound provided by minor keys and chords.

The Autoharp lends itself to many interesting strumming styles. Some songs suggest a banjo-style accompaniment. You can simulate this by using a plastic pick to produce alternately low- and high-sounding chords; strum first on the lower strings and then on the upper strings. Sometimes a particular strumming rhythm will create an especially appropriate accompaniment. In *The Many Ways to Play the Autoharp*[1] you will find excellent suggestions for creating folk-style accompaniments.

Tuning the Autoharp

Like any stringed instrument, the Autoharp must be tuned periodically. A new Autoharp will need to be tuned at least twice before the strings are set at the required tension for each pitch. Variations in temperature affect the tuning of the instrument; therefore, when not in use, the instrument should be stored in its case.

The quickest ways to tune the Autoharp are to match the pitch of a well-tuned piano or to use the tuning record available from the manufacturers.[2] A key to turn the tuning pegs is supplied with each instrument. Do not turn the peg too far or loosen it from the frame as you tune. Turning the tuning key in a clockwise direction will raise the pitch.

Begin with middle C and tune all strings for the C tonic chord (C–E–G) upward and downward from that position. Strike the piano key and then pluck the corresponding string, turning the key to raise the string to the pitch of the piano. If the pitch of the string is raised too much, turn it slightly counterclockwise to lower the pitch and then clockwise again to bring it exactly in tune. After you have tuned the tonic chord throughout the range of the instrument, begin near the middle of the Autoharp and tune each successive string so that it matches the pitch of the corresponding key on the piano. An Autoharp may need tuning every two to four weeks, depending upon climatic conditions and what kind of use it receives. If an Autoharp is noticeably out of tune it should not be used; if it is to be played along with other pitched instruments, it should be tuned to the same standard of pitch.

Transposing a Song

Since not all keys are represented on the Autoharp, it is often necessary to transpose a song in order to accommodate the instrument. When this is done, the chord numbers (I, IV, V^7) rather than chord letters (e.g., G, C, D^7) should be marked above the song. As an example, "Silent Night" (Example 6.7) is written in the key of C. By following the chord numbers you can transpose the song a whole step lower, to the key of B♭ (I = B♭, IV = E♭, V^7 = F^7). Placing chord letters for the key of B♭ above the song as written in the key of C can cause confusion, but chord numbers can refer to the chord needed in either key. Understanding chord numbers as well as chord letters will allow you to generalize your knowledge of harmony to any key.

For an example of the need for transposition, look at "I Ride an Old Paint" (Example 6.11), which is written in the key of A to accommodate the guitar. Since the key of A is not available on the Autoharp, Autoharpists must transpose the song to a nearby key. Your choices are shown here:

	I	V^7	
Key of G:	G	D^7	(a whole step lower)
Key of A:	A	E^7	(as written for guitar)
Key of B^b:	B^b	F^7	(a half-step higher)

Play the Autoharp and sing the song in both keys to determine which would be most comfortable for your voice. The song begins on the fifth step of the scale *sol, below the tonic (do),* so take care to get started on the right pitch within the key you choose.

You may also wish to change the key of a song to provide a more comfortable range for singing. For example, the melody of "Silent Night" (Example 6.7) has a wide range, and for some voices a lower key might be preferable. To change the key follow these procedures:

1. Determine the key in which the song is written (C) and the scale step on which the melody begins (G, which is *sol,* or *5*).

2. Judge whether transposition is really necessary; note the lowest tone (C) and the highest tone (F) in the melody. Might both be moved downward and still remain within acceptable limits? If so, will one half-step or a whole step lower better meet the singing requirements of the class? If moved down a whole step, the lowest note in the melody of "Silent Night" will be B^b and the highest E^b; both are sung only once, so this would be a better range for average voices. The key of B^b is available on the Autoharp. (If guitar accompaniment is used, the key of A would be easy to play and probably not too low for comfortable singing.)

3. Having decided what transposition is necessary, sound the new tonic chord and find the tonic note *(do or 1)* within that chord. This becomes the new home tone. All the notes in the song retain their original numbers or syllable names. C was the original key note and B^b, a whole step lower, is the new key-note *(do or 1)*. Within the new key, the first tone of the song remains *so (5):*

do   so   Si - lent night, ...

Although "Silent Night" is high in the key of C, it often appears in that key because it is easier to play on melody instruments. Also, when a song has a harmonizing part as this does, those who cannot sing the melody comfortably have the option of singing the lower part.

Pitch a new song lower or higher if the change seems justifiable, but then listen to discover whether the new range is suitable for the singers. If so, the song should thereafter be sung in that key. At Level III children can gain understanding about voice range and keys by discussing and experimenting to determine the key most appropriate to their voices.

Playing the Guitar

The guitar is an excellent, authentic accompanying instrument for many folk songs, especially in the United States and Latin America. It is a very useful accompanying instrument for elementary classroom singing, and some sixth graders who have learned the basic principles of chording on the Autoharp and keyboard instruments should be encouraged to begin learning to play the guitar.

The guitar to use in the elementary classroom is the classical guitar, which has a round soundhole, a flat top, and nylon strings. The diagram in Example 6.8 shows details of such a guitar. The flat-top guitar with a round soundhole and steel strings can also be used; the neck is narrower, and the steel strings may create more sore fingers for the novice player, but the instrument is useful with a wider variety of folk music. The tuning for both instruments is the same and is shown below.

EXAMPLE 6.8

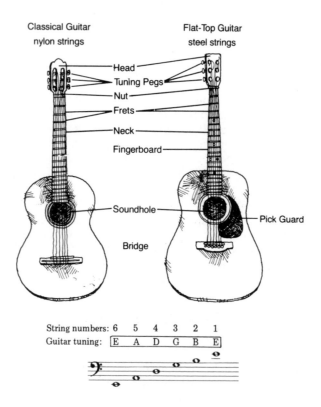

The baritone ukulele has four strings, tuned to the same pitches as the four upper strings on the guitar. It is smaller and easier to play than the guitar, but has more resonance and depth of tone than the soprano ukulele. The soprano uke is more of a novelty than a legitimate musical instrument. If you would like to learn a chording instrument a little less challenging than the guitar, consider the baritone uke.

As with the Autoharp, you should begin to play the guitar or baritone uke by learning some accompaniments utilizing one or two chords. The chords in the common keys that you use to learn to play the Autoharp or piano are not the easiest chords to play on the guitar. Even though you have great motivation for playing the guitar, do not dampen your enthusiasm by struggling too early with the more difficult chords.

The diagrams for chord fingerings on the guitar are shown in the chart in Example 6.9. The X-mark above a string in any diagram means that the string should not be sounded when that chord is played. A string having no finger number should be allowed to vibrate in its entire length when that chord is sounded.

EXAMPLE 6.9
GUITAR CHORD CHART

Numbering of left hand fingers in diagram

In order to use the easier guitar chords you will frequently need to transpose songs. This chart should help you do that, but when deciding which key to use, you should consider the range of the songs, discussed in Chapter 7 (pp. 229-231). For the beginner, the tonic (I) and the dominant-seventh (V^7) are the basic chords in each key in both major and minor. The tonic and dominant-seventh chord fingerings are easiest in the major keys of A and D. In Example 6.9 the diagrams for the minor chords on the right side of the chart are labeled with chord numbers for both the major key and the relative minor key that has the same key signature. These chords are used for minor keys, but the minor chords also are often used within the major key as the double chord numbers show at the top of the diagram.

When beginning to play the guitar, use songs that require only one chord, so that the left-hand fingers can learn to hold the strings down firmly while the right hand establishes a rhythmic strum. E minor is an easy chord to finger and can be used as an accompaniment throughout the old English round "Hey! Ho! Anybody Home?" (Example 6.10).

EXAMPLE 6.10

HEY! HO! ANYBODY HOME?
Old English Round

This song is in $\frac{2}{4}$ meter and, when you use one chord to accompany it, you should strum only on the first beat of each measure. Use your thumb to strum from the low-sounding to the high-sounding strings in a smooth, regular movment.

Any time you sing with an instrument, you must find the starting pitch in the key used. (The procedure was discussed in Chapter 5 and, in relation to the Autoharp, in this chapter.) In working with the guitar, you need to know the names of the strings and how to calculate the pitch of a string when it is pressed down in a finger pattern for a chord. Stopping the string at each successively higher fret on the guitar raises the pitch by a half-step. Sing "Hey! Ho! Anybody Home?" first in the key of E minor, and then in the key of D minor; observe on the following diagram how transposition affects the starting pitch and the range of the song. The arrow below the diagram shows the string that will sound the starting pitch in each key when the fingers are in place. In the key of E minor, the starting pitch, E, is the highest string with no fingers. For the key of D minor, note that the next-to-highest-sounding string on the guitar is B. When the finger stops the string at the third fret, the pitch is three half-steps higher, or D, the new starting pitch. Sing the first word of the song ("Hey!") on D as you strum the chord.

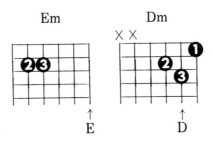

The range of this song, in E minor, is just an octave, B to B. In the key of D minor, it will be a whole step lower, with a range from A to A. Can you hear and feel a difference as you sing it? Which key seems most comfortable to you? What key do you think would be most appropriate for children?

"Are You Sleeping?" (Example 5.3) is a very familiar round that can be accompanied throughout by the D major chord. Note that the diagram for this chord gives the lowest string an x-mark, indicating that it should not be sounded. When singing this round with a one-chord accompaniment, strum on every other beat:

When two chords are needed in a song, you will have to practice moving your fingers from one chord position to the other smoothly without breaking the rhythm of the song. The A major chord does not appear on the Autoharp, but it is one of the easier chords to finger on the guitar. "Hush, Little Baby" (Example 6.4), "Hey, Lollee!" (Example 6.3), and "I Ride an Old Paint" can be accompanied by the A major and E^7 chords.

EXAMPLE 6.11

I RIDE AN OLD PAINT

Traditional Cowboy Song
Adapted by B. R. S. and D. S.

With a swing

I ride an old paint,___ I lead an old Dan,___ I'm

goin' to Mon - tan' for to throw the hoo - li - han, They

feed in the cool - ies, they wat - er in the draw. Their

tails are all mat - ted, their backs are all raw. Ride a -

round, lit - tle do - gies, ride a - round___ them slow, for the

fier - y and snuf - fy are rar - in' to go.

In each case you will need to find the correct starting pitch within the first chord. "I Ride an Old Paint" begins on E, the highest-sounding string on the guitar.

The tonic and dominant-seventh chords for D major (D and A^7) are reasonably easy to play on the guitar. "Water Come to Me Eye" (Example 6.24) and "Paw-Paw Patch" (Example 6.19) appear in the key of D, and "Shoo, Fly" (Example 3.9) can be transposed to this key.

The guitar fingering for the G major chord is a little less convenient, but with some practice you can learn to play songs using the tonic (G) and the dominant-seventh (D^7) in this key. "Polly Wolly Doodle" (Example 4.19) and "Down in the Valley" (Example 6.2) can be sung in the key of G.

A capo is a plastic-covered metal bar that is clamped over the guitar strings so that the vibrating length of the string is shortened and the pitch is raised. To give you an idea of the function of the capo, look at the relationship of the key of A and the key of C. Chords in the key of A are relatively easy to play on the guitar. Key of C chords are more difficult. If you wish to raise the pitch of the song from A to C, or play the accompaniment with Autoharpists, you could either use fingerings for the key of C or use fingerings for the key of A combined with the capo, placed as shown in Example 6.12.

EXAMPLE 6.12

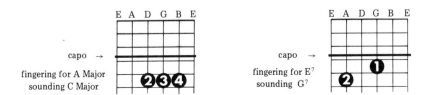

The note C is three half-steps higher than A. Each fret on the guitar represents a distance of one half-step; when the capo is placed behind the third fret, it stops the strings at that point, rather than at the end of the fingerboard. This raises the pitch of all the strings by three half-steps. You can therefore use fingerings for the key of A (placed three frets above the normal position), and this will give the actual pitches of chords in the key of C.

Although you should learn to use the capo fairly soon so that the fingerings you know can be used to play in more than one key, you should understand why many guitarists prefer not to use the capo. The capo shortens the string and the tone does not sound as resonant as the full-length string. The more open, full-length strings the player uses, the richer the tone that the guitar produces. For this reason it is best to learn as many separate chord fingerings as seems practical.

The scope of this book does not permit a detailed introduction to the guitar, but here are a few songs, utilizing the basic chords shown on page 193, that can be used as introductory material. The name of the first chord and the starting pitch within that scale is shown here; in some cases the key shown here is different from that in which the song is printed elsewhere in this book.

"Jack Be Nimble" $\frac{6}{8}$ C–5 (Example 4.6)

"Old House" $\frac{2}{4}$ Em–1 (Example 3.2)

"Row, Row, Row Your Boat" $\frac{6}{8}$ D–1 (Example 4.3)

"Scotland's Burning" $\frac{2}{4}$ A–5, (NDinM IV-155)

"A Ram Sam Sam" $\frac{4}{4}$ G–5, (Example 3.11)

"Chickama Craney Crow" $\frac{2}{4}$ D–1 (Example 4.2)

"Hey, Lollee!" D–5 (Example 6.3)

"Hokey Pokey" $\frac{4}{4}$ A–5, (Example 3.8)

The Keyboard Instruments

After children become acquainted with chords through using the Autoharp with its automatic chording mechanism, they can move on successfully to building chords on other instruments. The resonator bells with their adjustable tone bars are especially useful, but the piano can be used also.

To build chords on resonator bells, the children must know the letter names of the notes in each chord. This is called spelling the chord. The key signature must be taken into account; flats and sharps must be used to alter the names of the chord notes as necessary. Accompanying songs with harmonic chording thus provides motivation to learn the names of the lines and spaces of the staff and the key signatures (if these have not previously been learned). A chart like that shown in Example 6.5 can help fifth and sixth grade pupils see the relationships between the primary chords in the keys of C, D, F, and G, the keys they will work with most often.

Because the piano and the chromatic bells are fixed-scale instruments, children must know the positions of the tones in the chord as well as their names. On the piano certain arrangements of the tones in the chords make it easier to change from one chord to another. To play consecutive tonic and dominant seventh chords for "Down in the Valley" (Example 6.2), the beginning pianist would use the following placement of notes for the left hand. Notice that the player needs to move two fingers only one half-step in order to change from one chord to another:

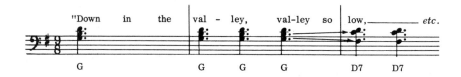

Example 6.13 shows positions of tones in chords in the keys of C, F, and G. In a simplified approach to piano chording, the chord tones shown there have the same fingering and relative position in every key. The drawing of the left hand shows the finger numbers as used in playing these chords.

EXAMPLE 6.13

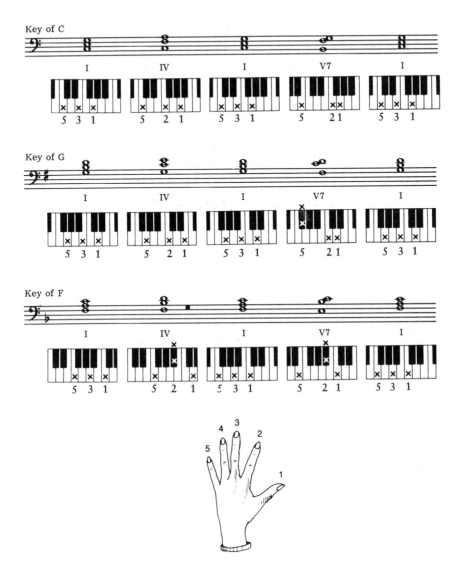

When the arrangement of the chords shown in Example 6.13 is used, you can change the accompaniment by changing the rhythm used in the chords. One of the patterns in Example 6.14 might be a more appropriate accompaniment than a simple block chord. Teachers and children who have some basic skill at the keyboard can learn to improvise accompaniments by using these chord positions and rhythms.

EXAMPLE 6.14

In this book the following songs in the key of F would allow you to try out chorded accompaniments using these different rhythms:

a. ($\frac{2}{4}$) "Love Somebody," Example 7.9 (uses I, V^7)

b. ($\frac{2}{4}$) "Shoo, Fly," Example 3.9 (uses I, V^7)

c. ($\frac{6}{8}$) "Night Herding Song," Example 4.17 (uses I, IV, V^7)

d. ($\frac{3}{4}$) "We Wish You a Merry Christmas," Example 7.5 (uses I, IV, V^7)

EXPERIENCES AT LEVEL I

In the kindergarten, first, and second grades, some general experiences with harmony can provide a readiness for more specific learning and skills to be developed at Levels II and III. The song accompaniments (Autoharp, guitar, or piano) you are able to provide will give these children opportunities to hear harmony, and you can direct their attention to the sound of harmony in several ways.

At Level I children can play simple accompaniments by strumming the Autoharp and playing a few selected tones on bell instruments. Although timbre, rhythm, and melody are the musical concepts to which principal attention is directed at this level, it is possible to develop a readiness for experiences with harmony.

Experiencing Harmony in Accompaniments

Throughout the country, people sing at home and in community gatherings. To accompany this informal singing, various instruments are used—guitar, banjo, or ukulele, as well as piano. The strumming instruments make a very appropriate accompaniment for folk songs, and song books designed for school use show chord markings that will help you provide such accompaniments. Different styles of strumming should be used, depending on the kind of song being accompanied. Strumming styles heard on recordings made by Burl Ives, Sam Hinton, and Pete Seeger are good examples.

The piano should be used as an enrichment rather than as a constant accompaniment to classroom singing. Folk and popular songs may appropriately be accompanied by broken chords on the piano, as shown earlier in this chapter. The manner of playing should support rather than cover up the voices. The left hand should play near the middle of the keyboard with a light, crisp touch for lively numbers and a legato touch for smooth flowing songs. Since each song should be expressive in its own way, the accompaniment should help to establish the appropriate mood and feeling. Accompaniment books for the basic music texts show piano parts that are varied and not difficult. If you don't play the piano, guitar, or other chording instrument, you will surely be able to find someone in the community who can come once or twice a month to play for group singing, using songs the children have previously learned in class.

First and second grade children can begin to hear the distinctive quality of the tonic and dominant-seventh chords. Sing and play the two-chord song "Hush, Little Baby" (Example 6.4), and notice the unfinished quality when you stop at the end of the first phrase (when the C^7 chord occurs in the accompaniment). The song really can't end there, but must go on to the conclusion of the second phrase, when the tonic or "home" chord, F, is used. The same effect is evident at the end of the second phrase of "When the Saints Go Marching In" (Example 3.12). Harmonically the song is quite unfinished at the second "marching in"; but if you pause at that point as though you intended to stop, you will notice that the harmony of the G^7 chord pushes the song on. Enact these harmonic effects by moving your hands apart at the end of the phrase on the cadence involving the dominant-seventh chord (a "half cadence"), and bringing the palms of the hands together in a closed position for the "full" cadence on the tonic chord.

Instructional Objectives: To focus the attention of the children on cadential harmony so that they hear the inconclusive quality of a cadence on a dominant-seventh chord (half cadence) and the finality of a cadence on the tonic (full cadence).

Behaviors providing evidence that these instructional objectives have been achieved: The children will

   □ demonstrate their awareness of these two different kinds of cadence by gestures indicating incompleteness or finality, when listening to a song that has not previously been approached in this way (e.g., "We Wish You a Merry Christmas," Example 7.5)

In a general way, direct the children's attention to accompaniments provided on song recordings, and help broaden their awareness of sounds that support their singing. Keep in mind the fact that before the age of seven, children may not be ready to perceive more than one dimension of music. If their attention is focused on the melody, they may not be able to notice the harmony at the same time. As a readiness procedure, you can direct attention to the two factors at different times, in order to initiate an awareness of musical accompaniment and qualities of harmony.

Exploring the Autoharp

Children of these ages like to strum the Autoharp; you will find they respond to the different quality of sound created by the different chords. The impact of the total sound, not the divisible components of the chord sound, is what they hear. It is essential that any instrument be touched and handled with care, and children who can be taught to respect the instrument can be allowed to explore its sound-making potential on their own.

If the Autoharp is available in the "music corner," individuals or small groups can strum the chords, listen, and compare the sounds. You can help shape their activity and observations by occasionally playing in succession two chords with different structures built on the same pitch, such as G major and G minor, or G^7, and asking if the chords are the same or different. If the children are to notice the quality of sound associated with the major or minor structures, it is important to limit the variables in this exercise or "game" by working with chords built on the same pitch. Also, try to use the same range of tones, and the same loudness, for if one chord is played in the high register and one in the low register, or one is loud and one soft, the "difference" the child hears may be one of these variables rather than the quality of sound resulting from the structure of the chords themselves.

If two Autoharps are available, and accurately tuned to the same standard of pitch, you can have a child play a chord on one instrument, then you can play the same or a different chord on the other instrument for the children to evaluate as the same or different. In this activity the cues for judgment of "same" or "different" should be aural rather than visual; i.e., the child who sees that different chord bars are depressed does not really need to listen; the main objective in this activity is to develop aural discrimination.

Instructional Objectives: To direct the children's attention to the harmonic sound of two different chords built on the same pitch (e.g., G major and G minor), and to teach them to identify two consecutively different chords as opposed to two consecutive chords that are the same.

Behaviors providing evidence that these instructional objectives have been achieved: The children will

□ correctly identify as "the same" or "different" two chords built on the same pitch, played consecutively (at the same loudness and in the same register) on the autoharp (piano or guitar)

You will need to show the children how to hold the chord bars down firmly so that a clear chord sound is produced, and you should provide a felt or leather pick so the sound they produce is pleasant to the ear. (Children's fingernails are rarely well enough developed to allow them to strum the Autoharp without the benefit of a pick.) Children at this level can learn to strum the Autoharp with a steady stroke to accompany a song, but it may be necessary for you to change the chord at the proper time. Let the children take turns being the "strummer" for songs the class sings with Autoharp accompaniment.

Put the Autoharp on a wooden table top and notice how the resonance of the wood amplifies the sound. When the children touch the table top lightly and feel the vibrations transmitted from the Autoharp, this can serve as an elementary lesson in the science of sound.

Singing and Playing in Two Parts

When a class of seven-year-olds has developed the ability to sing in tune with some independence, you can introduce simple two-part rounds such as "Are You Sleeping?" (Example 5.3) or "Row, Row, Row Your Boat" (Example 4.3). It is essential that the children be able to sing the song freely and accurately in unison (i.e., all together on a single tone or melody) before it is attempted as a round. As an introduction to round-singing, after the children know the song, you might sing one part as the children sing the other part and listen to the combined effect.

Songs that relate to one chord throughout can be accompanied by a "drone bass": two tones (tonic and dominant) played simultaneously. If the children have learned to keep a steady beat with rhythm sticks or drum, you may wish to have them supply a drone accompaniment for a pentatonic song. "Jack Be Nimble" is a lively song that could have the root and the fifth steps of the scale (C and G) sounded as a drone, as shown in Example 6.15.

EXAMPLE 6.15

JACK BE NIMBLE

The drone might be sounded four times before the singing begins, both to provide an introduction and to help make the children more aware of the accompaniment for the song. If the song is sung in the key of D, the Autoharp could be used to sound the drone: simultaneously depress the chord bars for D Major and D Minor as you strum. The combination of the major and minor chord bars eliminates the third in each chord.

Instructional Objectives: To provide children early experience hearing, singing with, and playing an accompaniment part that requires maintaining a reliable, steady beat.

Behaviors providing evidence that these instructional objectives have been achieved: The children will

☐ individually play, on two bars of an adjustable tuned instrument, a compatible drone bass in a steady beat while the class sings a familiar pentatonic or one-chord diatonic song

Other pentatonic songs that can be harmonized with a drone are:

"Bell Horses" (Example 5.8) C and G

"Chatter with the Angels" (Example 5.10) F and C

"Old MacDonald" (**SpM II-167**) G and D

"Ring Around a Rosy" (Example 5.9) C and G

The round "Are You Sleeping?" (Example 5.3) can be accompanied by repeatedly playing the last phrase as an introduction, an ostinato throughout the song, and as a coda.

EXAMPLE 6.16

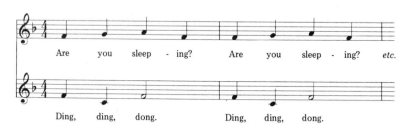

First use the resonator bells to play the pattern only when it occurs in the song. Then sing the pattern several times, being careful to give two beats to the half note at the end of the pattern. After that, the class can sing the song in unison while one or two individuals play the bell part as an ostinato.

The following and other rounds can be sung as unison songs in the key of C, or as rounds if the class is able to maintain independent parts, while a bell instrument is used to play an ostinato:

☐ "Little Tom Tinker"—Play high C followed by G in the pattern heard in the song on the word "ma-a."

◻ "Row, Row, Row Your Boat"—Play an alternating high and low C in a rhythm to fit the song.

You will find many more ideas for simple instrumental parts in the basic music series books at this level. Because these two-part activities require a certain amount of independence in playing within an established tempo and rhythm, they are best undertaken with mature six- or seven-year-old children.

EXPERIENCES AT LEVEL II

Children between the ages of seven and nine can be much more involved with harmony, due to their growing independence in singing and playing instruments. They can learn to play two- and three-chord song accompaniments on the Autoharp and to combine various melody instruments to create interesting harmonic effects. Rhythmic rhymes, chants, and pentatonic songs can be combined with drone and ostinato accompaniments, using adjustable instruments in ways recommended by the Carl Orff methodology. Various kinds of easy two-part singing can be introduced at this level. The preliminary experiences with harmony recommended for Level I can also be beneficial for these children if they have had no previous orientation to harmony.

Playing the Autoharp

Eight- or nine-year-old children can learn to play two- and three-chord Autoharp accompaniments with some proficiency. When teaching a class of children to play the Autoharp, demonstrate the procedures described earlier in this chapter. Select familiar rhythmic songs that can be accompanied by only two chords. Approach accompanying both by ear ("When do we have to change the chord in order to have it sound right with the melody we are singing?") and by chord indications in the book. Most school music books provide chord markings over the songs, and it is relatively easy to strum and change chords at the point where a new chord letter appears.

There is considerable variety among children's songs. The musical differences should be reflected in the Autoharp accompaniments. "A Ram Sam Sam" (Example 3.11) and "Paw-Paw Patch" (Example 6.19) should be played with a brisk stroke, producing a block chord effect. "Hush, Little Baby" (Example 6.4) should be accompanied by a gentle harp-like strum. The children can learn to hear the different quality of the minor chord, as used in "Simple Simon" (Example 5.5), and should learn to apply the term "minor" to chords of that type. Even though it is in a minor key, "Simple Simon" should be sung and played in a sprightly manner. "Minor" should not always be equated with "sad," and certainly this is not a sad song.

If only one or two Autoharps are available in the classroom, it is helpful to provide each child with a paper or tagboard mockup of the Autoharp chord mechanism, as shown in Example 6.1. The children then can see the relationship of the various chord bars and practice the necessary finger movement as they "strum" the imaginary instrument in preparation for taking their turn to play for the class. Provide time and place for individuals to practice on the instrument at other hours during the day.

In the early stages of learning to play, before two-hand coordination is established, one child can press the bars with the left hand and set up the necessary chords while another strokes the strings in the appropriate rhythm. Be sure the children understand the two functions of the accompaniment: to provide the key and harmony, and to establish the tempo and meter for the song.

With some guidance, children who learn to play the Autoharp can acquire musical concepts of these kinds:

1. the need for chord changes in accompanying a melody
2. the different musical sound of tonic, subdominant, and dominant-seventh chords within a key
3. the need to use a particular key to accommodate voice range
4. the need to tune voices or instruments to the key and chords used in a particular song
5. the need to coordinate the tempo and rhythm of the accompaniment with the singing
6. the musical effects of different styles of strumming
7. the quality of the minor key and chords

Children acquire this information through musical experiences, timely demonstration, and comments by the teacher, rather than through lecture or long explanations. If a teacher fails to pass along an understanding of what is being done, the process of learning to play the Autoharp can be largely a mechanical, rote acquisition of a skill. On the other hand, do not insist that all technical barriers be hurdled before the children take part in the pleasurable activity of playing. A fine balance in these matters will keep the children interested and at the same time develop concepts that will enable them to understand what they are doing musically.

Singing and Hearing Harmonizing Parts

Early experiences singing in harmony are provided by rounds, which can be sung in two or more parts, depending on the maturity and musical experience of the singers. After the melody has been learned in unison, the round may be sung in two parts. Encourage the children to listen to the blend of the two parts as they sing. Singing in harmony requires some concentration, but it is not necessary to plug the ears with the fingers in order to stay on one's part.

"White Coral Bells" is an especially beautiful English round to be sung in two parts. Notice the contrary movement of the two phrases; when sung as a round, the voices cross each other in an interesting way as shown in Example 6.18.

EXAMPLE 6.17

WHITE CORAL BELLS
English Round

Smoothly

1. White cor - al bells up - on a slen - der stalk,
2. Oh, don't you wish that you could hear them ring?

Lil - ies of the val - ley deck my gar - den walk.
That will hap - pen on - ly when the fair - ies sing.

As the song is sung in two parts, have the individuals singing each part enact the shape of the melody in the air with hand levels. Later, ask them to draw a contoured line showing this melodic movement.

EXAMPLE 6.18

The melody of "White Coral Bells" shown in a contour line.

As separate phrases: When sung simultaneously:

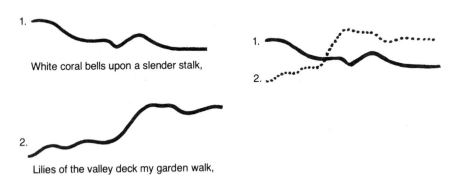

1.

White coral bells upon a slender stalk,

1.

2.

2.

Lilies of the valley deck my garden walk,

Compare this with other rounds such as "Are You Sleeping?" (Example 5.3), in which the combined effect is parallel thirds when the second voice joins the first at the end of the first phrase.

Instructional Objectives: To give children experience singing two-part rounds, and to develop their ability to sing one melody line, yet simultaneously be aware of the harmony created by the second part.

Behaviors providing evidence that these instructional objectives have been achieved: The children will

☐ successfully sing, in a group, a two-part round in tune and in the proper tempo and rhythm

☐ enact with hand levels the melody line they are singing and acknowledge the similar or different contour simultaneously shown in the other part

☐ draw contour lines of two parts of a round not previously treated in this manner, and make valid observations as to the relationship of the two parts

It is essential that the group know the melody well and be secure in singing it in unison before it is attempted as a round. Rounds are short and therefore are usually sung through twice or three times. To get a round started, you must listen as the first group sings and then bring the second group in on the correct pitch and on the right beat, so that the harmony between the two parts will be realized. Many rounds can be sung in three or four parts, creating a rich chord structure and texture; but the use of multiple parts should be undertaken only when the children have developed independence in singing and the ability to hear the more complex texture.

As a general rule rounds are not sung with a chorded accompaniment because the voices create the harmony. In a round like "White Coral Bells" you want to be able to hear the counterpoint between the two voices moving in opposite directions. Other rounds used as unison songs at Level I, but enjoyed as rounds by third and fourth graders, include:

"A Ram Sam Sam" (Example 3.11)   "Kookaburra" (ExM IV-11)
"Canoe Song" (Example 5.26)   "Tender Shepherd" (SBM IV-165)
"Die Musici" (NDinM IV-153)

Both the round and the canon feature strict imitation of a melody, starting at different points. A round is a "circle canon" in that the parts repeat from the beginning as many times as desired. Succeeding voices enter when the preceding voice reaches the end of the first phrase, and all parts stop together at the end of an assigned phrase. In a canon, imitation of one voice by another can be at the same or different pitch levels; the voices can enter in quick succession, and the end of the composition is written so that it provides for a satisfactory cadence without repeating the composition. "Farewell to the Old Year" (Example 4.15) is a canon.

Two different songs that have the same underlying harmony can be sung simultaneously as "partner songs." A simple example can be observed when "Paw-Paw Patch" (Example 6.19) and "Sandy Land" (Example 4.9) are sung simultaneously in the key of F.

EXAMPLE 6.19

PAW-PAW PATCH
American Singing Game

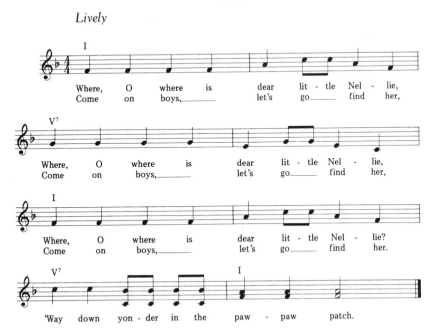

Lively

Where, O where is dear lit - tle Nel - lie,
Come on boys,_____ let's go_____ find her,

Where, O where is dear lit - tle Nel - lie,
Come on boys,_____ let's go_____ find her,

Where, O where is dear lit - tle Nel - lie?
Come on boys,_____ let's go_____ find her.

'Way down yon - der in the paw - paw patch.

In addition to creating compatible harmony throughout, "partner songs" can have rhythms that complement each other. Notice, also, the melodic contrast in "Sandy Land" and "Paw-Paw Patch"; when the melody of one moves upward or downward, the other has repeated notes. "The Angel Band" and "Swing Low, Sweet Chariot" are two pentatonic songs that can be used as "partner" songs (**NDinM IV-110**). Other examples will be found in *Partner Songs* and *More Partner Songs*.[3] When the individual songs are well known, it is fairly easy to combine them as an interesting experience in two-part singing.

Early experience singing in harmony can come in songs with simple two-part endings. The children should first hear the teacher sing the harmony part as they sing the melody, then a few of the children should join on the harmony part. Try "Paw-Paw Patch" and "Sing Your Way Home" (Example 4.10) and work out the easy two-part endings that bring these songs to a close. The musical objective of all part-singing is to learn to sing one part and at the same time be aware of the harmony that the two parts create.

Playing Root Tones, Drones, and Ostinati

In addition to using the Autoharp or guitar to accompany simple chorded songs, you can play single tones on bell instruments. For example, each time the G chord is needed in the harmony, just play that note (G, which is the root of the chord), and play the note D when the D^7 chord is indicated; sound a tone on each beat in the measure. If you are using an instrument with a long-lasting tone, such as the metallophone, it may be enough to play on the first beat of each measure.

"Roll Over" (Example 5.14) has a melody that relates to one chord all the way through. Provide an accompaniment for it by playing a "drone bass" as shown in Example 6.20.

EXAMPLE 6.20

There were three in the bed and the lit - tle one said, *etc.*

or

You could use the same drone for "Are You Sleeping?" (Example 5.3) because the tonic chord harmonizes the first and third beats throughout.

Songs based on the pentatonic scale are useful for early experience in creating accompaniment parts—almost any combination of the five tones makes an acceptable sound, and improvisation can go on without a knowledge of harmony. The Orff[4] approach to music education makes extensive use of the pentatonic scale for early improvisation. The parts shown in Example 6.21 can be used as an accompaniment for "Farewell to the Old Year" (Example 4.15) and are examples of ways tuned instruments can be used with pentatonic songs. The first part, a drone bass, could be played pizzicato on the two lower open strings of the cello, baritone uke, or on the guitar re-tuned to those pitches. The second part is a very simple ostinato that can be played on the soprano xylophone or resonator bells. The third part, played on the accent, reinforces the tonic pitch and could be played on a tuned drum. The fourth part adds rhythmic life to the ensemble and would sound well on the alto xylophone. Instrumental parts might enter in the order in which they are numbered, two measures apart, to establish an introduction before the singing begins, and could continue throughout the song.

EXAMPLE 6.21

Such an ensemble might begin with one or two instruments, and others could be added as the children become more capable in playing parts independently.

Instructional Objectives: To provide an opportunity for children to create an ensemble with multiple parts, to develop skill in playing a single line with rhythmic accuracy in an ensemble, and to broaden their hearing to include a more complex musical texture.

Behaviors providing evidence that these instructional objectives have been achieved: The children will

☐ sing and play "Farewell to the Old Year," as described, with two to four accompanying parts (as shown, or adapted to meet the tastes and needs of the group)

☐ play their part with rhythmic accuracy and at a dynamic level compatible with the ensemble

"Land of the Silver Birch" (Example 6.22) is a pentatonic song with B as a tonal center.

EXAMPLE 6.22

LAND OF THE SILVER BIRCH
Canadian Folk Song

Land of the sil - ver birch, home of the bea - ver

Where still the might - y moose wan - ders at will,

Blue lake and rock - y shore, I will re - turn once more.

Boom de de boom boom, Boom de de boom boom, Boom de de boom boom,

Boom_____ boom boom._____

From *Folk Songs of Canada* by Edith Fowke and Richard Johnston, 1954. Waterloo Music Company Ltd., Waterloo, Ontario. Reprinted by permission.

Easy accompanying parts can be created as follows: Play B and F♯ simultaneously on the first beat of each measure to create a drone. If you are fortunate enough to have tunable drums, you will find the drum's tone color excellent for this Canadian Indian song.

Bracketed within this song you will find two melodic motifs that can be played repeatedly as accompanying ostinati. Play either one of the patterns in Example 6.23 on a xylophone or bell instrument while the class sings the song.

EXAMPLE 6.23

xylophone:

glockenspiel:

tuned drums:

Note that in this example the ostinati are taken from the song itself. If adjustable instruments are used, take off all tone bars marked C and G, and substitute F# for F; you will then have the pentatonic scale used in "Land of the Silver Birch." Other ostinato patterns can be improvised and played, either above or below the melody, depending upon the tone quality and range of the instruments used.

At this level children can begin to sing rounds effectively and can add instrumental parts to the round. "Quarters and Dimes" (Example 5.15) offers several possibilities. Notice that there are four phrases, each two measures long and harmonized by a repeated use of the tonic and dominant-seventh chords. After the song has been learned in unison, undertake any one or some combination of the following activities:

1. Sing as a two-part round with the second group entering when the first voices start measure five.
2. Play the first two measures repeatedly on a bell instrument as an introduction, as an ostinato throughout the song, and as a coda.
3. Play a deep-toned bell instrument on the fifth of the scale (C) throughout the song.
4. Play any two-measure phrase in the song repeatedly on a bell instrument as an accompaniment for the voices singing in unison or in two parts.

This song is relatively easy, so it may be possible to combine several parts; but keep the performance within the capabilities of the class. Rounds are based on a simple chord progression that repeats in each phrase. Any harmony parts used must take the underlying harmony into consideration. You cannot use ostinato patterns as freely with rounds as with pentatonic songs.

Two important objectives govern any combination of voices or instruments that are used:

1. Players and singer must keep the beat steady, so that all the parts sound precisely together.
2. Participants should be able to hear the harmony that is created by any combination of parts sounded simultaneously.

Various tuned, as well as percussion, instruments can be used in such vocal–instrumental ensembles.

Musical Composition for Ensembles

Preliminary experiences in creative writing for ensemble performance can include the use of rhythm instruments for accompaniments and for dramatic effects (Chapter 4) and creating melodies for rhyme and chants (Chapter 5). The recording *Music for Children,*[5] made by children's classes trained in the method developed by Carl Orff and Gunild Keetman, provides excellent examples of ensemble performance based on rhythmic speech and simple use of melody instruments. On side 1 of that recording you will find the following techniques used in creating short musical settings for rhymes and chants:

- ☐ a two-tone xylophone ostinato
- ☐ an instrumental introduction and coda
- ☐ children's voices in a two-tone chant
- ☐ contrast between solo voices and voices in a group
- ☐ contrast of accompanied and unaccompanied voices
- ☐ use of contrasting vocal color for expressive effect
- ☐ drone accompaniment
- ☐ contrast of staccato and legato quality in words
- ☐ a three-tone children's chant
- ☐ use of chant at a higher level for climactic effect
- ☐ variety in percussive accompaniment (hand-clapping, rhythm instruments)
- ☐ contrast of instrumental timbres (xylophones versus glockenspiel)
- ☐ dynamic contrast in voices and instruments

After listening to that record and perhaps re-creating some of the examples to make sure you understand the techniques, form a small group and develop an expressive arrangement based on the following or some other rhyme or poem:

GOING BAREFOOT[6]

by Aileen Fisher

Bees in trees,
ants on plants,
frogs in bogs,
cats on mats,
wear feet bare.

They wear them late
and they wear them soon,
they don't have to wait
for a day in June
to go barefoot.

Make a diagram to show the musical events in your creative ensemble. If you use tuned instruments as a drone or in ostinato patterns, show what these are and where they begin in your composition. Make a tape recording so you can listen objectively to your work and share it with others.

Instructional Objectives: To provide an opportunity for children to express themselves creatively, and to combine previously learned vocal and instrumental techniques in a simple yet satisfying musical composition.

Behaviors providing evidence that these instructional objectives have been achieved: The children will

☐ create an original composition and record it for objective listening and sharing

□ express satisfaction with their composition's expressiveness, and offer constructive suggestions to improve it

□ identify at least three techniques that they used to create its expressive effect

Carl Orff described music that is combined with movement, dance, and speech as "elemental music." He said it is "pre-intellectual" and that it is the appropriate approach to music for children. The article "The Schulwerk—Its Origin and Aims"[7] will give you some orientation for this work. Principles of the Orff method are utilized with materials in the basic music series, and you will find additional information in the books[8] cited at the end of this chapter.

EXPERIENCES AT LEVEL III

All the activities and learnings described for Level II can be applied at Level III if the children have had no comparable experiences. Song materials compatible with the interests and tastes of nine- to eleven-year-olds should be used, of course. Children at this level can learn to play two- and three-chord songs on the Autoharp, and some begin to play the guitar.

As children combine melody instruments to create harmony, they learn to build chords in common keys and to relate this information to Autoharp accompaniments they worked with earlier. Creative melody writing, described in Chapter 5, can be expanded into creative ensemble work with instruments of various kinds.

The Guitar in Classroom Music

Fifth and sixth graders who have learned the basic principles of chording on the Autoharp and keyboard instruments have good potential for learning to play the guitar (or baritone uke). Information and procedures supplied earlier in this chapter will provide you with the necessary approach. If several children are interested in learning the instrument, a special class might be set up. *Guitar in the Classroom*[9] by Timmerman and Griffith is a good book to use for such a class.

Usually a few children who own a guitar have already learned to finger a few chords. You may have to help them tune the guitar, but by starting with one- and two-chord songs, you can make it possible for them to accompany the singing class. The SILVER BURDETT MUSIC series books for grades five and six each have a "satellite" section, "Playing the Guitar," which is addressed to students. There, boys and girls will find pictures and diagrams of finger positions, along with a useful repertoire of songs to play. With some time to experiment on their own, and a little guidance, they should become quite proficient with some basic chords and playing techniques.

Various simplified fingerings are often used by inexperienced players. Although these are helpful in the beginning stages, chords that use only three or four strings have a thin, less satisfactory sound. For this reason it is worth the effort for children to learn as soon as possible to play fuller chords that use more strings.

Begin with a one-chord round such as "Hey! Ho! Anybody Home?" and "Are You Sleeping?" as described on pages 194 and 195. Before they can provide an accompaniment for singing, the guitar players will need to (1) find the starting pitch for each song they learn to play, and (2) maintain a steady strum throughout the song.

The Jamaican folk song "Water Come to Me Eye" is a two-chord song well liked by children at this level. It is quite easy to play on the guitar, because its chord changes are very regular.

EXAMPLE 6.24

WATER COME TO ME EYE
Jamaican Folk Song
Words Adapted

2. Don't know why you went away, *etc.*
   When you comin' back to stay? *etc. Refrain.*

3. Time go slow when love is past, *etc.*
   When you come back, time go fast, *etc. Refrain.*

4. Listen 'cause I'm callin' you, *etc.*
   And my heart is callin' too, *etc. Refrain.*

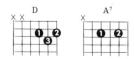

If the children have a little skill on the guitar, they might use a thumb pluck *(T)* on the tonic (D) and dominant (A) tones alternately with an upward strum of the fingers *(s)* while playing the D chord. Pluck the root (A) and the fifth (E) while playing the A^7 chord. Repeat this strumming pattern through the song:

D major A^7 D major

$\frac{4}{4}$ D   A | D   A | A   E | D   A
    T *s* *T* *s* | *T* *s* *T* *s* | *T* *s* *T* *s* | *T* *s* *T* *s*

When the class has learned to sing the song and when the chorded accompaniment is going well, you can develop a more interesting texture by adding parts such as the following:

1. Make this a call-response song by having a solo voice sing the first part of each phrase, answered by the group singing "Water come to me eye" each time it occurs.
2. Sing in two-part harmony following the easy alto part that is provided.
3. Add a rhythm accompaniment playing repeated patterns like these:

Any one or two of these procedures would add to the interest of the song. Attempt only as many parts as the group can do successfully.

Instructional Objectives: To enable children to create a multi-textured accompaniment for a folk song; to provide an opportunity for them to develop skill in playing ensemble parts with rhythmic and tonal accuracy; and to develop concepts of ensemble balance and the expressive shaping of a musical composition.

Behaviors providing evidence that these instructional objectives have been achieved: The children will

□ decide the number and kind of parts the group can perform satisfactorily as an accompaniment for "Water Come to Me Eye"

□ play or sing their choice of parts, compatible with the needs of the ensemble, with accurate pitch and rhythm, and appropriate dynamics

□ comment favorably upon the musical result, and suggest ways in which the arrangement might be improved at some future performance

"Water Come to Me Eye" could be played in the key of C using the C and G^7 chords, and it is a good experience for the players to develop the flexibility of tuning up and playing in different keys. Teach the children to use the capo, so that songs can be transposed into keys that are most comfortable for singing. Other two-chord songs using the easier keys of A and D are mentioned earlier in this chapter. Three-chord songs are easiest to play on the guitar in the following keys:

	I	IV	V^7
Key of D	D	G	A^7
Key of G	G	C	D^7
Key of A	A	D	E^7

A good example of a three-chord song in "blues" style is shown in Example 6.25. It can be most easily played on the guitar in the key of D, but when played and sung a whole step lower, in the key of C, the vocal range is more comfortable.

EXAMPLE 6.25

THE BLUES AIN'T NOTHIN' BUT A GOOD MAN FEELIN' BAD
Traditional Blues

2. I'm gonna go down to the levee,
   Take along a rockin' chair.
   If my babe don't come to me,
   Gonna rock away from there.
   'Cause the blues ain't nothin', *etc.*

3. Now when my baby said goodbye,
   Had to break right down and cry.
   When my baby said goodbye,
   I thought I'd surely die.
   Oh, the blues ain't nothin', *etc.*

Compare the chords needed for this song in the key of D and chords needed to play the I, IV, V^7 chords in the key of G (see chart above). You will see that the G major chord is used in both cases; however, "The Blues Ain't Nothin' . . ." uses G major as a IV chord, and in "Worried Man Blues" (Example 6.26) G major functions as a I (tonic) chord. Both songs use a D chord, but, again the function of the chord is different: D Major as I, and D^7 as V^7.

EXAMPLE 6.26

WORRIED MAN BLUES
Hillbilly Folk Song

With movement

© 1962 by James Leisy Music. Used by permission.

Well-known songs using three chords include:

"Every Night When the Sun Goes In"
$\frac{2}{2}$ D–*1*

"Michael Row the Boat Ashore"
$\frac{4}{4}$ A–*1*

"Kum Ba Yah" $\frac{3}{4}$ D–*1*

"On Top of Old Smokey" $\frac{3}{4}$ A–*1*

"Lonesome Valley" $\frac{4}{4}$ G–*5*

"She'll Be Coming Round the Mountain" $\frac{2}{4}$ G–*5*

After each title above, the meter signature is shown so that an appropriate strum can be set up. The key and starting pitch are essential information that will assure a singing range comfortable to most voices, although a song that has a narrow range may be sung in more than one key.

Playing and Singing Root Tones

Following their experiences in making harmony with the guitar or Autoharp, children can learn to play bass parts and build chords on other instruments. The resonator bells sound well when the tones are struck simultaneously in block chords. Other classroom melody instruments or orchestral stringed instruments can be used to accompany songs that use two or three chords. The value of such activities in building interest is as great as its value in increasing skills and understanding in harmony.

Orchestral stringed instruments are often available in an elementary classroom, and it is helpful to know what opportunities they can offer for playing easy accompaniments. These instruments are tuned as follows:

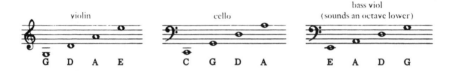

The open strings of these instruments can be used as root tones for chords in the following keys:

KEY	CHORD	ROOTS		INSTRUMENT
	(I)	(V⁷)	(IV)	
G	G	D		violin, cello, bass
D	D	A	G	violin, cello, bass
C	C	G		cello
A	A	E	D	violin, bass

Open strings of any of the instruments listed above can be used to play the root tones for "Streets of Laredo" (Example 6.27). The low tones of the bass viol would add depth and resonance to the chord accompaniment of the guitar or Autoharp. Notice that the tonic (G) and the dominant (D) alternate regularly throughout the song, except in the last phrase, where A, the root tone of the minor chord, is needed. The tone on these instruments can be produced most easily by plucking the string (pizzicato), but it can also be sustained by bowing the open string.

"Down in the Valley" (Example 6.2) is harmonized by the tonic and dominant chords in the key of G. This basic harmony can be used in several ways to create an accompaniment on tuned instruments that fifth and sixth grade children can play:

1. Follow the chord markings and pluck the open G and D strings on any of the stringed instruments, or sound these tones on a bell instrument in a lower octave, on the downbeat of each measure throughout the song.
2. Notice that the fifth of the scale (D) is a tone common to both chords; therefore, this tone can be sounded continuously throughout the song. The open D string of

the violin could be sustained, or D in the higher range of a bell instrument could be struck at the beginning of each measure.

3. On the first beat of each measure in which the chord is used, sound all the tones for each chord on resonator bells. Three children can play G, B, and D rhythmically during the first four measures, then four other children can play D, F$^{\sharp}$, A, and C on the downbeat until the tonic chord returns in the last measure of the song.

To involve as many players as possible, give each tone bar to a different individual. The chord will be created when three or four players tap their tone bars simultaneously, three beats in every measure. At other times a mallet with three heads can be used by one person to play simultaneously all the tones in a given chord.

Instructional Objectives: To provide children an opportunity to make musical decisions in creating an instrumental accompaniment for a folk song; to work in a meaningful way with notes and chords that fit together to create harmony; and to gain experience combining single parts into a rhythmic, cohesive whole.

Behaviors providing evidence that these instructional objectives have been achieved: The children will

  □ know and select the tone bars (or pitches on other instruments) that are needed in the chords of G major and D^7

  □ follow a conductor and play rhythmically, so that a clear chord and accurate chord changes are heard

  □ play so that they produce and hear a good ensemble balance of voices and instruments

  □ express interest in trying chords in different registers, using different timbres, or creating other arrangements of instruments for this accompaniment

After children in the intermediate grades have had experience playing chord accompaniments on the Autoharp and the bells, the next step is to show them how the simple harmonizing parts relate to the basic chord structure. Understanding the principles of harmonization leads to better singing and opens the road for singing "barbershop" harmony and other forms of improvisation.

Singing Descants and Part Songs

A simple melody written above and harmonizing with an original or principal melody is known as a descant. One principle of its construction is that it moves against the basic melody; hence, when the melody moves slowly the descant may move faster, and when the melody moves rapidly the descant may be in sustained tones. Also, as the melody moves upward the descant may be sustained or move downward. The arrangement of "Streets of Laredo" in Example 6.27 shows these characteristics in its descant.

EXAMPLE 6.27

STREETS OF LAREDO
American Cowboy Song

Simply

From *Music around the World.* © 1956, Silver Burdett Company.

Try this song with three or four voices singing the descant while a larger group sings the melody. The Autoharp or guitar can provide a good accompaniment for this song. Notice the effect of the A minor chord in the last phrase. A guitarist who can play the chords of D, A⁷, and E minor could play this song in the key of F, a whole step lower than it is shown above, by clamping a capo behind the third fret.

Instructional Objectives: To provide children with an opportunity to learn a well-known cowboy song; to sing and hear the effect of a descant as a harmonizing part; and to utilize the playing skill of one or more guitarists (or Autoharpists) in a musically satisfying performance, which will be recorded.

Behaviors providing evidence that these instructional objectives have been achieved: The children will

☐ sing or play their assigned parts with accuracy and in a style that fits the song

☐ comment favorably on the experience and suggest ways in which the performance might be improved

☐ express interest in repeating the performance for an audience or in having others hear the recording

The value of the descant is that it provides pleasing harmonic experience, but gives the less familiar part to the higher voices, which frequently sing with more independence. Since it lies in a higher range and is easily heard, the descant often is sung by only three or four voices. It should accompany and not dominate the melody. Bells, song flutes, and other melody instruments could play the descant with or without the voices. A solo instrumental counterpart is called an obbligato. When putting melodies together in this way, be particularly careful to count the rhythm correctly, holding the long notes for a proper amount of time so that the parts harmonize.

These well-known songs with descants can be found in the basic music series books for intermediate grades:

"Battle Hymn of the Republic"   "Roll On, Columbia" (ExM VI-6)
  (ExM V-34)
"Red River Valley" (DMT V-86)   "Wade in the Water" (NDinM V-138)

Singing a parallel harmonizing part above or below the melody line is another early experience in harmony. Sometimes harmony can be sung a third higher or a sixth lower than the melody for a pleasing effect; because the harmony parallels the melody, it is not difficult to sing. "Sing *Gemütlichkeit!*" (Example 5.22) can have an alto part added so that it moves consistently a third below the melody. Sing this in a group a few times until you can comfortably sing one part, and yet hear the harmony created by the two parts. Sometimes the melody can be sung by the larger group while one or more strong voices sing the alto. With such a song, both parts are equally easy to sing, providing you get started on the right pitch. To do this for "Sing *Gemütlichkeit!*" sound the key-note (C) and sing *do* on that pitch. As one group hums that pitch the other group can move up to *mi* to establish the harmony in thirds.

Individuals who have learned to do so find considerable satisfaction in harmonizing "by ear" in thirds or sixths above or below a melody. This skill is basic to "barbershop quartet" singing.

"Polly Wolly Doodle" (Example 4.19) can be sung with parallel thirds above or parallel sixths below the melody line. To accommodate the lower or higher parts, different keys need to be used in each case. Try it in these keys:

Thirds above the melody   *Sixths below the melody*

"Oh, I went down south,..."   "Oh, I went down south,..."

Current basic music series books show these easy arrangements for harmonizing in thirds and sixths:

"Gerakina" (SBM VI-113)   "Sambalele" (DMT VI-114)
"Little David" (NDinM VI-58)

The most important aspect of harmony singing is hearing the effect of the voices sounding simultaneously. To accomplish this, occasionally:

1. Hold chords at cadences or other convenient points in the song and listen to the harmony produced.
2. Sing a phrase in parallel thirds slowly, so that the movement of the harmony is heard.

Singing in harmony is a cooperative enterprise wherein the voices adjust to one another in making the harmony, and it is only through experience that one learns how each interval and chord should sound.

CHAPTER NOTES

1. Meg Peterson, **The Many Ways to Play the Autoharp** (Union, N.J.: Oscar Schmidt-International, Inc., 1966).
2. Oscar Schmidt-International. Music Education Group, 1415 Waukegan Road, Northbrook, Ill. 60062.
3. Frederick Beckman, **Partner Songs** and **More Partner Songs** (Boston: Ginn and Company, 1958 and 1962).
4. Carl Orff and Gunild Keetman, **Music for Children, I—Pentatonic,** English Adaptation by Doreen Hall and Arnold Walter (Mainz, Ger.: B. Schott's Söhne, Edition 4470, 1956; New York: Associated Music Publishers, Inc.)
5. Carl Orff and Gunild Keetman, **Music for Children,** Angel Records 3582B.
6. From **Going Barefoot** by Aileen Fisher. Text copyright © 1960 by Aileen Fisher. Used by permission of Thomas Y. Crowell, Publishers.
7. Carl Orff, translated by Arnold Walter, "The Schulwerk—Its Origin and Aims," **Music Educators Journal** vol. 49, no. 5 (April-May 1963).
8. Beth Landis and Polly Carder, **The Eclectic Curriculum in American Music Education: Contributions of Dalcroze, Kodály and Orff** (Washington, D.C.: Music Educators National Conference, 1972).

   Lawrence Wheeler and Lois Raebeck, **Orff and Kodály Adapted for the Elementary School** (Dubuque, Iowa: Wm. C. Brown Company, 1972, 1977).
9. Maurine Zimmerman and Celeste Griffith, **Guitar in the Classroom** (Dubuque, Iowa: Wm. C. Brown Company, 1971).

7

Songs and Singing Voices

Singing is a pleasurable activity that has an important place in the elementary school. In this setting it is not our concern that children become great singers, but that they become enthusiastic singers, and find this a natural way to express themselves. The classroom teacher can contribute a great deal to this goal by having the children sing every day, by using songs they enjoy, and by relating music to their other interests.

In the first part of this chapter you will find a discussion of characteristics you can expect to find in children's voices, together with procedures for classroom management of music and teaching songs. The musical experiences laid out in the latter part of this chapter focus separately on each of three levels, with discussion and examples of (1) ways to promote and improve children's singing; (2) practical approaches to teaching new songs; (3) the various kinds of songs that meet the needs of children at that level; and (4) musical learning that can arise from encounters with specific songs.

The experiences and songs in this chapter center on singing as an activity in itself. The related instructional objectives and listings of behaviors are designed to be continual reminders that in an educational setting you must point toward instructional goals, be they attitudes, increased awareness of the expressive factors in music and the ability to respond to them, or singing skills.

THE SINGING VOICES OF CHILDREN

It is generally accepted by those who work in elementary school music that all children can and should learn to sing. At Level I the general classroom and playground provide the setting for much of the basic development of singing voices, and this is one reason the classroom teacher needs to take an active interest in singing.

Some people account for the wide variation in children's singing in terms of "ability" or "talent." Many factors contribute to such an ability. Among them are (1) an early environment that provides a child with models for singing as well as speaking; (2) the child's motivation and freedom in using the singing voice, and (3) maturation of hearing and the ability to focus attention on what is heard. Sometimes motivation arises from the interest and encouragement of others, but often it results from the child's own inner urge for making music and expressing feelings. The many young and successful popular singers heard today may owe their success to these factors rather than to an intensive program of vocal training.

Quality and Range in the Voices of Children

Children's voices vary in quality, depending upon such factors as experience, available vocal examples, and physical structure. As long as the singing is free and unstrained, variety in tone quality is desirable because singing should be expressive of many ideas and moods.

For general singing, the practical vocal range of both girls and boys in the elementary school is from B♭ below middle C to D above the octave:

Nevertheless, we must expect a wide variation of singing skill among children when they first come to school. For a child who has never sung, the four or five tones centering around E or F are the first to be used.

"Hey, Lollee!" is a five-tone song which, when sung in the key of D (Example 7.1), utilizes just these tones. Try it, so that you can find this range of tones in your own voice.*

_____

*Note that the adult male voice will sound these notes an octave lower.

EXAMPLE 7.1

HEY, LOLLEE!

James Leisy
Based on a Bahamian Folk Tune

Lively

The range and general quality in the voices of boys and girls is essentially the same, but psychological factors can result in more vocal problems among the boys if singing voices are not well established in the primary grades. As they grow older, boys are less interested in developing a normal child's singing voice; they would rather cultivate a voice that is low and "manly." The best solution to this problem is to be sure all children have adequate singing experiences in early childhood and that appropriate procedures are used to overcome vocal problems in the primary grades.

The practical range of voices of children above the age of nine or ten is about the same as that shown above. Sing "Hey, Lollee!" in the key of G, so you can experience the upper tones of the average singing voice:

Greater use brings wider range and flexibility to the voice, just as exercise and training build skills and coordination in other muscular activities. Given adequate singing experience and guidance, some intermediate-grade children will begin to develop a more brilliant tone and may be able to sing tones somewhat lower or higher than those typical of younger or "average" singers:

Classroom singing normally does not utilize the upper notes of this expanded range; that will be experienced by the higher voices in special choral groups, usually directed by a music teacher. However, during preadolescent years you may need to accommodate some voices by taking songs to low A or G for comfortable classroom singing. When set in the key of A and sung in the lower octave, "Hey, Lollee!" uses five tones between A and E:

Hey, lol-lee! lol-lee! lol-lee!   Hey, lol-lee, lol-lee lo! *etc.*

Although this may feel more comfortable for your voice, it is not an optimal range for most children, and the singing lacks brightness and vitality. Try to accommodate the lower voices that begin to develop in the middle years by using the easy two-part songs and harmonizing procedures shown in Chapter 6.

Out-of-Tune Singers

The term "monotone" is an unfortunate one that should never be used, for it implies that the individual sings or speaks on one level with no pitch variation. You need only listen to the speaking voice of any child to hear the natural variation in pitch. Out-of-tune singers may be more accurately described as "conversational singers," who "sing" much as they speak. This condition can be found in children who did not learn to sing in a spontaneous, intuitive way at an early age.

Persons differ in sensitivity to pitch. Some children may need to have their attention directed to highness and lowness in pitch before they begin to notice that singing involves changes in pitch as well as in rhythm. Procedures to accomplish this can be undertaken at Level I.

Individually, children can engage in spontaneous vocal improvisation and crooning, which reveal the physical capacity to sing. In addition, to re-create a preestablished melody in the voice, tonal memory is necessary. This involves perception and memory of a succession of pitches within a rhythmic framework. Tonal memory arises out of early imitative vocal play and is developed to the point where the individual can remember an entire song or musical theme in an instrumental composition. Children in primary classes can begin to find their voices and develop tonal memory by using tone calls and games incorporated with classroom singing. The music specialist can work on an individual basis with older children who need special assistance, but the daily involvement and interest that the classroom teacher can generate in singing are as important as any remedial measure that might be taken.

MANAGEMENT OF THE SINGING SITUATION

In any group singing, someone needs to get the singing started at a good pitch level and at an appropriate tempo. When a piano or other chording instrument is used to accompany singing, the player always sounds the tonic chord or plays a brief introduction to establish the tonality of the song. When singing is to be accompanied by the Autoharp, guitar, or bells, the pitch should be taken from the instrument; when a record is used, the tonality is set by the recorded introduction, so no other tuning is necessary.

To assure a suitable singing range, songs should be sung in a predetermined key. As you work with various songs, try them in different keys in order to find the pitch level at which the song is most comfortable. Stay within the vocal ranges cited earlier for different groups of children. Although you may assume the responsibility for getting the singing started and playing an accompaniment for early childhood classes, nine- to eleven-year-olds can learn to provide this leadership for the class if they have had adequate musical experiences in earlier years and have harmonizing instruments to work with at this level.

To create an informal atmosphere for singing, you can have younger children sit in a semicircle on chairs or on a rug, much as they do during story-telling time. Since singing is dependent upon a proper use of the lungs and diaphragm, however, the children's posture when they sit on a rug is less desirable for singing than their posture when they sit in small chairs. An out-of-tune singer should sit next to a more accurate singer, and seating should be changed from time to time so you can hear different voices. You should sit or stand so you can easily communicate with every child in the group. "Communication" means eye contact, even when you are seated at a piano. Be sure the piano is in a position that allows you to look directly at the children when you play accompaniments. Use the soft pedal, so that the voices are not covered by the sound of the piano.

If you use the prevailing arrangement of desks in the room, you should be free to move among the children as they sing. You then can be aware of each child's vocal development, and will be able to give individual assistance and encouragement when necessary. Obtain a shoulder strap for your guitar or Autoharp so that you can have the instrument handy for tuning up or accompanying when needed.

In the primary classroom, it is neither appropriate nor necessary that formal voice testing be done. You can evaluate voices by listening as you move about the classroom while the children sing. In the fifth and especially the sixth grades, where some part-singing is done and where the tonal range of the songs may be greater, some grouping of higher and lower voices will be necessary. Listening and observation, trial of songs in different keys, and discussion with the children will reveal those who are more comfortable singing the lower part.

Selecting the Songs

In selecting songs for your class you will, of course, sing many songs the children already know and like. But the repertoire should gradually be expanded to meet the needs of the children as they mature and have a greater variety of interests. Although some songs are attractive to individuals of any age, the singing repertoire for children will differ somewhat from one level to another.

Basic series music books for classroom use (see Appendix B-I for listing) have been published for many years, and with changes in the teaching emphasis, the selection of songs has changed somewhat. In addition to folk songs and traditional children's songs, you will find at the present time a great many attractive songs from other cultures, as well as numerous songs written by successful commercial musicians. Although many of these songs may be new to you, they are easy to sing and attractive to children. The companies publishing these books supply recordings of all the songs in each book. These records can be an aid to the teacher with a limited singing ability, and they enrich the music program in the classroom of a competent singer as well. Other books and records are of value for children of different ages, and some of these will be mentioned in connection with musical experiences at the three levels.

The songs selected for classroom use should represent many moods and feelings. There should be game and nonsense songs, story songs and ballads, songs of patriotism, worship, and other celebrations, lullabies, and attractive contemporary popular songs appropriate and appealing to children. Among song collections for educational purposes, you will find many folk songs of the United States and other countries. Beatrice Landeck expressed the opinion that folk songs should be the basic song material for children:

> *After much experience with children and music, I came to rely almost entirely on folk songs. I've found in them colorful language, vivid imagery, humor, and warmth. They never seem to be outgrown. You hear them sung by adults with as much enthusiasm as by children.*
>
> *One reason American folk songs have such an appeal for children is that every child senses their vitality. Folk songs reflect every emotion from joyousness to despair. They may bounce up and down on the nonsense level or tread a stately pace.*[1]

It is not necessary to use only folk songs, but the fact that a song has existed long enough to become a "folk song" indicates that it has vitality beyond its original use. Among the many collections of folk songs for children are the books and records of Ruth Seeger, Pete Seeger, Ella Jenkins, Charity Bailey, Burl Ives, Sam Hinton, and others.

Generally speaking, you might expect that a song you like will have appeal for children, providing you have selected it for its intrinsic musical qualities rather than because it exemplifies safety or a trip to the zoo. Music has served didactic (instructional) purposes throughout the history of education, as evidenced by the alphabet and counting songs in all languages, but songs composed especially for didactic purposes usually lack grace, are soon outgrown, and have little meaning outside the specific situation in which they were originally used.

Undoubtedly you will need to use some songs of this type, but search for those that have lilt and musical charm. A song that is both popular with children and might be considered a "didactic" song is Melvina Reynolds' "The Magic Penny" (Example 4.13). The text of this song conveys a message about love that is meaningful to children, but it is set to a sprightly tune with a lilting rhythm that is memorable in itself. Learning the song will be a valid musical experience, and it seems possible that verbalizing these moral sentiments may be helpful in developing children's concepts about love. But children will also need to see examples of loving relationships if they are to truly know what love is.

The children's television programs *Sesame Street* and *The Electric Company* and the Hap Palmer educational records[2] make extensive use of music for didactic purposes. No doubt you recognize the value of this work and will use some of these songs, but do not limit classroom singing to the kind of music children hear daily on television.

As an outgrowth of a unit of study, some teachers have composed songs or written down songs created by their pupils. These are valid creative products in the atmosphere in which they took form, and you should look for opportunities for this kind of creative work in your own class. In this situation, however, the creative process is more significant than the product. When removed from the situation that inspired them, such songs usually lose their initial value as creative achievements and do not measure up as lasting song material.

Famous composers have written songs for children. Many of these find their place in the repertoire of special choral groups; some, however, are appropriate for general classroom singing and have been included in the basic series books. Also, certain contemporary popular songs are expressive and worthy of use in schools. Because no educational publication can keep up with the swift-paced change in popular music, you and the children must select those songs that will be learned by the entire class. Although some of these songs have lyrics that are not acceptable to everyone, you can help the children understand the need to choose those that are appropriate as well as appealing to them.

If this discussion brought to mind songs you remember and would like to share with children, you should begin a collection of those songs, and start a card file. The following basic information will be helpful:

1. title
2. composer or origin
3. source (publisher, book, edition, page)
4. key and starting pitch of the song
5. classroom use
   a. possible correlation with social studies, language arts, and so on
   b. musical concepts and skills to be developed

In this chapter you will find examples of songs that are appropriate at each of the three levels. With each, possibilities for musical as well as cultural learning have been pointed out; this is the kind of information you should include in the card file under item 5.

Teaching the Song

There is no single way to teach a new song. The variable factors are many: the song itself, the musical ability of the class, your ability to sing or play an instrument, the availability of recordings and books, and so forth. Songs are learned when children hear them sung or played from a recording and when a music book is used as a visual aid. Songs learned by imitation are often called "rote" songs. By definition this means "without thought of the meaning, or in a mechanical way." Even with young children, meaning and feeling should be a part of the song-learning process. Hence the term "rote" is not used in this book.

To work effectively in music with children, a teacher needs the flexible, natural voice of a good folk singer rather than the highly developed voice of the concert artist. A basic requirement is to express simply, through song, sentiments that are appropriate and appealing to children. Think in terms of "sharing" a song you like with children, rather than "teaching" it. How can you do this most effectively? The good enunciation and projection of ideas you use when telling stories to children are the same techniques to use in singing to children. Flexible, active use of the lips and tongue, vitality in facial expression, and eye contact with the children are essential. "Communication" is the name of the game in singing as well as in story-telling.

Older children can read the words from a song book or a chart and hear the melody sung. If there has been consistent use of music notation at each level, nine- to eleven-year-olds will learn a new song by a combination of hearing the music and seeing the printed page. You should try to have some visual representation of the music available at Levels II and III, so that the children can grow in their ability to use notation in learning new songs. Nevertheless, you will find that at every level you will need to use your voice, an instrument, or recordings, to help with the melody.

Using the Voice and Instruments. The best way to introduce a new song to young children is to sing it for them, because children match tones with another human voice more readily than with an instrument. Often you can first present a song with the voice and guitar or Autoharp accompaniment. If this is the method you prefer, sit with the accompanying instrument in a position that leaves you free to look at the children. The accompaniment should enhance the song and support, but not dominate, the voice. For this reason, it may not be completely satisfactory to use a piano accompaniment while presenting a song—unless you are a particularly skilled pianist and singer.

Some songs are most appropriate when sung unaccompanied. To assure a suitable singing range, decide ahead of time the key to be used and take the starting pitch from an instrument. Some children have excellent tonal memories that, if correctly developed, can lead to the possession of a fine sense of pitch. When a song is sung every day at a somewhat different pitch level, any development in this direction is thwarted. Furthermore, children with a good pitch sense can be confused, because for them the song sounds different each time it is sung in a different key.

When presenting a new song, sing it all the way through and then discuss with the children any interesting ideas in the lyrics or obvious characteristics of the music. Younger children should hear a song several times before they attempt to sing it. To achieve this, involve them with related visual aids, body movement, or other activities. If there are repeated phrases or an easy refrain, you can help the children learn to sing those parts first, and to listen or participate in other ways as you sing the harder phrases several times. It is not necessary that the children sing a song on the first day it is introduced; you can share it with them as you might a story, introduce a related activity, and talk about ideas in the song. If they hear the song several times before attempting to sing it, they will be more accurate in learning it.

Use of the Adult Male Voice. Children can learn songs from hearing the male voice, which sounds an octave lower. Because the range of the child voice lies within the range of the female voice, the woman teacher is at an advantage in providing a singing example. Children normally copy the male voice by singing at the octave above, if the song is in a comfortable middle range. Listen as the children sing; if you notice any difficulty, you can use some of the following techniques to help children place the song correctly in their voices:

1. Be sure you select a key that places the song in an appropriate range for the children's voices.
2. While you sing in your octave, play the melody on the piano or bells in the child voice range.
3. Train the children to take the pitch from a melody instrument (which sounds in their octave) and to sing the first note of the song on that pitch.
4. Use the voice of an accurate child singer as a sample for others learning a song.
5. Play the melody on the violin, flute, clarinet, recorder, or other instrument in the soprano register. If you cannot sing as you play, be sure the children have previously heard the song enough to know how the words fit with the melody.

Techniques in Using Records. Procedures for teaching a song with the aid of a record are as varied as those you might employ when using your own voice as a model. The recording does not fill the role of the teacher—it only provides the music example. In teaching with records you must

1. Be sure that the recorded version is in a key that provides a comfortable range for singing.
2. Know the song and be able to sing softly or mime singing at any point.
3. Effectively use a wide variety of techniques for interacting with children.

If you can help the children focus their attention on short, easy songs so that they hear the songs several times, the children probably will sing them quite readily. When introducing longer songs, you need to motivate listening by planning appropriate activities so that the children will hear the whole song several times before they attempt to sing it.

1. They may listen two or three times as they find out what the song is about and discuss it.
2. They may listen for rhythmic features, which they demonstrate through body movement or use of simple instruments.
3. They may listen for melodic characteristics, to discover same and different phrases.

Sometimes you can treat the song as a dialogue by finding easy phrases or refrains where you cue the children to join in the singing and then listen again as the artist sings the more difficult parts.

Another technique is "whispering" the words as the voice on the record sings. This method, useful after the children can follow the song text printed in the music book, serves two purposes:

1. It helps to establish the tempo and rhythm in the children's singing response. (Often when a group of children first sing with a record, they fall behind because they cannot hear the music enough to follow the tempo.)
2. When the rhythm and the text have been established in their minds, the children are able to connect them with the melody, which they can hear as they whisper.

This kind of participation is not unnatural for singers who have the words before them and are hearing a recorded song for the first or second time. You must use it with good judgment, however, because your objective should be a classroom of singing children, not silent mimics.

In general, a large group of young children should not hum with a new song. Until the tune is known, humming can result in an indefinable sound not closely resembling the melody desired, and the humming obscures the melody. After the children know a song well, humming can be an enjoyable activity that gives them experience with another vocal tone color.

Although you can use a recording to teach a new song and to get the singing started, when the children learn to sing the song, they should do so unaided by the recording. To do this, start the singing by playing the introduction on the record and then lifting the needle, or use an instrument to tune up in the same key. Sometimes you can use a record for the first presentation of a song, and then use your voice to help the children learn specific parts of the song.

In planning to teach a song, examine the possibilities for using instruments and body movement, so that you will be able to draw on these as supporting activities. Consider how music books might be used to make learning the song easier for older groups of children. In the following sections you will find procedures that might be used to teach songs at three levels in the elementary school. The examples will bring further details to your attention so that you will have a number of approaches to consider when you plan to teach a new song to a particular class. Above all, demonstration of some of these procedures in the methods class will be most helpful.

EXPERIENCES AT LEVEL I

In early childhood classes you must be prepared to (1) establish singing as a spontaneous, natural activity; (2) help children develop their voices, so that they find satisfaction in singing; and (3) provide children with a variety of songs that appeal to them. Since children at this level have short attention spans and are not yet able to use a printed page, you need to know techniques that will be useful in teaching songs of different kinds. In this section the procedures and materials described enlarge upon concerns discussed earlier in this chapter and relate them specifically to early childhood.

Spontaneous, Informal Singing

Since young children lack experience in cooperative activity, and often lack singing skill, they need much individual and small-group singing. Until children have discovered their individual singing voices, they can hardly be expected to master the more difficult task of singing together with others. Consequently, you must look for times and places to foster individual singing during the school day.

The Pillsbury Foundation study *Music of Young Children*[3] provides extensive documentation of children's spontaneous musical activities. In early childhood classes many of the informal periods, when children work alone or in small groups, provide opportunities for individual singing. As children build with blocks, play at housekeeping, paint, or color, they should feel free to sing and croon (hum or sing to oneself). If you and other adults set an example for such informal use of the voice, children are apt to do likewise.

In this informal setting a song need not be complete; phrases, repeated tone calls, make-up songs, and chants are natural and satisfying. The important thing is that the children sing because they feel free to sing; this continued vocalization leads to greater ease in using the voice. Chanting songs or short folk songs can be used when children sing about what they are doing or are going to do. "What Shall We Do?" (Example 7.2) and other children's songs lend themselves to improvisation on endless activities during the school play periods or with friends at home.

EXAMPLE 7.2

WHAT SHALL WE DO?
Traditional Game Song

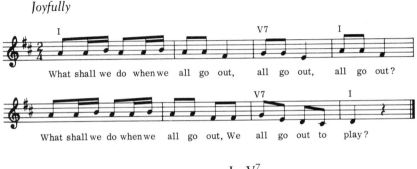

Joyfully

What shall we do when we all go out, all go out, all go out?

What shall we do when we all go out, We all go out to play?

$$\begin{array}{cc} \text{I} & \text{V}^7 \\ \hline \text{Key of D:} \quad \text{D} & \text{A}^7 \end{array}$$

This song can readily be accompanied by clapping, swaying, or marching. Try creating new words appropriate to different playground activities. "We will play on the jungle-gym," or "Turn somersaults on the trampoline" are words that would fit the tune.

Instructional Objectives: To provide children with a simple song that can be creatively adapted to their playtime activities, and that will entice children who previously have not sung to do so.

Behaviors providing evidence that these instructional objectives have been achieved: The children will

- □ sing the song spontaneously as they prepare for playground activities
- □ sing words that reflect the activities they will undertake
- □ sing the melody so that it is recognizable at whatever pitch level is comfortable for the individual

Singing Tone Calls and Chants

Children can most easily be helped to learn to sing if their first songs use the tonal range and intervals of the children's chant (refer to Chapter 5, page 146). To get started with the chant, use these two chanting tones to call roll or to sing "hello" and "goodbye."

The child who has success singing two tones will have established a concept about singing in tune; gaining this concept may lead to success with longer melodic fragments.

While the chanting tones are basic to singing in early childhood and should be given special attention, many other good tone calls can be found in songs. Such tone calls should be used for the development of voices and should be the first parts of songs that children learn to sing. As an example, in early childhood classes the familiar round "Are You Sleeping?" (Example 5.3) is often sung to the words "Where Is Thumbkin?" (Key of F, begins on F):

> Where is Thumbkin? Where is Thumbkin?
> Here I am! Here I am!
> How are you this morning? Very well, I thank you!
> Run away. Run away.

When you sing this song to children, use the finger play implicit in the lyrics: Close the fingers of each hand and let "Thumbkin" stand out alone. Put both hands behind your back as you begin to sing and bring each thumb out separately as you sing "Here I am" twice. Let one thumb bend when you sing, "How are you this morning?" and the other bend when you sing "Very well, I thank you." Both, of course, will disappear behind your back as you sing "Run away." Make this finger play very personal by looking directly at each "Thumbkin" when you address him.

In this song, easy repeated motifs can serve as tone calls that children can sing first when they are learning this song:

After singing the song for the children, you could say, "In this song Thumbkin sings to us, 'Here I am.' Let me hear you sing his part like this:" (example, followed by children's response). "Now sing the ending part where Thumbkin runs away like this:" (example, followed by children's response). As you sing the song again, the children can chime in on the two patterns they have rehearsed. They undoubtedly will create their own "Thumbkins" to dramatize their singing!

Instructional Objectives: To help young children find success in singing short melodic fragments, and to teach them a song that will give them pleasure.

Behaviors providing evidence that these instructional objectives have been achieved: The children will

- individually and in small groups, accurately sing tone calls extracted from the song
- sing the entire song as a basis for the finger play
- obviously enjoy the song, and ask to sing it at other times

In each of the following songs, encountered earlier in this book, look for a tone call that might provide a beginning for singing:

"Chickama Craney Crow" (Example 4.2)

"Jack Be Nimble" (Example 4.6)

"Old House" (Example 3.2)

"The Old Gray Cat" (Example 3.3)

Wherever you find it, a useful tone call has these characteristics:

1. It has unity and completeness in itself and thus is satisfying to sing.
2. It has a common melodic pattern found in many simple songs.
3. It lies in the most advantageous range of the voice.
4. It has rhythmic interest but is not difficult to sing.

When first singing the song for the children, you can make a game of a simple tone call. One small group after another may sing it, and individual children may sing it, imitating you or another child. The objectives of this tone call game are that children sing the song fragment in tune, and that they discover how it sounds and feels to sing it in tune.

It can be helpful to some nonsingers to participate in high tone calls that use the voice in a different way. Have them create high bird and animals sounds featuring the "ee" sound (cheep, peep, meow), or imitate the rising whine of a siren. When a high tone is sounded, the child should prolong that high pitch as someone else matches it. Two other procedures can be helpful: Show the child how to

1. enact the rising sound by raising the arms as the voice moves upward
2. use the resulting high sound as the beginning of a song; e.g., a siren might move upward until it becomes the opening tone call for "Bye'm Bye" (Example 5.6)

oh   Bye'm bye....

Tone calls from many songs should be used. A pleasant "game spirit" should prevail, so that the children do not become tense or anxious in any way, but can give full attention to the melodic fragments they are singing. The discussion and examples in "Tone Plays and Phrase Repetitions," pages 39 to 42 of *American Folk Songs for Children*,[4] are helpful.

A song has both words and melody, and the melody is comprised of both rhythm and pitch changes; thus the whole has three important dimensions. Since young children center their attention on one aspect of an object or situation at a time, it seems quite possible that those who sing rhythmically but not "tunefully" may be unaware of the quality of pitch change. By focusing on a short tone call, the child's attention can be centered on the component of pitch.

Other techniques can be used to direct attention to the melody of a song:

1. Occasionally sing with "la" or "loo" the first phrase or two of a familiar song; "Yankee Doodle" (Example 4.4) might be used. Ask the children to identify it and to sing it back to see if they can make it identifiable without the words.

2. At other times contrast singing with speaking by rhythmically *saying* a phrase such as "Old MacDonald had a farm . . ." Ask the children, "Did I *say* it or *sing* it?" They should then *say* it rhythmically. After that, sing the pattern and then ask the children to sing it.

3. Satis Coleman said "to speak in a singing voice with abandon, without having to conform to a set song, is a great help in freeing the voice."[5] Enlarge on this idea by having a singing "telling time" in which children sing their experiences or observations. *Music in Early Childhood*[6] describes sound play of this kind.

Choose a partner and spend a few minutes "conversing" in this manner. You may feel "silly" at first, but is there any reason why everyday communication should be limited to talking? If you use your voice freely in this manner, you may have a significant influence on what freedom children in your class find for using their singing voices.

Using Songs of Different Types

You will find teachers' manuals for music curricula designed especially for kindergarten and first grade classes (see Appendix B-I for listing). These books provide a wealth of songs and suggestions for teaching young children, and their organization of the material will help you see relationships among the songs. In addition, publishers have recognized children's interest in color and pictures related to the songs they sing, as well as the value of visual images in helping develop concepts about music. The result has been a number of attractive music books, either large chart-like books that the whole class can see, or individual "primers" for first graders.

These colorful books contain the words and melody for some songs; they also include diagrams and pictures related to the songs and recorded music to be heard. From the visual experience of diagrams and pictures, children can (1) learn to follow the left-to-right flow of melody on the page, (2) notice the rise or fall of a melody line, which can be visually related to the picture of a staircase or a ladder, and (3) learn to recognize rhythmic notation, in which some groups of notes represent a steady movement:

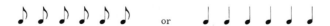

and other groups of notes represent an uneven, skipping or galloping kind of rhythm:

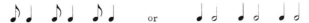

Whether or not you have music books for the children in your class to use, every song has some potential for developing children's understanding of the expressive qualities of the music, if you will sing and teach it so that these qualities are highlighted.

Young children are the center of their own universe; their interests and concerns do not range far. If there is a new baby at home, it is "my baby." A simple, repetitious song such as "Hush, Little Baby" (Example 6.4) is one that the child can share with the baby's entire family. This gentle song enables the singer to express affection for the baby and at the same time feel the quiet cradle-rocking movement associated with it. Sensing and responding to the rhythm and finding a way to express one's feelings through music are basic learnings at this level.

The singing voices of children are capable of considerable variation. Within musical limits this variation in vocal tone is desirable, for singing should express many ideas and moods. A high, light, flutelike voice quality is ideal for songs like "Hush, Little Baby" and "Bye'm Bye" (Example 5.6), and you should promote it through the mood and feeling expressed in these songs. Some children emulate a more vigorous voice quality, one suitable for exuberant songs. Their enthusiasm for such songs may be an important factor as they learn to use their singing voices. Chanting songs like "What Shall We Do?" (Example 7.2), songs such as "Train Is A Comin'" (Example 4.8), and the sea chantey "Up She Rises" (Example 7.3) are examples of rhythmic songs that should be sung with as much vigor as possible. Choose some "sailors" to pretend hoisting sails or strut to the beat of this song while the class sings.

EXAMPLE 7.3

UP SHE RISES
Sea Chantey

Vigorously

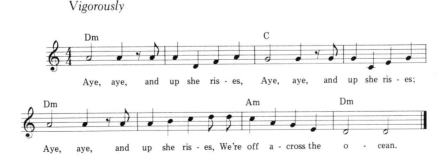

From MAKING MUSIC YOUR OWN. *Book I*, Teacher's Edition, © 1968, General Learning Corporation. Used by permission of Silver Burdett Company.

Mother Goose rhymes, such as "Mary Had a Little Lamb" (**ExM I-121**) and "Hickory, Dickory Dock" (Example 5.2), songs about characters from folklore, like "Mister Rabbit" (**SBM I-35**) and the folk ballad "The Little Pig" (Example 7.4), have a natural place in the singing repertoire of young children. A song that is longer and a bit more complicated will need to be broken into phrases and tone calls as the children learn to sing it. After the children have heard the song, any pleasing phrase or tone call can be a starting point for singing it.

EXAMPLE 7.4

THE LITTLE PIG
Texas

Moderately fast

There was an old wo-man and she had a lit-tle pig,___ Oink-oink-oink, There was an old wo-man and she had a lit-tle pig, Did-n't cost much 'cause it was-n't ver-y big,___ Oink-oink-oink.

2. The little old woman kept the piggy in the barn . . . (repeat)
   Prettiest thing she had on the farm . . .

3. The little old woman fed the piggy on clover . . . (repeat)
   He grew round and fat all over . . .

4. Now what can you do with a fat little pig? . . . (repeat)
   Sell him at the fair when he gets too big . . .

The phrase endings of "The Little Pig" are suitable fragments for early singing. Ask the group to listen for the story as you sing or play the recording the first time. Then you might say, "There is a part of this song that sounds as though the little pig had something to say. I wonder if you could sing it like this:" (you sing, then the children sing)

Oink, oink, oink

Make a game of it; sing the tone call several times, copycat style, at the pitch level of the song. Then you might say, "As I sing (or play the record of the song), you be ready to come in with the little pig's tune at just the right time." (A gesture from you, inviting their participation at this point in the song, will be helpful.)

Pictures of scenes and characters in a song, or hand puppets, can be of assistance in teaching a new song. A paper-bag puppet representing the little pig could be manipulated by one child when this part of the song is sung. The next day, sing the song with its several stanzas while one child manipulates the "little pig" hand puppet and the other children sing the phrase endings. After they have heard the song several times, the children should be able to sing the whole song along with you or the recording.

As new songs are learned, children can observe details of melody and rhythm. Notice that the second phrase of "The Little Pig" is higher than the first and third phrases. As you sing, enact the relative pitch levels by rhythmically moving your hand lower, then higher. The words "pig" and "big" are given two pitches in this song; show the drop in pitch by moving your hand down on the second tone. The children may imitate these gestures, but that is all right, because the gestures reinforce details in the melody they are hearing and singing.

Instructional Objectives: To give the children pleasure in learning a whimsical ballad song; to improve their skill in singing and their perception of details in melody.

Behaviors providing evidence that these instructional objectives have been achieved: The children will

- □ obviously enjoy the song and ask to sing it at other times
- □ be able to sing the tone call independently and accurately
- □ sing the second phrase at the necessary higher pitch
- □ show their awareness of the two tones on one word by singing correctly and enacting the fall in pitch with a hand movement

Small signs showing pictures or words can be mounted on tongue depressors or other small sticks for the children to display at certain times during the song. These can be helpful in holding the children's attention and can give individuals a special way to participate while they learn the song. What hand puppets, pictures, signs, or other props do you think would be useful with these songs?

"Bingo" (NDinM I-157)   "The Little White Duck" (ExM I-128)
"Bought Me a Cat" (DMT K-92)   "Over in the Meadow" (SpM K-13)

As the class becomes more proficient in singing, you can expand the repertoire of songs in several directions. In many areas we find families whose mother tongue is Spanish or the language of another minority group in this country. The use of songs in these languages is a fine way to have the whole class share another cultural heritage. "Muje Mukesin" (Example 5.13), "Duérmete, mi Niño" (Example 5.21), and "San Serení" (Example 4.14), are songs of the American Indian and Spanish heritages that young children could learn to sing. What minority groups are represented in your class? Learn a few of their songs and consider it an obligation to relate some of the classroom activities to the minority cultures of the community.

Among the important songs heard in the community are patriotic songs, Christmas carols, and songs of Thanksgiving and other holidays. Many of these have become traditional in the United States. Some of these melodies, however, lack the simplicity of folk songs; they are wide in range and more difficult to sing. When it seems appropriate, younger children may experience such songs by hearing others sing them, hearing recordings, or by singing only the refrain. "America" (**SBM I-127**) and the refrain of "God Bless America" (key of F, begins on *do*)* are two of the easiest of America's patriotic songs and will enable children to join in the singing at any community gathering.

Among the most familiar children's Christmas songs are "Jingle Bells" (**DMT K-139**) and "We Wish You a Merry Christmas" (Example 7.5). You can adapt this song to other holidays by changing the words, e.g., "We wish you a happy birthday," or "On Halloween the bats and witches fly," and so forth.

EXAMPLE 7.5

WE WISH YOU A MERRY CHRISTMAS
English Folk Song

Brightly

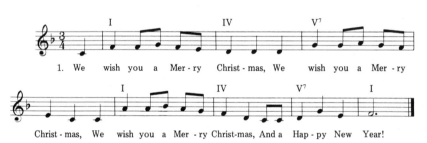

1. We wish you a Mer-ry Christ-mas, We wish you a Mer-ry Christ-mas, We wish you a Mer-ry Christ-mas, And a Hap-py New Year!

2. Oh, bring us some figgy pudding,
   Oh, bring us some figgy pudding,
   Oh, bring us some figgy pudding,
   And bring it right here.

3. We won't go until we get some,
   We won't go until we get some,
   We won't go until we get some,
   So bring it right here.

Repeat verse 1.

	I	IV	V⁷
Key of G:	G	C	D⁷
Key of F:	F	B♭	C⁷

---

* Because of copyright restrictions, this song and many contemporary popular songs are not found in basic series music books.

Notice that this song is in triple meter. Respond to the steady beat by clapping while you step or sway from side to side on the downbeat of each measure. The first line of the lyrics is sung three times, and the melody rises higher each time, giving a sense of insistence and urgency to the greeting. The singing can increase in intensity and the clapping hands can be raised higher on each repeated phrase. The last phrase has a child-like finality and expectation that will be enhanced when the clapping stops abruptly on the last words.

Instructional Objectives: To provide children with a practical holiday greeting song; to help them notice and respond to the triple meter and the sequentially rising line in this song.

Behaviors providing evidence that these instructional objectives have been achieved: The children will

☐ clap on the beat and step or sway from side to side on the downbeat in response to triple meter

☐ sing the song and respond to the expressive effect of the sequentially rising melody line, by singing a little louder on each repeated phrase

"The Friendly Beasts" (**DMT II-140**) and two spirituals, "Mary Had a Baby" (Example 5.12) and "The Angel Band" (**SpM I-145**), make good additions to the Christmas repertoire for young children. Contemporary holiday songs with the childlike simplicity of "The Little Drummer Boy" and "Rudolph the Red-Nosed Reindeer" are appropriate for school use.

Holidays are children's landmarks for the passing of time. They look forward to these celebrations and enjoy the associated symbols and songs. Minority cultures have songs of celebration that should be used in schools in which children of these groups study. Since many of the traditional songs are better suited to the singing abilities of older children, you will find numerous turkey, pumpkin and valentine songs written especially for young children. Unfortunately, these often are quite contrived. Do consider each song carefully in terms of its musical qualities, and make the best choice you can from among those you know or find in music books.

As you search for songs that appeal to children and are useful in promoting various musical activities and learnings, identify the important musical characteristics in the songs. The individual qualities of the song and the musical learnings the children are ready for will determine the approach to take in teaching that song.

EXPERIENCES AT LEVEL II

Children's voices grow in flexibility, control, and range between the ages of seven and nine and they should have opportunities to sing more challenging songs. If they have had an adequate, continuing program of vocal development at Level I, most eight-year-olds should be able to sing in tune. At Level II boys and girls must be given frequent opportunity to sing alone, in pairs, or in small groups, and they should be provided with opportunities to sing in larger groups outside the classroom.

Such singing experiences are essential to a varied program that will continue to hold the interest of these children.

Many of the procedures suggested for teaching songs at Level I also apply at Level II. These children, however, should be able to discriminate and respond to rhythms and melodies more quickly and accurately, and thus learn songs faster. Since children between ages seven and nine can read, they should learn many of their songs with the aid of music books.

The central instructional objective of singing experiences at Level II is to develop greater awareness of the expressive qualities of the songs learned. Every good song has musical qualities that make it unique, and that offer opportunity for the singers to learn more about the elements of music. The examples that follow will show you how to find these musical qualities and bring them to the attention of the children.

Developing Voices

It is well to keep in mind that the vocal mechanism that produces speech also produces singing. We find a link between the two in dramatic portrayal that utilizes different pitch and qualities of vocal sound. Such dramatic activities sometimes help nonsingers begin to sing.

Discuss with the children the different voices heard in their favorite TV cartoon and puppet shows. What characters do they identify with a high voice? with a low voice? Ask individuals to impersonate these voices, using typical phrases they identify with the character. Give special recognition to those who can imitate both high and low voice types.

Draw the nonsingers into this activity by giving them opportunities to impersonate at whatever vocal level they can. Encourage them to impersonate the character parts that use other levels of pitch. Vocal flexibility, movement up and down within the voice, is fundamental to singing.

Return to this activity periodically to hear how vocal flexibility is progressing. Show the children that spoken lines at a particular pitch can be lengthened into singing by prolonging the vowel sounds. Some of the children will be able to demonstrate this at low and high pitch levels. One objective is to get nonsingers manipulating their voices more freely, and to have them discover a singing tone. A broader objective for the whole class is to generate interest in the qualities that make a voice expressive.

In order to build confidence in singing alone and to give the weaker singers a chance to hear and find success in singing smaller fragments of songs, you should continue to use tone calls extracted from songs, as described at Level I. This must be done in a playful spirit, with individuals or small groups taking turns. Since children at this age still seek recognition and many of them enjoy a challenge, you should be able to do this as a regular part of your musical procedures. As an example, in the Halloween song, "The Ghost of John" (Example 7.6), the third phrase is a fine tone call. One or more voices could be assigned that phrase.

EXAMPLE 7.6

THE GHOST OF JOHN
Traditional Round

From *The Fireside Book of Children's Songs* by Marie Winn. Copyright
© 1966 by Marie Winn and Allan Miller. Reprinted by permission of
Simon & Schuster, a Division of Gulf & Western Corporation.

If you wish to have more solo parts, both the first and second phrases could be sung
by individuals or small groups, with the entire class joining in on the last phrase.

Singing voices are as distinctive as speaking voices. The benefits derived from
having children sing alone or in pairs are twofold: (1) other members of the class
have a chance to listen objectively to voices of various qualities, and (2) those who
sing learn to accept the quality of their own voices and develop confidence in their
ability to sing. Independence in singing a song and the ability to sing with an
accompaniment are skills that need to be built at this level. Both of these skills are
necessary for singing the rounds and other part-songs discussed in Chapter 6.

Using Music Books

Many school districts supply a basic series music book (see Appendix B-I for
listing) for each child from the second grade upward, and all of the music referred to
in these books is also available on records. It is not possible to find in one book the
variety of songs children should experience in a school year, and schools where
music series books are used effectively usually supply a set of supplementary books
to make available a wider choice of music.

In the second grade, if many of the children do not read words well, or they have not yet learned to find page numbers efficiently, you may find it advisable to delay the general use of music books until mid-year. Music books hold considerable interest for children, however, and in the current series books, visual materials designed by the authors are helpful; so use the books whenever they will enhance musical learning.

Even if you do not use books with the entire class at the beginning of the year, you may wish to make them available to children who are especially talented in music and have adequate general reading skills. With the materials now available, a child could successfully carry out an individualized study project that uses the music books and related recordings.

Teaching the melody of a new song with books in the hands of the children does not differ markedly from the techniques described earlier. You will be less concerned with other motivation, because diagrams and pictures in the book, along with readable words, provide much of the interest. Just how a song is presented depends upon its vocabulary and the children's reading level.

Before the books are opened, you can sing or play the recorded song and then discuss the song's topic and interesting aspects of the music. In this instance the children depend on their ears to tell them about the song. The development of aural perception is basic at all levels of participation in music; visual perception supports and defines in another way the sounds that the ear hears. When the books are opened, the children see the visual representation of what they heard, and you can gradually lead them to recognize notation for specific musical details.

At other times start by having the children open the books to the new song and direct their attention to the pictures, poems, questions, or other items of interest on the page. They can read the text and talk about it before they hear the music. This approach can be used when the vocabulary is within the reading ability of the children. As a preliminary exploration of the way the music goes, familiar tonal and rhythm patterns can be identified, discussed, and sounded.

Songs in many basic music books are laid out on the page so that the phrases conform to the length of the lines. This arrangement helps children see the construction of the song as a whole, its repeated phrases, contrasting movement, and melodic and rhythmic motives. It is helpful for the singers to be aware of the general structure as they begin to learn the song.

Let's assume that "Billy Barlow" (Example 7.7) is a song eight-year-olds will learn with the aid of the music book. Ask them to read the text and find out all they can about the song.

EXAMPLE 7.7

BILLY BARLOW
Texas

Moderately fast

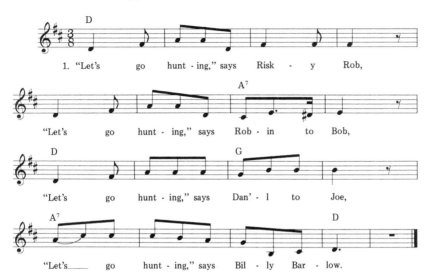

1. "Let's go hunt-ing," says Risk-y Rob,

"Let's go hunt-ing," says Rob-in to Bob,

"Let's go hunt-ing," says Dan'-l to Joe,

"Let's___ go hunt-ing," says Bil-ly Bar-low.

2. "What shall I hunt?" says Risky Rob,
   "What shall I hunt?" says Robin to Bob,
   "What shall I hunt?" says Dan'l to Joe,
   "Hunt for a rat," says Billy Barlow.

3. "How shall I get him?" says Risky Rob,
   "How shall I get him?" says Robin to Bob,
   "How shall I get him?" says Dan'l to Joe,
   "Go borrow a gun," says Billy Barlow.

4. "How shall I haul him?" *etc. (3 times)*
   "Go borrow a cart," said Billy Barlow.

5. "How shall we divide him?" *etc. (4 times)*

6. "I'll take shoulder," says Risky Rob,
   "I'll take side," says Robin to Bob,
   "I'll take ham," says Dan'l to Joe,
   "Tail bone mine," says Billy Barlow.

7. "How shall we cook him?" *etc. (4 times)*

8. "I'll broil shoulder," says Risky Rob,
   "I'll fry side," says Robin to Bob,
   "I'll boil ham," says Dan'l to Joe,
   "Tail bone raw," says Billy Barlow.

Plan a series of questions that can lead to a discussion of the song and discovery of some of its musical qualities.

1. Ask some general questions that permit a variety of answers: "What is the idea of the song? Who are the characters in the story, and what are they doing?"

2. Then ask some questions that require a certain amount of reasoning and drawing inferences: "Why do you suppose the title of the song is 'Billy Barlow' rather than 'A Hunting Song' or 'Risky Rob'? Does one really need a gun to get a rat, or a cart to haul him? What do these words tell you about the meaning and mood of the song?"

3. Finally, ask some questions that draw attention to the music: "There seems to be a great deal of repetition from one line to the next in the words of this song; is each phrase of the music the same? Which phrases are most alike and which are different? Which phrase is most distinctive in its melody and how does it differ from the other phrases? Who is speaking during that phrase?"

The discussion should begin to suggest the interpretation of the song: the melody should move with a carefree swing; as each of the characters repeats or amplifies the previous idea, the music can grow a little louder. The leader of this group of would-be big game hunters, Billy Barlow, always has the last word. The melody of his line has a broad, impressive sweep and should be sung with authority and conviction.

Sing the song as the children follow the melody line on the page. Repeat the last phrase and have the children sing it after you, so they feel the authoritative quality of Billy Barlow's response. Due to the wide skip in the melody, it may be necessary to sing the four notes for "Billy Barlow" as a tone call, with individuals and small groups echoing it:

Then the song can be sung in its entirety, possibly phrase by phrase to assure that the children sing it correctly. Later, different children could take turns singing the several lines that represent the different characters speaking, and one or two children might provide an accompaniment on the Autoharp. The voice and personality of one child in the class might be considered by the children to be particularly appropriate for "Billy Barlow." Such a choice would be a further indication that the children understood the musical expressiveness of this song.

As you see, much of the activity in learning "Billy Barlow" was related to reading and to interpreting verbal ideas, both of which are necessary preliminaries to learning the music.

Instructional Objectives: To teach a song the children will enjoy and will sing expressively in solo parts and as a group; to teach children how to approach a song through its printed notation.

Behaviors providing evidence that these instructional objectives have been achieved: The children will

☐ sing the song accurately and expressively, both as a group and using solo voices

☐ sing Billy Barlow's phrase in a manner reflecting Billy's character

☐ look for repeated phrases and for rhythm and tonal patterns when they approach another new song through its printed notation

In the early use of music notation, one problem that may arise is how to read consecutive stanzas in a song when more than one stanza is written under the music line, as in "Going to the Fair" (Example 7.8). The first song of this kind that children encounter should be a song for which they have previously learned two or more stanzas without books. Then when they see the printed song, the children will be able to follow the unaccustomed order of the text lines because they know the song.

In dealing with a new song in this format, cut page-width markers of construction paper for the children to hold under the words they sing and move down the page from line to line on each stanza. You will then be able to see by the position of the markers which children do not understand the order of the lines. This device can be used for a few weeks, with both familiar and new songs, until the children are used to reading the first line under the music score all the way through the song, and then returning to the top for the second stanza.

In learning some songs, the children can contribute more to the interpretation of the music itself. The following treatment of "Going to the Fair" will give you an idea of questions and procedures that might be used with such a song.

EXAMPLE 7.8

GOING TO THE FAIR
German Folk Song

From *Discovering Music Together*, Book 3, by Charles Leonhard, Beatrice Krone, Irving Wolfe, and Margaret Fullerton. © 1970 by Follett Publishing Company. Used by permission.

Have the children study the text and music and make whatever observations they can about it. They may notice the German exclamation "Ach ja!" meaning "Oh, yes!" How many times does it occur in each verse? Is the melody of that pattern the same each time? (The third occurrence of "Ach ja!" is different.) Sing, and have the children sing the two different fragments for "Ach ja!" with the necessary Autoharp chords as an accompaniment.

The rhythm of this song is very simple. If the boys and girls have had previous experience tapping similar rhythm patterns, they may be able to tap and verbalize the rhythm of the words for the first phrase. In this phrase the beats are evenly divided, and children could easily verbalize the rhythm pattern with ti and ta:

Next have them chant the words for that phrase as they tap the melody rhythm. Notice that the phrase beginning in measure four is just like the first; therefore, the singers can chant and clap the rhythm of those words, too.

The melody of the first part of the song (the *stanza*, which features different words each time it is sung), is substantially different from the melody of the *refrain* (which repeats its words as well as its melody each time it is sung). This is a two-part song form (A B) that has four phrases: a a b b'. Observing phrases that are alike and different will help the children learn the song. Sing the first verse and have them chime in on "Ach ja!" which they now know. They should then be able to sing the three verses of the stanza while you sing and accompany on the Autoharp.

At another lesson the children might sing the verses they know and then work out the rhythm of the refrain. Help them observe the small rhythm patterns that make up the refrain. Each of the two phrases has three patterns that they may be able to clap and chant:

Observe how the melody at the beginning of these two phrases differs in pitch (the second phrase starts a whole step lower). Sing, and have the class sing, each phrase, and then they will be ready to sing the whole song with you. The Autoharp or guitar can be used in this song-learning process, and since this is an easy two-chord song, some of the children could learn to play the Autoharp accompaniment. This song would be appropriate to use for developing a rhythm accompaniment and for a simple schottische dance, as described in Chapters 3 and 4.

Instructional Objectives: To help children learn a new song in a way that uses their previously acquired skills in dealing with rhythm, and their awareness of melodic movement; to develop children's confidence in their beginning ability to know what music symbols mean; and to help them develop a musical interpretation of a song that will give them pleasure.

Behaviors providing evidence that these instructional objectives have been achieved: The children will

   □ sing the melody of "Going to the Fair" accurately and with enthusiasm

□ subsequently approach another new song, of similar difficulty, with greater independence in dealing with basic rhythmic and melodic components

In learning songs at Level II, children should be helped to work out the melody and the rhythm along the lines outlined above. Different levels of ability can be found in every class, but the children should be encouraged to use whatever knowledge and skill they have. By using *sol-fa* syllables and tuned instruments to reinforce tonal patterns, as discussed in Chapter 6, you can help children to be more self-sufficient in learning new songs.

Expanding the Repertoire

The music of different cultural backgrounds can add a dimension to musical experience that is missing when the music used is limited to Western European songs and compositions. When social studies focus on people of other cultures, you should include experiences with the music and art of those cultures.

A unit of study about the American Indian is often used during grades two, three, or four. Usually a selection of Indian songs can be found in one of the basic series music books at this level. "Muje Mukesin" (Example 5.13) is an interesting Ojibway melody. The Indian concept of melody very often resulted in songs containing five different tones (pentatonic). Notice that in this song only the tones B—D E—G A B are used (B is repeated at the octave). The tonal center of this song is E. Play this succession of tones several times, so that you become familiar with the sound of this tonal organization. Then sing or play the melody until the words and the tune fit comfortably together.

Clap or use a drum to sound a steady beat on quarter-note values. Notice how the strong beat is placed in a way that alternately marks off sets of two and sets of three beats. Indian people had a freer concept of rhythm and did not find it necessary to keep the same organization of beats within one meter throughout the song.

Instructional Objectives: To help children become acquainted with the music of another culture and to experience the unique musical characteristics of its pentatonic melody and flexible rhythmic organization.

Behaviors providing evidence that these instructional objectives have been achieved: The children will

□ express interest in learning other Indian songs

□ identify a pentatonic arrangement of tones when it is played on a melody instrument

□ discriminate $\frac{2}{4}$ meter from a mixed meter such as that heard in this song

In this book you will find a number of songs from other cultures that would be useful at this level:

"A Ram Sam Sam," Moroccan (Example 3.11)

"Duérmete, mi Niño," Spanish (Example 5.21)

"San Sereni," Spanish (Example 4.14)

"Canoe Song," Canadian (Example 5.26)

The African people transported to America as slaves brought with them a deep love of music, and so began the Afro-American musical heritage of folk songs, spirituals, and blues. "Chatter with the Angels" (Example 5.10) is a cheerful Afro-American folk song that seems especially suited to children. In using this song and the song discussed below as part of a study of the Afro-American heritage, you should note that black people as slaves in America were deeply religious. Many of their songs allowed them to survive the harsh realities of this life by concentrating on the symbols and ideas within their religious beliefs.

"Mary Had a Baby" (Example 5.12) is a spiritual that can be used as a Christmas song. Notice that the first phrase of the text is repeated three times and that the repetitions build to a climax at the end of the third phrase. Each repeated phrase is followed by a response, "Yes, Lord," which changes each time. This is an example of a song form labeled "call and response." It arose in religious services when the preacher sang out an idea and people in the congregation sang back their agreement. Such songs were spontaneous and improvisatory, with the leader creating any text that seemed appropriate at the moment. With either of these two songs, individuals or small groups could be delegated to sing the repetitive phrases and the entire class could sing the response. Both should be sung with vigor, enthusiasm, and strong rhythmic drive.

Instructional Objectives: To help children understand the place of music in the life of Afro-American people, and to learn to sing two folk songs in a style appropriate to the culture.

Behaviors providing evidence that these instructional objectives have been achieved: The children will

☐ describe how black Americans, as slaves, used music to express their religious beliefs and to help make their lives happier

☐ demonstrate how a leader and a chorus take turns singing "call-response" songs

☐ sing with spirit, and with alternating solo and chorus parts appropriate to the songs

Among the special days that can be highlighted by appropriate songs, Thanksgiving has a number of traditional harvest songs that are part of the American heritage. "Praise and Thanksgiving," a round (**NDinM VI-222**), is appealing to all ages and can be sung as a unison song by younger children. From the third grade upward, children can learn to sing "Come, Ye Thankful People, Come" (**ExM IV-188**) or the old family favorite, "Over the River and Through the Wood" (**TMT II-164**). "The Ghost of John" (Example 7.6) is a very short song, or a round for those who are ready for two-part singing, that will add to the atmosphere of Halloween. "Love Somebody" is delightful and a much more satisfactory song for Valentine's Day than many others.

EXAMPLE 7.9

LOVE SOMEBODY
American Folk Song

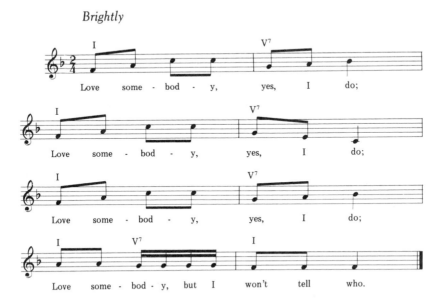

In contrast to many of the obviously contrived songs you will find for special days, these are expressive songs that individuals of any age will enjoy.

"America the Beautiful" (**SBM IV-139**) is the noblest of our patriotic songs and can be added to the repertoire of eight- and nine-year-olds. This is not a folk song, and the best accompaniment is provided by piano or organ.

Christmas brings a wealth of traditional songs, and some questions about how many of these have a place in the public school. Teachers in different communities find different answers. If a song is a thing of beauty and a joy to sing, it may be used regardless of its cultural or religious heritage. Many carols, however, are too difficult musically for young children and too deeply religious in text for school use. Christmas programs and pageants that center on the nativity story and related sacred music are generally not acceptable in public schools.

Carols and customs from Sweden, Mexico, and many other countries can broaden the appreciation of Christmas while also providing a basis for an acquaintance with people in other lands. A play, pageant, or tableau of almost any size can be developed around the topic "Christmas in Other Lands."

In addition to the Christmas celebration, you might consider the Jewish December Festival of Lights, as children are led to share an appreciation of traditional songs of holidays that receive less public attention. "Hanukkah" (**ExM III-74**), "O Hanukkah" (**TMT II-170**), and other songs are available in the basic song books. *A Treasury of Jewish Folklore*[7] by Nathan Ausubel is an aid to the teacher searching for interesting material about the Jewish faith and customs.

Easter is a holy day, rather than a holiday, and as such is even harder to deal with in the public schools, where all faiths are represented, than is Christmas. Songs that treat of Easter as a time of waking earth and flowers are usually quite acceptable.

Schools associated with a religious organization, of course, have the opportunity to use much fine religious music in the children's singing repertoire. Even in these schools you should take care that the music is appropriate for children, both in the text and in the simplicity of the melody.

EXPERIENCES AT LEVEL III

Nine- to eleven-year-olds are growing in independence and self-awareness. Feelings are near the surface, and these children need support and approval from peers as well as teachers. The expression of feeling through music, and the empathy achieved when several persons sing together of the same longings or convictions, are important at this age. A music teacher should be available to provide experience in special choral groups and to help individual children develop vocally; but the singing the classroom teacher can promote in conjunction with classroom activities and everyday living is as significant as other kinds of singing. The following are objectives that might be achieved through singing activities that can be carried on in the general classroom:

1. to help children find, express, and share their feelings as young developing personalities
2. to assist individuals in developing singing skills and styles of expression that meet their personal needs
3. to expand children's understanding of the elements of music and how these affect the expressive quality of the song
4. to teach a heritage of songs that brings children closer to feelings and values in their own contemporary world and other cultures
5. to build a feeling of community within the classroom and the school as a whole

Although some singing should be done by the whole class, more small-group singing can be fostered at this level. Not all children have the same tastes or feelings; since singing can serve such personal needs, it is wise to recognize these differences and help the children express themselves. The group encounter can be broadened when individuals or small groups share their songs with classmates, who usually are very respectful of the performance of their peers.

The Voices of Later Childhood

The outlook for good singing among nine- to eleven-year-olds is excellent, if motivation is present. Good singing is the result of clarity in enunciation and adequate breath support, which gives the musical phrase its continuity. When pupils are enthusiastic about singing, breath support is no problem, because the muscular framework is strong and flexible. If interest wanes, bodies sag in the chairs and tone quality deteriorates. In the intermediate grades, breath support is achieved only indirectly through (1) good posture, promoted as far as possible through interest and enthusiasm, and (2) the message of the song—how it should be sung to achieve an expressive melody or vital rhythm.

Precise enunciation of words is important. Children can be careless or simply untrained in proper habits of enunciation. A flexible use of tongue and lips is necessary for clear speaking as well as for good singing. Singing is intoned speech, and unless the words are understood it does not fulfill its intended function.

Singing has the added dimension of predetermined pitch, not found in speaking. Children need to learn to hear and sing the various steps and intervals of the scale in tune. Scale steps and intervals are found in all the songs they sing. (See Appendix A-III for a review of concepts about melody that can be developed at this level.) Learning songs accurately from good recordings, with the aid of a tuned instrument, or from a teacher with a good sense of pitch will do much to assure development of a sense of pitch relationships.

Boys' Voices. The range and general quality in the voices of elementary school boys and girls is essentially the same. However, at puberty the boy's larynx grows and the vocal cords lengthen and thicken so that his voice gradually drops an octave in pitch. During the fifth, sixth, and perhaps seventh grades, prior to the change in voice, he has his last opportunity to sing in the high register. At this time his soprano voice tends to develop more brilliance than the girls' and, when properly trained, may have an upward range to G or A above the treble staff. When these two facts are appreciated by the boys, there is usually little difficulty in promoting their interest in developing the unchanged voice.

Occasionally you may find a boy in the fifth or sixth grade whose voice and general physical development indicate his early approach to adolescence. At this time the voice may temporarily be limited to about an octave upward from G or A below the treble staff. Although the unusual quality of the voice may make it sound lower, this is still within the normal range of the mature alto voice. A fifth or sixth grade class also may include boys whose voices are not yet beginning to change, but who have not learned earlier to use their high singing voices. At this age they may have no inclination to do so. The teacher's problem then lies in helping them learn to sing in a lower limited range, knowing that within a year or two the normal lengthening of the vocal cords will permit them to extend the range downward. A practical range for these voices is:

Two obstacles can interfere with the development of both of these types of boys' voices: the normal singing range for the class does not include all the low notes of the range shown above; and almost every sixth grade song goes above this range. Here are four suggestions:

1. Help the boys identify their own effective vocal range, and encourage them to sing with the class whenever the song goes within that range.

2. Transpose songs with a short range, so that they can be sung in the lower octave by these voices and in the higher octave by the rest of the voices. "Hey, Lollee!" (Example 6.3), when sung in the key of A, has this range:

3. Some melodic sections of songs may be sung by these lower voices while the others sing harmony parts above the melody.

4. Two- and three-tone harmonizing parts can be arranged for these voices as shown under "Singing Chants and Root Tones" in Chapter 6.

Gifted Singers. Occasionally an intermediate child may possess an unusually beautiful voice that floats free and true without apparent effort. When such a voice is discovered, the teacher may be concerned about its proper development. Private lessons and any special training of the voice itself should be delayed until the singer is fifteen or sixteen years old, when the vocal cords have completely adjusted to the physical change of puberty. (It should be noted that there is growth in the larynx of the girl during puberty. The vocal cords do not lengthen, but in some individuals a strengthening of the lower tones of the voice gives evidence of the emergence of a true alto voice.) The general musical education of such children should be promoted, so that they will be in a position to use their voices to greatest advantage when they do mature.

Such gifted singers should be encouraged to sing in a natural, free voice and to develop a repertoire of folk and other songs they enjoy sharing with others. They can participate in the school choir, sing occasional short solos with the group to develop confidence in solo work, and participate in small ensembles with other good singers. Such a child might also study a musical instrument, in order to have further musical encounters and to become skilled in using music notation. The piano is a practical instrument for a singer to know, but musical skills can be broadened through the study of other instruments as well.

Musically gifted children should have broad experiences in listening to fine singers of all types and to a variety of instrumental music, so that they develop an intuitive sense of good musical expression. Classroom activities in music will combine to give these children basic understandings; later they may use these understandings to develop more specific music skills.

Undeveloped Voices. If a child at this level does not sing, the problem may lie in the lack of a concept about singing (how the vocal mechanism feels when one is producing a singing tone, or the effect of matching pitch with another voice or an instrument). To help a child establish such a concept, a teacher should

1. find a pitch level at which the individual can prolong the speaking voice into singing tones
2. ask the child to identify and sing a familiar melody limited to four or five different tones. "Hey, Lollee!" (Example 6.3) and "The Birch Tree" (Example 5.23) are five-tone melodies, and "Hot Cross Buns" (Example 5.4) uses three tones

3. identify singing success even if it consists of only three or four tones, and sing along with the child at that level

4. ask the child to repeat the successful phrase using quiet, relaxed singing

5. help the child sing more of the melody at the pitch level established

6. provide an accompaniment for the child's singing at the pitch level established

7. help the child find those pitches on an instrument that the child can play (e.g., guitar or bells), and suggest that he or she practice singing and playing the melody

8. later, begin singing at the previously successful level and

   a. move the pitch level of the song up or down a half-step at a time, exploring a broader range of pitch

   b. work with another melody at the same pitch level

It is possible to help an individual learn to sing, but we must begin at the point where success is most likely to occur. The ability to accompany a song in various keys can be very helpful when you adjust songs to the voices of inexperienced singers.

Learning New Songs and Expanding the Repertoire

Children in the intermediate grades learn songs by hearing them played from a recording or sung by their teacher, the music specialist, or a member of the class. The songs may be played on the piano, the bells, or another instrument. As they listen, the children should watch the notation, observing how what is heard relates to what is seen. Observing and listening this way will help them sing successfully at the earliest possible moment, and as they understand the notation, they will be better prepared to meet the next new song. Children who can read a song text and who have some familiarity with music notation should not have to learn a song without its printed version unless it is either very short and simple, or the situation makes it absolutely essential that they sing a song for which no copies are available.

At this level, songs can be approached as they might be by adults who have no specialized musical training. As the children listen to the song the first time, they might consider its text, noting any repeated lines; they might look at the general contour of its melody and the repeated or contrasting phrases that determine the song's form. These characteristics might be discussed, so that all will be aware of them before attempting to sing the song. The rhythmic characteristics of the song might be examined: establish the meter, and tap out repeated rhythm patterns that are identified. Survey it for familiar melodic patterns. When a group of notes is recognized as a scale line, or as related to a chord, or as beginning and ending at certain levels, that pattern or phrase might be sung or played on melody instruments. Songs built around the primary chords (I, IV, V^7) will be sung more easily if you use the Autoharp or guitar as a harmonic background.

However the song is studied, the experience should result in a feeling of satisfaction and accomplishment. Unrhythmic, note-by-note spelling out of a melody is not a musical experience. On the other hand, learning a song without any attempt to develop understanding about the music or its notation can hardly be considered music education. New songs should be approached in varied ways, with the use of effective techniques to solve melodic and rhythmic problems.

The following songs are examples of some that might be used with fifth or sixth graders. In the suggested procedures you will notice that as much attention is given to developing an understanding of the mood and meaning of the song as to learning the music itself. Music serves the human need for shaping and sharing feeling, whether it be in the joyfulness of a dance or in the quiet corner of personal experience.

Songs of Personal Relevance. During the years from nine to eleven, children are progressively more interested in exercising their own tastes and opinions and in finding their identity within the youth group of which they are a part. Many songs which we know as traditional will appeal to these boys and girls, but you should also make use of the contemporary popular music that is so much a part of their world. Girls mature faster than boys at this age and many girls like sentimental songs that boys reject. Due to different interests, then, the repertoire will be varied, but in song material of any type or style we can find opportunities for musical learning.

"Both Sides Now" (Example 7.10) by Joni Mitchell is a philosophic little song. Although not all boys and girls at these ages will admit to being interested in this sentiment, the song will be generally useful to them because each one has his or her own private illusions and frustrations.

EXAMPLE 7.10

BOTH SIDES NOW

Words and Music by Joni Mitchell

I've looked at clouds from both sides now,— From up and down,
I've looked at love from both sides now,— From give and take,

and still some-how— It's cloud il-lu-sions I re-call; I
and still some-how— It's love's il-lu-sions I re-call; I

real-ly— don't know clouds_____ at_ all._____
real-ly— don't know love_____ at_ all._____

	I	IV	V⁷
Key of A:	A	D	E^7
Key of B♭:	B^b	E^b	F^7
Key of C:	C	F	G^7

Approach this song by reading the text and discussing the bright and dark sides of life as mentioned in the song. Surely you can think of experiences in life that were more an illusion than reality.

Look at the form of the music; which phrases are alike? How long is the first phrase—four measures or eight measures? (Probably the completed phrase should be considered eight measures in length although there is a brief stopping place at the end of the fourth measure.) The first long eight-measure phrase is followed by another that is almost the same. Following it, the song has an eleven-measure phrase that is quite different from the preceding phrases. This could be considered the refrain, even though the words change the second time it is sung. Notice how each phrase has one main idea in the lyrics.

How does the melody of this song move, and what are the general qualities of the rhythm? Because the melody has such a wide range, it is written here in the key of A to accommodate unskilled voices. This is a good key for the guitar and a capo could be used to raise the pitch, especially if the refrain were sung in two parts, so that the lower voices could take the alto part.

Observe that although the range of the song is wide, the melodic contour of the stanza is quite a smooth flowing up and down. Two places in the stanza and several places in the refrain have wide downward leaps. Does this seem to have any relationship to the words at those points? Is it possible that the melody jumps around to reflect the fact that one's feelings are bounced around in one's experiences with life?

On a melody instrument, play the two-measure phrases in which the melody has wide leaps, then sing those phrases.

The song has considerable syncopation in the melody; notice how the verse alternates one measure in which the melody falls on the steady beats and one measure of syncopation. Tap a steady beat with your toe; count and clap the syncopated melody rhythm of the second measure, then clap it as you say the words:

In how many measures does this motif occur? Sing the words and clap the rhythm for this motif.

If there is a recording available of Joni Mitchell singing the song, play it to hear her particular interpretation. Then a guitarist and two or more singers in your group may want to work up their own rendition. "Both Sides Now" is just one example of a contemporary song that is expressive and musically interesting. Such songs come and go, but at a particular moment in time, a song can be very expressive and meaningful to young people. Look for others you think the children in your class will enjoy learning.

Instructional Objectives: To teach a song that will have personal relevance for children in the class; to help them analyze the song enough to understand how the musical elements of rhythm and melody support the meaning of the lyrics; and to use their knowledge of rhythm to help them learn the song.

Behaviors providing evidence that these instructional objectives have been achieved: The children will

- □ sing the song expressively, either in small groups or as a class
- □ distinguish large melodic intervals from smooth melodic lines and point out which lyrics need the wide intervals
- □ tap a straight four-beat measure followed by a syncopated measure and point to each in the musical notation

Songs of Social Relevance. Songs concerned with the the people and the building of this country will have meaning for boys and girls who are studying this history and will bring them closer to the feelings and concerns of the people they read about. "Shenandoah" (**TMT V-170**) is a nostalgic song of a river that was prominent in our history. "Streets of Laredo" (Example 6.27) tells the fate of the cowboy who roamed the frontiers of the West. "Don't Let Your Watch Run Down" (Example 5.24) relates the concern of members of the railroad gangs who toiled to link the East with the West by means of steel rail. "I'm On My Way" (Example 7.11) is a spiritual that suggests the hope the runaway slaves had in going north via the "Underground Railroad." Undoubtedly it will have personal appeal to the youngster who is trying to find personal identity in his or her world.

EXAMPLE 7.11

I'M ON MY WAY

Traditional Spiritual

With conviction

1. I'm on my way (I'm on my way) And I won't turn
2. I asked my brother [sister] To come with
3. I'm on my way To free-dom

back; (And I won't turn back;) I'm on my way (I'm on my
me . . . *etc.*
land . . . *etc.*

way) And I won't turn back; (And I won't turn back;) I'm on my

way (I'm on my way) And I won't turn back; (And I won't turn

back;) I'm on my way,— Great God, I'm on my way._____

	I	I⁷	IV	V	V⁷
Key of F:	F	F^7	$B^\flat$	C	C^7
Key of D:	D	D^7	G	A	A^7

This is a quiet, smooth-flowing melody that starts low and rises through three phrases to a climax. Each time the opening words are repeated, the melody is a little higher and more assertive. Notice how every phrase opens with a three note upbeat, leading to a strong sense of arrival and stability on the long note. At the climax the long note has a little special touch in the added grace note. All these details help shape this song into a statement of confidence and optimism, and it is worthwhile to bring them to the attention of the singers. The song is so simple that some member of the class probably could play the melody on the piano or an orchestral instrument.

If a lower key would make the song easier for some voices, try it in the key of D, which begins like this:

I'm on my way and I won't turn back...

Instructional Objectives: To teach a song that has both social and personal relevance for children; to help them understand the need American black people had to escape from slavery; and to notice how this single idea is expressed through a single melodic idea in the music.

Behaviors providing evidence that these instructional objectives have been achieved: The children will

☐ sing this song expressively, with a rise in intensity through the first three phrases

☐ ask questions and research the operation of the "Underground Railroad" as an escape route from southern slavery

There are, of course, many more songs of America, and it is a matter of selecting those which will have the most meaning for the boys and girls. Many of these songs can be accompanied by Autoharp or guitar, which a number of these children will be able to learn to play.

During their study of American history, nine- to eleven-year-olds can learn the important patriotic songs that grew out of that history. In some communities you may find groups who are not receptive to patriotic songs. The most reasonable time to learn the militant "Star-Spangled Banner" (Example 7.12) or the "Battle Hymn of the Republic" (**NDinM V-218**) is when children learn about the convictions and struggles that enabled the early patriots to establish an independent country. "The Star-Spangled Banner" is a difficult song with a wide range. Because it is the national anthem, it should be learned correctly at some point in the elementary school.

EXAMPLE 7.12

THE STAR-SPANGLED BANNER

Francis Scott Key
John Stafford Smith

With spirit

Gave   proof   thro' the   night   that our   flag   was   still   there.

Chorus

O   say,   does that   Star - Span - gled   Ban - ner   yet   wave,

O'er the   land   of the   free   and the   home   of the   brave?

2. O—thus be it ever when—free men shall stand
   Between their loved homes and the war's desolation!
   Blest with vict'ry and peace, may the heav'n-rescued land
   Praise the Pow'r that hath made and preserved us a nation!
   Then—conquer we must for our cause it is just,
   And this be our motto: "In—God is our trust!" *Refrain.*

"The Star-Spangled Banner" has four clearly defined phrases, each eight measures long, with this form: a   a   b   c. The phrase labeled "b" usually is played or sung smoothly (legato) in contrast to the more detached, accented style of the first and last phrases. Notice how many times the opening rhythm pattern is repeated:

This, together with the angular melody, gives the opening of the song its bold quality.

The extremely wide range of this song makes tuning-up procedures essential. The key of A$^\flat$ is the key most often used for singing this song, but some individuals may have difficulty with the highest tones. Although G below the treble staff is too low for some voices, you may want to try this song in the key of G to make the highest notes more accessible. The most appropriate accompaniment is the piano or an instrumental ensemble, rather than an Autoharp or guitar.

Instructional Objectives: To teach "The Star-Spangled Banner" so that the children sing it correctly, and with an understanding of the historical context that led it to be written.

Behaviors providing evidence that these instructional objectives have been achieved: The children will

  □ sing "The Star-Spangled Banner" correctly from memory
  □ tell about the historical events that led to the composition of the song

Songs of Other Cultures. Children of these ages will be studying civilizations and customs of people in other lands, and so you should take the opportunity to include music of those countries. Folkways, Lyrichord, Nonesuch, and other companies provide recordings of musicians from around the world singing and playing authentic instruments of their cultures. Try to use recordings of this type, and become acquainted with the tone color of voices and instruments that differ from those of musicians in this country. If it is impossible to see the instruments and the musicians in person, search in the library for pictures and books[8] that will help you know what the instruments look like.

The songs of Latin America and the Caribbean are rhythmic and colorful and should be a part of any study of people in those areas. Rhythm and chording instruments can be used as accompaniments, so that several children can be involved in different ways. "Water Come to Me Eye" (Example 6.24) is an easy Jamaican song with a syncopated rhythm pattern that can be picked up by players using claves or maracas. The song is easy to sing and, as shown in Chapter 6, it can be accompanied by two chords on the guitar or Autoharp.

Because performance practices differ from one musical tradition to another, certain aspects of music (that is, rhythm, melody, texture) from Asia, Africa, and other areas are unique. It can be very instructive to compare two recordings of a song, one by "Western" musicians and one by musicians from the country in which the song originated.

The Korean folk song "Arirang" (Example 7.13) appears in several basic school music series. Look for it and listen to the song as presented on the record that accompanies the book (**DMT VI-139, ExM VI-117, SBM VI-103**). What you hear and see is a "Western" transcription, primarily intended to help children learn to sing the song. These versions show the general melodic structure very well; Koreans, however, sing this song with more decorative tones in the melody. Translations of the text also differ; some versions give more consideration to the sound of the translation than to its literal meaning. The song as shown here is quite a literal translation of the Korean text and the melody can be labeled quasi-authentic (a concept to be explained later).

EXAMPLE 7.13

ARIRANG

Korean Folk Song
Transcribed and Translated by Dr. Kang-Sook Lee

Moderately

A - ri - rang, A - ri - rang, A - ra - ri - yo.

A - ri - rang ko - gae ro nŏ - mŏ kan - da.
Go - ing o - ver the A - ri - rang hill.

Na rŭl pŏ - ri - go ka - si - nŭn ni - mŭ - n,
If you're leav - ing me,

Sim - ni do mot - ga - sŏ pal - byŏng nan - da.
'Ere you get far a - way your feet will be sore.

Used by permission of Dr. Kang-Sook Lee.

In a performance by Korean musicians[9] you can hear a much more embellished version of this melody. Example 7.14 is a transcription of the first phrase of the melody, approximately as it is heard on the recording.

EXAMPLE 7.14

In addition to the greater melodic embellishment, notice that the quality of the voice and the sound of the accompaniment are markedly different from the tone colors we are accustomed to hearing in the Western European style.

The notation used here cannot show all the unique qualities of the melody heard in the recording. Dr. Kang-Sook Lee,[10] a music educator with Korean background, pointed out another difference in the music performed by the Korean musicians: "The important point to consider is that Korean modes are not based on equally tempered scales. . . . the pentatonic scale as found on the keys of the piano is fundamentally different from that of the Korean mode."

Although "Arirang" is based on a five-tone (pentatonic) scale, the tonal distances from one step of that scale to the next are slightly different from those of the "Western" pentatonic scale. In this musical example, the most obvious pitch deviation (less than a quarter-tone lower) occurs on those notes with downward arrows above them. Listen again to the Lyrichord record to hear this difference in pitch which, though subtle, is one quality that distinguishes the authentic Korean style from a quasi-authentic "Western" version of the same song.

Instructional Objectives: To have the children learn to sing a song from a culture different from their own; to help them understand that music of another culture can be quite different in its melodic components and performance practice; and to build a receptive attitude for music of other cultures.

Behaviors providing evidence that these instructional objectives have been achieved: The children will

- sing "Arirang" both with the English and the Korean texts
- understand and be able to state the chief distinguishing characteristics of this music: that (1) it is sung as an embellished melody, (2) it is based on a pentatonic scale that does not conform in pitch to tones played on the piano
- ask to hear other music of cultures different from their own

The following are examples of songs of other cultures that can be found in basic series music books and the related recordings at the intermediate level. Several of these can also be found on commercial recordings featuring musicians and instruments from these cultures.

"Flower Drum Song" *Feng Yang Drum),* Chinese (**ExM VI-120**)

"Guantanamera" (Lady of Guantanamo), Cuba (**EXM V-62**)

"Sakura" (Cherry Bloom), Japan (**NDinM VI-120**)

"Gerakina" *(Yerakina),* Greek (**SBM VI-112**)

"Musk Ox Hunt Song," Eskimo (**SBM V-107**)

"Bana Cimbusa," Zambia (**NDinM VI-70**)

Each song of another culture that is learned provides some opportunity for boys and girls to gain broader understanding about music around the world. Although most songs used in the classroom should be more traditionally a part of music in the United States, the justification is ample for including songs of more diverse cultures. When you do so, use recordings to provide an authentic flavor to the experience and broaden the children's understanding of different musical values and performance practices.

Broadening the Singing Experience

A special choir should be available for intermediate grade children who have a particular interest in singing. Such singing enriches their musical experience and also prepares them for choral work in the high school, church, and community. The music consultant or a musically talented teacher can organize an elementary school choir. Membership should be open to all fifth and sixth grade students on the basis of interest and, to some extent, singing ability. Whatever selection seems necessary should be done with due consideration for the needs as well as talents of individuals who are interested. Fourth grade students might be included, although their voices generally are less mature and the choir gains some prestige when membership is limited to older children.

To make satisfying progress, a choral group should meet two or three times weekly. It should not be a substitute for classroom music. Rehearsal during the school day is the most desirable arrangement. It may be necessary, however, to practice before school or at noon. After-school rehearsals are not recommended because boys and girls are too tired for satisfactory accomplishment. A compromise may be made by extending the thirty- or forty-minute rehearsal into the next school session for fifteen minutes in the morning, before or after lunch.

If more children seek membership in the choir than can be accommodated, membership may be selective as well as elective. Those who are not admitted must be given opportunities to improve their singing so that they can successfully seek membership at a later time.

In the United States, elementary school choirs traditionally sing many of their songs in two or three parts. Part-singing can be beautiful when the boys and girls are sufficiently experienced to listen to the total effect and to stay in tune. It is most effective when unaccompanied. In some schools, however, part-singing has been emphasized to the exclusion of unison singing. A select group of children's voices singing in unison a lovely art song such as "Children's Prayer" from *Hänsel and Gretel* is a musical treat for any audience and provides a genuine thrill for the performers as well.

An excellent collection of vocal music for unchanged voices from style periods of the pre-Renaissance through the contemporary can be found in the *Juilliard Repertory Library*.[11] Numerous publishers of choral music have works for children's voices. (See Appendix B for names and addresses of such firms.) Most fifth and sixth grade series music books contain some part-songs that can be used by such choral groups, but it is advisable to extend the repertoire beyond that used in the classroom music program.

The repertoire that the director selects should offer a balance of experiences for these young singers. They should not be asked to sing consistently difficult arrangements in which they fail to realize the full musical appeal of the song. An audience is a challenge if performances are well spaced and do not become the chief purpose of the choir's existence. Certainly such a choir should sing frequently for groups of children within the school. Some teachers think only in terms of public performance and fail to see the real values of the choir:

1. to provide an extended singing experience for talented and interested children
2. to acquaint all children, singers as well as listeners, with a more artistic and varied repertoire of songs than is ordinarily sung in the classroom
3. to develop musicianship and skill in reading notation through contact with a greater variety of music

CHAPTER NOTES

1. Beatrice Landeck, **Children and Music** (New York: William Sloane Associates, Inc., 1952), pp. 52 and 55. Copyright 1952 by Beatrice Landeck. Reprinted by permission.

2. Hap Palmer, Educational Activities, Inc., Freeport, L.I., New York.

3. Gladys Moorhead and Donald Pond, **Music of Young Children,** 6 vols. (Santa Barbara, Calif.: The Pillsbury Foundation for the Advancement of Music Education [P.O. Drawer A, 13102], 1941–1951; 5th printing, 1978).

4. Ruth Crawford Seeger, **American Folk Songs for Children** (New York: Doubleday and Company, Inc., 1948).

5. Satis N. Coleman, **Creative Music for Children** (New York: G.P. Putnam's Sons, 1922).

6. Barbara L. Andress et al., **Music in Early Childhood** (Reston, Va.: Music Educators National Conference, 1973), pp. 42–46.

7. Nathan Ausubel, **A Treasury of Jewish Folklore** (New York: Crown Publishers, 1948).

8. Alexander Buchner, **Folk Music Instruments** (New York: Crown Publishers, Inc., 1972).

9. **Korean Social and Folk Music,** Lyrichord Stereo LLST 7211.

10. Kang-Sook Lee, "The Development and Trial of Korean-Based Musical Activities for the Classroom" (Ph.D. diss., University of Michigan, 1975).

11. **Juilliard Repertory Library** (Cincinnati, Ohio: Canyon Press Inc., 1970).

8

Listening to Music

How do you listen to a musical composition that is new to you? Do you try to get a sense of the piece as a whole, or do you focus your attention on the progression of details that you hear? Do you notice the character and interaction of the rhythm, melody, harmony, dynamics, and other aspects of the music? Or do you immediately translate your response to these musical elements into impressions, moods, or mental pictures? Different people hear and interpret music in different ways—it is a private matter, but one that philosophers have been concerned with throughout history. Does music convey meaning? If so, what kind of meaning is conveyed?

Some people believe the meaning of music to be primarily intellectual, and that the value of music lies in understanding the interrelationships among the musical elements and in appreciating the musical form. Others believe that the intrinsic meaning of music is not only intellectual, but can be related to feeling as well. However, they contend that the feelings aroused are in direct response to the music itself, without reference to ideas and emotions present in the real world.

On the other side of the philosophical argument we find those who believe extramusical meaning is conveyed by music; if the composer hasn't provided a title or descriptive notes about the music, they create their own images as they listen. Richard Wagner, the exponent of 19th-century Music Drama, seemed to hold to the position that music is a representation of feelings and emotions set in "artistic perspective," rather than the direct expression of emotion itself.

Another philosophic position, related to psychology, sees music—with its rhythm and dynamics, harmonic tensions and resolutions, melodic climaxes and cadences—as resembling the human experience of movement from tension to release. Exponents of this position believe an individual can understand the musical structure of a composition and at the same time find that the music reflects certain aspects of feeling. Susanne Langer, a philosopher of this century, said, "Music is 'significant form,' and its significance is that of a symbol, a highly articulated sensuous object, which by virtue of its dynamic structure can express the forms of vital experience which language is particularly unfit to convey. Feeling, life, motion, and emotion constitute its import."[1] People of different cultures have developed different musical traditions to express these universal experiences. As you work with the material in this chapter you will find examples of music that seem to reflect each of the different philosophies.

THE MUSIC TO BE USED AND APPROACHES TO IT

In selecting music for classroom listening, plan to include as much variety as possible, to accommodate different tastes and to give children broad experiences with music. Listening lessons can focus on some musical characteristics that cannot be given adequate attention in other kinds of music lessons. Chief among these are composers' techniques in combining musical elements to create a composition.

The Scope of Music to Be Used

As you look for music for listening in your class, think in terms of four broad categories that will help you achieve variety in the selection.

Functional music serves family and community life. It would be hard to conceive of a parade, public ceremony, graduation exercise, a circus, or a carnival without music. Music is used in film, radio, and television to heighten the meaning and feeling conveyed in drama, documentaries, comedy, and commercial messages. Worship services of all faiths, wedding ceremonies, and funerals, all are underscored with appropriate music because music has the power to enhance the feelings associated with these human situations. In family life we need lullabies and love songs, music in work and in play. Help children in your classes tap this human heritage by introducing them to music for many uses.

Art music reflects human feeling and engages the mind. Some music is composed solely for its own expressive value and may have nothing to do with the functional aspects of life mentioned above. Like the play of shadows in the woods, or the blending of colors, line and design in a painting, the rhythms, timbres, and textures of a musical composition can simultaneously bring pleasure and engage the mind. Although the way the composer has used the musical elements and the structure of the composition can be studied and discussed, the subtle, elusive feelings that the music arouses differ for every individual and are not readily shared.

Contemporary popular music is designed to have an immediate appeal. The musical elements in popular music are the same as those in "art" music, but the compositional techniques used tend to be more limited and stereotyped. The lyrics and melody, or the rhythm of a particular piece may provide the chief interest. Some contemporary children's music and popular music should be used in the study of basic elements of music, and to help the children establish a useful perspective that includes different kinds of musical composition.

Music grows out of all cultures and is available in many styles. American music by traditional as well as contemporary composers, music of famous European composers of different historical periods, and music from other cultures all coexist. We can identify elements common to the music of all cultures (pitch, loudness, tone colors, durations of sound and silences, texture, and so forth); but the use of these elements is markedly different in the music of Europe and America as compared with music of the Orient, Africa and India. In teaching music we should use a broad sampling of music, so that when the children make their individual choices of music for listening, they will have enough experience and background to establish valid preferences and tastes.

You will need a good variety of recorded music. Look first at your own record collection and the music you know best; then get acquainted with the educational recordings listed in Appendix B-II of this book. These albums are widely available in schools and include teaching notes for a cross-section of music of different styles. The graded basic series music books also offer teaching suggestions for numerous recorded compositions that the authors consider appropriate for children at a particular level.

Materials and Equipment

Basic requirements for a program of music listening are a good-quality tape or record player and well-selected records. If a full, rich musical program is to be carried on, each classroom should have its own sound reproduction equipment ready for use at any time. A well-planned school record library has multiple copies of basic records and tapes that many teachers use regularly, as well as a wide variety of other recorded music.

The condition of the records and the record player is important, for the value of the musical experience is determined in considerable degree by the quality in the sound heard. When children are accustomed to stereophonic sound through radio, in the motion picture theater, and through home sound-reproduction equipment, they cannot be expected to listen with interest to antiquated recordings that are scratched and worn from numerous playings.

For classroom use, a disc record player that can operate at three or four speeds should be available. Cassette tape recordings are convenient and generally have a good quality of sound, provided they are played through an amplifying system that accommodates both low and high frequencies. Another useful piece of equipment is the phonograph or cassette player to which headsets are attached. This is an important tool for individualizing instruction.

Communication and Music

When you sit down to listen to music for personal enjoyment, there is no need for communicating your response in an overt way unless you wish to share your observations and feelings about the music. Your perceptions of the music and response to it can be complete, even when they are not generally observable. In an educational setting, however, sharing responses to music are often necessary, for at least three reasons:

1. Much music listening is done in a group and it is natural for humans to share and compare common experiences.
2. The teacher needs to be able to observe the children's responses to music in order to know how well they are learning.
3. In order to direct children's attention to features in the music that might enhance how they perceive and respond to it, the teacher needs to communicate about the music.

A teacher and pupils might communicate with regard to music in five ways:

1. Physically enact the ideas or feelings through movement, gesture, or pantomime.
2. Draw diagrams or pictures that convey the ideas or feelings.
3. Verbalize, discuss, and interpret one's personal responses to and observations about the music.
4. Perform musically, using the voice or an instrument to demonstrate or point up a musical idea.
5. Use written symbols, music notation, or words.

When you find it necessary to communicate about music, what is your most spontaneous way of doing so? As you survey a class of children, would you say all would communicate equally well in all these expressive modes? Probably not. Several factors must be considered. The age of the child will determine whether verbal skills are sufficiently developed to make a spoken or written response as effective as gesture and movement might be. On the other hand, natural abilities and experience may have much to do with how different people prefer to communicate. Some seem to have a talent for expressive movement or gesture, others for expressive use of visual art, and some may have a natural ability to communicate verbally. You must be prepared to accommodate these individual preferences.

Musical Elements and Compositional Techniques Highlighted in Classroom Listening

Many kinds of compositions are available to be heard—instrumental and vocal solos, small ensembles ranging from string quartets to Dixieland jazz groups and music of other cultures, and full orchestral performances. A large orchestra, whether a symphony orchestra or a Javanese gamelan, produces a very complex sound with rhythm, timbre, pitch, melody, texture, and dynamics sounding and changing with the flow of time. The listener should first get a general sense of the music, and then begin to notice the details that combine to create the musical effect. Children can distinguish one or two of the most prominent characteristics of the music if their attention can be directed to those features. Gesture, coordinated rhythmically with the feature you want children to hear, is one means; another is simple graphic design.

Musical texture (see Appendix A-IV) can be observed in greater variety in recorded instrumental music than in songs and student performance. Texture can be related to pictures and diagrams, which can be of help in developing the concept. Some of the current basic music series books have made contributions in pictures of this kind.[2] In listening, one can observe the transparent texture of two related melodic or rhythmic lines playing against one another; or the thick, tightly woven texture created by the sounding of many parts in a composition for full orchestra.

Musical form (see Appendix A-VI) is important in compositions used for listening lessons. Going beyond three-part sectional forms often found in songs, listeners encounter more complex structures like rondos, and developmental forms such as the theme and variations and the sonata form. Music teachers have developed visual guides and diagrams to help summarize these forms and guide the listener through the several sections that comprise the whole. Such visual aids help the inexperienced listener to remember and to compare the earlier musical statements with the end of a musical work, and thus to gain a better grasp of the overall form.

Timbre (see Appendix A-I) is varied due to the large number of different instruments in the orchestra and the instruments of diverse cultures, which are now available for everyone to hear on recordings. Hearing individual instruments separately in live performance, or in recorded performance with good pictures, is prerequisite to identifying them in a composition that combines the sounds of many instruments. For this reason, becoming acquainted with various instrumental sounds is particularly important at Level I and Level II. When a composition is played, you can draw attention to the tone color of a particular instrument by coordinating a hand gesture with the rhythmic or melodic (up-and-down) movement of the instrument's sound. You can also raise a hand or a picture or point to a name when a corresponding instrumental sound begins.

Articulation is important in highlighting and contrasting musical lines. Articulation means primarily the way the tone is made: staccato (short, crisp sounds), legato (smooth, connected sounds) and the use of accents. A rhythmic hand gesture that has the smooth or pointed qualities of the articulation is effective in drawing the attention to this musical element.

Tempo, rhythm, and dynamics were dealt with extensively in the discussion of body movement. Melody and harmony were explored in Chapters 5 and 6. Some techniques described earlier can be used in communicating about these elements in a listening lesson. Signs and symbols that have been learned (e.g., meter signatures, dynamic markings and chord symbols) can be incorporated into "call charts." These charts match numbers with different musical effects, and the numbers can be called out or pointed to while the music is being played.

There are many good techniques for communicating about music. It is inappropriate to talk when you expect children to be hearing the music. Any activity that detracts attention from the music can be detrimental; try to establish points to listen for before the music is played. You should not expect young children to focus on more than one detail at a time. Children will grow in their ability to hear and respond to the expressive qualities of music if you can achieve a good balance between directed listening, and giving children a chance to discover and respond to music in their own ways. All the techniques that enable the teacher to communicate about music with children, can in turn be used by children to communicate their musical discoveries with others.

EXPERIENCES AT LEVEL I

The listening experiences of young children should include the use of a good variety of well-recorded music and opportunities to hear and see live performers. Recorded music can be played for informal listening; or it can be the direct object of attention when children observe its basic qualities or relate it to a story or a picture.

Classroom Concerts and Learning About Instruments

Bring children and musicians together by arranging small concerts in the classroom or in a slightly larger room, where more than one class can assemble. Although it is appropriate for three or four classes to share a concert, avoid the more impersonal auditorium setting, which puts young children too far from the performers.

The music teacher might perform on his or her own instrument, or you might contact local musicians or music students at advanced levels who could play a concert for young children in your school. Music students in the local high school or college appreciate the opportunity to play for an audience. Prospective music teachers find this kind of performance a good pre-student-teaching laboratory experience, through which they can learn about communicating with a group of children, verbally as well as musically, and can have some experience pacing a lesson to maintain the children's interest.

Limit the concert to about thirty minutes so the children do not get restless, and orient the children to concert protocol. Let the children know ahead of time how you expect them to enter the room for the concert and where they will sit. They will need to know about the custom of clapping to show one's appreciation at the end of a piece, and the necessity for quiet during the performance. You will need to model this behavior for them.

Because children are inexperienced concert-goers, each piece should be quite brief, and there should be good variety among the compositions. The performers should be prepared to demonstrate the more important characteristics of the instrument each plays. The following are concepts about instruments and their sounds that might be developed in early childhood classes. Each concept should be demonstrated with a musical example.

Pitch:	high and low sounds	*Articulation:* staccato and legato playing (or other common techniques for that instrument, e.g., violin harmonics and pizzicato)
Dynamics:	loud and soft playing	
Tempo:	fast and slow playing	

Ask the performer to play brief, well-known compositions for that particular instrument which will provide examples of musical characteristics such as the above.

Sometimes it is possible to involve one or two children in the demonstration so the whole group feels more closely identified with the instrument. A child might be asked to hold an instrument, produce a sound on it, or otherwise "assist" the performer. If possible, make a tape recording of part of each performance, so that later you can review the sound with the children.

On the day following the concert, review the event with the children. If possible, show pictures of the instruments they saw; ask them to identify each and to demonstrate how it was played. Play a tape recording of part of each instrument's performance, and ask the children to give the name of the instrument or to pantomime how it was played. Review the concert again on another day and play a different recording of an instrument of the same kind and ask the children to identify it.

Instructional Objectives: To give the children an opportunity to hear live musical performances involving common instruments of the orchestra so they will recognize the instruments when heard individually, and understand the basic principles of playing the instruments.

Behaviors providing evidence that these instructional objectives have been achieved: The children will

☐ identify by naming the instrument or pantomiming how it is played, an instrument heard and seen in a concert, when its sound is heard on a tape recording

☐ identify a picture of such an instrument in the same way

As a general outcome of classroom concerts, you will find that recordings and pictures of instruments will be much more meaningful to children after they have encountered live musicians and have seen and heard the instrument played. Experience with one orchestral instrument of each type—strings, brass, woodwinds, or percussion—as well as any available folk instruments would be appropriate at Level I. Additional experience with instrumental sounds can be gained by using recorded music correlated with stories about instruments.[3]

Comparing Contrasting Elements in Music

Musical compositions selected for young children to study should be short and relatively simple. A single piece may have one or two prominent musical characteristics you might expect the children to notice. Often you can bring to their attention strongly contrasting musical elements or point out compositional techniques, either within one composition or shared by two different pieces. The concepts, in terms children at Level I can begin to understand, might include:

tempo:	fast—slow	dynamics:	loud—soft
pitch:	high—low	rhythm:	smooth—jerky
timbre:	piano, violin, etc.	melody:	up—down—curving

Play the following contrasting pieces and determine which musical qualitites characterize each composition.

"Pantomime" from *The Comedians*
by Kabalevsky (**AinM I-1**)

"Intermezzo" from *The Comedians*
by Kabalevsky (**BOL #53**)

It is not necessary to take the titles into consideration; just listen to the music. The first piece moves slowly; it features low-pitched instruments. These characteristics can be discussed and demonstrated by moving or by using words to describe the music.

In what ways is "Intermezzo" different from "Pantomime"? "Intermezzo" may be described as having a moderately fast running rhythm. It features higher-pitched instruments. How might a drawing that represents this music differ from a drawing depicting "Pantomime"? Which diagram shown in Example 8.1 suggests each of these compositions? Identify two elements in each diagram that correspond to a musical characteristic you hear in that composition.

EXAMPLE 8.1

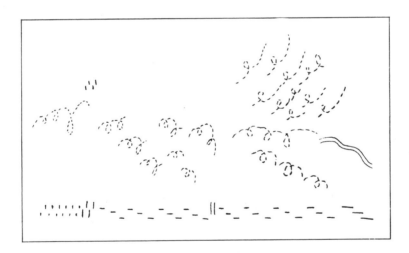

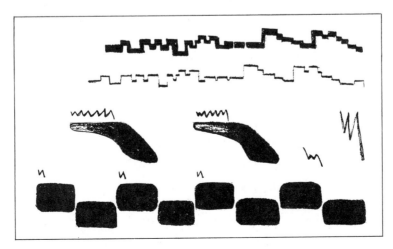

Even though a composer may give the music a descriptive title, some of the musical characteristics listed above will be manipulated to achieve the desired expressive effect.

Carnival of the Animals by Camille Saint-Saëns (**BOL #51**) features several short, contrasting episodes. You might start with "The Elephant," which is a waltz in a very slow tempo; the melody is played by the low-pitched, ponderous voice of the bass viol. In contrast, "Aquarium" features gently rippling sounds of the flute, violin and celesta. The music is higher in pitch, smooth in rhythm, and generally softer. Make two diagrams that in color, line, and design will clearly distinguish between these two pieces of music. Show the two drawings as the music is replayed; could an observer pair the art work with the piece of music that inspired it?

A marked contrast can occur within one short piece, as in "Walking Song" from *Acadian Songs and Dances* by Thomson (**AinM I-1**). This composition has three parts with a contrasting middle section, so that the form can be labeled A B A. The marked change here occurs in the rhythm, which swings along in an energetic walk at the beginning. In the middle section the forward movement of rhythm seems to stop, and upward moving pitches suggest stretching and growing. After that, the walking rhythm returns and the music has both contrast and repetition of musical elements. You might present the children with two copies of two diagrams, one representing section A and one section B. Ask them to arrange the diagrams to show what happens in the music.

Such contrast is a basic principle of musical form that can be encountered in many compositions. Appropriate visual representations of the music make it possible for the children to identify what they hear, and to codify the form in a concrete way. Other ways of expressing the changes heard in the music would be to (1) move in different ways to the music of the two sections, or (2) create a story that takes into account the change in movement and subsequent return to the first musical idea.

Instructional Objectives: To enable children to hear short compositions with contrasting musical characteristics, so that they will be able to identify one musical difference between two such compositions.

Behaviors providing evidence that these instructional objectives have been achieved: The children will

☐ verbalize or demonstrate with movement that one piece differs from another in terms of tempo, dynamics, or rhythm

☐ point to one of two different diagrams or pictures, or verbalize that one piece differs from another in terms of the instrument played, the general pitch level, or the shape of the melody

Musical Details that Relate to Stories and Characterizations

Prokofiev composed *Peter and the Wolf*[3] especially for children. He associated each character in the story with a particular instrument so children would learn the sound of the instrument. Although the narration tells the story, the instruments themselves supply many additional details of the action: Listen for the dialogue between the flute and the oboe when the "bird" and the "duck" argue. When the "cat" climbs the tree to escape from the "wolf," the clarinet plays a rapid, running passage from low to high in its register.

These details, of course, are most apparent to individuals who readily distinguish the sounds of the instruments involved. The introductory portion of the recording should be heard more than once, and even dramatized, so that the listeners know which sounds represent each character. Draw or have the children draw pictures of the characters. As the children follow the story line, you can point to the character whose music is heard at any particular time, thus helping relate the character with the sounds Prokofiev associated with the "duck," the "cat," and so on.

Instructional Objectives: To introduce the children to a classical musical story and to help them find meaning and descriptive detail in the music as well as in the narration.

Behaviors providing evidence that these instructional objectives have been achieved: The children will

□ individually listen to the composition at other times because they enjoy it

□ dramatize portions of the story, and in doing so, coordinate dramatic movement with details in the music as well as in the narration

□ identify the characters in instrumental sections of the composition that do not include the narration

The Nutcracker Suite by Tchaikovsky (**BOL #58**) may first be heard in relation to its story, which can be found on record jackets or various other sources.[4] The "Miniature Overture" can describe the children's party, and the "March" can suggest the midnight magic when the toy soldiers parade around the Christmas tree and the great battle ensues between the mice and Prince Nutcracker's army of toys. The remaining sections are a part of the entertainment provided Marie during her dream visit to the land of the "Sugar-Plum Fairy." Toys and dolls from exotic lands (Russia, Arabia, China) dance, and the finale consists of a brilliant "Waltz of the Flowers." In each of these movements the composer featured different instruments and used the musical elements in different ways. Look again at the list on page 276 and listen to two or three of these dances. What are the main musical characteristics you hear in each?

Musical literature abounds in impressions of characters or animals and their activities.[5] Classroom topics, special days, pictures, and songs may suggest musical sketches that can be used in the classroom in many ways and at different times.

When people go to an art gallery and see a picture, they look at it from various angles. They make themselves receptive to the feeling the artist was trying to convey and perhaps agree that the painter succeeded in giving the subject life and feeling on the canvas. A similar process should take place when you hear a musical sketch; you should listen, and if you are in a receptive frame of mind, the characterization in the music should have meaning for you. The meaning will be personalized and based on your own experiences.

Brief discussions and sharing of ideas about the music can include some attention to the means the composer employed to achieve the musical effect. Saint Saëns, for example, called one piece "Aquarium" in *The Carnival of the Animals* (**BOL #51**). He suggested the liquid sounds of water by using a rippling accompaniment in the piano part. A very smooth melody and light curving sounds played on gentle high-pitched instruments suggest fish swimming, bubbles rising, and other aquarium sounds.

As important as any other objective in these music listening activities is the fact that children learn to enjoy listening to music, that they learn to focus their attention on it, and to respond to it with feeling and imagination.

EXPERIENCES AT LEVEL II

If eight- and nine-year-olds have not had an opportunity to hear and know some of the music recommended for use at Level I, e.g., *Peter and the Wolf* and *The Nutcracker Suite,* they certainly should become acquainted with such pieces at this level. Live concerts are equally valuable at this level, and the recommendations made in the discussion at Level I can be adapted for these children. However, a greater variety of recorded music can be used to expand and consolidate the knowledge eight- and nine-year-olds have of musical instruments.

In this section you will find suggestions of music to use in helping children discover principles of musical form and to understand how a composer creates program music. Supporting materials and techniques for using this music are described in the hope that you will design some lesson plans that you will be able to try out, either in the college class or in the musical instruction of children.

Knowing the Sounds of Orchestral Instruments

Getting acquainted with the instruments of the orchestra is a natural extension of exploring sound in simple instruments. Many basic series music books give helpful material for elementary studies both in the science of sound and in instruments of the orchestra. In addition, specialized recordings,[6] motion pictures,[7] pictures,[8] and books[9] should be in the school library to be studied by the whole class or individuals with special interest in musical instruments.

In addition to hearing recorded stories and sounds of the instruments, it is important that children have an opportunity to see the instruments first hand. Older children in the school may bring violins, clarinets, or trumpets into the classroom and show the essentials of the instruments. Demonstrations help not only the children who see the instrument close at hand, but also the older child who explains the instrument. Young Audiences, Inc.[10] is a national organization that provides live concerts of fine music for children in schools. The performers are professional musicians who also have the ability to communicate verbally with children. Approved groups (numbering from three to five members) are available in many parts of the country. The compositions heard on the programs are often organized around topics such as studies of musical instruments, elements of music (rhythm, melody, harmony, and so on), and forms of music.

Children should study the four "families" of instruments in a symphony orchestra. An outline such as this may be followed:

THE STRINGS	THE WOODWINDS	THE BRASS WINDS	PERCUSSION
violin	piccolo	trumpet	snare drum
viola	flute	French horn	bass drum
cello	clarinet	trombone	timpani
bass viol	oboe	tuba	cymbals and gong
	English horn		assorted small rhythm instruments
	bassoon		xylophone, orchestral bells, celesta

In some classes children make their own bulletin board displays of pictures of the instruments. They might develop a chart or a three-dimensional layout showing a seating of the players of the various instruments in the orchestra.

EXAMPLE 8.2

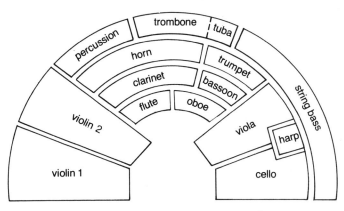

A Conventional Seating Plan for Symphony Orchestra

Instructional Objectives: To provide children with a comprehensive view of instruments of the orchestra so they will know the four basic types, have a concept of the sound of instruments in each family, and understand how tone is produced on them.

Behaviors providing evidence that these instructional objectives have been achieved: The children will

☐ name the four families of instruments and describe their basic characteristics

☐ name and identify by sight at least two instruments in each category

☐ categorize, when heard on a record, the sound of instruments as belonging to one of the four groups

As a result of their studies of the instruments, children can be led to feel that learning to play an instrument is a privilege and a challenge. They should understand the means of tone production and recognize the unique sound of each type of instrument.

A listening unit on singing voices and different choral organizations is suggested at Level III in this book, but at Level II you should provide opportunities for children to hear different voice types in live concerts and recordings. The song recordings that accompany the basic series music books contribute toward this end. Commercial recordings of concert and opera singers as well as folk and popular singers should also be used, so that different voice types can be compared. Whenever a live concert can be arranged, children will benefit from hearing a good singer in person.

Discovering Principles of Musical Form

The basic principles of musical form are simply repetition of an idea (melody, rhythm, or other musical element) and contrast (following one musical idea or effect with something different). These principles of repetition and contrast can be dealt with on the level of the motif, the phrase, or on the broader basis of the section. Following are three musical examples in which you can hear both repetition and contrast at more than one level.

Ralph Vaughan Williams was a very successful English composer of the 20th century. "March Past of the Kitchen Utensils," third movement of the suite *The Wasps,* originally was composed as incidental music for an old Greek play. You can read the descriptive background in the *Teacher's Guide* for ADVENTURES IN MUSIC, Grade 3, Volume 1.

As you may be able to tell from the character of the music, this march is a satire. It concerns a mock trial in which kitchen utensils march before a jury to testify about a dog who stole food from the kitchen. Listen to the music and discover what specific qualities it has that suggest officious pomp, satire, and mockery. Discuss these qualities with others and listen again to pinpoint as many musical details as you can.

You may have noticed that the music has a contrasting middle section. This is a very clear example of A B A form. Example 8.3 shows one way of diagramming the form of this march.

EXAMPLE 8.3

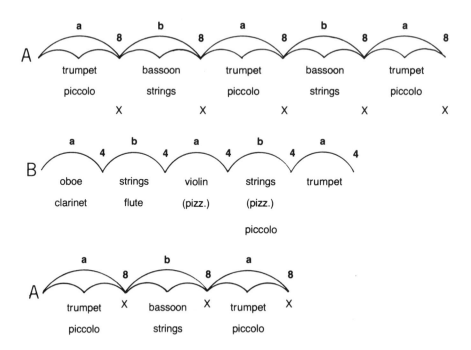

Read through the diagram; notice that phrases are labeled with lowercase letters, and sections are labeled with capital letters. There are four beats to a measure in this music, and the length of each phrase is shown on the diagram. (Predominant instrumental sounds are also indicated.) Watch the diagram as you listen to the music, and see if you can tell when each new section and phrase begins.

Although the general character of the music is related to its descriptive background, the composer was very much concerned with a clearcut form in this piece. The form is shaped by the melodic and rhythmic contrast between the large sections; within each section, the form is clarified by selective instrumentation of the phrases. The themes in this composition alternate regularly, but each retains its identity as a whole. In contrast, in the other two compositions laid out later in this section, the themes are sometimes broken up and used in smaller segments.

Instructional Objectives: To give the children experience in listening purposefully to music; to help them notice the structure of the music; to help them comprehend the principles of repetition and contrast as applied to melody and instrumentation on two different levels.

Behaviors providing evidence that these instructional objectives have been achieved: The children will

□ listen to the music and raise their right hands when theme "a" occurs, and raise their left hands when theme "b" occurs

☐ follow the diagram and point to the section that is heard at a particular moment

"March Past of the Kitchen Utensils" is a fine piece to dance to, as discussed in Chapter 3, or to score for percussion instruments as suggested in Chapter 4. By participating in a composition in one of these ways children become very aware of its form because they must change their participation as the music changes.

Within the broad sectional divisions of their music, composers use thematic materials in different ways. They employ rhythmic changes, fragment, combine, extend, and embellish the original melodic ideas, and use different combinations of instruments.

In *Hungarian Dance No. 5* by Brahms (**BOL #55**) you can hear the broad sectional outline, A B A, moving from minor to major and back to minor. Within that framework there are individualistic uses of the instruments, as well as contrast, embellishment, and extension in the handling of the themes. You can help children understand a composer's varied treatment of a musical theme by suggesting the analogies, such as making two different dresses from one basic pattern, or ordering a different hamburger. In using the hamburger as an example, pickles, onions, and catsup might be "embellishment," a "double-decker" might be "extension," and "medium rare," "well done," or an onion roll as opposed to a plain bun might be analogous to the use of different instrumental colors.

As you listen to *Hungarian Dance* try to notice these details: Theme "a" consists of one musical idea that is immediately repeated, embellished, and extended. Theme "b" of Section A has three short phrases based on one musical idea. This idea first moves lower, then ritards, then is supplied with a fast ending. Here is a diagram of the entire composition to show you how these details might be depicted:

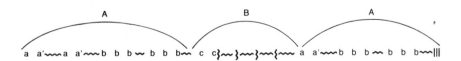

In section B the rapidly moving phrases of theme "c" are followed by curious accordion-like effects. Brahms composed this work as one of a series during the 1870s. It is music of the Romantic period, when composers sought to reflect the spirit of folk music in their concert pieces. This music was inspired by Hungarian gypsy dance tunes, and the effects heard at this point suggest the traditional use of violin and accordion by Hungarian folk musicians.

If you wish to have the children in your class hear this music and notice these details, play the music. As you listen, mark each part of the diagram on the chalkboard (or overhead projector) precisely at the beginning of the music it represents. You should finish with a flourish, marking the three closing slashes on the diagram as the three closing chords are played.

Ask the class what you have done, and they will tell you that what you have drawn somehow represents the music. Proceed then, one section at a time, to help them hear the relationship among the various phrases.

Provide a simple example of embellishment and extension as applied to a melody they know well. "Sandy Land" might be treated in this way (Example 8.4):

EXAMPLE 8.4

Instructional Objectives: To give the children experience hearing simple examples of thematic modification; to develop concepts of embellishment and extension; and to help children know a simple composition by a notable composer.

Behaviors providing evidence that these instructional objectives have been achieved: The children will

☐ identify *Hungarian Dance No. 5* by name when they hear it
☐ identify techniques of embellishment and extension when applied to a familiar melody

A symphony orchestra is a large group of instrumentalists playing together under the direction of a conductor, but "symphony" is also the name of a musical form. A symphony usually has four large contrasting movements (sometimes only three), each of which is a recognizable musical form in itself. During the time of Haydn and Mozart (1750–1800) the first movement of the symphony developed into a form that has been used for some of the world's greatest music.

Harl McDonald, a contemporary American composer, created *Children's Symphony* (**AinM II-2; ExM II-53, 115**). This work is useful in helping children understand some of the features of the symphony as a composition. The symphony's first-movement form includes two contrasting melodies or "themes," one in a major key and the other in a related major or minor key. The first movement of *Children's Symphony* is based on two well-known melodies, "London Bridge" and "Baa, Baa, Black Sheep."

As an introduction to the work, ask the children to notice any familiar melodies as they listen to the recording. After they have heard the complete movement, ask some open-ended, data-gathering questions: "What did you hear? How many different melodies were there? What instruments did you hear?" and so on. Accept all the answers as possibilities (you might write a list on the chalkboard). After hearing from all who have ideas about the music, ask the children to listen again to confirm the points they made, and to find out how many times each of the familiar melodies is played. (You can be quite specific in assigning individuals to listen for different things, e.g., some to count the appearance of each melody, and others to confirm the instruments heard at specific points.)

In the first movement of a symphony, the two themes are heard complete in the "exposition" (the section in which the composer exposes or lays out the basic musical ideas). The music moves from the first theme to the second by means of a transition section (a "bridge"). In the "development," the two themes are fragmented and changed. "Recapitulation" means a review or return of the musical ideas in their original form. Exposition and recapitulation are demonstrated in the *Children's Symphony*, along with a "coda," which is a "tail" or ending of the movement.

During the second discussion period, review and discuss the answers the class arrived at by listening. The children may observe that sometimes only parts of the melody were heard. You might then suggest the idea that, by having different instruments play many bits (fragments) of the melody, the composer creates a new piece. "Has anyone ever made a collage of bits of colored glass, paper or cut-up magazine pictures? Could you break a familiar tune into fragments? Try it with 'Three Blind Mice.' " Some repeatable fragments are marked off in Example 8.5; sing or play some of them fast and some slow.

EXAMPLE 8.5

THREE BLIND MICE
Old English Round

On another day you might review the composition and what was previously discovered about it, and then listen while following a chart that shows the musical events as they occur. Read over the items on the chart with the class first. Ask, "What do you suppose a musical 'bridge' is? What does an ordinary bridge do? Yes, it takes us from one place to another, and that is what happens in this music . . . the bridge takes us from melody 'a' ('London Bridge') to Melody 'b' ('Baa, Baa, Black Sheep'). What do you suppose a 'coda' is?—Let's listen and find out. I will point on the chart to each item as we hear it in the music." (A listing such as this is considered a "call chart" because the teacher can guide the listening by calling out or pointing to the numbers.)

1. Introduction: three loud chords
2. Melody a: woodwinds
3. Melody a: full orchestra
    : change to minor mode
    : melodic fragments, woodwinds
4. Melody a: woodwinds, minor mode
5. Melody a: full orchestra
6. Bridge   : percussion
7. Melody b: violin
    : violas and cellos respond
    : strings complete the melody
    : brass repeat final phrases
8. Bridge   : percussion
9. Melody a: full orchestra
    : fragments
    : full orchestra
10. Coda

Although this composition is not a complete example of the first movement symphony form (it leaves out the heart of that form, the "development"), it does show some of the ways in which this form differs from the simple A B A sectional forms that were heard in the two previous compositions.

Instructional Objectives: To introduce children to some attributes of the first movement form of the symphony; to develop (1) the ability to identify melodic fragmentation of a familiar melody, (2) concepts of "bridge" and "coda," (3) further skill in identifying instruments of the orchestra; and to develop interest in listening to music both for pleasure and to hear how it is put together.

Behaviors providing evidence that these instructional objectives have been achieved: The children will

☐ identify melodic fragmentation heard in an unfamiliar but clear-cut example

□ employ the concept of "bridge" and "coda" in creative ensemble play-ing of the kind suggested in Chapter 7

□ identify the timbre of common instruments of the orchestra when heard in unfamiliar, but fairly obvious recorded compositions

□ express interest in studying the musical details of other compositions

These are just three different examples of compositions that lend themselves to an elementary study of musical form. They were selected for three reasons:

1. The music is appealing to children.
2. The structure of each of the three selections is sufficiently unique to provide some scope in a consideration of musical form compatible with abilities to hear and understand at Level II.
3. The compositions represent music of three different styles.

Select two or three compositions that you might like to use in a study of musical form at Level II. The basic series music books have good examples, both in the recorded songs and the instrumental compositions. You can choose music with readily observable structure from the libraries of recorded music listed in Appendix B-II.[11]

How the Composer Projects a Picture or a Story

Some composers give their music descriptive titles, and if the music is closely related to the story or scene listeners may feel they can hear musical details of the event. Camille Saint-Saëns, a French composer of the 19th century, knew a poem by Henri Cazalis concerned with ghostly revelry on Halloween.

DANSE MACABRE

by Henri Cazalis
(translated by Lillian Baldwin)[12]

Zig-a-zig, zig-a-zig-a-zig,
Death sits on the tombstone and drums with his heel.
Zig-a-zig, zig-a-zig-a-zig,
Death tunes up his fiddle and plays a weird reel.
'Tis midnight and sadly the winter wind moans;
From shadowy lindens, with loud sighs and groans,
The skeleton dancers in white, whirling crowds,
Come leaping and skipping and waving their shrouds.

Zig-a-zig-a-zig, what a horrible sound,
The rattle of bones as they dance 'round and 'round!

But hark! Bold young chanticleer heralds the day,
And Death and his dancers have vanished away!

In his composition *Danse Macabre* (**BOL #59**), Saint-Saëns made the music depict a number of the details of this poem. Read the captions in the chart of themes in Example 8.6 to get an idea of the programmatic details contained in this music.

EXAMPLE 8.6

DANSE MACABRE
Camille Saint-Saëns

A. PRELUDE

1. The clock strikes twelve (harp)

2. Something stirs in the graveyard (cellos and basses, pizz.)

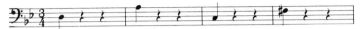

3. Death tunes his fiddle (solo violin)

B. THE DANCE

4. The dancing begins (flute)

5. A chanting tune in waltz time (solo violin)

6. Laughter sounds above the dancing (flute and clarinets)

A'. POSTLUDE

7. The cock crows (oboe)

8. The dancers disappear (violins, softly)

Have someone play these fragments on an instrument, so that you will know what to listen for when you hear the entire composition. Notice that there are three parts to this piece: an introduction or "Prelude" that sets the scene; the "Dance"; and the "Postlude," which subtly recaps musical ideas heard at the beginning.

Saint-Saëns skillfully utilized the tone colors of all the families of instruments in orchestrating this music. You may need to listen to it a number of times to hear the interplay of the different instruments that does so much to portray the programmatic details of this composition. The piece is held together musically by two main themes (items 4 and 5 on the chart) that recur throughout in various forms, played by different instruments. Sometimes the themes are played in their entirety, and at other times only fragments are heard, but these two melodies have the function of unifying a composition that consists of numerous other musical "effects."

Two other musical elements help shape this composition into a unified whole. Try to hear them in the music:

1. Dynamic shape—the music begins very softly, gradually grows to a climax, fortississimo *(fff)*, and then retreats to a very quiet ending *(ppp)*.
2. Rhythmic *accelerando*—the music begins and ends at a moderate pace, but speeds up as it approaches the musical climax.

Listen to the entire composition while you follow the musical outline. The themes are first heard rather early in the composition, so a considerable period of development takes place between item 5 and item 7, which signals the approach of the end of the composition.

Instructional Objectives: To acquaint the children with a well-known programmatic composition that they will enjoy; to relate music to the expression of a story through poetry and visual art; and to help the children understand how the composer created the descriptive effects in the music.

Behaviors providing evidence that these instructional objectives have been achieved: The children will

☐ request to hear *Danse Macabre* at other times

☐ recognize, out of context, both principal themes of the composition

☐ identify musical effects that depict specific events in the story

☐ be eager to create pictures that reflect the programmatic content of the poem and the music

Charts of musical themes can be helpful in listening if the sound is associated with the notation, so that it has meaning for the listeners. The BOWMAR ORCHESTRAL LIBRARY has theme charts (or projection transparencies) to accompany all the music recorded in that series. Both ADVENTURES IN MUSIC and the BOWMAR series show the principal themes in the descriptive notes for each composition, and the listening selections in the basic music series books often show musical themes to guide children's listening.

With younger or less musically experienced children you might want to use a call chart with pictures that represent the progression of events in a composition.

The outline of *Danse Macabre* readily suggests different sketches that could be used for each of the eight points. If you have a talent for drawing, make such a chart as an example for the class. The children, of course, may want to create their own pictures to accompany this music.

Danse Macabre was composed at about the same time as Brahms's *Hungarian Dances,* and both represent the Romantic period of music composition. Although *Hungarian Dance No. 5* has some programmatic connotation, the composer's play with the musical themes is of greater interest. *Danse Macabre,* on the other hand, is dominated by the composer's intent to make the story as real as possible; it was composed to entertain the listener. We are able to identify the principal themes and the general shape of the composition, but it is much less important to study the details of structure in such music. Of greater interest are the techniques the composer used to create the programmatic effects.

The same might be said of "The Banshee,"[13] a 20th-century composition in a completely different style by the American composer Henry Cowell. The chief objective in this music is to convey a single descriptive impression. According to Irish folklore, a banshee is a spirit foretelling death. Unlike *Danse Macabre,* this music has no specific programmatic details. Only one instrument is used in this piece, a grand piano. Some eerie effects are achieved because the "player" strokes and plucks the strings rather than playing the keys in the normal manner.

Since the main objective of this music is to affect the feelings, you might plan to play it when you sense an appropriate, contemplative mood in the class. Without revealing the title, simply ask the children to listen to the music and see what impressions the music gives them. The room must be very quiet to allow the listeners to hear the beginning of the music.

Invite the class to share their impressions. Do not overtly evaluate the responses, either by facial expression or what you say, but ask, "What in the music gives you that impression?" You probably will find that the group needs to hear it again to refine their impressions and to begin to arrive at answers to your question.

In a second discussion period you can ask more specific questions: "What instrument was used? How? Is there a melody? Can you feel a beat in the music? Is there any dynamic change? Describe the dynamic change you heard." After playing the music a third time, you might point out musical effects not mentioned and give the title and its implications.

You will note that the composer used several contrasting musical elements: high and low sounds are heard; some effects are soft and shimmering, others are loud and rumbling. At three points in the music, three or four distinct pitches are sounded by plucking the strings. These definite pitches are in sharp contrast to the sliding, wailing sounds achieved by rubbing the strings.

As a final level of questions, ask the class: "What is the composer's purpose in writing this music? Why should people want to listen to it?" If you get the beginning of a philosophical position that pleasurable listening experiences are enjoyable and beneficial, you will know that the children are beginning to value music for its own sake.

This is experimental, impressionistic music; there is no melody or rhythm in the ordinary sense, but the piece does create feeling and movement. If you never have "played the inside" of a piano, you might try it to see if you can reproduce some of

Mr. Cowell's ghostly effects. Similar effects might be achieved on a smaller scale, by "playing" an Autoharp in the same way.

Instructional Objectives: To get the children sensitively involved with a piece of music; to have them listen intently, respond to the aesthetic impact of the music, discover some of the means by which the composer creates the musical effect, and to have them discover that listening to music can be a rewarding experience.

Behaviors providing evidence that these instructional objectives have been achieved: The children will

- ☐ listen intently to the music
- ☐ respond thoughtfully to questions about the music and its effect
- ☐ ask to hear the music at a later time
- ☐ comment about hearing other music that has some relationship to this composition

Although the music in "The Banshee" and *Danse Macabre* focuses on the programmatic implications of each title, both composers utilized a number of musical elements and traditional as well as innovative compositional techniques to achieve their musical objectives. Do all you can to make it possible for the children to enjoy the descriptive qualities of such music, but try to go beyond the programmatic ideas and help the children discover to some extent how the composer achieved these effects.

Experiences that Relate Art and Music

In the previous section it was suggested that children draw pictures related to the programmatic music they hear. This section describes a second approach to art and music, in which line, design, and color are used to represent musical rhythms, melodies, tone colors, and other elements.

Just as in the visual arts we have colors that are "cool," "warm," "restful," or "active," so in music the composer has a whole palette of tone colors with which to work . . . the distinctive tone colors of the various orchestral instruments. Musical rhythm and the flow of melody find their parallels in art in the rhythm and dynamics of line and design.

Simple contrasts demonstrate how music's tone color, rhythm, and melodic movement can be interpreted in terms of color and design. The two black-and-white designs used under Experience at Level I (see page 277) may help you understand what is intended here. Choose two short, contrasting musical compositions, neither of which contains a contrasting section. "Träumerei" by Schumann (**AinM IV-2**) and "March" from *The Love for Three Oranges* by Prokofiev (**BOL #54**) are good examples. Two separate pieces of drawing paper and a variety of colors (e.g., crayons, finger paint, chalk) should be available for each listener.

Play the two compositions consecutively, so that the contrast is quite evident. The titles should not be given, for the visual interpretations should arise out of impressions received directly from the music. After the initial hearing, each composition should be played two or three times as the color design for it is completed.

Individuals who have had considerable work in art might feel quite free in making designs on two papers, one to represent each musical composition. Others may need guidance, which might be given by asking them to interpret the music first through body movement. Discussion may follow: "How would the graceful movements be shown on paper?" Color qualities can be brought in—cool colors, warm colors, and feelings associated with each.

Many times adults as well as children, in their initial experience of relating design to music, immediately respond to the rhythm by making the crayon, brush, or fingers move in time to the music. This is a natural reaction because people are accustomed to keeping time to the music, but it does not lead to the most expressive design. The essential process is to hear the music, notice the characteristics of the melody and rhythm, and recreate the design as line and color on the paper; the art work, then, becomes a synthesis of the total effect of rhythm, timbre, dynamics, and other elements, as heard in the music.

When the two designs are finished, hold them up in pairs to see the difference in design and color. Which design represents each piece of music? What tells us? The comparison of *color* in the two designs should be an important item. "Träumerei" is restful and graceful in rhythm and melody. Repose may suggest pastel colors, lightly applied. When crayons are used, the flat side of a broken piece produces a broad, restful line. In contrast, "March" is very active, and has dissonant tonal combinations. Red and orange may be considered active colors; intensely applied blues and greens give more feeling of activity than do light strokes of the same colors. Combinations of certain colors promote a greater feeling of activity.

The arrangement of *lines* may provide contrast between the pictures. "Träumerei" has a flowing melody line; the phrases rise in two levels and then fall back in smooth spiraling movements. Curved lines may express this type of melodic movement. On the other hand, "March" is erratic and angular; visual design related to it may have sharp corners bumping into other lines.

How the *space* in a design is used may suggest the relationship of the elements in the music. If the music sounds "busy," that quality might be conveyed by small intricate shapes. A piece of music that is not broken up by an interplay of parts may be interpreted on paper with no clear-cut divisions of the space.

Go beyond one successful "experiment" with color and design, for it may take three or four experiences for individuals to feel at ease making designs to music; only then do they begin to interpret sensitively what they hear. In the educational record collections you can find contrasting numbers featuring pastel and smooth-flowing rhythms,[14] and lively color contrast and angular design.[15]

EXPERIENCES AT LEVEL III

Greater variety of music and more depth of study can characterize listening experiences at Level III. The examples provided here can help you begin to work out useful units of study related to several different topics: (1) the study of different types of singing voices and choral ensembles, (2) an introduction to music of other cultures, (3) development of a concept of style in the Western European musical tradition, and (4) an introduction to the music of different composers and styles of 20th-century America.

Types of Singing Voices and Choral Ensembles

Voices are as individual as fingerprints—neither the speaking nor the singing voice of one individual is exactly like that of another person. Voices can be classified according to range (highness and lowness) and timbre (color or quality). The style of singing (operatic, pops, blues, and so on) influences the way the voice is used and, consequently, its sound. In addition, people in different cultures have distinct ideals of vocal quality and production, as we discover when we listen to recordings or have an opportunity to hear live performances of music from other countries.

A Classification of Voice Types. Adult voices are categorized according to range (highness or lowness of the voice), and fall into four general types utilized in choral work:

Soprano	(high female voice)	*Tenor*	(high male voice)
Alto	(low female voice)	*Bass*	(low male voice)

Further categories of *mezzo soprano* (medium-high female voice) and *baritone* (medium-high male voice) are often applied to soloists and voices in ensembles with a greater number of parts.

Operatic voices are labeled according to the quality and character of the voice, and these determine the operatic roles sung. As an example, the coloratura soprano voice has a very high range and great agility (Joan Sutherland or Beverly Sills singing "The Bell Song" from *Lakmé* by Délibes), and the lyric soprano voice has a flexible, lighter quality in a high range (Leontyne Price singing Violetta's farewell aria, "Addio del pasato" from *La Traviata* by Verdi, or her favorite hymns).

The mezzo soprano voice is strong and full, with a slightly darker color and the potential of great dramatic contrast (the title role in *Carmen* by Bizet, sung by Jean Madiera or Marilyn Horne), and the contralto is a female voice in a lower range, with a dark quality of sound (Marian Anderson singing art songs by Brahms and Schubert, as well as spirituals).

The lyric tenor voice (Luciano Pavarotti, an Italian operatic tenor, or Jan Peerce singing opera as well as musicals such as "Fiddler on the Roof") is a male voice with a relatively high range, but lighter in quality than a "heroic tenor." The baritone is a full, medium-high male voice (popular singers such as Bing Crosby, Ed Ames, and Frank Sinatra, as well as concert artists such as Robert Merrill). Among bass voices, the basso profundo is the lowest and has a dark, somber quality (William Warfield in *Porgy and Bess* or Martti Talvela as the High Priest in the *Magic Flute,* or as *Boris Godounov*).

Instructional Objectives: To direct children's attention to several kinds of male and female voices singing famous arias and songs, and to enable them to identify a tenor voice as distinct from a bass, or a soprano as different from an alto.

Behaviors providing evidence that these instructional objectives have been achieved: The children will

□ hear a series of three different voices and circle on a chart the correct name of the voice-type heard

□ request, by name, recordings of two well-known arias or songs to which they have listened during the course of the unit

The Stylistic Use of a Voice. In this country alone, one can hear many different kinds of singing, and each style can be identified rather easily. Following are some examples:

□ *operatic style*—Any of the selections from opera suggested in the previous section

□ *blues singer*—Bessie Smith and Dinah Washington were famous "blues" singers (Aretha Franklin sings "soul," which grew out of the blues style.)

□ *crooner*—Bing Crosby

□ *country-western*—Johnny Cash and Hank Williams

□ *contemporary rock*—Rock singers use their voices with great abandon; sometimes the male voice soars into the treble register through the use of the falsetto technique. (The falsetto is produced by constricting the vocal cords; although the sound is high, it sounds thin and tight. Specialists in early English music, Alfred Deller and the "The King's Singers," make regular use of the male falsetto.)

The concert and operatic styles of singing heard in this country are generally the same as those in the European countries in which these styles developed. In some musical cultures vocal styles are markedly different; e.g., in the recorded music of Korea you can hear the unique sound of the "P'ansori" singer (which is a storytelling or musical drama kind of singing).

You may be able to think of other vocal styles, such as the liturgical chant of the priest, the Swiss yodel, the cantillation of the Jewish cantor, or the raspy voice of Louis Armstrong. All are expressive uses of the voice, but each has a distinctive sound. Children should understand that there are many different musical ways to use the singing voice.

Vocal Ensembles. Numerous kinds of vocal ensembles exist, as does a great variety of musical literature for choruses and choirs. The a cappella choir (unaccompanied male and female voices in four or more parts) is a standard choral ensemble found in many high schools and colleges. Recordings featuring the Robert Shaw Chorale, the Roger Wagner Chorale, the Mormon Tabernacle Choir and other ensembles make available great accompanied and unaccompanied choral works as well as excellent arrangements of folk songs and hymns. To hear and compare the distinctive quality of the four vocal parts, listen to a recording of the "Hallelujah Chorus" from Handel's *Messiah* in the polyphonic sections, where each voice type has a chance to sing a particular musical line.

The Gospel choir also utilizes four vocal parts, but the enthusiasm and abandon with which the gospel choirs sing, together with a more open tone quality, sets such groups apart as a unique style in choral singing. The four-part male chorus has less variety of tone color than the mixed chorus or choir, but there is a large repertoire of both sacred and secular composition available to such a group. The "barbershop quartet" features four male voices (first and second tenor, baritone, and bass) and is a popular form of recreational singing.

Among contemporary choral groups, the Swingle Singers have a repertoire that includes vocal jazz arrangements of famous madrigals and choral compositions. Sometimes voices are used to imitate instrumental sounds, as in the Gregg Smith Singers' recording of György Ligeti's "Lux Aeterna," heard at the opening of the film *2001*. Children's choirs of unchanged voices, such as the Vienna Boys' Choir, provide a contrast in tone color when compared with the more mature four-part adult choirs.

Instructional Objectives: To enable children to hear and identify two or more choral groups of different composition, distinctive voice types, and associated musical style.

Behaviors providing evidence that these instructional objectives have been achieved: The children will

☐ hear three choral groups featuring different voice types and circle on a chart the correct type of group heard (e.g., accompanied mixed voices, a capella, gospel choir, male chorus, children's choir)

☐ identify the style of three pieces by placing a number in front of each type on a list to show the order in which they were heard (e.g., barbershop style, traditional madrigal, choral jazz)

Cultural Diversity in Music Listening

Wonderful varied music from all over the world now is available on recordings. You should have access to some representative recordings of music from other cultures and, by continued sampling, you and the children in your class can acquire a taste for it. The music is different, but it still uses instruments and voices (although the timbres may be unlike those of "Western" music). Look in the library for books[16] showing pictures of instruments and performers.

All music has some kind of rhythm, although it may not be based on metric groupings or even have the steady beat which prevails in Western music. Texture is an important quality in music of other cultures; some have "layers" of sound, interrelated rhythmically and by melodic motifs. A good sampling of music from countries around the world can be found in *The Nonesuch Explorer*.[17] After an acquaintance with the many kinds of music recorded there, you can find complete albums devoted to the music of the different ethnic styles. Much useful information can be found on record jackets. Here are a few samples of music from other cultures that you may be able to obtain for study.

Sakura (BOL #66). This is a Japanese folk song featuring a Japanese flute (*shakuhachi*) accompanied by a thirteen-stringed instrument called a *koto*. This is a delicate-sounding music and you may characterize the melody as "oriental." It is a type of pentatonic (five-tone) melody, tuned somewhat differently from such scales in our culture.

The *shakuhachi* is a five-holed bamboo flute blown from the end in the manner of a recorder. This flute sound is well balanced by the sound of the koto, on which the tones are plucked. The koto player uses three picks on the right hand, while the left hand is free to adjust the pitch of the strings by moving bridges and applying pressure to make subtle changes in the tone. Look for other examples of Japanese music[18] recorded in the country itself, rather than a Western adaptation of the music.

Gambongan Gamelan Anklung.[19] Moving farther south in the Pacific, we encounter quite a different sound in the Balinese gamelan (orchestra). The instruments heard in this recording are knobbed brass gongs *(trompong)* and pairs or quartets of bronze keys set over resonator boxes. Both are played with wooden mallets. The shimmering throb heard in this music is caused by tuning the bronze keyed instruments at two slightly different levels of pitch (one group is called *gender* and the other is called *gangsa*).

Listen and try to hear the following, which are the most obvious characteristics of the music:

1. a fast, repetitive pattern played on the brass gongs
2. two-toned drums
3. the main melodic idea, a slow-moving, three-tone pattern of shimmering sound played by the bronze-keyed instruments
4. the layers of sound around the slow melody
5. another repetitive pattern on a single pitch
6. sectional form in three parts:
   introduction, *(a)* fast, *(b)* slow, and *(c)* fast

Other recordings[20] of Balinese music as well as books[21] are available and will provide background information about the music and life of the people.

The music of Africa encompasses many tribes and many different styles. In Chapter 4 "Sara," ceremonial music from Nigeria, was recommended as a musical example using percussion instruments.

After you are comfortable with this music, search for a few other African compositions you would like to study and share with members of the class. Some general sources are cited in the Chapter Notes,[22] and current basic series music books, with their coordinated recordings, make available a good variety of music from other cultures.[23]

Instructional Objectives: To enable children to become familiar with music of selected cultures, identify each culture's music by its overall sound, and recognize the general type of instruments used.

Behaviors providing evidence that these instructional objectives have been achieved: The children will

☐ hear an unfamiliar composition from a culture previously studied, and identify the country of origin and the predominant instrumental sound

☐ discuss music they hear on recordings, radio, television, or in movies that is based on music of other cultures they have studied

What Is Style in Music?

Style in music is the result of particular ways of using the elements of music and procedures for improvisation or composition. People often think of musical style in terms of the periods of Western European art history—baroque, Viennese classic, romantic, and so on. These are distinctive and important, but American music also has styles—jazz, blues, country and western, and others—and so does the music of other cultures: music of the *gagaku* in Japan and Balinese gamelan music are only two. Each uses the elements of music in distinctive ways that one can learn to recognize.

Appendix A-VII lists concepts about style in music that children might acquire through units of study in the elementary school. In the following discussion well-known exemplar compositions of three European style periods have been selected, and your attention is directed to the distinguishing characteristics of each style. A fourth style, the romantic period (consisting of much music composed between 1820 and 1900) was represented by several works discussed at Level II. Although no exemplar composition of the romantic period is included here, music and related teaching notes are readily available in the educational record series[24] and in the basic series music books.[25]

"Jesu, Joy of Man's Desiring" (**AinM V-1, BOL #62**) was composed by Johann Sebastian Bach. Hearing the music without knowing the title, one might conclude that it has the solemnity and majesty associated with some formal religious services. The composition is in fact a hymn tune (chorale) that Bach embellished with a long flowing countermelody and used as a prelude for the church service. So although this is chosen as an example of music of a particular style period, it is also an example of music that served a functional purpose.

Stringed instruments begin the composition by playing the countermelody, and then the chorale melody comes, first in the woodwinds and then the brass. Listen for ten different appearances of phrases from this chorale, played alternately by woodwinds and brass, always framed by the decorative countermelody in the strings. Here is the first phrase of the chorale melody:

Je - su,   joy   of   man's de - sir - ing,   Ho - ly   wis - dom,   love   most   bright,

This chorale prelude moves along in a steady rhythm with a firm bass line. The decorative upper line seems to flow with few resting points. It is really an embellishing melody set over the basic harmonies of the chorale.

In these qualities we find the main features of the late baroque style in music composed between 1680 and 1750. It is related in some ways to baroque art and architecture, which is strong, heavily decorated, and activated by the flow of detail. Teaching notes for other compositions in this style are readily available.[26] (See Appendix A-VII for a summary of the baroque style and representative composers.)

About the time of America's founding, the Viennese classic style was at its height (1750–1820). Among the composers of that period were Haydn, Mozart and Beethoven. Mozart's *Eine kleine Nachtmusik* ("A Little Night Music") (**AinM IV-1, BOL #86**) was written as a serenade to entertain the guests at an outdoor garden party. It, too, is "functional" music in that it had a social purpose. The second movement, "Romanze," as the title implies, is a gentle romantic piece of music. Listen to the music and try to decide which characteristics of each pair below best describe the music:

1. *Melody:*	☐ one theme	or	☐	several themes
	☐ fragmentary		☐	long lines
2. *Rhythm:*	☐ regular		☐	syncopated
3. *Instruments:*	☐ brass and woodwinds		☐	strings
4. *Phrases:*	☐ regular, balanced		☐	irregular, uneven lengths

The melodies of Viennese classic music are expressive but simple and clear-cut. Often two different themes are set in contrast to one another. In "Romanze" you will find three different themes organized into six sections. The first theme has two parts: the first a stepping kind of movement, and the second an upward winding movement. Listen again to the first theme, so you have it well in mind; then hear the entire composition and decide which musical form is used:

☐ A B A B A Coda   or   ☐ A B A C A Coda

A number of compositions by Viennese classic composers are included in the educational record series.[27]

The French artists Claude Monet, Auguste Renoir and Edgar Degas, who worked in the last half of the 19th century, are known as Impressionist painters. This style in art features flickering patches of color that are rich yet subdued, pastel, and misty. Outlines are blurred, giving an impression of a scene or a subject rather than providing all the details.

Music has its impressionistic composers, Debussy, Delius, Ravel, and others, whose music (mostly composed between 1890 and 1910) has characteristics somehow like the work of the impressionistic painters. The melodies tend to be wispy, consisting of short motifs rather than long singing lines. Rhythms often have a vague pulse obscured by syncopation, and tone colors are mixed and blended together.

"Nuages" by Debussy (**Bol #70**) is a good example of impressionistic music. Listen to the music and decide which characteristic in each pair below best fits this music:

1. *Beats:*	☐ strong	☐ weak
2. *Accents:*	☐ few	☐ many
3. *Melodies:*	☐ fragmentary	☐ clear-cut
4. *Instruments:*	☐ strings and woodwinds	☐ brass and percussion
5. *Articulation:*	☐ staccato	☐ legato
6. *Dynamic changes:*	☐ abrupt	☐ gradual

Other music of the impressionistic style is readily available in the educational record series.[28]

Opera (a staged drama that is sung throughout with instrumental accompaniment) is another musical form with roots in all these style periods. Mozart's opera *The Magic Flute* is often programmed by opera companies and can be seen in an excellent screen version. The songs and recorded music from *Hänsel and Gretel* by Humperdinck, an opera written for and about children, are readily available and can be combined with a study of the opera.[29]

Amahl and the Night Visitors[30] is a short opera by the contemporary composer Gian-Carlo Menotti. It is usually presented on television during the Christmas season and provides a very accessible introduction to opera for children. The music of *Carmen* by Georges Bizet is captivating and can be combined with the story in a listening unit. Portions of the vocal solos can be used; at this age, however, children tend to prefer orchestral versions, unless the teacher can help them arrive at an appreciation for the operatic voice. The opera singer spends years developing a voice that is strong and versatile. Since opera singers are dramatic actors as well, and sing (usually without amplification) from a stage in a large auditorium, they must be able to express and project to the audience all shades of feeling. Children who have an opportunity to hear and see an operatic singer on stage (or in a good television production) will more readily understand this kind of drama. Stories of operas and adaptations of operas for young people are available for class use or individual study.[31]

American Music of the 20th Century

Music of this country, in this century, has moved away from the traditions of the "classics" into new forms. Composers use new sound sources such as varied percussion sounds, sounds created by nontraditional uses of standard instruments, and electronically produced sounds. Rhythm is characterized by changing meters and other complexities, and harmonies are derived from chords built in different ways.

Examples of different kinds of music by American composers are suggested and discussed in this section. All of this is meant to encourage you to find a few 20th-century compositions that you will enjoy sharing with children in your classes.

Music from the American Ballet Theater. Aaron Copland wrote the music for the ballet *Rodeo* at the request of the choreographer Agnes de Mille. The first performance was at the Metropolitan Opera House in New York City. Later, the composer rearranged the music in "Four Dance Episodes" for symphony orchestra. In this and some of his other compositions, Copland used American folk tunes as a source of melodic ideas. He combined these with energetic, syncopated rhythms and brilliant use of orchestral instruments.

The final dance episode, "Hoe-Down" (**AinM V-2**), accompanied a square-dance scene in the ballet. Listen to the music once to get a general impression of its style and length, then review the points laid out on the following call chart.

"Hoe-Down," episode 4 from Rodeo

by Aaron Copland

Introduction (17 measures)

1. galloping rhythm (4 measures)
2. tuning-up sounds (9 measures)
3. galloping rhythm (4 measures)

Rhythmic Vamp (21 measures)

4. piano and strings pizzicato and *col legno* (striking strings with the bow stick)

Section A (59 measures)

5. theme a (8 measures)
6. theme b (8 measures)
7. theme a (8 measures)
8. theme b (16 measures)
9. theme a (8 measures)
10. theme a, with bridge to next section (11 measures)

Section B (32 measures)

11. theme c (8 measures)
12. theme c interplay (8 measures)
13. theme c interplay (8 measures)
14. rhythmic extension (20 measures)

Rhythmic Vamp (16 measures)

15. piano, percussion, brass (8 measures)
16. ending with ritard and hold (8 measures)

Section A (26 measures)

17. theme a (8 measures)
18. theme b (12 measures)
19. theme a, with extension and ending (16 measures)

Listen again to the music to see if you can identify the musical events. If necessary, ask someone who is familiar with the music to call or point to the numbers as the specific details are heard in the music.

Now, consider further the means the composer used to create this piece of music. On the chart below, by underlining the best answers under each heading, indicate which musical techniques Copland used:

Rhythm

☐ Beat: strong   weak
☐ Tempo: fast   moderate   slow   changing
☐ Meter: duple   triple   regular   changing
☐ Melody rhythm: straight   syncopated   mixed

Pitch and Melody

☐ Melodic material: one theme   contrasting themes
☐ Melodic Movement: stepwise   chordwise   disjunct   mixed
                                    upward   downward   repeated tones   mixed
☐ Register: high   low   middle   changing

Tone Color

☐ Use: one color   many colors
☐ Type: strings   brass   woodwinds   percussion   voices

Dynamics

☐ Level: loud   medium   soft   varied
☐ Changing: getting louder   getting softer   both   no changes

Form

☐ Phrases: regular—long   regular—short   irregular
☐ Sections: AAB   ABA   ABAC

Harmony

☐ Mode: major   minor   trade-off   other mode
☐ Effect: consonant   dissonant

Texture

☐ Type: polyphonic   homophonic   monophonic
☐ Effect: thick   thin   both   changing

Articulation

☐ Type: legato   staccato   accents
☐ Effect: strong   weak

Read the background material in the record album so you will know the story of the ballet. Then listen again to the music, relating it to a stylized square-dance scene such as Agnes de Mille might have created for her dancers. Because you have no visual representation of the dance scene, you are free to create your own—either by mental pictures or in your kinesthetic memory of movement. The spirit of the composition, rather than its precise construction, is of greatest importance to the listener. In sharing the music with children, you may choose to direct their listening only to the six large sections outlined on the call chart.

Numerous American composers have used themes from folk music in their compositions or have composed music for films, and examples are currently available on recordings with related teaching notes.[32]

Instructional Objectives: To give children an opportunity to hear the music of a well-known American composer; to identify melodic material and basic structural features in the music; and to learn about the use of music in theatrical dance production.

Behaviors providing evidence that these instructional objectives have been achieved: The children will

☐ follow a call chart as they hear the composition and identify which of the following is being heard each of four times the needle is lifted:

	1	2	3	4
Theme a	_____	_____	_____	_____
Theme b	_____	_____	_____	_____
Theme c	_____	_____	_____	_____
Rhythmic vamp	_____	_____	_____	_____

☐ describe ballet as expressive dancing that conveys both feeling and story ideas

Using Unconventional Instruments. Harry Partch was a highly original composer who invented new instruments and adapted old ones to create the sounds to be used in his music. "Cloud-chamber bowls" were a basic sound source for "Cloud-Chamber Music,"[33] composed in 1950. The bottoms and tops cut from 12-gallon Pyrex bottles were hung suspended on a rack. The bell-like tone was produced when the glass was struck with a soft mallet.

Listen to the music to get a general impression of it. Notice the moving, gliding tones and the brief vocal chant at the end. Does this music have a similarity to any you have heard? There seems to be an introduction and two sections to this music as shown on the call chart below. The cloud-chamber bowls signal each change.

Cloud-Chamber Music

by Harry Partch

Introduction

1. rhythmic bell ringing—cloud-chamber bowls

Study in gliding tones

2. glissando on stringed instruments
   marimba and kithara accompaniment
3. transition sounded by cloud-chamber bowls

A dancing tune

4. tune played on stringed instrument with accompaniment by bass marimba
5. tune played on marimba with bass marimba accompaniment
6. tune played on stringed instrument with accompaniment by marimba, kithara and cloud-chamber bowls
7. repeated rhythmic figure in marimba with deer-hooves rattle. Tune played on stringed instrument
8. transition signaled by cloud-chamber bowls

Climactic Statement

9. vocal chant with marimba and stringed instrument accompaniment

Listen to the music a second time as you follow the call chart.

   After you have grasped the mood and character of the music, try to analyze the techniques used in the composition of Section A and Section B. In what way do these two sections differ with respect to the following musical elements:

Rhythm	SECTION A	SECTION B
☐ Beat: strong weak no beat	_____	_____
☐ Tempo: fast moderate		
slow changing	_____	_____
☐ Meter: duple triple		
changing no meter	_____	_____

Pitch		
☐ high low middle changing	_____	_____

Tone Color		
☐ strings winds percussion voices	_____	_____

Dynamics   SECTION A   SECTION B

☐ loud   medium   soft   changing   _____   _____

Texture

☐ Type: polyphonic homophonic monophonic   _____   _____
☐ thin   changing   _____   _____

Using one or more instruments, find a way to demonstrate the different qualities possible under each musical element; e.g. show strong beat, weak beat, or no beat in a creative musical context.

Finding New Ways to Use Musical Pitches. Composers in the 20th century have looked for approaches to musical composition that differ from the melody and harmony as used in earlier musical-style periods. Arnold Schonberg invented the system of composition called the "twelve-tone row," which was designed to minimize the sense of tonality in music. The melodic component of each piece was determined by arranging the twelve chromatic tones of an octave according to certain rules. To establish a "tone row," each of the twelve possible pitches must be used before any pitch can be repeated.[34]

Gunther Schuller is one of many contemporary composers who adopted the "twelve-tone" compositional technique. An example of this compositional device is found in "The Twittering Machine" (**AinM II-2**), one of *Seven Studies on Themes of Paul Klee* composed by Schuller in 1959. Schuller set out to create, in musical terms, a more or less literal translation of an imaginary twittering machine represented in a painting. The composition has the following tone row as its basic tonal material. Notice the large intervals between pitches, which give the music a disjoined, mechanical sound.

Some interesting instrumental sounds can be heard in the composition, which has a simple repetitive form:

Introduction

1. winding-up effect (strings and oboe)

Section A

2. tone row played on wind instruments using very short sounds (pointillism) with woodblock and gourd added to tone color
3. unique articulation of instrumental sounds
   trumpet flutter-tongue
   trombone glissando

4. the "machine" slows down (the pitch lowers) and stops

Section A'

5. winding-up effect (strings and oboe)
6. woodwind twittering begins again, accompanied by woodblock and gourd, together with special effects on trumpet and trombone

Ending

7. brief wind-up effect (strings and oboe), followed by two pointillistic woodwind chords

Although this music has no melody or harmony in the traditional sense, it does give an impression of the subject, which was the composer's intent. In the following list of musical characteristics, underline those that apply to this composition:

Rhythm

□ Beat: strong   weak   no beat
□ Tempo: fast   moderate   slow   changing

Pitch

□ Movement: stepwise   chordwise   disjunct   mixed
                 upward   downward   repeated tones   mixed
□ Register: high   low   middle   changing

Tone Color

□ strings   brass   woodwinds   percussion   voices

Dynamics

□ loud   medium   soft   varied

Texture

□ Type: polyphonic   homophonic   monophonic
□ Effect: thick   thin   changing

Articulation

□ legato   staccato   accents

Instructional Objectives: To acquaint children with American music in which the composer is frankly creative and innovative; to encourage them to create original instruments or scales; and to teach them how musical elements can be varied for expressive purposes.

Behaviors providing evidence that these objectives have been achieved: The children will

☐ create a twelve-tone row on resonator bells or adjustable xylophone, or

☐ create an instrument (percussion, string, wind) and use it in an ensemble to compose a brief piece of music

☐ use their instruments to demonstrate contrasts of rhythm, pitch, dynamics, tone color, and texture

Creating Music by Electronic Means. "Electronic" music is of three types: (1) music created by altering sound by means of tape recorders, (2) music created on a synthesizer, and (3) music composed through use of a computer. An early electronic music composer, Milton Babbitt, discussed the differences in an interview with the editor of the *Music Educators Journal*. This November, 1968, issue of the magazine (now available as a separate publication)[35] provides many articles, a glossary of terms, and a bibliography and discography that are valuable resources on electronic music.

You may have heard the recording, "Switched-On Bach" (Columbia MS 7194), in which Walter Carlos recreated on a synthesizer several well-known compositions by Bach. That record was a good example of synthesized sounds used in a traditional musical context.

Many composers have created original music using these new sound sources, and the basic series music books provide some examples.[36] In addition, excellent electronic realizations of famous symphonic compositions and some original film music created on a synthesizer can be found among commercial recordings.[37]

You can study electronic music, as any music, from the point of view of its tone color, texture, dynamics, form, rhythm, melody, and harmony. This is the "new" music of this century; it is music that is heard on radio and television and in films. Children should learn that it has properties in common with other music, and that all kinds of music convey mood and feeling and can be valued because they combine musical elements in creative, expressive ways.

Using Current Popular Music. Music of all cultures and all styles uses the elements of music discussed so extensively in this book. Among the compositions currently popular with fifth and sixth grade children, you can find examples that will help in studying one or more musical elements and their effects. The one-time popular "Both Sides Now" by Joni Mitchell was discussed in Chapter 7, and characteristics of the melody that seemed to reflect the sentiment of the lyrics were pointed out. In "Take Five" (Chapters 3 and 4) various rhythmic characteristics were explored and little attention was paid to melody. The more interesting contemporary popular music has individual features that can be identified as contributing to its expressive qualities.

Some teaching aids incorporate popular music in study units. Among these is a series of recorded study units, THE WORLD OF POPULAR MUSIC,[38] that has been useful to many teachers. Michael Bennett produces *Pop Hit Listening Guide*,[39] a monthly listening guide with the selections chosen from current "hit" records. This can keep you up to date with new recorded releases.

Whether you get listening guides from such publications, or make them yourself, they can consist of outlines and call charts like those shown in this chapter. You can guide listening by placing questions in the outline of the musical form; these should give the children a chance at various points within the composition, to make choices that reveal their listening skill and knowledge of obvious musical elements. An example of a "call chart" in which the listener makes a choice describing what is heard at particular points in a composition can be found in **SBM VI-250** in the *Learning to Listen* section "What Do You Hear?" This call chart analyzes the rock composition "The Garden of Earthly Delights."

In using hit tunes you will be dealing with music about which the children have strong feelings. It is therefore advisable to approach the study as an effort to discover what musical techniques the composer and the arranger use to generate those feelings in the listener.

CHAPTER NOTES

1. Susanne K. Langer, **Feeling and Form** (New York: Charles Scribner's Sons, 1953), p. 32.

2. **NDiM V-114** and **115; SBM VI-107** to **117.**

3. "Pan the Piper," "Peter and the Wolf," and "Tubby the Tuba," Columbia CL 671.

   "The King's Trumpet" and others, Children's Record Guild CRG 5040.

   "The Wonderful Violin" and others, the Greystone Corporation, Young People's Records YPR 311.

4. Syd Skolsky, **The Music Box Book** (New York: E. P. Dutton and Co., Inc., 1946); Lillian Baldwin, Music for Young Listeners, **The Crimson Book** (Morristown, N.J.: Silver Burdett Company, 1951), p. 84.

5. "Diary of a Fly" (**AinM I-2**) and "Bear Dance" from **Hungarian Sketches** by Bartók (**AinM III-2**).

   "Golliwog's Cakewalk" from **Children's Corner Suite** by Debussy (**BOL #63**).

   "Fairies and Giants" from **The Wand of Youth Suite** by Elgar (**AinM III-1**).

   "The Little White Donkey" from **Histories No. 2** by Ibert (**AinM II-1**).

   "Clown" from **Marionettes** by MacDowell, and **Under the Big Top** by Donaldson (**BOL #51**).

   "The Royal March of the Lion," "Hens and Cocks," "The Elephant," and "The Swan" from **Carnival of the Animals** by Saint-Saëns (**BOL #51**).

   "The Alligator and the Coon" from **Acadian Songs and Dances** by Thomson (**AinM III-2**).

6. **Licorice Stick, Story of the Clarinet** (Young People's Records YPR 420), **Said the Piano to the Harpsichord** (YPR 411), and others in this series contain musical examples and verbal explanations of essential points.

   Instruments of the Orchestra (Columbia, Victor, Decca), single instruments playing excerpts from symphonic literature.

   Instruments of the Symphony Orchestra (Jam Handy records with filmstrips).

   Meet the Instruments (Bowman Records with filmstrips).

7. **Music for Young People Series** (distributed by NET Films), "Introducing the Woodwinds," "Percussion, the Pulse of Music," and others.

We Make Music (distributed by Film Associates), "The Bassoon," "The Violin," and others.

What is Music? (distributed by Churchill Films), "Wind Sounds," "String Sounds," and others.

8. **Meet the Instruments** (Bowmar Records, full-color charts).

   Instruments of the Orchestra (charts from J. W. Pepper and Son).

9. Harriet Huntington, **Tune Up** (New York: Doubleday & Company, Inc., 1942). Contains excellent photographs and brief descriptions.

   Marion Lacey, **Picture Book of Musical Instruments** (New York: Lothrop, Lee and Shepard Co., Inc., 1951). Contains pen sketches of the instruments with a historical resumé on each.

   Benjamin Britten and Imogen Holst, **The Wonderful World of Music** (New York: Garden City Books, 1958). Tells of the development of the instruments in an interesting, beautifully illustrated historical study.

   Robert W. Surplus, ed., **Musical Books for Young People** (Minneapolis: Lerner Publication Co., 1963). A series of small books about instruments and other musical subjects.

10. Young Audiences, Inc., 115 East 92nd St., New York, N.Y. 10028, or 21 Columbus Ave., San Francisco, Calif. 94111.

11. "Andalucia" from **Suite Andalucia** by Lecuona (**AinM IV-1**).

    "Copacabana" from **Saudades do Brazil** by Milhaud (**AinM IV-2**).

    "March" from **Ballet Suite** by Lully (**AinM III-2**).

    "March of the Dwarfs" by Grieg (**BOL #52**).

    "Sailing" from **Harbor Vignettes** by Donaldson (**BOL #53**).

    "Trepak" from **Nutcracker Suite** by Tchaikovsky.

    "Grand Waltz" from **Mlle. Angot Suite** by Lecocq (**BOL #56**).

    "Swanhilda's Waltz" from **Coppélia** by Délibes (**AinM II-2**).

12. Lillian Baldwin, **A Listener's Anthology of Music**, II (Morristown, N.J.: Silver Burdett Company, 1948). Reprinted by permission.

13. Henry Cowell, "The Banshee," available in **Sounds of New Music**, Folkways Records FX 6160. Also found in Exploring Music, Book 3, Record 8.

14. "Sehr Langsam" from **Five Movements for String Orchestra** by Webern (**AinM II-2**).

    "The Swan" from **Carnival of the Animals** by Saint-Saëns (**AinM III-2** or **BOL #51**).

15. "Chinese Dance" from **The Nutcracker Suite** by Tchaikovsky (**BOL #58**).

    "Dagger Dance" from **Natoma** by Herbert (**AinM III-1**).

    "Fire" from **Gayne Ballet Suite No. 2** by Khachaturian.

    "Polka" from **The Golden Age** by Shostakovich.

16. Alexander Buchner, **Folk Music Instruments of the World** (New York: Crown Publishers, Inc., 1972).

17. **The Nonesuch Explorer,** Nonesuch Records H7-11.

18. "Flower Dance," in **Japanese Folk Melodies,** Nonesuch Records H-72020.

19. From LEARNING TO LISTEN TO MUSIC (Morristown, N.J.: The Silver Burdett Co., 1969).

20. The Nonesuch Explorer Series: **Golden Rain,** H-72028, and **Music from the Morning of the World,** H-72015.

21. William Malm, **Music Cultures of the Pacific, the Near East and Asia** (Englewood Cliffs, N.J.: Prentice-Hall, Inc., 1967); Colin McPhee, **Music of Bali** (New Haven, Conn.: Yale University Press, 1966) and **A House in Bali** (New York: John Day Co., 1946).

22. James A. Standifer and Barbara Reeder, **Source Book of African and Afro-American Materials for Music Educators** (Washington, D.C.: Music Educators National Confer-

ence, 1972); Sidney Fox, Barbara Reeder Lundquist, and James A. Standifer, THE WORLD OF POPULAR MUSIC, **Afro-American** (Chicago: Follett Publishing Co., 1974).

23. "Music of the Pacific World" (**ExM VI-113**).

"Music of Africa and the Middle East" (**ExM VI-131**).

"Music of Latin America" (**ExM VI-151**).

"Responding to African Music" (**SBM V-23**).

"Eskimo and American Indian Music" (**SBM V-106**).

"Music of India" (**SBM V-136**).

"Music of Africa" (**NDinM V-69, NDinM VI-65**).

"Music of the Orient" (**NDinM V-107**).

"Music of China and Japan" (**NDinM VI-115**).

"Music of the Middle East" (**NDinM V-157, NDinM VI-155**).

"Music of India" (**NDinM V-189, NDinM VI-187**).

"Music of the Near East" (**SBM VI-22**).

"Instrumental Music of the Mexican Indians" (**SBM VI-124**).

24. Examples of romantic compositions in educational record series:

First movement from **Symphony No. 5** by Beethoven (**BOL #72**).

Roman Carnival Overture by Berlioz (**BOL #76**).

Hungarian Dance No. 1 by Brahms (**AinM V-2**).

Night on Bald Mountain by Moussorgsky (**BOL #82**).

Scheherazade by Rimsky-Korsakov (**BOL #77**).

First movement from **Symphony No. 5** by Schubert (**AinM VI-1**).

Prelude to Act II from **Lohengrin** by Wagner (**AinM VI-1**).

25. Examples of romantic compositions discussed in basic music series:

"Andante Cantabile" from Quintet in E^b by Beethoven (**SBM V-94**).

"Farandole" from **L'Arlesienne Suite** by Bizet (**ExM VI-31**).

"Aeolian Harp" by Chopin (**NDinM VI-27**).

First movement from **Piano Concerto in E^b** by Liszt (**NDinM VI-181**).

The Moldau by Smetana (**ExM VI-103**).

Till Eulenspiegel's Merry Pranks by R. Strauss (**ExM V-182**).

26. **Suite for Strings** by Corelli-Pinelli (**AinM V-2, BOL #63**).

Chorale, "Awake Thou Wintry Earth" by Bach (**BOL #83**).

Royal Fireworks Music by Handel (**AinM III-2**).

Concerto in C for Two Trumpets by Vivaldi (**BOL #84**).

27. "Musette" from **Armide Ballet Suite** by Gluck (**AinM II-2**).

Symphony No. 99 by Haydn (**BOL #73**).

Second movement ("Variations") from **The Surprise Symphony** by Haydn (**BOL #62**).

Overture from **The Marriage of Figaro** by Mozart (**BOL #76**).

28. "Claire de Lune" (**BOL #52**), "Clouds" and "Festivals" (**BOL #70**), and "La Mer" (**AinM VI-2, BOL #70**) by Debussy.

Mother Goose Suite by Ravel (**AinM IV-2, V-1, BOL #57**).

"The White Peacock" by Griffes (**AinM VI-1**).

29. **Hänsel and Gretel** by Humperdinck, story and music (**ExM III-121 to 129, BOL #58, AinM V-2**).

30. Gian-Carlo Menotti, **Amahl and the Night Visitors,** narrative adaption by Frances Frost (New York: Whittlesey House, McGraw-Hill Book Co., Inc., 1962).

31. Harriet Nordholm, Birchard Opera Series, **Hansel and Gretel, The Magic Flute, Carmen,** and others (Evanston, Ill.: Summy-Birchard Company, 1951).

    Opera Stories for Young People, **The Magic Flute** by Stephen Spender, **The Bartered Bride** by Johanna Johnston, and others (New York: G. P. Putnam's Sons, 1966).

32. "Symphonic Dances" from **West Side Story** by Bernstein (**BOL #74**).

    Variations on "Pop, Goes the Weasel" by Cailliet (**AinM IV-1**).

    "El Salon Mexico" (**BOL #74**).

    "American Salute" by Gould (**BOL #64, AinM V-1**).

    "Putnam's Camp" from **Three Places in New England** by Ives (**BOL #75**).

33. **Music of Harry Partch,** Composers Recordings, Inc., CRI 193 (170 West 74th Street, New York, N.Y. 10023).

34. Further information on the use of the twelve-tone row and creative applications in the classroom can be found in Mary Val Marsh, **Explore and Discover Music** (New York: The Macmillan Company, 1970).

35. **Electronic Music** (Washington, D.C.: Music Educators National Conference, 1969).

36. Exploring Music, **Book VI** (pp. 192–3, record 14): "Composition for Synthesizer" by Babbitt, "A Piece for Tape Recorder" by Ussachevsky, and "Three Synchronisms for Instruments and Electronic Sounds" by Davidovsky.

    Silver Burdett Music, **Book VI:** "Dripsody" by LeCaine, p. 118, record 5; "The Hammer without a Master" by Boulez, p. 247, record 12; "Mexican Cactus," p. 130, record 6; and "Syn-Rock" by Hays, p. 20, record 1.

37. **Clockwork Orange** by Walter Carlos, Columbia KC 31480.

    The Bermuda Triangle by Isao Tomita, RCA ARL 1-2885, and the following electronic realizations by Tomita: **Pictures at an Exhibition** (Mussorgsky), RCA ARL 1-0838; **The Firebird** (Stravinsky), RCA ARL 1-1312.

38. The World of Popular Music, **Rock, Afro-American, Folk and Country, Jazz,** by Sidney Fox, et al. (Chicago: Follett Publishing Company, 1973–74).

39. Michael Bennett, **Pop Hit Listening Guide** (Pop Hits Publications, current subscription service, 3149 Southern Avenue, Memphis, Tenn. 38111).

9

Implementing the Program

We have traveled a long road in delineating the kind of education in music that should be provided for preschool and elementary children. The challenges of the first chapter return in these final pages: a music program cannot be extracted from a textbook, but must be created by the inner promptings of teachers charged with the responsibility for it. At this time it should be possible for you to come to some conclusions about the value of music for children you will teach, and the broad objectives for the music program you would like to carry out.

Relationships between music, the social studies, and other areas of the curriculum have been referred to frequently. We know that experience with the music of other peoples can bring an individual into dynamic association with the spirit and feelings of those peoples. For this reason you will find music to be an important adjunct to social studies. Daniel Prescott said:

If we teach art subjects in such a way as to induce feelings, surely our children will understand the stream of history, will sense the on-goingness of civilization as they never can through mere verbal symbols describing those times. . . . Indeed, the aesthetic arts should render the same service of interpretation and crystallization to the point of feeling within our own culture.[1]

This chapter will deal in part with the interrelationship of music with studies in science and the social studies.

Now that you have studied the music education curriculum, you will need to develop plans to relate this information to your particular teaching assignment. Such planning should be so broad that it can include general arrangements for the full year, as well as the details of daily teaching procedures. Sample plans for music lessons you could teach should certainly include procedures for the evaluation of musical learning. Evaluation is necessary not only because most school administrators and parents expect a report of growth on the part of the children, but also because evaluative procedures help you know in what areas your work is most effective and where you may need to challenge yourself to seek more adequate techniques and materials.

MUSIC AND OTHER AREAS OF THE CURRICULUM

In the school curriculum music can be related to physical education and dance, visual and language arts, as well as science and the social studies. The relationship of music to physical education and dance was given considerable attention in Chapter 3 of this book. Several suggestions were made in Chapter 8 for using art activities and story-telling in connection with listening to music. Poems, nursery rhymes, and chants were suggested as material for creative melody-writing in Chapters 5 and 6.

All these activities can be expanded if teachers and children have the interest and resources to do so. The basic music series and other curriculum publications offer additional approaches and materials. Science and the social studies have important relationships to music that will be considered briefly in this chapter.

Music and Science

As follow-up to the activities related to the analysis of sound (Chapter 2), the scientific principles of tone production and amplification can be studied in elementary science projects at different grade levels. Music has been associated with mathematics and astronomy since the day of Aristotle, but not because of its rhythmic aspect—that two quarter-notes equal a half-note, and so on. Although the durations of notes are named as fractions (quarter, half, eighth, . . .), rhythm is too flexible to be arithmetic; the meter signatures (e.g., $\frac{2}{4}$, $\frac{3}{4}$, $\frac{6}{8}$) do not function as fractions. Rather, the association of music with mathematics is based on the fact that each pitch is generated by the vibration of a sound source (e.g., a stretched string, membrane, a piece of metal) at a particular rate. The octave is the basis for the division of pitch into musical scales, and precise mathematical relationships exist among the tones of a scale. When children of the intermediate grades learn intervals (the octave, fifth, fourth, third, and so on), they begin to work with divisions of the scale that are determined by the harmonic series in music, the real basis of a relationship between music and mathematics. Some simple science exhibits show how a plucked string vibrates in its entire length and in partials (i.e., in halves, thirds, fourths, and so on), creating not only the fundamental pitch that we hear, but also a complex of other almost inaudible pitches called harmonics.

Several science books written for children[2] make the basic principles quite understandable. You will need to decide to what extent a study of sound can be incorporated in the science projects recommended for the grade you expect to teach. What relationships can be drawn between musical tone and the physics of sound?

Intellectually gifted children at Level III will be interested in relating science to musical sound. Ask the school librarian to provide books on acoustics and on the principles of hi-fi and stereo, as well as how recording is done. When the children have completed their research, let them make a report to the class; let them use mock-ups and models to demonstrate the scientific principles, if possible, or visit a recording studio to gather first-hand information.

Social Studies: Resources and Organization

At every grade level you will find opportunities to use music in social studies to help children expand their cultural horizons and help them understand themselves and other people. The social studies program at Level I is determined by the interests of children of these ages. In the kindergarten and first grade, social studies center on the home, the family, and the school. As you attempt to bridge the gap between home and school in our multi-cultural society, it is important that you draw on the musical heritage of races and nationalities other than just your own.

Second and third grade social studies center in part around the community and its resources: the city with its services and activities; the farm and the various people, animals, and work associated with it. Many third grade classes study native American cultures. Authentic Indian songs tend to be modal in quality (that is, their melodies are based on scales having arrangements of intervals different from the familiar major or minor), and so the children experience a different musical sound when these songs are used in the classroom. It is much better that children have an opportunity to sing authentic songs of these peoples, when simple, appropriate examples can be found, than to merely sing songs composed about the Indians. The specially composed songs may lack musical quality, and they do not project the imagery and feeling of the ethnic group. Many basic series music books at Level II contain groups of songs that can be used, and Louis Ballard[3] has done a great deal to make American Indian music available to teachers.

Ethnic songs need not be sung only when a social studies unit is in progress. Peoples all over the world have similar activities and concerns; their songs can be shared by children here merely because they are appealing. The songs in this book were selected to exemplify cultural diversity within a music curriculum; they can also serve broader purposes when they are related to other cultural studies.

Songs and dance music of other peoples will enrich both singing and the listening. UNESCO[4] has published a series of records, *Hi, Neighbor,* that includes children's songs from many countries. This is only one of many interesting resources you can use. Basic series music books include original texts for some folk songs. When the words can be presented correctly, such songs should be sung in the original language both for interest and for the cultural enrichment that the language brings to the music program. Foreign language curricula routinely use songs as a vehicle for learning the language. These too are "music" if sung expressively.

In the social studies of the intermediate grades, students are concerned with the people of their own community and with peoples as far distant as Asia and Europe. Historical and geographical considerations are important in such a study. When the children see how different aspects of music have developed and are related through history, they will more surely understand the close relationship among peoples. Most city, county, and state curriculum planners have determined the topics to be used in each grade. Once the study is limited to a region or a historical period, you can determine what values musical resources might have in the total study. Sometimes the use of related music offers good opportunities for children to identify with a particular culture, and for a time most of the musical activities of the class may be centered around the study.

The classified indexes of the basic music books list appropriate songs for many subjects. Some recent books and listings from recording firms suggest specific recordings. Since no one source contains all the most desirable music, it is advisable that you provide yourself with specialized supplementary books; city and county libraries are usually good sources.

Music related to social studies need not be limited to folk music. A country's composers make important contributions to its culture; children should hear representative instrumental and vocal music of these composers. This book discusses composed music of Spanish, Russian, Mexican, French, Indonesian, and German as well as American origin. As far as possible, the children should understand how the composer's nationality and time, as well as events in history, influenced the music. Such understanding depends on the background and maturity of the children and the extent to which they can understand such basic social considerations. Some of these factors are taken into account when we categorize music as belonging to a certain "style" period.

Regional Studies. At Level II social studies often are related to the country, region, or state in which the children live, or to type-regions of the world, such as the hot, dry countries or the cold countries.

Material about local areas is compiled in state or county courses of study and generally is not available in national publications. Often there is a shortage of good usable musical material that is authentic rather than "arranged" and adapted. Local libraries, historical societies, and museums may have information bearing on music of the locality. Available material will center around (1) native peoples, American Indian or Spanish Americans, if any; (2) immigrants (early or more recent) who brought their folk music with them; and (3) local historical events commemorated in song.

Some of the type-regions studied offer good opportunities for considering related music. Curriculum bulletins frequently list all the music available on each topic, but many such listings can be unselective and often include a large number of songs of little authenticity and musical value. Such lists are useful as resources, but each song or musical reference must be judged in terms of its genuine worth in the topic concerned.

In addition to musical criteria, you can evaluate songs in terms of the following:

1. Is this a song actually sung by the people being studied, or has it merely been composed about them?
2. If it is sung by the people themselves, what is its significance? Does it reveal them as a particular kind of people, of a particular occupation? Does it genuinely express human feeling and experience? Is it a good representative of its type?
3. If the song has been composed about the life and circumstances of a particular people, is it a good song in itself? Does its musical and poetic quality make a genuine contribution to the study at hand?

Recorded music typical of the countries or regions studied is also important. Short examples designed to give children the flavor of authentic music can be valuable and impressive. Someone must select the music to be heard by the class as a whole; in some cases a small committee of children can help determine what will be most interesting to the entire group.

When music of other cultures is heard, it should be studied with respect to its rhythmic elements, melody, harmony or lack of it, and instrumentation. Older pupils can deal with these questions much more extensively than younger pupils. The Korean folk song "Arirang," discussed in Chapter 7, is a good example of a folk song of another culture that can be learned by children as an adjunct to their study of that culture.

Music in the United States. In many schools fifth grade children study America from the landing of the Pilgrims to the present day and from the East Coast to the West. The music applicable to this study is varied and should constitute a large part of the musical experiences during the year. Several fifth grade music books center around music of the United States, and therefore it is not difficult to obtain appropriate literature.

Several points must be noted regarding the use of American folk music. Genuine folk music is an expression of a people; it expresses their concerns, moods, love, and relationship to their work, family, and the world. Insofar as it truly expresses these human qualities, the music has lasting value as a part of American life.

Such music has a place in education and should be studied in a way that brings these expressive factors to the attention of the children. Certainly not all cowboy or riverboat songs are important, but good examples of each type of song can be chosen. Some songs may be included because they have historical significance. Others may be included for their particular musical characteristics. You should use not only songs that best represent each category, but also songs that give the children varied musical experiences in melody, mood, rhythm, and accompaniment. Because the United States is a collection of immigrants from many countries, folk music of other lands has its place in a study of American music; well-known melodies of other countries complement the study of folk music in this country.

A number of resource books are available.[5] For teaching purposes the study should be divided into smaller units such as "Music of the Colonial Period" and "Music of the Western Frontier." Sound filmstrips on these topics include relevant music. The music will be enhanced if the cassette or record is heard on a good-quality player. Most cassette players used for individual study of unit work do not reproduce the music adequately.

Patriotic and service songs may be learned by fifth grade children. Often the occasion and purpose of a song's origin is as important as the song itself, for only in that setting are some songs fully appreciated. The children should hear recordings of fine soloists and choirs singing these songs and read the historical background of this music.[6]

Widening Horizons of People and Music. Sixth grade music books reflect a broader source of music. Some sixth grades study Canada, Mexico, or countries in Central and South America. Other classes look closely at the Philippines, Japan, Africa, or Australia. Perhaps only one or two such topics will be considered, but the related music is plentiful and interesting. Topical indexes in the basic music series suggest authentic songs. Other sources[7] discuss the important characteristics of the music of several regions of the world. The Library of Congress and commercial companies such as Folkways, Columbia, Nonesuch, and Lyrichord have recorded music in many lands. A number of films are also available as enrichment for such a study. Films showing musical activities by native performers are especially useful.

Sixth grade children can be very capable musicians; when previous training has been good, they can sing and play melodies and rhythms with little guidance from their teacher or the music specialist. Individuals may do research reading, listening, or viewing on selected topics and report their findings. The extent of such activities, of course, depends on the resources available at a suitable reading level. Because of the relative maturity and the greater musical skills of these children, a study of music can have considerable significance in a social studies unit.

Developing a Resource Unit. When building a resource unit in which you relate music to social studies and other classroom activities, you should consider the following questions:

1. In the selection of the literature, which music is authentic and appropriate? Are there possibilities for student reports on the backgrounds of this music? If so, what readings are available? Where?

2. Are recordings of authentic music available? Which would be most appropriate for use with this class? Are there reliable sources of information about this music?

3. How are the character, customs, and life of the people reflected in the music? Are they generally peaceful or warlike, agrarian or hunters? Are religious and social customs revealed? If they were immigrants and settlers, what were their life purposes and outlook, social and religious customs, occupations, and everyday concerns with living?

4. What are the distinctive melodic, rhythmic, and harmonic characteristics of this music? How much of this information should be brought to the attention of the pupils?

5. What use of musical instruments was made in the period or region? Did instruments vary with the music and the occasion? Are similar instruments available, or can they be made by the students?

6. What possibilities exist for using body movement and playing instruments in authentic or nearly authentic ways with this music?

A culminating program can be arranged around the activities of the study. The children sing, perform typical dances, and dramatize events related to the topic, and parents or other classes may be invited to the classroom. If these programs are closely related to everyday studies and activities, they are quite justifiable educational enterprises, a sharing of what has been learned in a particular study rather than a "performance" in the formal sense. Drama, art, poetry, music, and dance may be combined to provide a colorful and interesting presentation.

Social studies topics vary in their musical importance. Occasionally a topic may have rich musical potential, and for a time little unrelated music is studied. Other topics may offer little of genuine musical interest, and the attention should be focused in other directions. Explore the possibilities for musical enrichment with whatever units of study you plan for your class.

"EXCEPTIONAL" CHILDREN AND MUSIC EDUCATION

The philosophy, objectives, subject matter, materials, and procedures of music education recommended in this book are intended to meet the needs of the wide range of children considered "normal." There are other children who are "exceptional" in various ways. These children, too, need music as a basic component in their education. "Exceptional" is a relative term applied to children who deviate in some way, mentally, physically, or socially, from "normal." Among exceptional children are those who are handicapped and those who are gifted. A few individuals are both handicapped and gifted, as in the case of the famous violinist Itzhak Perlman. He is handicapped in that he is obliged to walk with crutches, but he is enormously gifted musically and in the physical coordination required to play the violin.

There are children with such great handicaps that they, in the past, would not have been educated in the public schools. With the passage of Public Law 94-142, *Education of All Handicapped Children Act of 1975,* public education is guaranteed for handicapped children. Federal funds have been authorized to assist state and local educational organizations in meeting the requirements of this law. Whatever specialized services are needed for handicapped children will be supplied, including written, individualized educational programs for each child, when necessary. In addition, school districts must maximize the opportunities these children have to be educated with normal children.

In the past, exceptional children could be isolated in a special class, having little or no contact with normal children. Public Law 94-142 specifies that exceptional children shall have as much opportunity as their individual cases will allow to be educated in regular classrooms. The procedure, called "mainstreaming," will bring some exceptional children into many regular, graded classrooms for at least part of the school day.

In Chapter 1 we considered the value of music to the population as a whole; these values extend as well to exceptional children, be they handicapped or gifted. Though the contribution of music education to the social, physical, intellectual, and emotional domains of life is acknowledged as significant, its ultimate value is its potential as an alternative, nonverbal way of knowing oneself and the world. Whether normal or exceptional, all children need life enriched by the arts; the objectives of music education for exceptional children, therefore, can be considered to be the same as those for normal children.

In addition, music can be used in a program of therapy for children with social, psychological, or physical problems. The implementor of such a program is the music therapist. A by-product of the music therapist's work may be aesthetic responsiveness, but the main thrust of this specialist's use of music with handicapped children is functional improvement of one kind or another.

We now see music in the schools from three points of view:

1. The chief concern of the music teacher, and the classroom teacher who assumes the role of music teacher, is music as a life-enriching, aesthetically rewarding encounter.
2. The classroom teacher views music in the context of general education. While it is needed for a well-balanced education, music also has a functional use in the development of reading, physical coordination, socialization, and a positive self-concept.
3. The music therapist prescribes music to resolve the particular problems of the handicapped child.

All these are legitimate uses of music in education, but the objectives are distinct in each case. Conditions and means for achieving the objectives differ. In this book our chief concern is Item 1 above, but we recognize the value and need for each of the other emphases.

Children who are exceptional in some way may have limitations not encountered in normal children. These must be taken into account, and the teacher whose goal is to develop musical responsiveness in children will need to work around any limitation, and not allow the problem to intervene between the child and musical participation. Following is a survey of the various exceptional children you are likely to encounter in the elementary classroom, together with suggestions of modifications that might be needed to accommodate such a child in the music education program. There are a number of good sources of more detailed information on music for exceptional children.[8]

The speech-impaired child might be the victim of one or more disorders. These involve problems of articulation (distortions, substitutions, omissions, or additions of sound); vocal disorders involving pitch, loudness, or quality; problems of fluency (stuttering); cleft palate, which can result in a variety of speech problems; cerebral palsy, which interferes with muscle control over speech and breathing; and various impairments resulting from brain disorder or damage.

Some use of vocal music may be prescribed by the music therapist to help overcome the disorder. The goals of the music education program, however, should be success, pleasure, expanded understanding and ability to respond to music. To this end, the activities of the music program should be varied enough to allow these children to participate in ways in which they can be successful—exploring and manipulating sound, playing instruments, moving, or listening to music. The speech-impaired child can enter fully into many of the musical experiences described in preceding chapters. Although certain musical activity may be helpful as therapy, do not limit the child's musical encounters to activities prescribed for therapy. Do not, on the other hand, require verbal responses that will limit the musical success of the verbally handicapped.

Emotionally disturbed children may be physically aggressive or extremely withdrawn. Many are obviously tense, anxious, and unable to control their impulsive behavior. A certain amount of structure, together with motivation provided by musical activities they find attractive, can be helpful. A child may learn to modify undesirable behavior for the sake of musical participation in a group.

As the teacher, you must establish an understanding with the emotionally disturbed child, recognizing the need for control of behavior in group music-making, but also assuring the child that you will find ways in which he or she can participate successfully. You might have the child play a drone bass on the metallophone, teaming up with a stable, reliable child to assure success. The activity should be simple and brief, and you should unobtrusively commend acceptable behavior.

We know that music can shape people's mood, and you should consider this when working with emotionally disturbed children. One way in which some of these individuals can begin to realize success is to have them take part in simple in-place music-related body movement at an activity level slightly above their own level of activity. Gradually lower the activity level of the music, and the child may adjust accordingly; this establishes that it is possible for the child to respond flexibly to music. The appeal of musical sound and the activities of the music program often provide motivation and success that these children may not find elsewhere.

Mentally retarded children are classified in two groups: Educably Mentally Retarded (EMR) are those having an I.Q. above 50; Trainable Mentally Retarded (TMR) with an I.Q. of 50 or below. The teacher's attitude in working with such children is extremely important. An enthusiastic, positive attitude, and the expression of pleasure in musical activity must be conveyed, because these children need a model for their positive behavior.

EMR children must be helped to find activities in which they can be successful and thus develop greater self-confidence. All can learn to respond to music at some level. With a slight adjustment of musical materials, the kind of program recommended for normal children of a younger chronological age can be adapted for mentally retarded children. When grouped with children of their own chronological age, a retarded child can do simple musical tasks that support more advanced activities of normal children. As an example, the EMR child can keep a steady beat on an instrument while others improvise more complex patterns, or strum the Autoharp as you or a capable normal child hold down and change the chord bars.

Children with learning disabilities "exhibit a disorder in one or more of the basic psychological processes involved in understanding or in using spoken or written language."[9] This dysfunction may be in perception, integration of information, or in expression.

Since music does not convey specific meanings, but does require perception and integration of musical sounds and rhythms, it can provide an area of success for such children. You will need to provide ways for the child to respond directly to the music, bypassing the problem areas of spoken or written language. Good possibilities include demonstrative rhythmic response in large body movement and playing larger rhythm or tuned instruments that are easy to strike.

The child with impaired hearing can perceive music by feeling or touch. It is rare that such individuals are totally deaf, and arrangements should be made so they can experience sound and its related vibrations at close range. Pitches in the bass staff are more likely to be heard by these children, so have them listen to or play low-pitched sounds.

Experimentation with sound and playing instruments of various kinds are activities within the abilities of many of these children. They particularly enjoy rhythm, which is transmitted to them when they feel the vibration of a musical instrument directly, or transmitted through a table top or a wooden floor. Movement, dance, and dramatization are areas of good potential for these children. Have them feel the steady beat of music via a balloon that they hold lightly in their hands as they move to the music.

Deaf children learn to depend upon visual cues, so tap the steady beat or accent with your foot to enable the child to follow while rhythm or tuned instruments are played. Dynamics can be shown through gesture. Read Carol Epley's article, "In a Soundless World of Musical Enjoyment" to learn why a deaf child would seek participation in a musical ensemble.[10]

Blind and partially sighted children can be as successful in music as normal children if the teacher will make adjustments to accommodate their particular needs. Those who have partial sight must be in a position with good light to make optimum use of their limited sight. Music-related materials they can touch, together with the vast amount of recorded music available today, are immensely helpful in enabling sight-impaired children to enjoy rich musical experiences.

Much individualized work in music can be done, but blind children can take part in musical ensembles if they can pick up cues to performance through physical contact with adjacent participants, as in a choir where individuals stand or sit close together so that breathing, articulation, and phrasing can be physically felt by the blind student.

Braille notation was first developed by Louis Braille to enable him to have notation for music. An explanation of how the system of six dots is applied to music can be found in an article by Doris Herlein.[11] Musical materials for the blind can be made available by the school or special agencies.

Crippled children are no less feeling, responding individuals than normal children, unless the handicap has been allowed to intrude on life to the extent that psychological damage has been done. A music program that has a variety of participatory activities and instruments that require different playing techniques should be able to accommodate in some way most physically disabled children. Although the challenge to master a skill may be strong, the use of music that will evoke feelings must also be part of the musical experience.

Ruth Anne Dykman[12] recommends involving normal children in musical activities for the handicapped. She described wheelchair dances in which a normal child was paired with a child confined to a wheelchair, and felt both children benefited from the experience.

Gifted children may be intellectually innovative and creative, or they may possess high-quality motor skills that set them apart. Music can accommodate the needs of either, because it has its own logic systems which challenge the scholar, and it also requires development of performance skills. Individualized work and special opportunities should be provided to meet the needs of these children.

In *Explore and Discover Music*[13] Mary Val Marsh describes summer musical activities for the academically talented. She found that these children grasp new ideas faster and their creative work is more varied and original than normal children. Margery Vaughan[14] suggests three phases of activity in music for the gifted: (1) set-breaking, (2) realignment, and (3) reconstruction. As an example of set-breaking she suggests working in mixed meters or with cross-accents, and working in the whole-tone scale or twelve-tone scale. She says, "Realignment should generate all kinds of hypotheses and reconstruction should test them."

As teachers we must view exceptional children as individuals with all the human needs and feelings of other individuals. Juliette Alvin has written in *Music for the Handicapped Child:*[15] "Music can be adapted to make the best of any ability the child possesses, and to suit any mental, emotional or physical handicap." In music we have something unique and beautiful to share, and no exceptional trait should deprive a child of musical opportunities.

PLANNING MUSIC INSTRUCTION

As you look ahead to music instruction during the school year, you must first view the span of time and the relationship of music to the children's lives. In addition to the knowledge and musical skills to be developed, seasons and holidays must be commemorated with music, and social and personal interests highlighted. Then you must consider the variety of musical activities children can engage in, which vary in their appeal and suitability for different children. A class of twenty-five or thirty children is a dynamic group that must gradually learn to work together and to accommodate their individual differences.

You should plan with regard to several spans of time. First the year can be blocked out into five or six periods framed by established school grading periods or holidays and vacations.

The opening period of two or three weeks should be planned to accomplish several objectives:

1. reestablish the varied school musical activities, review familiar musical material, and rebuild skills that have not been used during the summer
2. acquaint you with the differing musical abilities of the children
3. serve as an evaluation–planning period during which you can decide the pace of activities and materials to be used during the year

The closing two or three weeks of the school year can be used to summarize and review the musical learnings that have taken place during the year and to reinforce them whenever possible by new musical settings.

In each of the four remaining periods study should be centered on the development of musical skills and concepts that you determine to be appropriate for this particular group of children. The best way to assure that these goals are achieved is to construct a unit plan utilizing materials and activities chosen with the goals in mind. The basic music series books usually organize the musical material around a series of such units of study, so that it is often necessary for a teacher only to adapt such an instructional unit to meet the needs of the class. Each learning period should be planned to include all the different musical activities (singing; playing instruments; responding to music through movement, visual art, and verbalization; listening to music; and creating music) at a level appropriate to the class, and utilizing varied attractive music literature.

The next level of planning should be on a weekly basis. In this plan you should block out objectives for the week in terms of the instructional unit in progress. To assure variety and interest, one or two new musical compositions (song or recording) should be introduced each week. These pieces can vary in length and difficulty depending on the musical skill of the class. Other musical materials will include (1) familiar musical material used in a new context and (2) songs or other music that supplement the instructional unit.

All instructional materials (special records, books, charts, and instruments) that will be needed should be gathered together as you make your weekly plan. Continuity within the weekly plan can be achieved in a couple of ways:

1. by using some of the same materials for several days, but varying the activities or focus of the study in terms of the elements of music that are considered
2. by centering on the same activities or study of musical elements, but giving examples and experiences with different songs or recorded material

Music should have a place in the daily schedule of every class. Ten or fifteen minutes may be long enough for a special music period in kindergarten and first grade, if music is used frequently at other times during the day. Generally a daily twenty-minute music lesson should be planned for the primary grades and a twenty-five or thirty-minute lesson for the intermediate grades.

Before going on to more specifics on lesson planning, we should consider choices you will need to make in developing such plans. Your philosophy of music education and knowledge of the way children learn, as well as teaching strategies and materials for music education, are drawn into this process. In addition, as you plan you should consider the need to evaluate children's general music development, as well as their achievement of the objectives of your instruction.

The Teacher's Art as Balance

Everything you do in the instructional role takes into account your personal adjustment to life and your individual teaching style and philosophy of education. Rarely is an extreme position necessary; nevertheless, you probably will find your place on the continuum of possibilities to be a bit different from that of another teacher. Here are some of the variables within which any teacher works in music education:

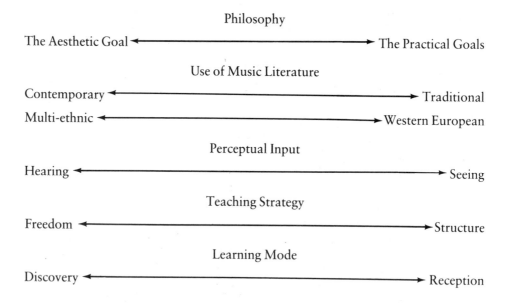

In the philosophy of music teaching you will need to find a position on the continuum between the aesthetic and the practical that provides a viable rationale for the music program you can carry out. If there is any doubt in your mind about these alternatives, re-read the first section of Chapter 1, "The Value of Music."

Throughout this book you have been urged to utilize music literature of varied types and styles. Exclusive use of any one style—United States folk, contemporary popular, Western European classical—or any other single type—group instrumental, vocal, or accompanied solo—can deprive children of the opportunity to become familiar with the broad spectrum of music available. You may, of course, have your musical preferences; but this instructional material, as in any subject, should represent what is appropriate for children.

Music is an aural art, and hearing is basic to it, of course; but music notation and visual representations of musical effects clarify and help us grasp musical ideas and notice details that the nonmusician can miss in a purely aural approach. Our ultimate objective is keen musical perception in response to hearing music; but you should be sensitive to achieving the most productive balance between aural and visual stimuli in the music instruction you provide.

In all learning situations some kind of structure is necessary. This may be imposed by the discipline studied, by the learning style of the student, or by the teacher. As you work with individuals and groups you should try to strike a comfortable, productive balance along the continuum between complete freedom and rigid structure, neither extreme being characteristic of a good learning situation.

As exemplified in the musical experiences for children described in this book, the chief mode of learning in early childhood and elementary classes is discovery through planned experiences. The experiences should be sequenced and related so that children develop a useful cognitive structure and effectively build skills related to music. Receptive learning, as explained in Chapter 1, is the assimilation of information through verbal instruction and lecture. Although you may incorporate "telling" as one mode of instruction for children, the primary emphasis should be learning through concrete experiences or "doing."

In all these decisions it is important that you realize what position you have taken in relation to the alternatives on the continuum of possibilities, and why that choice meets the needs of the children you teach and your own teaching style.

Evaluation

In the elementary school, evaluation of progress made in music is not so much a grading of the pupil as it is a grading of the program itself and of the implementation of that program through effective teaching. Because of its varied, natural appeal, children respond with enthusiasm to music when it is brought to them in vital, meaningful ways.

Evaluation and planning are reciprocal parts of the teacher's work. The growth and achievements of children shine forth in their musical activities and responses; you must continually evaluate this progress in order to make valid plans for the next stage of the music studies. In your first musical contact with the group you should be able to discern the general level of response in the activities undertaken. Succeeding lessons then are planned for reinforcement or for introducing new activities and material that lead to gradual development of new skills and concepts.

Singing, playing instruments, responding to music through body movement, verbalization, and visual art, as well as creative work in music, are ways in which children reveal growing musical knowledge and skills. You must realize, however, that response in any single activity cannot be taken as a measure of a child's total musical achievement. There may be a child who, for lack of early vocal experiences, does not yet sing well; but other activities and responses may suggest that the child's growth in musical concepts and skills is quite satisfactory.

If you have worked with the activities chapters in this book in conjunction with the content of Appendix A, you will have an adequate basis for evaluation, whether you give a test designed to measure the child's achievement in each area, or whether you are familiar enough with each individual in the class to note progress as demonstrated in classroom musical activities. In an evaluation based on the outline of concepts and skills related to rhythm, what general skill in response to rhythm might you look for at a given grade level? When might a child discriminate and respond at will to the metric beat, the melody rhythm, and the accent? At what point might a child clap a rhythm (1) in response to a pattern heard? (2) in response to a pattern seen in notation? A study of the recommended teaching techniques and activities in this book should suggest other ways in which children might reveal their development in rhythm.

In each area of musical concepts, growth should be evaluated in terms of the child's responses to music. The ability to respond and to make music, and to understand the sound and function of music, are far more important than facts that may have been memorized. The behavior lists following the instructional objectives in this book provide concrete examples of good evaluative procedures.

Most classes are supplied with books for music study. These provide an outline of work as well as a basis for evaluation. Each of the series contains short tests or other procedures that can aid in evaluation (see especially the pages and related recordings "What Do You Hear?" in SILVER BURDETT MUSIC, and pages for "Evaluation of Children's Musical Growth" in the EXPLORING MUSIC series). In addition, each unit of study that you design should include evaluative materials and procedures. Study of the sample unit and lesson plans in this chapter will reveal the relationship between instructional and evaluative material and procedures.

If the school administration requires formal grades in music, you should consider the child's musical potential and evaluate in terms of individual achievement. One point of caution should be observed: it is a mistake to give the highest possible grade in music to a pupil who has a limited musical potential. The highest grade should be reserved for those who both have and use their natural ability; next highest grades may go to those who have enthusiasm and who participate in spite of lower natural endowment. When children who are not capable of doing first-quality work are given the highest grade, they and their parents are given the erroneous impression that they have superior musical potential. For children in primary classes, a brief written report or a conversation with a parent is better than a number or letter grade in music.

In the last analysis, you must evaluate the program in terms of what music is doing and can continue to do for the individual. If music is to continue to have beneficial effects throughout life, the individual must grow continuously in response to it, and in the ability to participate in it in progressively more mature ways.

Organizing a Unit of Study

A unit plan requires objectives and materials appropriate to instruction, as well as materials for evaluation. You should state at least one instructional objective; it should be supported by behavioral objectives as demonstrated throughout this book. The focus of the instruction may be toward developing a particular musical concept, developing or refining a skill, or both. Authors of the basic series music books define the learnings to be developed from the material in those books. As an example, each composition in NEW DIMENSIONS IN MUSIC is accompanied by a list of "Learnings and Skills" that can be used as behavioral objectives in planning and in evaluating learning.

Instructional material should be of two types: (1) Plan to use some musical material that is familiar to the children, but use it in a new way. (2) Select at least one new musical composition that clearly exemplifies the concept to be developed, or that permits exercise of the skill on which the unit focuses.

By using different musical material in evaluation you permit children to apply the new knowledge or skill in a new musical setting. (If you attempt to evaluate in the same context in which the concept was learned, you may be evaluating memory alone rather than understanding.) As with instructional material, a familiar composition can be used in a new context or new material can be selected.

You should develop at least one instructional unit for the teaching level of your choice. If you are working with children in a classroom setting you can design the plans specifically for them. Be realistic in your planning: (1) collect all material needed and construct any visual aids you plan to use; (2) the procedures you describe for the teacher should accommodate your musical skills and reflect what you are realistically able to do. You may adapt any of the musical materials used in this book, or seek appropriate songs and recordings elsewhere. Following is a sample unit plan consisting of three instructional and one evaluative lesson. Adapt the format provided here to the unit you prepare.

SAMPLE INSTRUCTIONAL UNIT (LEVEL I)

Topic: Direction in Melodic Movement

INSTRUCTIONAL OBJECTIVES
exemplified by
Behavioral Objectives

1. The child will correctly identify the upward or downward direction of melodic patterns in evaluative material by:

☐ choosing the diagram that represents the melodic movement heard

☐ demonstrating the melodic direction by using hand levels

☐ saying that the melody moves from low to high or upward as opposed to downward

☐ playing the pattern on adjustable tone bars

MATERIALS

1. Instructional material

Familiar songs
"Who's That?" (Example 2.1)
Upward leap: D A *(1-5)*
"Sing It High, Sing It Low" (Example 9.1)
Upward pattern: C E G *(1-3-5)*

New Song
"Bye'm Bye" (Example 5.6)
Downward leap: D A *(8–5)*

2. Evaluative material (new applications of learning)

Familiar song
"Roll Over" (Example 5.14)
Downward pattern: C A F *(5–3–1)*

New song
"Love Somebody" (Example 7.9)
Upward pattern: F A C *(1–3–5)*

EXAMPLE 9.1

SING IT HIGH, SING IT LOW

Words & music by Karen Wolff

Slow and easy

Used by permission of Karen Wolff.

For this unit, three "familiar" songs were chosen, two for instruction and one for evaluation. You are to assume that the first graders involved in this unit became acquainted with these songs in another context.

"Who's That?" was used in Chapter 2 (Example 2.1) as a song that suggested two different sound effects; assume that the children learned the song in conjunction with such activities. In this unit the rising repeated pattern (D A) is the focus of attention. Assume that "Sing It High, Sing It Low" (Example 9.1) was used for early experience in singing tone calls. In this unit, the upward-moving repeated tonal pattern (C E G) is identified. "Roll Over" (Example 5.14), in duple meter, previously may have been used for rhythmic clapping or as a counting song. In this unit the descending repeated melodic pattern (C A F) will be used to evaluate the children's grasp of upward versus downward melodic patterns. As you see, some of these songs were used earlier in this book for musical learning at Level II; the educational context in which the song is used, rather than the music itself, helps determine the educational level where it will be useful.

Hand levels and adjustable bells are concrete tools for children to use to reinforce the concept of up and down in melodic direction and can reveal their grasp of these concepts when you wish to evaluate them. Words also are used to label upward and downward melodic movement. All these processes, including the use of diagrams, have a place in the instructional lessons of this unit.

Since "Roll Over" and the new song, "Love Somebody" (Example 7.9), are to be used for evaluation, you must avoid using any of the above techniques when you introduce these songs. The children should be familiar with both songs before evaluation, but only during evaluation should you ask, "How does the melody move in this song?"

This unit is planned for use in early February to provide a Valentine's Day context for learning "Love Somebody." Since three songs in the unit are familiar to the children, the unit can be completed in three instructional lessons and one evaluative lesson. It is not essential that the entire unit be presented on consecutive days; but it would be preferable to have the final instructional lesson on the day before the evaluation. The evaluative material is shown next, so that you can relate the instructional units to the evaluative goal.

Evaluative Materials and Procedures

Since all children in the class can respond simultaneously to a paper and pencil test, the form shown below will be used with this unit. Before you proceed to the test items, you should demonstrate the correct response to the practice example by singing and showing hand levels, as necessary.

The children will sing each evaluative song once, together with the teacher; they will then be instructed to draw a circle around the diagram that shows how the melody for those words moves. The teacher then should sing or play the correct pattern twice while the children mark their papers. Do not gesture or give other visual cues that would support the correct answer.

1. Practice Example

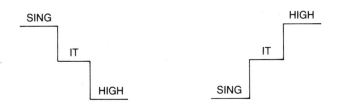

2. Test Item 1

3. Test Item 2

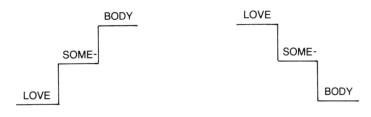

My name is _____ .

THE LESSON PLANS
LESSON ONE

Materials: *Autoharp or guitar*
Songs—"Who's That?" "Bye'm Bye,"
"Sing It High, Sing It Low"
Adjustable bells, vertically mounted

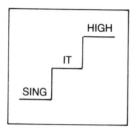 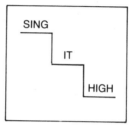

Diagrams on tagboard

PROCEDURES:

TEACHER	CHILDREN
1. Review familiar song with familiar activity. Play accompaniment and sing "Who's That?" (*D–1*).	1. All sing "Who's That?" At appropriate points in song, three children *tap* using chopsticks; three children *knock* using tone-blocks.
Suggest that children sing the second verse; ask one child to play the pattern (D A) on bells to sound like a door chime. Others should sing and show with hand levels how the melody moves on that pattern.	One child plays D A when "Who's That?" occurs in the song. Others sing and use their hands to show how the pattern moves up from D to A.
Ask children which way the melody moves; sing and enact with hand levels as one child plays the pattern (correct and incorrect).	Children respond that the first goes up, and that's the way it is in the song.

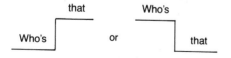

| 2. Introduce new song: "Bye'm Bye" (*D–8*). Ask children to be ready to tell something about the | 2. Children watch and listen. |

song. Sing entire song and play bells simultaneously on repeated pattern :

D   A
"Bye'm Bye."

"What is the song about?

How many "stars" did you count?

"How does this pattern move? Show me with your hands." Play D A and sing "Bye'm Bye."

Ask children to sing pattern and show the melodic direction with hands; play bells as children sing.

Sing entire song as one child plays D A pattern on bells each time it occurs.

3. Play accompaniment and invite children to rock rhythmically and sing familiar song "Sing It High, Sing It Low" (C–1).

Show two diagrams

Respond to questions.

Move hands from high to low. Respond that the pattern goes down.

Children respond.

One child plays pattern. Others sing pattern and enact high-to-low movement.

3. Children sing and respond.

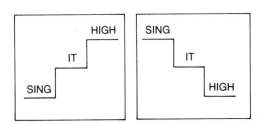

Ask children to sing song again and decide which diagram shows the way the melody moves when "Sing It High" is sung.

Select one child to hold up the correct diagram and another to play C E G on the bells each time that part of the song is sung;

Play accompaniment for song.

4. Summarize: "Today we learned about different kinds of melodic patterns. How were they different?"

Children sing.
Point to diagram that moves upward and say, "It goes up."

Sing entire song, enacting melodic movement for pattern with hand levels as child holds up diagram at appropriate points and another plays the bells on one pattern.

Children interpret:
Some patterns go up, other patterns go down.

LESSON TWO

Materials: Autoharp or guitar
Songs—"Love Somebody," "Sing It High, Sing It Low,"
    "Bye'm Bye"
Adjustable bells, vertically mounted
Diagrams for "Sing It High" used previously
Red paper hearts with child's name on reverse of each
Five cards, numbered 1 to 5

PROCEDURES:

TEACHER	CHILDREN
1. Tell the children Valentine's Day is coming and there are a song and game for that day.	1. Children hang red hearts on pegboard with name against the board.
Sing "Love Somebody" accompanied by guitar or autoharp.	
Choose a child to start the game; repeat song.	One child chooses a heart from the board and gives it to child whose name is on reverse.
Repeat song several times.	Each time song is sung, one heart is taken from pegboard.
Announce that the game will be continued two more days, until only one heart remains. The child whose name is on it will receive some kind of award.	
2. Accompany and sing "Sing It High, Sing It Low" with two visible diagrams of the melodic pattern.	2. Sing and enact melodic movement for opening pattern.
Present "step" bells or other vertically mounted bells and ask for a volunteer to play the pattern for "Sing It High."	One child picks pattern that represents the melody.
Select child to play pattern whenever it occurs in the song. Sing entire song as child plays pattern whenever it occurs.	One or more volunteers play pattern individually.
3. Play "Bye'm Bye" pattern on bells and ask children to show and be able to tell how the melody moves.	3. Respond to show downward movement.
Replay pattern twice and have children sing and show hand levels.	Children sing pattern and enact melodic movement.
Ask five children to sit in front of the class holding cards numbered 1 through 5.	

Accompany and sing repeated middle section of song.

Selected children stand when their number is sung.

Repeat while rest of class sings along on that part of song.

All sing the song.

The five children sit and then stand as their number is sung.

Sing entire song with children involved in singing and activities.

All sing; one child plays bells on opening melodic pattern; five children hold number cards and stand on cue.

4. Summarize: "This melodic pattern moves downward." Play pattern.

4. Sing pattern and enact with hand levels.

LESSON THREE

Materials: *Autoharp or guitar*
Songs—"Love Somebody," "Roll Over," "Bye'm Bye"
Red paper hearts on pegboard
Adjustable bells, vertically mounted
Diagrams of melodic pattern

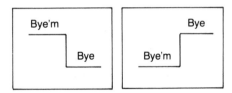

PROCEDURES:

TEACHER

CHILDREN

1. Accompany and sing as game is played for "Love Somebody" (avoid any physical or visual indication of melodic direction in this song).

1. Individuals choose hearts from pegboard as in last lesson.

Children begin to sing the song along with the teacher.

2. Accompany and sing familiar song, "Roll Over" (avoid any physical or visual indication of melodic direction).

2. Children sing and engage in appropriate rhythmic activity.

3. Play opening pattern of "Bye'm Bye" on bells and ask what song you are playing; ask how they know what the song is to be?

3. Children identify pattern as opening of "Bye'm Bye." Respond that they know "by the way the melody moves—downward."

Show the two diagrams and ask for volunteers to (1) pick the correct diagram, and (2) play the pattern on the bells.

Individuals are chosen and respond.

Sing and accompany song. Repeat as time allows with other children chosen to play the bell pattern.

Individual plays opening pattern while others sing entire song and enact melodic direction of pattern with hand levels.

4. Summarize: Ask, "How does this melodic pattern move?"

4. Reply that "it goes down, from high to low."

After these three lessons you might record your evaluation of each child's grasp of the concept of upward–downward melodic movement, basing your observation on the musical behavior seen in class. Later you can compare your evaluation with the results of the paper-and-pencil test to be given.

EVALUATION LESSON

Materials: *Autoharp or guitar*
Songs—"Sing It High, Sing It Low," "Roll Over," "Love Somebody"
Evaluation sheets (see p. 329)
Remaining hearts for Valentine game
Prize for winner of Valentine game

PROCEDURES:

TEACHER

CHILDREN

1. Accompany "Sing It High, Sing It Low."

1. Sing and sway to rhythm of "Sing It High, Sing It Low."

Distribute evaluation forms and see that each child has a pencil.

Write name on bottom of evaluation form.

2. Follow procedures for evaluation (see page 329).

2. Respond to evaluative procedures.

3. Complete the game for "Love Somebody"; accompany the song as children sing. Award prize to winner.

3. Sing "Love Somebody" and find game's winner, whose name stayed on pegboard the longest.

Ask the children to sing the song once more while they think of the person they love the most. Suggest that they make a valentine to give to that person.

Children sing together accompanied by Autoharp or guitar.

As a result of the evaluation, you now know which children need additional experiences to help them grasp the concept of upward–downward melodic movement. Many songs you will use for other instructional purposes will also provide continued opportunities to develop this concept. In addition, children can be directed to listen for upward- and downward-moving melodies in recorded music.

No teacher uses exactly the same procedures in any two lessons, although some patterns of teaching develop over time. Certain basic principles are worth noting, however, and an attempt has been made to incorporate such principles into the lessons described above.

1. Begin each lesson in a manner that will gain the attention of the children.

2. End by pointing up the most important concept dealt with in the lesson.

3. Devise many ways in which individual children can be singled out for participation and recognition.

4. In choosing individuals to perform or respond, be sure all get an opportunity on an equal basis; but give harder tasks, at first, to those most likely to succeed and provide a model for those who are less apt. You thus individualize instruction because you give slower pupils more opportunity to develop the ability or understanding needed for success. Represent the concept in a variety of ways: enactive, iconic, symbolic (see Chapter 1, pages 7–8), but always relate the movement, diagram, or verbalization to the musical sound.

5. Use at least three different encounters to develop a musical concept or skill —introduce the idea in the first lesson, explore in further depth at the second lesson, and summarize in a third lesson.

6. Develop the concept in two or three different musical contexts, showing both what it is and what it is not.

7. Vary the musical material used in a single lesson. Do not "exhaust" the song (or the children) by repeating it more than three or four times in one lesson. By using a composition in a later lesson you give children a chance (1) to reflect on the music and connect it with previous experience, and (2) to experience it within the psychological "set" of another day.

8. Arrange procedures so the children will hear the whole song when it is first introduced; later it can be used in smaller sections or phrases. End by using the whole song again.

9. Sometimes direct children's attention by asking them to listen for something specific (a structured approach); at other times ask them what they noticed (an unstructured approach).

10. Even though a unit of study is directed toward acquiring a musical concept, do not neglect the aesthetic impact of the music. At some time during its use, the children should feel the expressive quality of each song in this unit.

Levels and Strategies in Questioning

One technique for guiding and structuring learning is effective use of questioning. The type of question asked should be determined by the progress of instruction. At the beginning of inquiry into a subject, data-gathering questions (DGQ) are appropriate. Such questions often are open-ended, eliciting a variety of possible answers that encourage many of the children to think and respond. On the other hand, a series of narrower data-gathering questions cause the children to recall facts and circumstances or observe specifics about the present object (instrument, diagram, or other item) or experience (music heard, presently performed, otherwise encountered).

When enough information has been collected and as many children as possible have been involved in the effort, data-processing questions (DPQ) may be asked. Such questions encourage the children to work with the information, to analyze, compare, and discuss relationships in the present experience or object.

Finally, questions should be asked that cause the children to apply the concept or principle to a new situation. In a unit plan that develops a particular concept, the second or third examples presented would provide an opportunity to use this kind of question. Such data-applying questions (DAQ) are of a more advanced type, and they are used in limited ways with children who have not achieved the intellectual stage of "formal operations" (refer to Chapter 1).

Skillful use of these three kinds of questions will allow you to interact with children at different levels of intellectual development. Less mature children should be encouraged to contribute in response to data-gathering questions that accommodate many possible answers. Individualize the instruction to challenge the gifted child when you ask questions that apply data.

From Class Instruction to Individualized Instruction

What children experience and learn about music has been the focus of attention throughout this book. Of the procedures suggested, some accommodate interaction of a larger group of children, and others apply to individualized instruction. In one sense, the most efficient instruction is that allowing one teacher to orient a large group to a procedure or an idea. On the other hand, instructional materials may ultimately be more efficient when they meet the needs of individuals who work at their own level and pace. The teaching–learning situation reaps the greatest benefits when a combination of approaches is used: large-group, small-group, and individualized study.

Large-group instruction can provide a framework at the beginning (orientation) and end (sharing) of a unit of study. In between, a development period can allow small groups to interact creatively and report, or can permit individuals to develop skills and concepts as well as work creatively. The foregoing lesson plans offer examples of some basic principles of group instruction. In developing individualized units of music study, you can draw on a variety of sources.[16]

In instructional units for children's independent work, ideas and procedures must be laid out carefully and sequentially. Current basic series music books address the student directly and provide a significant amount of material for individualized study. "The Five Sense Store" is an Aesthetic Education Program developed by CEMREL.[17] Filmstrips, records, and tapes are also available to allow individuals to study a number of music topics.

In reviewing the materials and procedures discussed in this book, you will find the following readily adapted to individualized study and small-group participation:

INDIVIDUALIZED STUDY	INTERACTION IN A SMALL GROUP

Chapter 2
  Sound Exploration
  Exploring Sound Through Electronic
    Alteration
	Chapter 2
	  Group Use of Instruments
	  Making a "Sound-Story"
	  What Can You Do With Sound?
	  Using Sound in Drama

Chapter 3
  Learning to Conduct Songs
	Chapter 3
	  Characterization and Drama in Music

Chapter 4
  Construction of a Rhythm Instrument
  Percussion Accompaniments with
    Recorded Compositions
	Chapter 4
	  Playing the Accent and Knowing Meter
	  Developing an Orchestration
	  Relating Beat, Accent and Meter

Chapter 5
  Playing Melodies
  First Steps in Melody Writing
  Playing Small Wind Instruments	

Chapter 6
  Playing the Autoharp
  Playing the Guitar
	Chapter 6
	  Musical Composition for Ensembles
	  Singing Descants and Partner Songs

Chapter 8
  Relating Art and Music
  Many Listening Experiences	

Chapter 9
  Research on Music Related to Science
    and Social Studies.	

Children who have exceptional musical ability, and who take private music lessons, need opportunities to work independently with classroom musical materials. Individualized projects related to group study will allow them to proceed at their own pace and get into musical activities that may not be included in their private music lessons. In addition, they may serve as leaders in small-group assignments or help other children on individual projects. Instruction that provides diversity in group size, interest, and activity will more likely meet the needs of more children in your class than instruction that is predominantly teacher-centered.

Talent from Varied Sources

The discussion in this book has been based on the premise that the classroom teacher is an important motivator of music in children's education. A classroom teacher who knows what kind of music program can be developed can go a long way toward achieving it in spite of personal musical limitations, because specific music skills can usually be found in others: a music consultant or special music teacher, the classroom teacher next door, a parent, or an upper grade student.

A special music teacher usually is employed to work in several classrooms on a regular schedule as a member of the teaching team for each group of children. Part of the responsibility of this specialist is to initiate musical activities that the children and the classroom teacher can carry on. Under such an arrangement the music program must be tailored to the needs of each class, and the two teachers must discover how their individual teaching talents can complement one another.

The music consultant is an assistant, a resource person, and an advisor to teachers. The consultant should have no more than seventy-five teachers to assist. He or she should come to each school once or twice a week, go into the rooms of teachers who need aid and (1) assist in planning the music program for the class, (2) suggest and provide new, varied materials to meet specific needs in that classroom, and (3) do some teaching to supplement the experiences that the classroom teacher is able to provide. In pursuit of these objectives, the music consultant's greatest assets will be a warmth of personality and the ability to help the teacher and children feel confident in their own musical activities.

A music consultant who is available but does not visit often enough to do more than assist in the planning might be able to help a teacher find music skills in others:

In one school district the music consultant had two needs in mind when she arranged to have talented fifth and sixth grade pianists aid the primary teachers in music. The teachers knew that they needed more help than the consultant could give personally, and the consultant felt that the older students needed an outlet for their musical talent and training. These students could both sing and play the piano. Although it was necessary to plan the work so that it did not interfere with their regular studies, the whole project was a challenge to the older students and very helpful to the primary teachers.

Occasionally a parent who has special skill can be invited to come into the classroom on a more or less regular basis to provide instrumental accompaniments, sing, or help notate original songs. In utilizing the musical abilities of others, the classroom teacher remains responsible for the program, but plans together with the musician to use this special skill in the most advantageous ways.

A New Teacher Beginning the Year

School administrators generally are pleased to employ a classroom teacher who is prepared to teach music, along with other required subjects, and some beginning teachers can do this. Others may have a good understanding of the music education curriculum but, lacking certain musical skills, they should ask whether a music specialist is available.

As you become acquainted with the school to which you are assigned, find out what music books are in use, what classroom instruments are available, whether you will have access to a good record player, and what records are available. As you establish yourself in the classroom, arrange different centers of activity and interest. Among these, there should be a music center where you place a few well-chosen items: an easy-to-play instrument or two, a colorful song book, pictures or posters giving promise of musical activities to come.

On your visits to the district or county school libraries you should look for books that will help develop musical interest and knowledge. Enrichment reading books, many cited in this text, can be among those you make available to your pupils. Supplementary song books can be evaluated and reserved for use at a specific time during the school year.

You should have a record player and some records for use the first day of school. It may be a short day, but certainly there will be a few minutes when music can be used. The children may enjoy singing with the Autoharp or a guitar that a student can play, and you can begin to find out who are the musical leaders and what songs they know. If kindergarten or first grade children become tired, an action song or finger play will wake them up, or a lullaby will relax them.

During the first week, plan a series of lessons that will reveal the musical abilities of your pupils and, thinking in terms of the music consultant's first visit, jot down musical problems and needs. Too often teachers do not make it easy for the consultant to help them. Either they cover up their problems when the consultant is present, or they fail to give any prior thought to the assistance this person can give. If the consultant is scheduled to arrive on a particular day, make an effort to find out when you can have a conference and what kind of service the consultant is in the habit of giving. If you want a sample lesson in a particular musical activity, let the consultant know a day ahead, so that he or she can come prepared.

The music consultant may be able to help in getting books, records, and instruments, or in setting up a systematic plan for acquiring them later. With these material aids, a judicious use of available music talent, and a keen sense of the value of music, classroom teachers can do much to make music a significant part of education in the elementary school.

As stated in Chapter 1, the special music teacher, the classroom teacher, and the principal must work as a team to make music an integral part of elementary education. Mutual respect and good will are necessary on the part of each. One of the most important things you can do in the opening days of the school year is to establish a positive relationship with other members of the team. Thereafter, the happiness and satisfaction a good program in music brings to the children should assure continued support and cooperation.

CHAPTER NOTES

1. Daniel A. Prescott, **Emotion and the Educative Process** (Washington, D.C.: American Council on Education, 1938), p. 225. Reprinted by permission.

2. Larry Kettelkamp, **The Magic of Sound** (New York: William Morrow and Company, 1956); **Singing Strings** (1958); **Drums, Rattles, and Bells** (1960); **Flutes, Whistles, and Reeds** (1962).

   Melvin Berger and Frank Clark, **Science and Music: From Tom-Tom to Hi-Fi** (New York: McGraw-Hill Book Co., Inc., 1961).

   Tillie S. Pine and Joseph Levine, **Sounds All Around** (New York: McGraw-Hill Book Co., Inc., 1959).

   Ira Freeman, **All About Sound and Ultrasonics** (New York: Random House, 1961).

3. Louis W. Ballard, "Put American Indian Music in the Classroom," **Music Educators Journal** (March 1970), p. 38; and "American Indian Music for the Classroom," songs, recordings, and teacher's guide, distributed by Canyon Records.

4. UNESCO, United Nations Educational Scientific and Cultural Organization, Place de Fontenoy, Paris 73, France, or 2201 United Nations Building, New York, N.Y. 10017.

5. Ruth Tooze and Beatrice Krone, **Literature and Music as Resources for Social Studies** (Englewood Cliffs, N.J.: Prentice-Hall, Inc., 1955).

6. John Henry Lyons, **Stories of Our American Patriotic Songs** (New York: The Vanguard Press, 1942).

7. "Music in World Cultures," a special issue of the **Music Educators Journal** (October 1972), featuring many articles and listing books, records and films on the topic.

8. "Music in Special Education," **Music Educators Journal,** special issue (April 1972); Richard M. Graham, **Music for the Exceptional Child** (Reston, Va.: Music Educators National Conference, 1975); Richard M. Graham and Alice S. Beer, **Teaching Music to the Exceptional Child: A Handbook for Mainstreaming** (Englewood Cliffs, N.J.: Prentice-Hall, Inc., 1980).

9. Dale Bryant, "Learning Disabilities," **The Instructor,** April 1972, p. 51, quoting The National Advisory Committee on Handicapped Children, January 1968.

10. Carol Epley, "In a Soundless World of Musical Enjoyment," **Music Educators Journal** (April 1972), p. 55.

11. Doris G. Herlein, "Music Reading for the Sightless—Braille Notation," **Music Educators Journal** (September 1975), p. 42.

12. Ruth Anne Dykman, "In Step with 92–142, Two by Two," **Music Educators Journal** (January 1979), p. 58.

13. Mary Val Marsh, **Explore and Discover Music** (New York: The Macmillan Company, 1970).

14. Margery M. Vaughan, "Music for Gifted Children—A Bridge to Consciousness," **Music Educators Journal** (April 1972), p. 70; and "Music for Gifted Children," in Richard M. Graham, **Music for the Exceptional Child,** (Reston, Va.: Music Educators National Conference, 1975).

15. Juliette Alvin, **Music for the Handicapped Child** (London: Oxford University Press, 1965), p. 3.

16. **Music Educators Journal** special issues: "Individualization in Music Education" (November 1972) and "Music in Open Education" (April 1974); Joseph W. Landon, **How to Write Learning Activity Packages for Music Education** (Costa Mesa, Calif.: Educational Media Press, 1973); Eunice Boardman Meske and Carroll Rinehart, **Individualized Instruction in Music** (Reston, Va.: Music Educators National Conference, 1975).

17. CEMREL, Inc., **The Five Sense Store, The Aesthetic Education Program** (New York: The Viking Press).

Appendix A
A Catalog of Musical Concepts

Examples of musical concepts that children might acquire from musical experiences up through the sixth grade have been grouped under the following headings. This listing of concepts is representative, but not all-inclusive, of what children might learn about music.

1. Tone color in voices and instruments
2. Rhythm and tempo
3. Melody
4. Texture and harmony
5. Dynamics
6. Form in music
7. Style in music

As far as possible, the concepts are stated as generalizations of what is heard (the aural). Marginal notations show the level at which an idea might first be encountered. All the concepts listed may be introduced at the level indicated, but they must be reconsidered in the grades above, for children develop deeper musical understanding and better skills as they mature. Learning is cyclical, and what may be encountered in a musical setting appropriate for Level I must be dealt with again by older children for broader as well as more precise application in different musical contexts.

Musical experience is the vehicle for this learning. The musical activities described in Chapters 2 through 8 include many that will facilitate development of concepts recommended as appropriate for each of the three levels of development.

I. TONE COLOR IN VOICES AND INSTRUMENTS

A. Tone: General

1. Sounds can be produced by hitting, scraping, or blowing different objects.   Level I
2. The same object can produce more than one sound if struck or scraped in different ways.
3. Instruments are objects that people have made to produce particular kinds of sounds.
4. Instruments are made of different kinds of material (wood, metal, etc.).
5. People use their voices in many different ways; the singing voice sounds different than the speaking voice.
6. Sound is heard when vibrations in the air contact a person's eardrum. These air   Level II
vibrations are created by the vibration of the instrument.
7. Instruments vibrate in different ways:
   a. Sometimes the body of an instrument produces the vibrations, as in a tone-block, gong, rattle, or bells.
   b. Sometimes the skin head attached to the instrument vibrates, as in a drum.
   c. Sometimes a string stretched between two points on an instrument vibrates, as in a guitar, Autoharp, or violin.
   d. Sometimes a column of air vibrates as a result of blowing, as in a flute or whistle.
   e. Sometimes air is blown through a reed, which vibrates and produces a tone, as in an oboe.
   f. Everyone has vocal cords that vibrate when air from the lungs passes between them.
   g. Sometimes electronic means is used for tone production, as in a chord organ.

B. Tone: Loudness (Intensity)

1. Some instruments produce loud sounds and some produce soft sounds.   Level I
2. The singing voice can be made to sound loud or soft, or any degree of loudness in between.
3. Some instruments can be made to sound loud or soft, depending upon how hard they are struck or shaken.
4. Loudness depends upon the size (amplitude) of the vibrations.   Level II
5. Two instruments played together will sound louder than one played by itself.

C. Tone: Duration

1. The tone of an instrument lasts as long as the instrument continues to vibrate.   Level I
2. A singing tone can last as long as the singer has breath to make the sound.

3. The tone of some instruments dies away quickly, and the tone of others lasts much longer.

4. Some instruments have to be struck, shaken, or scraped repeatedly to make the sound last.

5. Most instruments can make both long and short tones, depending upon how they are played.

D. Tone: Pitch

1. A tone can be high or low in pitch.   Level I

2. Some instruments produce tones of higher pitch than others.

3. Some instruments produce more than one pitch.

4. Some voices sound higher in pitch than others; the voice of a child or a woman is higher than the voice of a man.

5. Voices can sing tones on many different pitches.

6. Some instruments produce tones with definite pitch and others produce tones of   Level II
indefinite pitch.

7. Low tones are produced when the sound-maker vibrates slowly; high tones are produced when the vibrations are fast.

E. Tone: Timbre (color)

1. The tone color of one instrument is different from that of another.   Level I

2. You can identify an instrument by its tone color.

3. You can identify a person by the tone color of his or her voice.

4. Some instruments produce a ringing sound.

5. Some instruments produce a dry, clicking sound.

6. Some instruments produce a resonant thud or boom.

7. The way an instrument is played or the kind of mallet used to strike it can affect   Level II
the tone color.

8. The vowel a person uses to sing a tone influences the color of the tone.

F. Vocal Tone

1. A voice can be made to sound soft and gentle, or loud and brilliant, or exciting,   Level I
depending upon the feeling that is to be conveyed in the song. (This list of adjectives identifying vocal expression should be expanded in successive grades.)

2. Voices of different people have different qualities of sound; some voices have a smooth, velvety sound, others may sound rough or nasal, or dark and veiled. (Other adjectives can be used to describe vocal tone quality as children hear a greater variety of voices in successive grades.)

3. When people sing together under the direction of a leader, they may be singing   Level II
in a chorus or a choir. Groups that sing sacred music are called choirs. (Later, as children hear different singing groups, they can learn what voice parts make up

a children's choir and an adult chorus or choir. An a cappella choir is unaccompanied.)

4. Girls, some women, and boys with unchanged voices are classifed as sopranos. Such voices are high, light, and bright in quality.

5. Women with lower, darker, or heavier singing voices are classified as altos. Some children who sing lower tones better than upper tones take the lower (alto) part in two-part music.

6. The highest and brightest man's voice is the tenor; a man's voice that sounds four or five tones lower and is deeper and more somber in quality is called a bass.

7. When people sing together in small groups, with each voice on a different part, they may sing in a duet, a trio, a quartet, a quintet, or a sextet. (Pupils may become acquainted with "barbershop" quartets and famous ensembles from opera or oratorio.)

8. Among highly trained singers, voices are classified according to musical expression and the dramatic roles played. The voice of the coloratura soprano is brilliant and agile with a very high range; the lyric soprano voice is sweeter and lighter in quality. The dramatic soprano has a heavier voice.

9. The quality of voices among men singers is likewise varied. There are lyric, heroic, and robust tenor voices; each voice reflects to some extent the qualities associated with the name. The baritone is the full, middle-range male voice, and the basso profundo is the deep, powerful male voice often playing the solemn role of a king or priest in opera.

10. Singers from different cultures may have different ways of singing; the tone as well as the way the voice moves from one pitch to the next may be unique.

Level III

G. The Strings

1. On some instruments a musical tone is made when a tightly stretched string is plucked with the finger, set in vibration by a bow drawn across it, or struck by a small felt hammer. (In successive grades, children can become further acquainted with the plucked or strummed instruments, such as guitar, ukulele, banjo, Autoharp, psaltery, zither, and harp; they should learn to differentiate between the tones of the bowed stringed instruments and the keyboard instruments.)

2. Strings that are long and thick produce heavy, low tones of long duration; strings that are short and very thin produce high, bright tones of shorter duration. (In successive grades, the concept of pitch is related to high- and low-sounding strings on different instruments; children learn how strings are stopped by the fingers at higher or lower positions on plucked or bowed instruments to make higher or lower tones.)

3. All stringed instruments have a soundboard or a resonating body that vibrates when the string is sounded, reinforcing the tone so it is loud enough to be heard. (Children touch different instruments to feel the vibrations created; later they learn how the player controls the volume of the tone by various playing techniques.)

4. On many stringed instruments the duration of the tone depends upon the length of time the string continues to vibrate after it has been struck or plucked; the

Level I

Level II

violin and other bowed instruments can produce a singing tone because the player can use the bow to draw a smooth, continuous tone. (In successive grades, children can hear how the bow is used on instruments of the violin family to create very short, dry tones called staccato; long, connected tones called legato; or light, lifted tones called spiccato.)

5. The piano has the widest range of tones from low to high; it has a different string (usually double or triple) for each pitch. The strings of the harp are similar to the strings of the piano, but the harp is played by plucking the strings with the fingers rather than by striking them with a hammer, as on the piano. (Later, children can learn to recognize such musical effects as glissandos, arpeggios, and running scale passages on both instruments, and the use of the piano pedals.)

6. Among the bowed stringed instruments, the violin is the highest in pitch and tonally the most versatile; its tones can be soft and lyric, soulful, or dramatic and exciting. The viola, which is a little larger, has a darker, more sonorous tone. The cello, not so agile or brilliant in tone as the violin, can sound dramatic, robust, or tender and soulful. The double bass has the lowest and most powerful tones of this group of instruments.

7. The harpsichord looks like a grand piano, but its tone is produced by a mechanical plucking of the strings with leather plectrums. The tone, although limited in dynamic range, is crisp and sparkling; the harpsichord is considered the ideal keyboard instrument for much music by Bach, Handel, and other composers of the baroque period.

Level III

8. The bowed strings make up half of the symphony orchestra, providing the basic tone quality for that group.

9. The string quartet is an ideal small group because the tones of the instruments blend to form a well-balanced musical ensemble. The quartet consists of first violin, second violin, viola, and cello. Their parts are comparable to soprano, alto, tenor, and bass in vocal groups.

H. The Woodwinds

1. On some instruments a musical tone is made when a person blows across a hole in a short pipe, as across a bottle. The flute and its half-sized relative, the piccolo, are played this way. The higher tones of the flute can be very bright and penetrating; the lower tones may sound hollow and dark. (In successive grades, children can learn more about playing the flute and about its tone quality; they can compare it with the recorder, an end-blown flute with a soft, more intimate tone quality.)

Level I

2. In all woodwinds, the player raises or lowers the tone by opening or closing holes down the length of the instrument. Since the mechanism that closes the holes lies conveniently under the fingers, the musician can play very rapidly, leaping from low to high tones easily. (Later, children can learn the different musical effects of legato and staccato played on these instruments.)

3. Some wind instruments have a single-reed mouthpiece at the end of the instrument. The clarinet is the most important of this group; its tone is rich and full, but quite bright on the high notes. (Later, children can learn to know the different qualities of the clarinet in its three registers; they can become acquainted with the rich, low tones of the bass clarinet and the mellow but sometimes reedy tone of the saxophone.)

Level II

4. Other wind instruments have a double-reed (flattened "soda-straw"-type) mouthpiece. Of this group the oboe is well known. It is about the size of a clarinet, but it has a relatively unchanging tone that is somewhat nasal and sometimes pastoral or oriental in quality. (In successive grades children can become acquainted with the plaintive, reedy tone of the English horn.)

5. The bassoon is a larger double-reed instrument; it has a wide dynamic range and such tonal versatility, from grandiose to plaintive or humorous, that it is sometimes called the clown of the orchestra. (In successive grades, children can become acquainted with the heavy, somber tones of the contrabassoon.)

6. The woodwind instruments are important "color" instruments in the symphony orchestra because their tones contrast well with the string tone. They can also carry the melody line or provide modest fill-in parts for the whole ensemble. Concert or marching bands, which seldom use strings, depend upon the many woodwind instruments to set the basic tone quality.

Level III

I. The Brasses

1. The most brilliant, commanding tone of any instrument comes from the trumpet. This instrument is related to the bugle, which, being limited to only five tones, is used for signaling, e.g., reveille and taps. Because it has three valves, the trumpet can sound any tone and carry a melody beautifully. (At a later time, children learn that the cornet is similar to the trumpet, but slightly shorter and less brilliant.)

Level I

2. One of the largest instruments of the orchestra is the tuba. It is an armful of wound brass tubing with a flaring bell. Because its tone is so heavy and slow-moving, the tuba is used primarily to support the bass rather than to carry melody. (Later, children can learn that the sousaphone is a tuba wound so it can be carried on the player's shoulders in a marching band.)

3. A characteristic common to brass instruments is the cup-shaped mouthpiece. The lips of the player produce the tonal vibrations; the tubing and bell amplify the tones; the size and shape of both mouthpiece and instrument determine tone quality.

Level II

4. The trombone is the baritone-bass of the brass family. It has a sliding cylindrical tube that is used to form different pitches. The tone quality of the trombone is rich and powerful, but more solemn and dignified than the trumpet; it can sound brilliant when played loudly. (The baritone horn sounds in the same range as the trombone and is a standard instrument in bands.)

5. The French horn is descended from the natural hunting horn; it is circularly wound, has a large flaring bell and, with its three circular valves, can sound all tones of the scale. Its tone, lower than that of the trumpet, is noble and full, sometimes majestic and brassy. It can be muted for an effect of distance or solitude.

Level III

6. The trumpet, the tuba, the trombone, and the French horn add body and brilliance to the orchestral sound. These and other brass instruments are used in greater numbers in the band, where they often provide massive effects.

J. The Percussion

1. Some drums emit a deep, resonant tone of long duration; other drums have a tone that is short and penetrating, with a dry quality. (In higher grades, children

Level I

can become acquainted with the tone quality of untuned drums such as tom-toms, bongo and congo drums, and the snare and bass drums of the symphony orchestra. They learn that the size of the drum, the type of material in the drumhead, and the method of beating all are factors contributing to the different tone qualities.)

2. Some single-toned percussion instruments produce short, dry sounds, and others produce ringing sounds of longer duration. (Later, children learn to recognize subtle differences in the tones of instruments such as the claves, castanets, woodblock, maracas, triangle, sleighbells, cymbals, and gong. They observe how different qualities of sound can be produced through different uses of the instruments.)

3. Some percussion instruments are tuned, and melodies can be played on them. Glockenspiels, bells, and resonator bars have a bright, bell-like tone. The tone of the xylophone is dry; it can be either brittle or muffled, depending upon the type of mallets used. (Later, children learn that pitch in these instruments is related to the length of the tone bar or size of the bell.) `Level II`

4. There are two kinds of drums in a symphony orchestra: tuned drums and those of indefinite pitch. Both the snare drum and the bass drum are of indefinite pitch. The kettledrums (timpani) are tuned drums with the shape of large copper kettles. A symphony orchestra usually has two or three, tuned to different pitches; the tone is deep, resonant, and important to majestic or triumphant expression by the orchestra.

5. Many single-toned percussion instruments, such as castanets, triangle, cymbals, and gong, are used in the symphony orchestra for special effects. The xylophone and glockenspiel are used occasionally.

6. Among the tuned instruments with bell-like tones is the celesta, which is essentially a glockenspiel attached to a keyboard (it looks like a small piano). Its tone is very delicate, with little carrying power. The orchestral chimes, tuned metal tubes, are struck with a wooden hammer to produce a tone of great resonance and duration. `Level III`

K. Tone: In Composition

1. When instruments having one general tone color are used, the effect created is different from that heard when several kinds of instruments are used. `Level III`

2. When all instruments used are high in pitch, the effect created is different from that of instruments sounding both high and low tones.

3. Contrast in duration of tone among the instruments can create musical interest.

4. A composer can shape the musical effect of a piece by using the loud and soft sounds of the instruments in different ways.

II. RHYTHM AND TEMPO

A. Pace and Character of Movement

1. Music can move fast or slowly. (Later, pace in music is called tempo.) `Level I`

2. Some fast music may be light; other fast music may be heavy and vigorous.

3. Slow music may be calm and quiet, or it may be ponderous and heavy.

4. Some music has a steady, even movement like running or walking, but other music may have a steady, uneven short–long movement, like galloping or jumping.

5. One piece of music can be played or sung at faster or slower speeds, arousing different feelings at each different speed.   Level II

6. Usually the rhythm of a piece of music moves at the same speed throughout, but sometimes it slows down gradually near the end or at some place in the middle. (Later this effect is identified as a ritard.)

7. Sometimes the rhythm of a part of a composition is speeded up gradually, often to make up for a previous slowing down. (Later this effect is called *accelerando*.)

8. Sometimes the melody is alternately accelerated and slowed, while the accompaniment keeps a steady pace. (Later this effect is called *rubato*.)   Level III

9. Different speeds and qualities of movement in music are designated by certain English and Italian terms:

grave—slow, solemn	*allegretto*—moderately fast
largo—very slow and broad	*animato*—animated
lento—slow	*allegro*—quick, lively
adagio—leisurely	*vivace*—brisk, fast
andante—moderate and flowing	*presto*—very fast
cantabile—in a singing manner	*leggiero*—light, graceful
dolce—sweetly	*maestoso*—majestic
grazioso—gracefully	*molto*—very much
moderato—moderate	*poco*—a little

10. A moderate tempo is about the speed of a heartbeat (72 pulses per minute). Sometimes the composer specifies the tempo as a certain number of beats per minute.

B. *Rhythmic Motif or Pattern*

1. Rhythm in music consists of groups of rhythm patterns; the tones in some rhythm patterns are regular and even, but in other patterns some tones are short and some are long.   Level I

2. A rhythm pattern may consist of tones that are long– and slow–moving; a piece with such rhythm patterns can be restful and quiet, reverent and solemn.   Level II

3. A rhythm pattern may consist of tones that are short– and fast–moving; a piece with such rhythm patterns can be brilliant and exciting, lively and dancing.

4. A rhythm pattern usually can be played by itself as a satisfactory repeated figure; sometimes the syllables and words in a song help determine the length of a rhythm pattern.   Level III

5. One tone in a rhythm pattern usually seems heavier than other tones; the heavier tone often is the second or third, but sometimes it is the first or last tone in the pattern.

6. A rhythm pattern that has regular and even tones is less exciting than one in which the tones are irregular in length and occurrence.

7. A rhythm pattern may repeat once or several times in one composition; it may alternate with other patterns.

8. Two short rhythm patterns may be grouped together to form a longer pattern; sometimes only part of the pattern is repeated.

9. Rhythm patterns within a phrase may be symmetrical, even in number, and balanced; sometimes an unbalanced, asymmetrical effect is desired, and rhythm patterns may be designed to help achieve this effect.

10. A rhythm pattern can be varied (developed) in a number of ways: it may be lengthened (extended), shortened (fragmented), played twice as fast, or played half as fast.

C. Beat, Meter, and Accent

1. The beat is regular and continuous throughout most pieces of music; in marches and dances this regular beat is felt strongly.   Level I

2. Lullabies and other gentle pieces have an underlying beat, but in these it is less obvious.

3. The beat must be set at a suitable speed (tempo) for each piece; it can vary considerably from one composition to another.   Level II

4. When beats are grouped in sets of two the music is said to be in duple meter. The steady beat for a march or a dancing song in duple meter is sounded "one-two, one-two." (Older pupils can discover that $\frac{2}{4}$, $\frac{2}{8}$, fast $\frac{2}{2}$, $\math0{C}\!\!\!|$, and fast $\frac{6}{8}$ represent duple meter.)

5. When beats are grouped in sets of three, the music is said to be in triple meter. A waltz or a minuet is sounded "one-two-three, one-two-three." (Older pupils can discover that $\frac{3}{4}$, $\frac{3}{8}$, fast $\frac{3}{2}$, and fast $\frac{9}{8}$ represent triple meter.)

6. In any meter the first beat is slightly stronger than the other beats in the set; it is called the accent. Measure bars mark off accents and metric units.

7. In quadruple meter the beats are grouped in sets of four with an accent on the first beat and a lesser accent on the third beat. (Older pupils can discover that quadruple meter is represented by $\frac{4}{4}$, C, $\frac{4}{8}$, fast $\frac{4}{2}$, and fast $\frac{12}{8}$.)

8. A slow duple meter that has a swing is counted in six beats: "one-two-three, four-five-six." In this meter there is an accent on the first beat and a lesser accent on the fourth beat. (Slow compound duple meter is shown by $\frac{6}{8}$ and $\frac{6}{4}$. Compound triple meter is shown by $\frac{9}{8}$.)   Level III

9. In some folk and contemporary music, meters containing sets of five or seven beats are encountered. In such meters as $\frac{5}{4}$ and $\frac{7}{4}$ the beat is steady, but the occurrence of the accent on an odd-numbered beat gives an asymmetric rhythmic effect.

10. In uneven meters the beats can be grouped around the primary and secondary accents in different ways:

$$\underset{\frac{5}{4}\;1}{\overset{>}{}}\;\;\underset{2}{}\;\;\underset{3}{\overset{>}{}}\;\;\underset{4}{}\;\;\underset{5}{}\;\;\text{or}\;\;\underset{1}{}\;\;\underset{2}{}\;\;\underset{3}{\overset{>}{}}\;\;\underset{4}{\overset{>}{}}\;\;\underset{5}{}$$

$$\overset{>}{\underset{4}{7}}\overset{}{1}\ 2\ 3\ \overset{>}{4}\ 5\ \overset{>}{6}\ 7\quad \text{or}\quad \overset{}{1}\ 2\ \overset{>}{3}\ 4\ \overset{>}{5}\ 6\ \overset{>}{7}$$

$$\text{or}\quad \overset{}{1}\ 2\ \overset{>}{3}\ 4\ 5\ \overset{>}{6}\ 7$$

11. When the beat continues at a steady pace throughout a composition while the meter changes so that the accent is shifted, an exciting, asymmetrical rhythm is achieved. This effect is found in some folk dances and contemporary music.

12. In the music of some other cultures rhythmic ideas may extend over twelve, fifteen, or more beats without being related to smaller groups of beats.

D. Rhythm Patterns Related to Meter

1. A rhythm pattern can have a smooth movement when its tones flow evenly, twice as fast as the beat. (Later, various patterns of even quarter, eighth, and sixteenth notes in $\frac{2}{4}$, $\frac{3}{4}$, and $\frac{4}{4}$ meter can be shown to have this characteristic.)   Level II

2. A rhythm pattern can give a feeling of roundness and flow when the tones of the pattern divide the beat into three parts. Many nursery rhymes have rhythm patterns of this kind. (Later, various eighth, quarter, and dotted quarter note patterns in $\frac{6}{8}$, $\frac{9}{8}$, or $\frac{12}{8}$ can be shown to give this effect.)

3. A rhythm pattern may have tones that move exactly with the beat; in other patterns, some tones may move half as fast as the beat, and they can be combined with faster and even, slower tones. Various combinations of quarter, half, dotted half, and whole notes are used in such patterns.

4. A rhythm pattern may not take up all the beats in a measure; sometimes the pattern is repeated, another pattern is sounded, or a period of silence (called a rest) occurs.

5. Occasionally a rhythm pattern begins with its most important tone on the first beat of the meter; in many other rhythm patterns one, two, or three quick light tones precede the most important tone. Such short tones leading to the accent are said to be on the upbeat (anacrusis). Rhythm patterns with upbeats may cut across measure bars.   Level III

6. Many rhythm patterns have tones that divide the beat unevenly. In one common pattern the beat is divided into four parts, with the long tone getting three parts of the beat, and the short tone one part. Various combinations of eighth and dotted quarter notes or sixteenth and dotted eighth notes represent such patterns.

7. When a rhythm pattern is arranged so that its important tone does not coincide with the strong beat in the meter, the pattern is said to be syncopated. Many syncopated Latin-American rhythm patterns have a short tone on the beat, followed by a longer tone on the unaccented part of the beat; others may have a rest on the beat, with tones sounded after the beat.

III. MELODY

A. The Shape of Melody

1. A melody may rise, it may fall, or it may stay generally on one level.   Level I

2. In rising or falling, a melody can move by small steps or it can move by larger steps or leaps.

3. Every melody has resting points (later these can be identified as cadences).   Level II

4. When each successive tone in a melody is higher than the one preceding it, we say the melody rises.

5. When each successive tone in a melody is lower than the one preceding it, we say the melody falls.

6. A melody may have several resting places (cadences), some more final than others.   Level III

7. A melody often has a high point of interest (later identified as a climax). This may occur early in the melody, but more often it comes near the end.

8. The mood a melody arouses is determined to some extent by the way it moves:

   a. a slow-moving melody that remains near one level, using repeated tones and neighboring tones, can seem calm and restful;

   b. a melody that has wide intervals or a persistently rising melody can give a sense of boldness and strength.

9. A melody may have both very high tones and very low tones; such a melody is said to have a wide range.

10. A melody using only high tones is said to be in a high register, whereas a melody using only low tones is said to be in a low register. (E.g., a soprano sings or a flute plays in a high register, and a bass voice sings or a tuba plays in a low register.)

B. The Function of Rhythm in Melodic Shape and Pattern

1. Melody is comprised of both longer and shorter tones; we call these long–short patterns the "melody rhythm."   Level I

2. Sometimes we can identify a familiar melody by hearing just its rhythm.

3. Some melodies are smooth and have a slow melody rhythm.

4. Other melodies are made up of shorter groups of tonal–rhythmic patterns that are easy to clap.

5. Some tonal patterns are longer than others; some are as short as two tones, while others may be six or seven tones long.   Level II

6. Rhythm is part of a tonal pattern; if the pitches remain the same but the rhythm changes, the pattern is different.

7. In a motif (or a tonal pattern), one tone is usually more important than the others; this important tone may be in the middle of the motif, at the beginning, or at the end.   Level III

C. Tonality and Intervals in Melodic Construction

1. Certain tones in every melody are restful, but other tones seem restless and tend to lead toward a restful tone.   Level II

2. The tones of a melody can be related to a scale. Different kinds of scales exist; the most common is the major scale (labeled with syllables—*do, re, mi, fa, so,*

la, ti, do—or by playing from C to C on consecutive white keys on the piano, producing the C-major scale, one of twelve possible major scales).

3. The most restful tone in a melody is the key-tone (tonic), and all the other tones are related to it.

4. The distance from low *do (1)* to high *do (8)* is a very wide leap. (Older children can count the beginning and the ending scale steps and all the steps between, to find that there are eight tones in this interval, which is called an *octave*.)

5. The distance from *do (1)* up to *re (2)*, and the distance from *re (2)* up to *mi (3)* is one step. (Later this interval is identified as a major second.)

6. The distance from *do (1)* up to *mi (3)* is an easy skip; it is the first part of the tonic chord and is used for tuning up to sing. (Later it is identified as a major third.)

7. The distance from *mi (3)* up to *fa (4)* is a half-step, and the distance from *ti (7)* up to *do (8)* is a half-step; this is a very small interval. (Later it is identified as a minor second, which is one half-step smaller than a major second.)

8. The distance from *mi (3)* up to *so (5)* is a small skip, as is the distance from *la (6)* up to *do (8)*. Brahms' "Cradle Song" has this skip as its first ascending interval. (Later it is identified as a minor third, which is a half-step smaller than a major third.)

9. Some melodies have a different, darker sound than others; they are said to be in the minor mode. (The natural minor scale can be sounded by playing from A to A on consecutive white keys on the piano, producing the A-minor scale, one of twelve possible natural minor scales.)

10. Some melodies use only five different tones and have larger gaps between tones. (Later children can learn that these melodies are in the pentatonic scale.)

11. A melody that moves steadily upward or downward from one scale tone to another is said to be stepwise or scalewise (in the manner of a scale).

Level III

12. A melody that moves through the tones of a chord is said to move chordwise.

13. A melody often has a framework of chord tones that is filled in by other tones.

14. The distance from *do (1)* up to *so (5)* is a firm leap; this interval is heard when the open strings of the violin are tuned. (Later it is identified as a perfect fifth.)

15. The distance from *so (5)* up to *do (8)* is a leap, as is the distance from *do (1)* up to *fa (4)*. This interval is the first ascending interval in "Taps." (Later it is identified as a perfect fourth.)

16. The distance from *do (1)* up to *la (6)* is a comfortable, wide leap, as is the distance from *so (5)* up to *mi (3)*. This interval is heard in the first two tones of "My Bonnie Lies Over the Ocean." (Later it is identified as a major sixth.)

17. A minor scale has more harmonic strength when the seventh step of the scale is raised (it is then called the leading tone); raising this tone creates another form of the minor scale, the harmonic minor.

18. The harmonic minor scale can be made in another way: by beginning on the first tone of the major scale and lowering the third and the sixth scale degrees by a half-step.

19. Melodies based on major and minor scales are said to be tonal; the first tone of the scale is the tonal center and all the other pitches are related to it.

20. Most scales on which melodies are built consist of a series of whole steps and half-steps; another scale consists entirely of whole steps (the whole tone scale).

21. The chromatic scale consists of twelve tones, each a half-step apart. A twelve-tone row is a particular kind of melody based on the twelve different tones in the chromatic scale.

22. A melody based on a twelve-tone row has no tonal center and is said to be atonal.

D. The Way Melodic Material is Used

1. Musical phrases can be short or long.   Level I

2. Music is made of smaller parts that are combined to make the whole piece. Level II

3. In many songs each syllable in each word is given one tone, but in some music one syllable is given several tones.

4. When a motif or a theme is changed by adding something, we say it has been extended.

5. When a theme is broken into parts and some of the parts are used individually, we say it has been fragmented.

6. When a theme or a motif is turned upside down, we say it has been inverted. Level III

7. Any melodic idea can be repeated immediately, or at a later point in the composition, thereby providing unity in the melodic material.

8. Variety and interest can be provided by introducing a contrasting idea into the melodic material.

9. When a pattern is repeated on a higher or lower level, the repetition is called a sequence.

E. Notation for Pitch

1. The pitch of musical tone, referred to as high or low, is shown as high or low on a music staff. Each step of a scale is represented by the consecutive lines and spaces of the staff.   Level II

2. The first seven letters of the alphabet are used to name the lines and spaces of the staff, just as they are used to name the piano keys and resonator bars. These are repeated at higher and lower levels.

3. When a tone is so high or low that it cannot be shown on the staff, leger lines are added above or below the staff to show the pitch. Music for bass voices or instruments is written on another staff.   Level III

4. A clef sign at the beginning of the staff shows what tones are represented by the lines and spaces of a staff. The treble clef (G clef) is used for high voices and instruments; the bass clef (F clef) is used for low voices and instruments.

5. The lines and spaces of both staffs conform to the whole- and half-step arrangement of the C major scale; that is, half steps occur between E–F and B–C; all other consecutive lines and spaces represent whole steps.

6. When notes other than those in the scale of C major are to be written, half-step changes of pitch can be shown by a sharp or a flat placed on a line or space before the note.

7. When a melody is written in a scale other than C major, the necessary sharps or flats are placed at the left of the staff (as the key signature) rather than before

every note that needs to have a sharp or a flat. The music is then said to be in the key of the tonic note of that scale.

IV. TEXTURE AND HARMONY

A. Types of Texture

1. Music can have one sound coming after another or it can have several sounds happening at the same time.   Level I

2. Our ears can hear more than one sound at a time.

3. When one instrument plays alone, it creates an effect different from that of several instruments playing at the same time.   Level II

4. When many instruments or voices are used at once and the tones happen close together, a thick texture is created.

5. When a few instruments or voices are used and the tones occur farther apart, a thin texture is created.

6. When a chord accompaniment supports one main melody, the effect is called harmony. (In more advanced study, this is called homophonic texture.)

7. Changes in texture of a composition can create interesting musical effects.

8. Solo with accompaniment is created when an instrument is featured throughout much of a composition and other instruments play supporting parts.   Level III

9. When a melody is harmonized, the harmony may have different qualities of texture: slow-moving chords that are held while the melody moves through several tones; chords that are played on almost every tone of the melody; chords that are broken and played in arpeggios or in repeated accompaniment figures.

10. Two or more melodies of equal importance sounding at the same time create counterpoint. The round and the canon are simple types of counterpoint. (In more advanced study, this is called polyphonic texture.)

11. An accompaniment that consists of a rhythmic–melodic pattern repeated over and over is called an *ostinato.*

12. When parts are added to music the texture becomes thicker, and the music is expressive in a different way.

13. Sometimes two or more voices in a composition move for a short or a long time in parallel motion. The intervals between the voices usually are thirds or sixths, which are consonant intervals. This kind of harmony is found in two-part songs for children's voices and between the upper parts of "barbershop quartet" arrangements.

14. Sometimes two parts in a composition move in opposite directions, or in contrary motion; a descant is often set in contrary motion to the melody.

B. Chords and Their Relationships

1. A chord is a group of tones sounded together. The tonic chord (I) is the "home" chord and gives a feeling of restfulness and arrival. Musical compositions often begin with tonic-chord harmony and usually end on it.   Level II

2. The dominant chord (V) is an active, restless chord; its tones tend to lead to tones in other chords, usually the tonic.

3. The subdominant chord (IV) is a smooth, pleasant sound and is heard as the first chord in the "amen" at the end of a hymn.

4. The tonic chord (I), the dominant chord (V), and the subdominant chord (IV) are the three chords most often used in simple harmonies of hymns and folk music. All of these are bright-sounding major chords when a major scale is used.   Level III

5. When a melody is harmonized, chords that fit with its important tones must be used. Some tones that are short or that do not occur on accented beats in the melody can be treated as passing tones or neighboring tones, which are not harmonized.

6. When a minor scale is used, the tonic chord (I) and the subdominant chord (IV) are minor chords; such chords have a sweet, pleasant sound that is darker in quality than the sound of major chords.

7. When the harmony moves from the dominant chord to the tonic chord at the end of a piece, it creates a feeling of arrival and finality (later identified as a full cadence).

8. When the harmony moves from subdominant (IV) to tonic (I), the result is a less strong, "amen" cadence (later identified as a plagal cadence).

9. Sometimes a phrase or larger section of a composition ends on tones of the dominant chord; this is a temporary kind of ending (later identified as a half cadence).

10. In a major key the supertonic chord (II) is a minor chord, and it sometimes is used to provide a quality of sound that contrasts with the major chords.

11. Some chords in modern music produce tense, clashing sounds that are called dissonant. The composer uses dissonance to produce an effect or create feeling through the music; it is not necessarily unpleasant.

12. Composers of modern music sometimes use chords from two different keys at the same time (polytonality). Such combinations of tones create variety and interesting musical effects, although they may seem dissonant and jarring to listeners accustomed to traditional harmonies.

C. The Structure of Chords

1. The simplest chord, a triad, consists of three tones built up in thirds from any step of a scale. The tone on which a chord is built is called its root.   Level II

2. Chords are labeled in three ways: with a Roman numeral, indicating the scale step on which the chord is built; with a capital letter (as seen on the Autoharp) showing the letter name of the note on which the chord is built; or by a name indicating its harmonic function, such as tonic (I) or dominant (V).

3. The dominant-seventh chord (V^7) has four tones and is used instead of the   Level III
dominant (V) when a richer, more dynamic quality is desired. (This is the form of the chord available on the Autoharp.) The dominant-seventh is a major chord with an added third on top, which is an interval of a seventh from the root of the chord; this is a dissonant chord that forces the harmony to move.

4. Some chords having the same letter name and formation are found in different keys. The function and harmonic effect of a chord depend upon its relationship

to the tonal center of the key in which it is used, just as each tone of the scale has its own relationship to the key tone (tonal center).

5. A chord can have some tones doubled, or it can be inverted, and still retain its general characteristics and function.

V. DYNAMICS

A. Relative Strength of Sound

1. Some music should be played or sung loudly in order to create an appropriate mood for the piece. Marches and heavy work songs might be quite loud.   Level I

2. Some music should be played or sung softly in order to create an appropriate mood for the piece. Lullabies and other gentle pieces usually should be sung softly.

3. In a musical composition some phrases or sections may be sung or played louder than others in order to convey contrasting ideas or moods.   Level II

4. There are various degrees of loudness and softness in music. The performer must select the level of loudness or softness that is most appropriate to the mood and ideas in the music. (At Level III, signs for various gradations of loudness and softness can be learned.)

5. When many instruments or voices play or sing together, they may sound louder than a single instrument or voice. In playing or singing, however, either an individual or a group can vary the loudness or softness in order to produce the desired mood in the music.

B. Types of Dynamic Change

1. Music may become suddenly louder or suddenly softer in a composition because the players simultaneously play or sing louder or softer to obtain a desired effect.   Level I

2. Music may become suddenly louder or suddenly softer in a composition because singers or players are added or dropped out of a performing group. (At Level III, children may learn that the "terrace" dynamics of some music in the baroque style is created by the alternate playing of large and small groups.)   Level II

3. Music may become gradually louder or gradually softer within a composition. This effect is called *crescendo* (louder) or *diminuendo* (softer); it is achieved by careful control on the part of each player or singer so that the gradual change is achieved.

C. Interrelationship of Dynamics with Other Musical Elements

1. Music that goes faster may become louder unless the performers take care to maintain the same dynamic level.   Level III

2. A melody that goes higher sometimes sounds louder because of a difference in the tone quality of certain voices and instruments in a higher register.

3. The texture of the music may influence the effect that the dynamics of a composition produce. A single line played loudly by many instruments, for example, will produce an effect strikingly different from that of many instruments playing several different parts at the same dynamic level.

4. By using dynamic changes interrelated with other factors in music (melody, rhythm, harmony, texture, and timbre), the composer and the performer achieve expressive effects that help convey the mood and meaning of the music.

VI. FORM IN MUSIC

A. General

1. Every composition has a beginning and an ending. Level I
2. Sometimes a composition sounds much the same from the beginning to the end.
3. Contrast can be created by changing:
   a. the number of instruments played
   b. the kind of instruments played
   c. the way they are played
   d. how loud they are played

B. The Phrase as a Unit of Musical Form

1. Music is built of phrases and sections that, together, make up a whole composition. Level I

2. A song or other short piece of music usually consists of several well-defined phrases, some alike and some different.

3. Often a composition has an even number of phrases, but sometimes the number is uneven. Level II

4. Within one composition, the phrases usually are the same length, but sometimes a phrase is longer or shorter than others.

5. A phrase can be repeated exactly (aa); it can be repeated, but with some changes (aa'); or it can be followed by another that is in contrast to it (ab).

6. Sometimes two phrases sound like a question and an answer within a longer musical unit. (Later these are identified as antecedent and consequent phrases within a musical period.)

7. Some phrases give the impression of a long flowing line; others readily divide into short melodic motives. Level III

8. A phrase may consist of one important motive that is repeated and expanded, or it may consist of two or more different motives.

C. Sectional Forms in Music

1. Some songs and short instrumental pieces seem symmetrical and balanced, because a second section completes or answers the first section; some marches, Level I

dances, and songs having a stanza followed by a refrain have this form. (Later this may be called *two-part* or *binary form* and represented in analysis as A B.)

2. A musical composition may have a satisfying first section that is followed by a contrasting second section. When the first section is repeated at the end, the whole piece seems well balanced and complete. Some cradle songs, waltzes, minuets, preludes, and other short pieces are written in this form. (Later this may be called *three-part* or *ternary form* and represented in analysis as A B A.)

3. Sometimes a first section is alternated with two or more other sections. Since the first section comes around after each different section is played, this form is called a *rondo*. The rondo usually is lively and cheerful in nature. (Later the rondo form may be diagrammed as A B A C A D A, or as some other form of this basic pattern, with A recurring.)

4. A composer can use any arrangement of sections that is suitable to the musical material. Some compositions that are clearly divisible into sections do not fit any of the prescribed plans. (Later this structure can be called free sectional form and analyzed as A B B, A B C A, and so on.)

5. Sometimes a composer selects a short song or dance (or composes an original one) and writes a series of variations on it. Each section is the same length as the original melody, but each is treated in a different way:

   a. The theme may be ornamented; passing tones, turns, and other decorations can be added to the melody or the accompaniment.

   b. The theme may have a change in its basic rhythm, melody, or mode.

   c. The accompaniment may be altered by a change in rhythm, harmony, tone color, or dynamics.

6. Two large sectional forms in music are the sonata and the symphony. The sonata is written for one or two instruments; the symphony is written for full orchestra. These large forms consist of three or four related but separate movements. A single movement might be a three-part form, a rondo, a theme with variations, or a sonata-allegro form. In the sonata-allegro form, usually the first movement in a symphony, the composer contrasts and develops the themes in some generally prescribed ways. (More specific consideration of these large developmental forms is undertaken in music appreciation classes at the secondary or college level.)

D. Nonsectional Forms in Music

1. Sometimes a melody in one voice (vocal or instrumental part) is followed by successive voices that enter separately, imitating the first voice throughout. The different voices, singing in counterpoint to one another, overlap any phrase endings so that the whole seems to be one continuous composition. (This can be identified as a *canon,* one form of which is the round.)

2. A short composition may sound unified and unbroken if the composer has used a single pattern of rhythmic movement and textural treatment throughout. (Bach composed some well-known preludes on continuous broken-chord patterns.)

3. One or two musical motives can be so skillfully handled by the composer that they grow into one small unified composition, with no repetitions or contrasting sections. (Debussy composed some piano preludes in this way.)

Level II

Level III

Level II

Level III

4. A composer using a story or other descriptive idea as the basis for a composition may choose not to follow a prescribed design in music. The composer may construct the piece in a single movement in order to have greater freedom to develop the musical continuity and feeling that express the programmatic ideas. (Tone poems often are written in such a free form.)

5. In another kind of continuous, imitative counterpoint, a composer may present a theme in a single voice (A) that is imitated in turn by two or three other voices; often, when one voice (A) turns the main theme over to another (B), the first voice then carries a countertheme until the main theme moves on to the third voice (C); then the first voice (A) has a free part (nonimitative) until the main theme again returns to it (A). (These can be identified as important characteristics of a *fugue*.)

E. Suites and Dramatic Forms

1. Many composers have written music based on episodes and stories to be portrayed in ballet. When the music offers listening pleasure without the dancing, the composer may arrange its strongest parts into a ballet suite of contrasting movements for concert orchestra.   Level II

2. Any collection of related musical compositions might be a suite. The dance suite, a popular musical form at the time of Bach, consists of a group of contrasting dances such as the sarabande, the minuet, and the gigue. In more recent times, composers have written descriptive suites that might be called musical pictures of one subject.

3. Almost every motion picture film is accompanied by background music that contributes to the ideas and feelings conveyed by the film. A composer may arrange an orchestral suite from the film music. In earlier times, incidental music written for plays was arranged into a suite for separate concert performances.

4. When drama, stage sets, costumes, singing, orchestral music, and dancing are all combined, the impressive stage production is called *opera*. Opera includes music for solo voices, small vocal ensembles, chorus, and orchestra to create dramatic effects while portraying a story. The main musical themes of an opera often are introduced in the overture, which the orchestra plays before the curtain rises.   Level III

5. When a large dramatic work is based on a contemplative or religious subject, it may be performed as a concert without costumes, stage sets, or drama. In such music, called an *oratorio*, solo voices and ensembles, chorus and orchestra, and sometimes a narrator are used.

VII. STYLE IN MUSIC

A. General Concepts

1. The music of every culture employs the basic elements of pitch, timbre, time, simultaneous sequential use of sound, a sense of form, and usually simultaneous sounds, but in many different ways.   Level III

2. Pieces of music of the same style tend to use the elements of music in similar ways.

3. Folk music, popular music, and classical music can be identified as belonging to particular styles, because of their characteristic uses of the musical elements.

4. Every broad stylistic type of music has identifiable substyles within it.

5. To know the music of a particular culture, one must hear and study it in terms of its own characteristics.

6. A person who knows the characteristics of music in various styles can identify music that belongs to a style, even without knowing the composer or the piece of music itself.

B. The Baroque Style

1. Baroque music has a strong, steady rhythm and a firm bass line. The treble voice is somewhat florid, using distinctive figurations and embellishments of the melody.   Level III

2. A baroque composition features a single theme that is extended, elaborated, and intensively explored. The variation form and the fugue lend themselves to such treatment.

3. In instrumental music of the baroque period, solo passages often alternate with ensemble passages.

4. Baroque composers liked to give a vivid representation of words, ideas, and feelings in the music itself.

5. Some of the more prominent composers of the baroque style were Bach, Corelli, Couperin, Handel, Lully, Scarlatti, and Vivaldi.

C. The Viennese Classic Style

1. Melodies of Viennese classic composers have some qualities of the folk songs and dances of that day; they have a simple expressiveness and clear-cut beauty of line.   Level III

2. Regular metric groupings provide the rhythmic basis for Viennese classic music. The effect of clear, well-balanced phrases, periods, and larger sections is characteristic of the style.

3. Music of the Viennese classic style makes ingenious use of motives and themes that are set in contrast to one another, elaborated, and developed throughout an entire section of the work.

4. The predominant texture of Viennese classic music is homophonic—that is, one melodic line stands out. Melodic material, however, is shared by instruments of the ensemble, and skillful use is made of counterpoint that is subsidiary to the leading voice.

5. Some of the more prominent composers of the Viennese classic style were Beethoven (except latest works), Gluck, Grétry, Haydn and Mozart.

D. The Romantic Style

1. The large orchestral piece of one grand, unbroken movement is characteristic of   Level III

the romantic style; picturesque episodes within the composition suggest different aspects of an idea or event.

2. Instrumental tone color is used to convey feeling and effect in this music; massive, rich, low-pitched sound may provide heroic effects, and unusual combinations of high and low may be used for brilliant contrasts and flashes of color.

3. Chromatic tones, indefinite cadences, and some irregularity of rhythmic flow contribute to a mood or pictorial image. Chords are used for their color effects and emotional qualities; certain complex, dissonant chords create rich, enchanting sound as well as strong musical movement.

4. Groups of short pieces in different moods, written for solo voice or instrument, especially the piano, are characteristic of the romantic style.

5. Some of the more prominent composers of the romantic style were Berlioz, Bizet, Borodin, Brahms, Chopin, Dvořák, Franck, Grieg, Mahler, Mendelssohn, Moussorgsky, Rimsky-Korsakov, Saint-Saëns, Schubert, Schumann, Sibelius, Tchaikovsky, Wagner, Wolf, and Verdi.

E. *The Impressionist Style*

1. Impressionist melodies tend to be vague; they consist of short motives rather than long singing lines.   Level III

2. Rhythms of the impressionist style often have a vague pulse and are obscured by syncopation. Subtle use is made of dynamic changes.

3. Chords are used for their color value and sonority rather than for the dynamic quality of movement. When sectional forms are used, the outlines are blurred.

4. Tone color in impressionist music is rich but subdued, pastel, and misty. The harp is frequently heard; many instruments are muted; piano solos use much pedal to sustain and mix chord colors and tonal outlines.

5. Some of the prominent composers of the impressionistic style were Debussy, Delius, Falla, Griffes, Ravel, and Respighi.

F. *Contemporary Music*

1. Rhythm is energetic and driving in music of the 20th century. Often it seems erratic. Sometimes there is no regular duple or triple grouping of beats; accents seem shifted or misplaced.   Level III

2. Tone sometimes is generated by media that in an earlier age would be considered nonmusical sources, including electronically produced sound.

3. Melodies in contemporary music tend to be jagged and fragmentary. Sometimes folk tunes and motives are used, but seldom in long, flowing lines.

4. Contemporary harmony can be dissonant and clashing. Much use is made of counterpoint, and it, too, may produce dissonance. Opposing musical lines may be written in different scales; different sections of the orchestra may play chords simultaneously in different keys.

5. Contemporary music often shows sectional forms. Phrases can be heard in a question-and-answer relationship. Sections may end with an abrupt shift to a different harmony or texture rather than with a cadence.

6. Some of the prominent composers of contemporary music are Bartók, Britten, Cage, Copland, Cowell, Ginastera, Guarnieri, Harris, Honegger, Ives, Kabalevsky, Khachaturian, Kodály, McBride, Menotti, Milhaud, Prokofiev, Schoenberg, Shostakovich, Stravinsky, Thomson, Varèse, Vaughan Williams, Villa-Lobos, and Walton.

G. Folk Music of Different Cultures

1. Tone color is determined by the traditional instruments of the culture and the way they are played, as well as particular ways of using the voice.   Level III

2. Pitch and standards for tuning scales differ from one culture to another.

3. Uses of rhythm can differ widely, with some cultures featuring rhythmic complexity, polyrhythms, and the layering of simultaneous lines to create rich textures of sound.

4. Simultaneous sounds are heard in the music of most cultures, but principles of "harmony" apply to those musical cultures growing out of Western European musical traditions.

5. The music of most cultures features qualities of rhythmic and melodic tension and release.

6. Although specific forms of music differ, the construction of music of most cultures utilizes basic principles of unity and variety.

H. Popular Music of America

1. The popular music of America grew out of Negro spirituals, gospel, and blues, combined with Western folk music.   Level III

2. The styles of popular music continue to change, but basic categories are rock, soul, folk, country and western, and jazz.

3. These musical styles have qualities in common:

   a. they are based on metered rhythm
   b. they use diatonic scales
   c. they are harmonically oriented
   d. they use Western instruments,
   e. they have simple musical forms

4. These musical styles differ in

   a. their use of vocal timbre and expression
   b. the extent to which they are improvised
   c. their rhythmic complexity

Appendix B
Guide to Materials

I. BASIC MUSIC SERIES* (with reference code)

Addison-Wesley Publishing Company, 2725 Sand Hill Rd., Menlo Park, Calif. 94025. **Comprehensive Musicianship Through Classroom Music** Series, Dorothy Gillett, Leon Burton, et al., 1972.
CMP—*The Comprehensive Musicianship Program, Kindergarten* and *Grades 1–6.*

Allyn and Bacon, Inc., 470 Atlantic Ave., Boston, Mass. 02210. **This Is Music for Today** Series, William R. Sur et al., 1970.
TMT—*This is Music for Today, Kindergarten* and *Grades 1–6.*

American Book Company, 150 West 50th St., New York, N.Y. 10020. **New Dimensions in Music** Series, Robert A. Choate et al., 1979.
NDinM—*New Dimensions in Music, Kindergarten* and *Grades 1–6.*

Follett Publishing Company, 1010 West Washington Blvd., Chicago, Ill. 60607. **Discovering Music Together** Series, Charles Leonhard et al., 1974.
DMT—**Discovering Music Together, Early Childhood** and **Grades 1–6.**

Ginn and Company, 191 Spring St., Lexington, Mass. 02173. **The Magic of Music** Series, Lorrain E. Watters et al., 1966.
MoM—*The Magic of Music, Kindergarten* and *Grades 1–6.*

Holt, Rinehart and Winston, Inc., 383 Madison Ave., New York, N.Y. 10017. **Exploring Music** Series, Eunice Boardman and Beth Landis, 1975.
ExM—*Exploring Music, Kindergarten* and *Grades 1–6.*

The Macmillan Company, Inc., 200F Brown St., Riverside, N.J. 08075. **The Spectrum of Music** Series, Mary Val Marsh et al., 1975.
SpM—*The Spectrum of Music, Kindergarten* and *Grades 1–6.*

---

* Graded music series books published by these companies are also available for seventh, eighth, and sometimes the ninth grade.

Prentice-Hall, Inc., Englewood Cliffs, N.J. 07632. **Growing with Music** Series, Harry Wilson et al., 1966.
  GwM—*Growing with Music, Kindergarten* and *Grades 1–6.*

Silver Burdett, Division of General Learning Corp., 250 James St., Morristown, N.J. 07960. **Silver Burdett Music** Series, Bennett Reimer et al., 1978.
  SBM—*Silver Burdett Music, Early Childhood* and *Grades 1–6.*
  Making Music Your Own Series, Beatrice Landeck et al., 1965.
  MMYO—*Making Music Your Own, Kindergarten* and *Grades 1–6.*

II. RECORD SERIES* (with reference code)

Adventures in Music, A New Record Library for Elementary Schools, RCA Victor Recording Corporation (Le = "long play," Les = "stereo"). A teacher's guide is included in the folder for each volume. (See alphabetical listing of music on following pages.)
  Grade 1, Volume 1 (Le/Les 1000) (**AinM I-1**)
  Grade 1, Volume 2 (Le/Les 1010) (**AinM I-2**)
  Grade 2, Volume 1 (Le/Les 1001) (**AinM II-1**)
  Grade 2, Volume 2 (Le/Les 1011) (**AinM II-2**)
  Grade 3, Volume 1 (Le/Les 1002) (**AinM III-1**)
  Grade 3, Volume 2 (Le/Les 1003) (**AinM III-2**)
  Grade 4, Volume 1 (Le/Les 1004) (**AinM IV-1**)
  Grade 4, Volume 2 (Le/Les 1005) (**AinM IV-2**)
  Grade 5, Volume 1 (Le/Les 1006) (**AinM V-1**)
  Grade 5, Volume 2 (Le/Les 1007) (**AinM V-2**)
  Grade 6, Volume 1 (Le/Les 1008) (**AinM VI-1**)
  Grade 6, Volume 2 (Le/Les 1009) (**AinM VI-2**)

Bowmar Orchestral Library (BOL), Bowmar Educational Records. Each album is accompanied by wall charts of the themes and suggestions to the teacher. (See listing of music on following pages.)

Adventures in Music—Musical Contents

Anderson: Irish Suite—THE GIRL I LEFT BEHIND ME, Gr. 5, Vol. 2

Arnold: English Suite—GRAZIOSO (7th movement), Gr. 1, Vol. 2
  English Suite—ALLEGRO NON TROPPO (5th movement), Gr. 2, Vol. 2

Bach: Cantata No. 147—JESU, JOY OF MAN'S DESIRING, Gr. 5, Vol. 1
  LITTLE FUGUE IN G MINOR (arr. by L. Cailliet), Gr. 6, Vol. 1
  Suite No. 2—BADINERIE, Gr. 3, Vol. 1
  Suite No. 2—RONDEAU, Gr. 2, Vol. 2
  Suite No. 2—GIGUE, Gr. 1, Vol. 1

Bartók: Hungarian Sketches—BEAR DANCE, Gr. 3, Vol. 2
  Hungarian Sketches—EVENING IN THE VILLAGE, Gr. 5, Vol. 2
  Mikrokosmos Suite No. 2—JACK-IN-THE-BOX, Gr. 2, Vol. 1
  Mikrokosmos—DIARY OF A FLY (Moto perpetuo, No. 142), Gr. 1, Vol. 2

---

* See Section III for listing of other firms offering useful records.

Beethoven: Symphony No. 8—SECOND MOVEMENT, Gr. 6, Vol. 1

Berlioz: The Damnation of Faust—BALLET OF THE SYLPHS, Gr. 1, Vol. 1

Bizet: L'Arlesienne Suite No. 1—MINUETTO, Gr. 4, Vol. 2
    L'Arlesienne Suite No. 2—FARANDOLE, Gr. 6, Vol. 1
    Carmen—CHANGING OF THE GUARD, Gr. 3, Vol. 2
    Carmen Suite—DRAGOONS OF ALCALA, Gr. 2, Vol. 2
    Children's Games—THE BALL; CRADLE SONG; LEAP FROG, Gr. 1, Vol. 1

Borodin: IN THE STEPPES OF CENTRAL ASIA, Gr. 6, Vol. 1

Brahms: HUNGARIAN DANCE No. 1, Gr. 5, Vol. 2

Cailliet: POP! GOES THE WEASEL—Variations, Gr. 4, Vol. 1

Carpenter: Adventures in a Perambulator—THE HURDY-GURDY, Gr. 5, Vol. 2

Chabrier: ESPAÑA RAPSODIE, Gr. 5, Vol. 1
    MARCHE JOYEUSE, Gr. 4, Vol. 1

Charpentier: Impressions of Italy—ON MULEBACK, Gr. 5, Vol. 1

Cimarosa: Cimarosiana—NON TROPPO MOSSO (3rd movement), Gr. 2, Vol. 2

Coates: London Suite—KNIGHTSBRIDGE MARCH, Gr. 5, Vol. 2

Copland: Billy the Kid Ballet Suite—STREET IN A FRONTIER TOWN, Gr. 6, Vol. 1
    The Red Pony Suite—CIRCUS MUSIC, Gr. 3, Vol. 1
    The Red Pony Suite—DREAM MARCH, Gr. 2, Vol. 2
    Rodeo—HOE-DOWN, Gr. 5, Vol. 2

Corelli-Pinelli: Suite for Strings—SARABANDE, Gr. 6, Vol. 2

Debussy: Children's Corner Suite—THE SNOW IS DANCING, Gr. 3, Vol. 1
    La Mer—PLAY OF THE WAVES, Gr. 6, Vol. 2

Delibes: Coppélia—WALTZ OF THE DOLL, Gr. 1, Vol. 1
    Coppélia—SWANHILDE'S WALTZ, Gr. 2, Vol. 2
    The King Is Amused—LESQUERCARDE, Gr. 1, Vol. 2

Dvořák: SLAVONIC DANCE No. 7, Gr. 4, Vol. 2

Elgar: Wand of Youth Suite No. 1—FAIRIES AND GIANTS, Gr. 3, Vol. 1
    Wand of Youth Suite No. 2—FOUNTAIN DANCE, Gr. 2, Vol. 1
    Wand of Youth Suite—SUN DANCE, Gr. 2, Vol. 2

Falla: La Vida Breve—SPANISH DANCE No. 1, Gr. 6, Vol. 1

Fauré: Dolly—BERCEUSE, Gr. 2, Vol. 1

German: Henry VIII Suite—MORRIS DANCE, Gr. 1, Vol. 2

Ginastera: Estancia—WHEAT DANCE, Gr. 4, Vol. 1

Glière: The Red Poppy—RUSSIAN SAILORS' DANCE, Gr. 6, Vol. 2

Gluck: Armide Ballet Suite—MUSETTE, Gr. 2, Vol. 2
    Iphigenie in Aulis—AIR GAI, Gr. 1, Vol. 1

Gottschalk-Kay: Cakewalk Ballet Suite—GRAND WALKAROUND, Gr. 5, Vol. 1

Gould: AMERICAN SALUTE, Gr. 5, Vol. 1

Gounod: Faust Ballet Suite—WALTZ No. 1, Gr. 3, Vol. 1

Grainger: LONDONDERRY AIR, Gr. 4, Vol. 2

Grétry: Céphale et Procris—GIGUE (arr. by Mottl), Gr. 1, Vol. 1
    Céphale et Procris—TAMBOURIN (arr. by Mottl), Gr. 2, Vol. 1

Grieg: Lyric Suite—NORWEGIAN RUSTIC MARCH, Gr. 4, Vol. 1
    Peer Gynt Suite—ANITRA'S DANCE, Gr. 1, Vol. 2
    Peer Gynt Suite—IN THE HALL OF THE MOUNTAIN KING, Gr. 3, Vol. 2

Griffes: THE WHITE PEACOCK, Gr. 6, Vol. 1

Grofé: Death Valley Suite—DESERT WATER HOLE, Gr. 4, Vol. 1

Guarnieri: BRAZILIAN DANCE, Gr. 6, Vol. 2

Handel: Royal Fireworks Music—BOURRÉE, MENUETTO No. 2, Gr. 3, Vol. 2
    Water Music—HORNPIPE, Gr. 2, Vol. 1

Hanson: For the First Time—BELLS, Gr. 1, Vol. 2
    Merry Mount Suite—CHILDREN'S DANCE, Gr. 3, Vol. 1

Herbert: Babes in Toyland—MARCH OF THE TOYS, Gr. 2, Vol. 1
    Natoma—DAGGER DANCE, Gr. 3, Vol. 1

Holst: The Perfect Fool—SPIRITS OF THE EARTH, Gr. 6, Vol. 2

Howe: SAND, Gr. 2, Vol. 2

Humperdinck: Hänsel and Gretel—PRELUDE, Gr. 5, Vol. 2

Ibert: Divertissement—PARADE, Gr. 1, Vol. 1
    Histories No. 2—THE LITTLE WHITE DONKEY, Gr. 2, Vol. 1

Kabalevsky: The Comedians—MARCH AND COMEDIANS' GALOP, Gr. 3, Vol. 1
    The Comedians—PANTOMIME, Gr. 1, Vol. 1
    The Comedians—WALTZ, Gr. 1, Vol. 2

Khachaturian: Gayne—DANCE OF THE ROSE MAIDENS, Gr. 1, Vol. 2
    Masquerade Suite—WALTZ, Gr. 4, Vol. 2

Kodály: Háry János Suite—ENTRANCE OF THE EMPEROR AND HIS COURT, Gr. 4, Vol. 2
    Háry János Suite—VIENNESE MUSICAL CLOCK, Gr. 2, Vol. 1

Lecuona: Suite Andalucia—ANDALUCIA, Gr. 4, Vol. 1

Liadov: Eight Russian Folk Songs—BERCEUSE, Gr. 1, Vol. 2

Lully: Ballet Suite—MARCH, Gr. 3, Vol. 2

McBride: PUMPKIN EATER'S LITTLE FUGUE, Gr. 2, Vol. 2
    Punch and the Judy—PONY EXPRESS, Gr. 1, Vol. 2

McDonald: Children's Symphony—ALLEGRO, Gr. 3, Vol. 2
    Children's Symphony (3rd Movement)—FARMER IN THE DELL, JINGLE BELLS, Gr. 2, Vol. 1

MacDowell: Second (Indian) Suite—IN WARTIME, Gr. 5, Vol. 1

Massenet: Le Cid—ARAGONAISE, Gr. 1, Vol. 1

Menotti: Amahl and the Night Visitors—MARCH OF THE KINGS, Gr. 1, Vol. 2
    Amahl and the Night Visitors—SHEPHERD'S DANCE, Gr. 4, Vol. 2

Meyerbeer: Les Patineurs—WALTZ, Gr. 2, Vol. 1

Milhaud: Saudades do Brazil—COPACABANA, Gr. 4, Vol. 2
    Saudades do Brazil—LARANJEIRAS, Gr. 2, Vol. 1
    Suite Provençale—MODERE (3rd movement), Gr. 1, Vol. 2

Moore: Farm Journal—HARVEST SONG, Gr. 1, Vol. 2

Moussorgsky: Pictures at an Exhibition (orchestrated by Ravel)—BALLET OF THE

UNHATCHED CHICKS, Gr. 1, Vol. 1; BYDLO, Gr. 2, Vol. 1; PROMENADE No. 1, Gr. 1, Vol. 2

Mozart: Divertimento No. 17—MENUETTO No. 1, Gr. 5, Vol. 2
Eine kleine Nachtmusik—ROMANZE, Gr. 4, Vol. 1
The Little Nothings—PANTOMIME, Gr. 1, Vol. 2

Offenbach: The Tales of Hoffman—BARCAROLLE, Gr. 3, Vol. 1

Pierné: Cydalise—ENTRANCE OF LITTLE FAUNS, Gr. 2, Vol. 2

Prokofiev: Children's Suite—WALTZ ON THE ICE, Gr. 3, Vol. 2
Summer Day Suite—MARCH, Gr. 1, Vol. 1
Lieutenant Kije—TROIKA, Gr. 2, Vol. 2
Winter Holiday—DEPARTURE, Gr. 2, Vol. 1

Ravel: Mother Goose Suite—THE CONVERSATIONS OF BEAUTY AND THE BEAST, Gr. 5, Vol. 1
Mother Goose Suite—LAIDERONNETTE, EMPRESS OF THE PAGODAS, Gr. 4, Vol. 2

Respighi: Brazilian Impressions—DANZA, Gr. 5, Vol. 2
Pines of Rome—PINES OF THE VILLA BORGHESE, GR. 4, Vol. 1
The Birds—PRELUDE, Gr. 2, Vol. 2

Rimsky-Korsakov: Le Coq d'Or Suite—BRIDAL PROCESSION, Gr. 4, Vol. 1
Snow Maiden—DANCE OF THE BUFFOONS, Gr. 2, Vol. 2

Rossini: William Tell Overture—FINALE, Gr. 3, Vol. 1

Rossini-Britten: Matinees Musicales—WALTZ, Gr. 1, Vol. 2
Soirées Musicales—BOLERO, Gr. 2, Vol. 2
Soirées Musicales—MARCH, Gr. 1, Vol. 1

Rossini-Respighi: The Fantastic Toyshop—CAN-CAN, Gr. 2, Vol. 1
The Fantastic Toyshop—TARANTELLA, Gr. 3, Vol. 2

Saint-Saëns: Carnival of the Animals—THE ELEPHANT, Gr. 1, Vol. 2
Carnival of the Animals—THE SWAN, Gr. 3, Vol. 2

Scarlatti-Tommasini: The Good-Humored Ladies—NON PRESTO IN TEMPO DI BALLO, Gr. 4, Vol. 2

Schubert: Symphony No. 5—FIRST MOVEMENT, Gr. 6, Vol. 1

Schuller: Seven Studies on Themes of Paul Klee—TWITTERING MACHINE, Gr. 2, Vol. 2

Schumann: Scenes from Childhood—TRÄUMEREI, Gr. 4, Vol. 2

Shostakovich: Ballet Suite No. 1—PETITE BALLERINA, Gr. 2, Vol. 1
Ballet Suite No. 1—PIZZICATO POLKA, Gr. 1, Vol. 1

Sibelius: Karelia Suite—ALLA MARCIA, Gr. 5, Vol. 1

Smetana: The Bartered Bride—DANCE OF THE COMEDIANS, Gr. 6, Vol. 2

Sousa: SEMPER FIDELIS, Gr. 3, Vol. 2
THE STARS AND STRIPES FOREVER, Gr. 4, Vol. 2

Strauss, R.: Der Rosenkavalier—SUITE, Gr. 6, Vol. 1

Stravinsky: The Firebird Suite—BERCEUSE, Gr. 1, Vol. 1
The Firebird Suite—INFERNAL DANCE OF KING KASTCHEI, Gr. 5, Vol. 2
Petrouchka—RUSSIAN DANCE, Gr. 1, Vol. 2

Taylor: Through the Looking Glass—GARDEN OF LIVE FLOWERS, Gr. 3, Vol. 2

Tchaikovsky: Nutcracker Suite—DANCE OF THE SUGAR PLUM FAIRY, Gr. 1, Vol. 2
   Nutcracker Suite—DANCE OF THE REED FLUTES, Gr. 1, Vol. 2
   The Sleeping Beauty—PUSS-IN-BOOTS, THE WHITE CAT, Gr. 3, Vol. 1
   The Sleeping Beauty—WALTZ, Gr. 4, Vol. 1
   Swan Lake—DANCE OF THE LITTLE SWANS, Gr. 1, Vol. 1
   Symphony No. 4—FOURTH MOVEMENT, Gr. 6, Vol. 2

Thomson: Acadian Songs and Dances—THE ALLIGATOR AND THE 'COON, Gr. 3, Vol. 2
   Acadian Songs and Dances—WALKING SONG, Gr. 1, Vol. 1

Vaughan Williams: FANTASIA ON "GREENSLEEVES," Gr. 6, Vol. 2
   The Wasps—MARCH PAST OF THE KITCHEN UTENSILS, Gr. 3, Vol. 1

Villa-Lobos: Bachianas Brasileiras No. 2—THE LITTLE TRAIN OF CAIPIRA, Gr. 3, Vol. 1

Wagner: Lohengrin—PRELUDE TO ACT III, Gr. 6, Vol. 1

Walton: Façade Suite—VALSE, Gr. 6, Vol. 2

Webern: Five Movements for String Orchestra—SEHR LANGSAM (4th movement), Gr. 2, Vol. 2

Bowmar Orchestral Library—Musical Contents

BOL #51   ANIMALS AND CIRCUS
Saint-Saëns, CARNIVAL OF THE ANIMALS: Introduction, Royal March of the Lion, Hens and Cocks, Fleet Footed Animals, Turtles, The Elephant, Kangaroos, Aquarium, Long Eared Personages, Cuckoo in the Deep Woods, Aviary, Pianists, Fossils, The Swan, Finale
Stravinsky, CIRCUS POLKA
Donaldson, UNDER THE BIG TOP: Marching Band, Acrobats, Juggler, Merry-Go-Round, Elephants, Clowns, Camels, Tightrope Walker, Pony Trot, Marching Band

BOL #52   NATURE AND MAKE-BELIEVE
Grieg, MARCH OF THE DWARFS
Donaldson, ONCE UPON A TIME SUITE: Chicken Little, Three Billy Boats Gruff, Little Train, Hare and the Tortoise
Tchaikovsky, THE LARK SONG (Scenes of Youth)
Grieg, LITTLE BIRD (Vöglein)
Liadov, DANCE OF THE MOSQUITO
Rimsky-Korsakov, FLIGHT OF THE BUMBLE BEE
Donaldson, SEASON FANTASIES: Magic Piper, The Poet and His Lyre, The Anxious Leaf, The Snowmaiden
Torjussen, TO THE RISING SUN (Fjord and Mountain, Norwegian Suite #2)
Debussy, CLAIRE DE LUNE

BOL #53   PICTURES AND PATTERNS
Rossini-Respighi, PIZZICATO (Fantastic Toyshop)
Bizet, MARCH—TRUMPET AND DRUM (Jeux d'Enfants), IMPROMPTU—THE TOP (Jeux d'Enfants)

Lecocq, POLKA (Mlle. Angot Suite), GAVOTTE (Mlle. Angot Suite)
Kabalevsky, INTERMEZZO (The Comedians)
Schumann-Glazounov, GERMAN WALTZ—PAGANINI (Carnaval)
Donaldson, BALLET PETIT
Mozart, MINUET
Handel, A GROUND
Schumann-Glazounov, CHOPIN (Carnaval)
Liadov, VILLAGE DANCE
Debussy, EN BATEAU ("In a Boat")
Donaldson, HARBOR VIGNETTES: Fog and Storm, Song of the Bell Buoy, Sailing

BOL #54   MARCHES
Pierné, ENTRANCE OF THE LITTLE FAUNS
Prokofiev, MARCH
Elgar, POMP AND CIRCUMSTANCE, NO. 1
Berlioz, HUNGARIAN MARCH (Rakoczy)
Alford, COLONEL BOGEY MARCH
Pierné, MARCH OF THE LITTLE LEAD SOLDIERS
Prokofiev, MARCH (The Love for Three Oranges)
Ippolitov-Ivanov, CORTEGE OF THE SARDAR (Caucasian Sketches)
Schubert, MARCHE MILITAIRE
Sousa, THE STARS AND STRIPES FOREVER
Rodgers, THE MARCH OF THE SIAMESE CHILDREN (The King and I)

BOL #55   DANCES, PART I
Wolf-Ferrari, DANCE OF THE CAMMORISTI
Guarnieri, DANÇA BRASILEIRA
Kabalevsky, GAVOTTE
Dvořák, SLAVONIC DANCE NO. 1
Copland, HOE-DOWN (Rodeo)
Walton, FAÇADE SUITE: Polka, Country Dance, Popular Song
Brahms, HUNGARIAN DANCE NO. 5
Waldteufel, SKATER'S WALTZES
Khatchaturian, MAZURKA, GALOP (Masquerade Suite)

BOL #56   DANCES, PART II
Vaughan Williams, FOLK DANCES FROM SOMERSET (English Folk Song Suite)
Benjamin, JAMAICAN RUMBA
Corelli, BADINERIE
Smetana, DANCE OF THE COMEDIANS
Lecocq, CAN-CAN GRAND WALTZ (Mlle. Angot Suite)
Strauss, TRITSCH-TRATSCH POLKA
Rossini-Respighi, TARANTELLA, WALTZ (Fantastic Toyshop)
Waldteufel, ESPAÑA WALTZES
Guion, ARKANSAS TRAVELER
Khatchaturian, RUSSIAN DANCE (Gayne Suite #2)

BOL #57   FAIRY TALES IN MUSIC
Coates, CINDERELLA
Mendelssohn, SCHERZO (Midsummer Night's Dream)
Ravel, MOTHER GOOSE SUITE: Pavane of the Sleeping Beauty, Hop o' My
    Thumb, Laideronette, Empress of the Pagodas, Beauty and the Beast, The Fairy
    Garden

BOL #58   STORIES IN BALLET AND OPERA
Menotti, SUITE FROM AMAHL AND THE NIGHT VISITORS: Introduction, March of the Three Kings, Dance of the Shepherds
Humperdinck, HÄNSEL AND GRETEL OVERTURE
Tchaikovsky, NUTCRACKER SUITE: Overture Miniature, March, Dance of the Sugar-Plum Fairy, Trepak, Arabian Dance, Chinese Dance, Dance of the Toy Flutes, Waltz of the FLowers

BOL #59   LEGENDS IN MUSIC
Saint-Saëns, DANSE MACABRE
Grieg, PEER GYNT SUITE NO. 1: Morning, Ase's Death, Anitra's Dance, In the Hall of the Mountain King
Dukas, SORCERER'S APPRENTICE
Saint-Saëns, PHAETON

BOL #60   UNDER MANY FLAGS
Smetana, THE MOLDAU
Torjussen, LAPLAND IDYLL, FOLK SONG (Fjord and Mountain, Norwegian Suite No. 2)
Grainger, LONDONDERRY AIR
Sibelius, FINLANDIA
Coates, LONDON SUITE: Covent Garden, Westminster, Knightsbridge March

BOL #61   AMERICAN SCENES
Grofé, GRAND CANYON SUITE: Sunrise, Painted Desert, On the Trail, Sunset, Cloudburst; MISSISSIPPI SUITE: Father of Waters, Huckleberry Finn, Old Creole Days, Mardi Gras

BOL #62   MASTERS IN MUSIC
Bach, JESU, JOY OF MAN'S DESIRING
Handel, BOURRÉE (Fireworks Music)
Haydn, VARIATIONS ("Surprise" Symphony)
Mozart, MINUET (Symphony No. 40)
Beethoven, SCHERZO (Seventh Symphony)
Grieg, WEDDING DAY AT TROLDHAUGEN
Schubert, MINUET (Symphony No. 5)
Wagner, RIDE OF THE VALKYRIES
Verdi, TRIUMPHAL MARCH (Aida)
Brahms, HUNGARIAN DANCE NO. 6
Mahler, SECOND MOVEMENT (Symphony No. 1)

BOL #63   CONCERT MATINEE
Debussy, CHILDREN'S CORNER SUITE
Corelli-Pinelli, SUITE FOR STRING ORCHESTRA: Sarabande, Gigue, Badinerie
Haydn, MINUET ("Surprise" Symphony)
Verdi, ANVIL CHORUS
Grieg, NORWEGIAN DANCE IN A (NO. 2)
Schumann, TRÄUMEREI

BOL #64   MINIATURES IN MUSIC
Zador, CHILDREN'S SYMPHONY
Schubert, THE BEE
Haydn, GYPSY RONDO
Schumann, THE WILD HORSEMAN, THE HAPPY FARMER
Couperin, LITTLE WINDMILLS

Leo, ARIETTA
Liadov, MUSIC BOX
Gounod, FUNERAL MARCH OF THE MARIONETTES
Elwell, DANCE OF THE MERRY DWARFS (Happy Hypocrite)
Villa-Lobos, LITTLE TRAIN OF CAIPIRA

BOL #65   MUSIC, USA
Copland, SHAKER TUNE (Appalachian Spring)
Thomson, CATTLE AND BLUES (Plow That Broke the Plains), FUGUE AND
    CHORALE ON YANKEE DOODLE (Tuesday in November)
McBride, PUMPKIN-EATER'S LITTLE FUGUE
Gould, AMERICAN SALUTE
Cailliet, POP! GOES THE WEASEL
Ives, LAST MOVEMENT, (Symphony No. 2)

BOL #66   ORIENTAL SCENES
Koyama, WOODCUTTER'S SONG
Donaldson, THE EMPEROR'S NIGHTINGALE
Folk tune, SAKURA

BOL #67   FANTASY IN MUSIC
Coates, THREE BEARS
Prokofiev, CINDERELLA: Sewing Scene, Cinderella's Gavotte, Midnight Waltz,
    Fairy Godmother
Donaldson, MOON LEGEND
Tchaikovsky, SLEEPING BEAUTY WALTZ

BOL #68   CLASSROOM CONCERT
Tchaikovsky, ALBUM FOR THE YOUNG
Stravinsky, DEVIL DANCE
Bartók, THREE COMPOSITIONS
Pinto, MEMORIES OF CHILDHOOD

BOL #69   MUSIC OF THE DANCE: *Stravinsky*
FIREBIRD SUITE: Koschai's Enchanted Garden, Dance of the Firebird, Dance of the
    Princesses, Infernal Dance of Koschai, Magic Sleep of the Princess Tzarevna,
    Finale: Escape of Koschai's Captives
SACRIFICIAL DANCE (The Rite of Spring)
VILLAGE FESTIVAL (The Fairy's Kiss)
PALACE OF THE CHINESE EMPEROR (The Nightingale)
TANGO, WALTZ AND RAGTIME (The Soldier's Tale)

BOL #70   MUSIC OF THE SEA AND SKY
Debussy, CLOUDS, FESTIVALS
Holst, MERCURY (The Planets)
Wagner, OVERTURE (The Flying Dutchman)
Thomson, SEA PIECE WITH BIRDS
Debussy, DIALOGUE OF THE WIND AND THE SEA (La Mer)

BOL #71   SYMPHONIC MOVEMENTS, NO. 1
Tchaikovsky, THIRD MOVEMENT, (Symphony No. 4)
Beethoven, SECOND MOVEMENT, (Symphony No. 8)
Mozart, FIRST MOVEMENT, (Symphony No. 40)
Schumann, SECOND MOVEMENT, (Symphony No. 4)
Brahms, THIRD MOVEMENT, (Symphony No. 3)
Saint-Saëns, FOURTH MOVEMENT, (Symphony No. 3)

BOL #72   SYMPHONIC MOVEMENTS, NO. 2
Dvořák, FIRST MOVEMENT, (Symphony No. 9 From the New World)
Beethoven, FIRST MOVEMENT, (Symphony No. 5)
Britten, FIRST MOVEMENT, Boisterous Bourrée (A Simple Symphony)
Hanson, SECOND MOVEMENT, (Symphony No. 2 Romantic)
Sibelius, FIRST MOVEMENT, (Symphony No. 2)

BOL #73   SYMPHONIC STYLES
Haydn, SYMPHONY NO. 99 (Imperial)
Prokofiev, CLASSICAL SYMPHONY

BOL #74   TWENTIETH CENTURY AMERICA
Copland, EL SALÓN MÉXICO
Bernstein, DANZON (Fancy Free), SYMPHONIC DANCES (excerpts) (West Side Story)
Gershwin, AN AMERICAN IN PARIS

BOL #75   U.S. HISTORY IN MUSIC
Copland, A LINCOLN PORTRAIT
Schuman, CHESTER (New England Triptych)
Ives, PUTNAM'S CAMP (Three Places in New England)
Harris, INTERLUDE (Folk Song Symphony)
Phillips, MIDNIGHT RIDE OF PAUL REVERE (Selections from McGuffey's Readers)

BOL #76   OVERTURES
Strauss, OVERTURE (The Bat)
Brahms, ACADEMIC FESTIVAL OVERTURE
Mozart, OVERTURE (The Marriage of Figaro)
Berlioz, ROMAN CARNIVAL OVERTURE
Rossini, OVERTURE (William Tell)

BOL #77   SCHEHERAZADE by *Rimsky-Korsakov*

BOL #78   MUSICAL KALEIDOSCOPE
Borodin, ON THE STEPPES OF CENTRAL ASIA
Ippolitov-Ivanov, IN THE VILLAGE (Caucasian Sketches)
Borodin, EXCERPTS, POLOVTSIAN DANCES (Prince Igor)
Glière, RUSSIAN SAILORS' DANCE (The Red Poppy)
Bizet, CARILLON, MINUET (L'Arlesienne Suite No. 1), FARANDOLE (L'Arlesienne Suite No. 2), PRELUDE TO ACT I (Carmen)
Berlioz, MARCH TO THE SCAFFOLD (Symphony Fantastique)

BOL #79   MUSIC OF THE DRAMA: *Wagner*
LOHENGRIN: Overture to Act I, Prelude to Act 3
THE TWILIGHT OF THE GODS: Siegfried's Rhine Journey
THE MASTERSINGERS OF NUREMBERG: Prelude, Dance of the Apprentices and Entrance of the Mastersingers
TRISTAN AND ISOLDE: Love Death

BOL #80   PETROUCHKA by *Stravinsky* (Complete ballet score with narration)

BOL #81   ROGUES IN MUSIC
Strauss, TILL EULENSPIEGEL
Prokofiev, LIEUTENANT KIJE SUITE: Birth of Kije, Troika

Kodály, HÁRY JÁNOS SUITE: Viennese Musical Clock, Battle and Defeat of Napoleon, Intermezzo, Entrance of the Emperor

BOL #82 MUSICAL PICTURES: *Moussorgsky,* PICTURES AT AN EXHIBITION: NIGHT ON BALD MOUNTAIN

BOL #83 ENSEMBLES, LARGE AND SMALL
Britten, YOUNG PERSON'S GUIDE TO THE ORCHESTRA
Gabrieli, CANZONA IN C MAJOR FOR BRASS ENSEMBLE AND ORGAN
Bach, CHORALE: AWAKE, THOU WINTRY EARTH
Schubert, FOURTH MOVEMENT, "TROUT" QUINTET
Kraft, THEME AND VARIATIONS FOR PERCUSSION QUARTET
Mozart, THEME AND VARIATIONS (Serenade for Wind Instruments) (K361)

BOL #84 CONCERTOS
Grieg, FIRST MOVEMENT, (Piano Concerto)
Brahms, FOURTH MOVEMENT, (Piano Concerto No. 2)
Mendelssohn, THIRD MOVEMENT, (Violin Concerto)
Castelnuovo-Tedesco, SECOND MOVEMENT, (Guitar Concerto)
Vivaldi, THIRD MOVEMENT, (Concerto in C for Two Trumpets)

BOL #85 MUSICAL IMPRESSIONS; *Respighi,* THE BIRDS (Prelude), PINES OF ROME, FOUNTAINS OF ROME

BOL #86 FASHIONS IN MUSIC
Tchaikovsky, ROMEO AND JULIET (Fantasy-Overture)
Bach, LITTLE FUGUE IN G MINOR
Ravel, SUITE NO. 2 (Daphnis and Chloe)
Mozart, ROMANZE (A Little Night Music)
Schoenberg, PERIPETIA (Five Pieces for Orchestra)

III. *RECORD COMPANIES AND SOURCES OF CATALOGS FOR EDUCATIONAL USE*

Bowmar, 4563 Colorado Blvd., Los Angeles, Calif. 90039. **Bowmar Orchestral Library** and sound filmstrips. Catalog available.

Bourne Company, 136 West 52nd St., New York, N.Y. 10019.

Capitol Records, Educational Department, Capitol Tower, 1750 North Vine St., Hollywood, Calif. 90028. Capitol and Angel Records Educational Catalog.

Children's Music Center, 5373 West Pico Blvd., Los Angeles, Calif. 90019. Records, books, and other materials. Catalog available.

Columbia Records, Inc., Educational Department, 799 Seventh Ave., New York, N.Y. 10019.

Decca Records, a division of MCA, Inc., 445 Park Ave., New York, N.Y. 10007.

Educational Activities, Inc., Box 392, Freeport, N.Y. 11520. Distributors of **Activity Records,** including Hap Palmer, **Learning Basic Skills Through Music.** Catalog available.

Educational Records Sales, 157 Chambers St., New York, N.Y. 10007.

Electra Records, 1855 Broadway, New York, N.Y. 10019.

Encyclopaedia Britannica, Inc., 425 North Michigan Ave., Chicago, Ill. 60611.

Folkcraft Records, 1159 Broad St., Newark, N.J. 07114.

Folkways Records, 43 West 64th St., New York, N.Y. 10023. Recorded music of many cultures.

The Franson Corporation, Institutional Trade Division, 225 Park Ave. South, New York, N.Y. 10003. Distributors of **Children's Record Guild** and **Young People's Records.**

Highland Music Company, 1311 North Highland Ave., Hollywood, Calif. 90028.

Mercury Record Productions, Inc., 110 West 57th St., New York, N.Y. 10019.

MGM Records, 1350 Avenue of the Americas, New York, N.Y. 10019.

Pop Hit Publications, 3149 Southern Ave., Memphis, Tenn, 38111. Listening guides utilizing popular music.

RCA Music Service, Educational Dept. A, 1133 Avenue of the Americas, New York, N.Y. 10036.

Scholastic Audio-Visual, 50 West 44th St., New York, N.Y. 10036.

Vox Productions, Inc., 211 East 43rd St., New York, N.Y. 10017. Recorded instructional units on composers.

IV. MEDIA MATERIALS, FILMS, AND FILMSTRIPS FOR EDUCATIONAL USE

AIMS Instructional Media Services, Inc., P.O. Box 1010, Hollywood, Calif. 90026.

BFA Educational Media, 2211 Michigan Ave., Santa Monica, Calif. 90404. Films featuring music of other cultures.

Bowmar, 4563 Colorado Boulevard, Los Angeles, Calif. 90039. **Bowmar Orchestral Library** and sound filmstrips. Catalog available.

Brandon Films, Inc., 221 West 57th St., New York, N.Y. 10019. Catalog available.

Contemporary Films, a division of McGraw-Hill, Inc., 330 West 42nd St., New York, N.Y. 10036; 828 Custer St., Evanston, Ill. 60202; and 1211 Polk St., San Francisco, Calif. 94109.

Coronet Films, 65 East South Water St., Chicago, Ill. 60601. Catalog available.

Creative Audio Visuals, 12000 Edgewater Drive, Cleveland, Ohio 44107, Individualized materials for music study.

Educational Audio Visual, Inc., Pleasantville, N.Y. 10570.

Educational Productions, Inc., P.O. Box 12138, Atlanta, Ga. 30305.

Educom, Ltd., Box 388, Mt. Kisco, N.Y. 10549. Transparencies for overhead projectors featuring songs and teaching units for opera.

Elkan-Vogel Co., Inc., 1712 Sansom St., Philadelphia, Pa. 19103.

EMC Corporation, 180 East Sixth St., St. Paul, Minn. 55101. Filmstrips, records, and cassettes.

Film Associates, 11559 Santa Monica Blvd., Los Angeles, Calif. 90025. Short teaching films in color.

Sam Fox Publishing Co., Inc., 1841 Broadway, New York, N.Y. 10023.

The Jam Handy Organization, 2821 East Grand Blvd., Detroit, Mich. 48211. Filmstrips with recordings.

Keyboard Publications, 1346 Chapel St., New Haven, Conn. 06511. Multimedia enrichment materials. Catalog available.

Learning Arts, P.O. Box 179, Wichita, Kan. 67201. Sound filmstrips, records, and cassettes.

Hal Leonard Publications, Inc., 5525 West Blue Mound Rd., Milwaukee, Wisc. 53213.

Library of Congress, 1291 Taylor St., N.W., Washington, D.C. 20540. Catalog to motion pictures and film strips.

McGraw-Hill Films, 1221 Avenue of the Americas, New York, N.Y. 10020.

Music Educators National Conference, 1902 Association Dr., Reston, Va. 22091. Film guide and selected lists of instructional resources; many professional publications.

National Geographic Society, Washington, D.C. 20036. Films of music in other cultures.

NET Film Service, Audio-Visual Service, Indiana University, Bloomington, Ind. 47401.

Warren Schloat Productions, Inc., 115 Tompkins Ave., Pleasantville, N.Y. 10570.

Society for Visual Education, Inc., 1345 Diversey Parkway, Chicago, Ill. 60614. Filmstrips featuring folk music in America.

Teaching Film Custodians, Inc., 25 West 43rd St., New York, N.Y. 10036. Annotated listing, "Motion Pictures for Music Classes," available on request.

Washington Films, University of Washington Press, Seattle, Wash. 98195. Films and records of music of other cultures.

H. W. Wilson Company, 950 University Ave., New York, N.Y. 10052. "The Educational Film Guide." Generally available in libraries.

V. COMPANIES SUPPLYING CLASSROOM INSTRUMENTS AND OTHER EQUIPMENT

Children's Music Center, 5373 West Pico Blvd., Los Angeles, Calif. 90019. Records, books, and other materials. Catalog available.

C. G. Conn, Ltd., 616 Enterprise Drive, Oak Brook, Ill. 60521. Guitars and other instruments.

Educational Music Bureau, Inc., 434 South Wabash Ave., Chicago, Ill. 60605.

Electronic Music Laboratories, Inc., P.O. Box H, Vernon, Conn. 06066.

Gamble Music Co., Inc., 312 South Wabash Ave., Chicago, Ill. 60604. Classroom instruments, library materials, teaching aids. Catalog available.

Hargail Music Press, 28 West 38th St., New York, N.Y. 10018. Specialists in recorders and music for recorders and other instruments.

M. Hohner, Inc., Andrews Rd., Hicksville, Long Island, N.Y. 11802. Representative for Sonor musical instruments for schools.

Hughes Dulcimer Co., 4419 West Colfax Ave., Denver, Colo. 80204. Folk instrument kits and related publications.

Jensen Mfg. Division, The Muter Co., 6601 South Laramie St., Chicago, Ill. 60638. Manufacturer of recorders.

Kitching Educational, a division of Ludwig Drum Co., 1728 North Damen Ave., Chicago, Ill. 60647. Mallet-played instruments and rhythm instruments.

Wm. Kratt Co., 988 Johnson Place, Union, N.J. 07083. Chromatic pitch pipes, harmonicas.

Lyons, 530 Riverview Ave., Elkhart, Ind. 46515. Classroom instruments of all kinds, educational recordings, other materials, and equipment. Catalog available.

Magnamusic-Baton, Inc., 10370 Page Industrial Blvd., St. Louis, Mo. 63132. Distributor of Studio 49 Orff instruments and related materials. Catalog available.

Music Education Group, 1415 Waukegan Rd., Northbrook, Ill. 60062. Autoharps and other instruments and related publications. Catalog available.

Peripole, Inc., Brown Mills, N.J. 08015. Rhythm, melody, harmony instruments, and related materials. Catalog available.

Rhythm-Band, Inc., P.O. Box 126, Forth Worth, Tex. 76101. Distributors of all kinds of classroom instruments, materials, and equipment. Catalog available.

Scientific Music Industries, Inc., 823 South Wabash Ave., Chicago, Ill. 60605. Manufacturers of Tone Educator Bells and other classroom instruments. Catalog available.

Targ and Dinner Inc., 2451 North Sacramento Ave., Chicago, Ill. 60647. Distributors of American-Prep Tone Bells.

Temporal Acuity Products, Inc., 1535 121st St., S.E., Bellevue, Wash. 98005. TAP Master rhythm training materials.

The Viking Press, 625 Madison Ave., New York, N.Y. 10022. Publishers of **The Five Sense Store,** the Aesthetic Educational Program developed by CEMREL.

Wenger Corporation, 577 Park Dr., Owatonna, Minn. 55060. Choral risers, acoustical shells, sound modules. Catalog available.

Wexler, David, and Company, 823 South Wabash Ave., Chicago, Ill. 60605.

Willis Music Co., 440 Main St., Cincinnati, Ohio 45202. Educational music, records, teaching aids. Catalog available.

The Wurlitzer Company, Music and Education Department, 1700 Pleasant St., De Kalb, Ill. 60115. Electronic pianos and other equipment.

VI. PUBLISHERS OF MUSIC FOR ELEMENTARY SCHOOLS

Alfred Publishing Company, Inc., 15335 Morrison St., Sherman Oaks, Calif. 91403. Unison and two-part music and other publications.

Associated Music Publishers, Inc., a subsidiary of G. Schirmer, Inc., 866 Third Ave., New York, N.Y. 10022. "Choral Music Catalog" lists music for children's chorus.

Belwin Mills Publishing Corporation, Melville, N.Y. 11746. Music for elementary schools including musical plays, operettas, and foreign-language music study books with records.

Bourne Company, 136 West 52nd St., New York, N.Y. 10019.

Canyon Press, Inc., Box 1235, Cincinnati, Ohio 45201. Publishers of the **Juilliard Repertory Project** and other instructional programs.

Continental Press, Inc., 520 East Brainbridge St., Elizabethtown, Pa. 17022.

European American Music Distributors Corporation, 195 Allwood Rd., Clifton, N.J. 07012. Vocal and instrumental music, Orff Schulwerk publications, recorder music. Catalog available.

Carl Fischer of Chicago, 312 South Wabash Ave., Chicago, Ill. 60604. Octavo editions and collections for unchanged voices. Catalog available.

Hargail Music Press, 28 West 38th St., New York, N.Y. 10018. Specialists in recorders and music for recorders and other instruments.

Byron Hoyt Sheet Music Service, 190 Tenth St., San Francisco, Calif. 94103.

Neil A. Kjos Music Co., 525 Busse St., Park Ridge, Ill. 60068. Collections include descants and other arrangements by Beatrice and Max Krone.

Malecki Music, Inc., 2040 Division Ave. South, Grand Rapids, Mich. 49507. Mail order service in choral music.

Marks Music Corporation, 1790 Broadway, New York, N.Y. 10019. Folk song collections, choral collections, operettas, music for recorders and other instruments. Descriptive list available.

Oxford University Press, Inc., 200 Madison Ave., New York, N.Y. 10016. Octavo editions of folk and composed music as well as song collections and musical plays.

Plymouth Music Co., 170 Northeast 33rd St., Fort Lauderdale, Fla. 33334.

Theodore Presser Company, Presser Place, Bryn Mawr, Pa. 19010. Octavo editions and collections. Some musical plays and operettas. Catalog available.

Schmitt, Hall and McCreary Co., 527 Park Ave., Minneapolis, Minn. 55415.

Shawnee Press, Inc., Delaware Water Gap, Pa. 18327. Choral collections, recordings and books for children, including a vocal sight-reading course, grades 3–5.

Southern Music Co., P.O. Box 329, San Antonio, Tex. 78292.

Warner Bros. Publications Inc., Dept. AR, 75 Rockefeller Plaza, New York, N.Y. 10019. Contemporary music for two- and three-part choruses. Catalog available.

Appendix C
Reference Material for Music Theory and Notation

I. METER AND RHYTHM

metric beat—the underlying framework of regular pulses around which the rhythm of music is organized. The beat is usually represented by one of the following symbols:

♪ = an eighth note (numerically indicated by 8).

♩ = a quarter note (numerically indicated by 4).

𝅗𝅥 = a half note (numerically indicated by 2).

tempo—the speed of the metric beat, designated by:
   a. metronome marking indicating the number of beats per minute, e.g., MM = 72.
   b. traditional Italian terms that suggest mood and type of movement as well as pace:

grave—slow, solemn
largo—very slow and broad
largamente—slow and stately
lento—slow
adagio—leisurely
andante—moderate and flowing
andantino—slight modification of
   andante, generally quicker

moderato—moderate
allegretto—moderately fast
animato—animated
allegro—quick, lively
scherzando—playful, lively
vive—lively, brisk
vivace—brisk, fast
presto—very fast

c. words qualifying the above and suggesting more definite expression:

assai—very
cantabile—in a singing manner
dolce—sweet
giocoso—humorous, playful
grazioso—graceful
leggiero—light, graceful
maestoso—majestic
meno mosso—less movement

molto—very much
non troppo—not too much
più—more
poco—little
sempre—always
sostenuto—sustained
tranquillo—calm, quiet
très—(French) very, most

d. simple English equivalents of the Italian terms.

e. variations within the established tempo indicated by:

accelerando, accel.—increase tempo gradually
ritardando, rit., rallentando, rall.—decrease tempo gradually
a tempo—in the original tempo after a change
ad libitum—at will, with freedom from strict metric regularity
rubato—fluctuating or not in strict time

f. rhythmic treatment of an individual note:

> an accent

⌢ *fermata*—hold or lengthen

sf *sforzando*—a heavy accent

meter—a systematic grouping of the metric beats.

measure—one unit of metric beats.

bar lines—vertical lines to frame the measure.

meter signature—figure given at the beginning of a composition to indicate the metric organization.

simple duple meter:

or ¢ which is *alla breve*
(sometimes called "cut time")

simple triple meter:

quadruple meter:

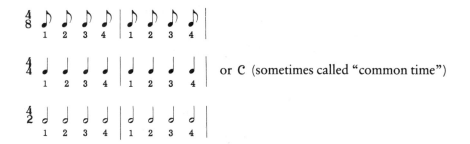

or C (sometimes called "common time")

duration—the length of time assigned to a note or rest:

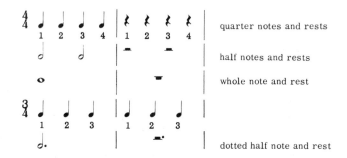

quarter notes and rests

half notes and rests

whole note and rest

dotted half note and rest

even division within the beat, showing eighth (♪) and sixteenth (♬) notes with flags and beams, rhythm syllables:

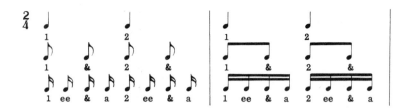

uneven division within the beat, showing the use of the *dot* to indicate the additional time of one-half the value of the note it follows, a *tie* binding together two notes on one pitch level, and eighth and sixteenth rests:

compound meters:

> *duple:*

> *triple:*

comparison of subdivided duple meter and compound duple meter:

triplet division within one beat:

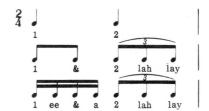

combination meters—groupings of two or three beats within one measure:

rhythm—the flow of the tones in music in short patterns or in longer phrases toward a point of release. Rhythm is related to the underlying metric structure but is not limited to it. Whereas meter is framed by measure bars, rhythm flows across them. Rhythm patterns may cut across measures.

anacrusis—an upbeat leading to the accent:

syncopation—a shift of the accent from what would be its normal position in the underlying metric scheme. Achieved by:

a. failure to begin a tone on the normal accent:

b. prolonging a tone on the unaccented part of the measure:

II. DYNAMICS

Signs and terms relating to strength of sound in music:

pianissimo (pp)—very soft

piano (p)—soft

mezzo piano (mp)—medium soft

mezzo forte (mf)—medium loud

forte (f)—loud

fortissimo (ff)—very loud

crescendo, cresc., ◁———————▷ —an increase in loudness.

diminuendo, dim., decrescendo, decresc., ▷———————◁ —a decrease in loudness.

III. PITCH

The *grand staff* and a diagram of the piano keyboard:

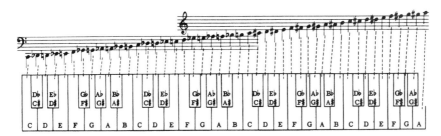

G clef establishes the pitch for higher voices. So named because a Gothic letter G was used to locate that tone on the *treble staff.*

F clef establishes the pitch for lower voices. So named because the Gothic letter F was used to locate that tone on the *bass staff.*

staff degree—a line or space on the staff, named by one of the first seven letters of the alphabet. (See grand staff, which shows names of all staff degrees on the related keyboard.)

leger line—a short line above or below the staff used to extend the range of tones notated. (See grand staff.)

octave—an interval designated by duplication of each letter name every eighth scale degree. (See grand staff.)

half-step—the tonal distance between each consecutive key (whether black or white) on the piano keyboard.

accidental—a tonal alteration of the pitch indicated by a given staff degree. Its influence lasts during the measure in which it appears and is canceled by the bar line.

sharp (♯)—raises the tone one half-step.

flat (♭)—lowers the tone one half-step.

double sharp (✖)—raises the tone one whole step.

double flat (♭♭)—lowers the tone one whole step.

natural (♮)—cancels other accidentals or the influence of a sharp or flat in the key signature.

enharmonic tones—a single pitch notated in different ways and called by two or more different names, depending on the key in which the composer is working.

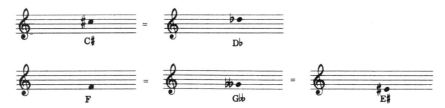

IV. SCALES AND CHORDS

major scale—a group of seven different tones in a particular pattern of whole and half steps. Half steps occur between the third and fourth and the seventh and eighth tones of the major scale:

$$1 \quad 2 \quad \overset{\wedge}{3\ 4} \quad 5 \quad 6 \quad \overset{\wedge}{7\ 8}$$

key center—the tone on which a scale is built (also called the tonic note, tonic tone, tonal center, or key-note).

scale numbers—numbers used to name the tones within a scale.

sol-fa syllables—Italian syllables naming the tones within a scale.

C-major scale (showing number, syllable, and letter names on two staves:)

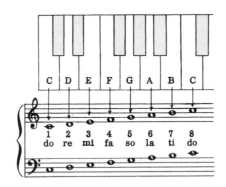

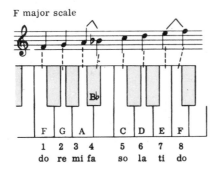

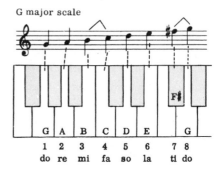

key signature—sharps or flats placed on the staff immediately after the clef sign to
designate the key center and to alter the pitches of the staff degrees to provide
the correct arrangement of whole and half steps:

common major-key signatures (in addition to those already shown):

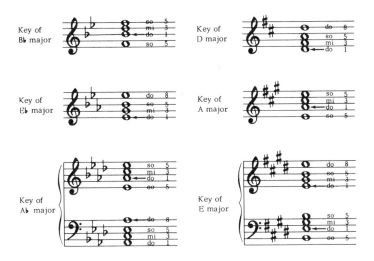

circle of keys showing the number of sharps or flats in all key signatures; major keys
shown outside circle, minor keys inside circle:

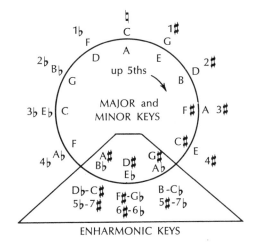

From Howard A. Murphy and Edwin J. Stringham, *Creative Harmony
and Musicianship: An Introduction to the Structure of Music* (Englewood
Cliffs, N.J.: Prentice-Hall, Inc., 1951). Used by permission.

chromatic scale—a group of twelve tones, all one half-step apart. (See grand staff under Section III, p. 000.)

sol-fa syllables for chromatic scale (showing ascending and descending forms) and hand signs for tones of the major scale:

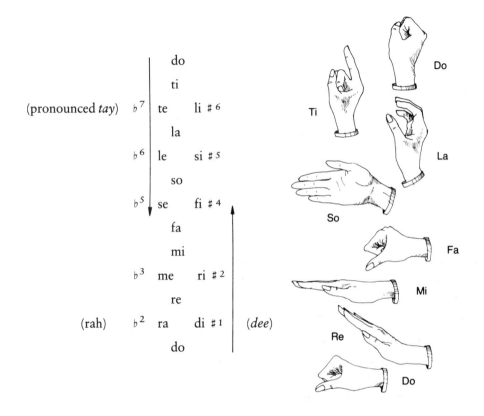

(pronounced *tay*)

(rah)

(*dee*)

interval—the distance between two tones, determined by the number of staff degrees involved.

Intervals between the key tone of the major scale and each of the other tones (illustrated for C major):

unison   second   third   fourth   fifth   sixth   seventh   octave

Qualifying sizes of intervals in the major scale (as above):

perfect (P): unison, fourth, fifth, octave.

major (M): second, third, sixth, seventh.

minor (m): one half-step smaller than major intervals.

diminished (d): one half-step smaller than minor or perfect intervals.

augmented (A): one half-step larger than major or perfect intervals.

Other common intervals between notes of the major scale:

$$3 - 5 = m3 \qquad 5 - 8 = P4$$
mi   so   so   do

$$6 - 8 = m3 \qquad 4 - 8 = P5$$
la   do   fa   do

triad—a chord of three tones, built in thirds.

root—the tone on which the chord is built.

third—the tone of the chord a third above the root.

fifth—the tone of the chord a fifth above the root.

major triad—a chord in which the lower third is major and the upper third is minor: *minor triad*—position of major and minor third reversed:

diminished chord—the triad consisting of two minor-third intervals; it occurs naturally in major keys when built on the seventh step of the scale.

augmented chord—the triad consisting of two major-third intervals.

triads of the major scale—classified as to size with scale numbers, chord numbers and names:

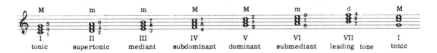

dominant seventh chord—a four-tone chord built on the fifth step of the scale:

minor scales:

    natural minor—containing the same tones as the major scale but with a tonal center a minor third lower; half-steps fall between second and third, and between fifth and sixth steps of the scale:

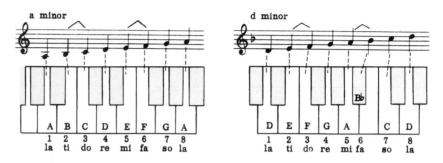

harmonic minor—same as the natural minor but with the seventh step of the scale raised so that the following pattern is formed:

(descent is the same)

melodic minor—the sixth and seventh steps of the scale are raised in ascent and unaltered in descent:

pentatonic scale—a scale built of five tones. The most common pentatonic scale represents the major scale with the fourth and seventh scale steps omitted:

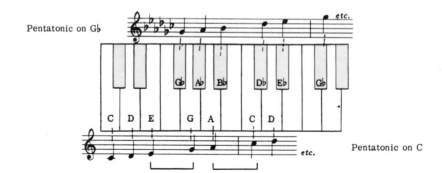

Glossary*

a cappella—choral singing without instrumental accompaniment.

acoustics—the science of sound.

Aeolian mode—a seven-tone scale represented on the piano by the white keys between A and A (the *natural minor* scale).

Alberti bass—continuous broken-chord accompaniment in the left hand of a keyboard instrument.

aleatory music—20th century music in which some elements are not specified by the composer, but, within certain limits, are left to chance or choice in the performance.

arco—playing a stringed instrument with the bow.

aria—an extended solo melody for voice with instrumental accompaniment, usually from an opera, oratorio, or cantata.

arpeggio—a chord in which the notes are played one after another in rapid succession, rather than simultaneously.

art song—a composed song in which the poetry, melody, and accompaniment are balanced and contribute mutually to the complete expressive effect.

atonality—in musical composition, the absence of any defined key center.

augmentation—the effect of slowing down the tempo of a musical subject by changing to note values twice as long.

authentic cadence—the strongest harmonic effect of arrival at the close of a musical phrase; a dominant chord in root position moving to a tonic chord in root position. Qualified as *perfect* or *full* when the melody comes to rest on the tonic note, and as *imperfect* when the melody ends on the third or fifth of the tonic chord.

ballad—a simple, narrative song of several stanzas.

band—a group of instrumental players, chiefly wind and percussion instruments.

* This list contains only terms that are not clearly defined or exemplified elsewhere in this book; please see Index of Subjects for excluded terms.

baroque—the style of art, architecture, and music following the Renaissance; generally in a grand style, highly decorated, and colorful. Applicable to much music composed between 1600 and 1750.

binary form—a basic musical form of two sections, the second being the logical completion of the first; sometimes called two-part song form.

blue notes—a characteristic of some jazz, derived from a type of early American Negro song, wherein certain degrees of the scale are used both flatted and natural, resulting in "blue notes" or chords.

bourdon—a low tone of long duration, such as the drone bass of the bagpipe.

bourrée—a 17th century French dance in quick duple meter beginning with an upbeat; used as a movement in instrument suites.

cadence—a pause or point of rest in melody and harmony; it is temporary or final, depending upon its position at the end of a phrase, period, or musical work as a whole (see "authentic cadence," "half cadence," and "plagal cadence.")

canon—meaning "according to law," the musical application of which is the exact imitation of one voice by another at the same or at a different pitch level, with each voice starting at a different time.

choir—a group of singers performing together with more than one person singing each part, or a group of related instruments.

chorale—a hymn tune characteristic of the German Protestant church.

chorale prelude—an organ composition based on a chorale melody and designed as a prelude to the congregation's singing of the chorale.

classic—in a general sense, music of established value; specifically, music of the Viennese classic period (Haydn, Mozart, Beethoven).

coda—a concluding section designed to bring a musical composition to a satisfactory close.

concerto—a large composition, generally in three movements, for one or more solo players and orchestra.

conjunct movement—melodic movement by half steps or whole steps.

consonance—a relative term, in opposition to dissonance, applied to a simultaneously sounded combination of tones that conveys stability and repose.

courante—an early French or Italian dance in quick triple meter, found as a movement in instrumental suites.

da capo or *D.C.*—indicates a return to the beginning of a composition.

dal segno or *D.S.*—indicates a return to a sign: 𝄋

diatonic—music based on a scale of seven tones within an octave, consisting of five whole steps and two half-steps in an arrangement found in the white keys on the piano.

diminution—the effect of speeding up the tempo of a musical subject by reducing the time values of all the notes by an equal amount.

disjunct movement—melodic movement by intervals larger than a whole step.

dissonance—a relative term, in opposition to consonance, applied to a simultaneously sounded combination of tones that conveys instability and disturbance.

dominant—the fifth degree of a major or minor scale.

Dorian mode—a seven-tone scale, represented on the piano by the white keys between D and D.

duet—a composition for two performers, with or without accompaniment.

electronic music—music in which some or all of the sounds are produced by electronic sound media.

ethnic music—music characteristic of a race, a nation, or a people.

etude—a study or short piece usually devoted to one special aspect of instrumental technique.

exposition—the opening section of a musical work, setting forth the musical subjects to be developed later.

finale—the last movement of a large musical work, or the final section of an operatic act.

fine—end, close.

frequency—in acoustics, the number of sound-producing vibrations per second.

fugue—a composition employing imitation, but more free than a canon. "Fugue" means "flight"; two or more parts seem to chase each other, but may diverge after each entrance.

gamelan—Balinese or Javanese musical ensembles of pitched and unpitched percussion instruments.

gigue—a movement in the early dance suite, in triple meter with some imitation.

glissando—sliding from one pitch to another vocally or on an instrument such as a violin or a trombone.

ground bass—a bass part consisting of a few notes and used as a recurring theme over which new melodies are created.

half cadence—a temporary close of a musical phrase, ending on the dominant chord and thus demanding continuation, as from a question to an answer.

harmony—the vertical relationship of simultaneously sounded tones in a musical composition (chords), their succession and the relationships between them.

harpsichord—a keyboard instrument, forerunner of the grand piano, in which the strings are sounded by a quill or leather plectrum; a characteristic instrument for Baroque music.

homophonic—the texture of music in which a single melody is supported by chords in the other parts; in contrast to polyphonic texture.

imitation—a way of writing music in which the established theme is taken up in turn by successive voices or instruments.

impressionism—a style of composition, principally by Debussy and Ravel, designed to evoke a mood or atmosphere by subtle use of musical tone color and texture and unorthodox techniques in harmony. Painting has its parallel in Monet and Renoir.

improvisation—spontaneous creation of music in performance, without reference to previously existing notation or to memory.

incidental music—instrumental music designed for performance before and between acts of a play and at necessary points within the drama.

intonation—the accuracy with which one sings or plays in tune, with an instrument or with other voices.

inversion—a change in the relative position of notes in a chord or of voice-parts in a composition; or, in a musical subject, playing all the upward intervals downward and vice versa.

jazz—an important popular musical style that evolved in the early 20th century, featuring syncopation, certain melodic nuances, and much improvisation within a basic structure.

leading tone—the seventh degree of the scale, which is a half-step below the tonic note and has a strong tendency to lead to that note.

legato—smooth and connected; indicated by a *slur* above or below a group of notes:

libretto—the text, or words, of a long composition such as an opera or an oratorio.

lied—a German word for "song."

Lydian mode—a seven-tone scale, represented on the piano by the white keys between F and F.

marcato—notes "marked" or emphasized in performance.

march—music with a simple, strong, duple rhythm, in regular phrases, designed to accompany marching.

mazurka—a Polish dance in moderate triple meter with accents on the second and third beats.

melismatic—referring to a vocal melody in which many notes are often given to one syllable in the text (also "florid.")

metronome—a mechanical or electrical device used to establish tempos in music.

mezzo—medium or half; therefore, *mezzo-piano (mp)*—medium soft; *mezzo-soprano*—medium-range soprano.

minuet—a French dance in moderate triple meter, originating about 1650; often used as a movement in early symphonies.

Mixolydian mode—a seven-tone scale, represented on the piano by the white keys between G and G.

mode, modal—an arrangement of tones in a scale, consisting of the tonal material used in a particular musical work. Major and minor scales of western European music are modes, as are pentatonic and oriental scales and the scales that are the basis of medieval church music, including Gregorian chant. The adjective *modal* usually applies to music based on the modes of medieval church music, but is not limited to church music.

modern music—music composed between 1890 and the present; a general classification, because modern music comprises a variety of styles.

modulation—moving from one key to another within a composition.

monophonic—a musical texture involving a single melodic line.

motif (motive)—a salient, germinating feature, derived from thematic material, which is expanded and developed throughout a musical work.

musique concrète—electronic music composed of natural sounds that have been modified electronically or by means of tape manipulation.

mute—a device put on, or in, an instrument to soften or modify the tone.

neighboring tone—the tone a staff degree above or below a tone in a chord the melody comes from and returns to:

obbligato—in early music the term mean "obliged," or a part not to be left out; general usage has reversed the meaning, so that it now refers to an optional ornamental part, usually on a solo instrument, accompanying a given melody.

opera—a staged drama in which music, sung dialogue, arias, and duets with instrumental accompaniment are combined with other theatrical representations (costumes, scenery, and dancing) to produce an integrated art form.

operetta—a musical-dramatic work with spoken dialogue, vocal solos, ensembles, and dancing, with instrumental accompaniment; generally with a nonserious plot and in a popular style.

opus—a "work," usually used in reference to the chronological works of a single composer.

oratorio—a serious musical-dramatic work utilizing vocal recitative, arias, chorus, duets, and so forth, with instrumental accompaniment, but without staging or costumes.

orchestra—a large group of musicians playing string, woodwind, brass, and percussion instruments.

overtone—in acoustics, a higher frequency of pitch, above the fundamental tone, which contributes to the tone color.

passing tone—a tone which is touched in passing stepwise from one chord tone to another:

pavane—a stately court dance of the Renaissance; usually in duple meter, and sometimes appearing as an introductory movement of a suite.

period—a unit of two or more phrases which presents a complete musical idea (analogous to a sentence in language). Within a period two phrases may provide contrast and balance wherein the first serves as the *antecedent* and the second the *consequent* phrase (in a sense, "question and answer").

phrase—a short musical idea with a well-defined point of arrival, but not complete in itself.

pitch—the property of musical sound determined by the rate of vibration of the sound waves, defined in terms of twelve semitones within an octave: A, A♯, B, C, and so forth.

pizzicato—playing a bowed stringed instrument by plucking the string with the finger instead of using the bow.

plagal cadence—the ending of a phrase or composition in which the subdominant chord moves to the tonic (IV-I); typified by the "amen" ending of a hymn.

polka—a lively Bohemian dance in duple meter, originating in the early 19th century.

polonaise—a stately Polish processional dance in triple meter; important as a stylized form of instrumental composition among the works of J. S. Bach, Chopin, and others.

polyphonic—the texture of music woven in horizontal melodic lines with apparent independence of each part but a compatibility of the whole.

polyrhythmic—the use of cross rhythm, two or more strikingly different rhythms employed in different parts at the same time.

polytonality—the simultaneous use of two or more keys in a single musical passage.

prelude—an introductory movement to a suite, opera, or other work; also a short independent piece for solo or instrumental ensemble.

program music—music in which the aesthetic impact of tone color, melody, rhythm, and structure (found in all music) is specifically directed to convey an idea, mental image, or feeling of the composer. Such music is sometimes accompanied by descriptive titles or program notes by the composer.

quartet—a composition for four vocal or instrumental performers.

quintet—a composition for five vocal or instrumental performers.

ragtime—a style of American popular music, usually for piano, that preceded jazz around 1900.

range—the total span of pitches from the lowest to the highest, either in a piece of music, or in the tones of a voice or an instrument.

recapitulation—in sonata form, the third section, in which the initial musical ideas return.

recitative—intoned speech, used in narrative and declamatory sections of opera or oratorio, wherein melody is abandoned in favor of a few pitches on which the words are recited; provided with a very simple instrumental accompaniment.

repeat—a sign indicating that the passage is to be repeated:

resolution—movement from an active or dissonant note or chord to one of consonance and stability.

rest—a symbol representing silence in music.

retrograde—reversal of order in the tones of a musical subject.

rococo—ornamental 18th century architecture, furniture, and music of elegance and refinement; in music, also called the "gallant style," represented by some aspects of some compositions by Haydn and Mozart.

romanticism—the characteristic style in literature, art, and music of the 19th century, representing a break with formalism and classical aims in favor of individual expression of sentiment and imagination, characterized by music with programmatic implications, rich orchestral sonority, full and somewhat blurred outlines in harmony.

rondo—the form resulting from a prescribed repetition of different sections in a composition. Usually the first section is heard alternately with other sections: A B A C A D A, and so forth.

scherzo—a lively, humorous composition in triple meter, often used as the third movement in a sonata or symphony.

score—the composite musical notation for a piece that involves several or many different parts.

semitone—a half-step, the smallest interval in the tonal system of western European music.

sequence—the reproduction of a pattern of tones at a higher or lower pitch level.

sextet—a composition for six vocal or instrumental performers.

sine-wave—a sound wave that produces a pure tone incapable of further simplification; it is generated electronically.

slur—a curved line over two or more notes, indicating that they are to be sung on one syllable or played smoothly.

solo—a composition for one vocal or instrumental performer, with or without accompaniment.

sonata—a composition for one or two instruments, generally in three independent but related sections called movements. The first and often the second or third movements are in "sonata form," the most important organizational plan in musical composition of the 18th and 19th centuries.

square-wave—a complex tone, consisting of an infinite number of sine-waves; produced electronically.

staccato—a note to be played short, not connected; indicated by dots above or below the notes:

staff—the horizontal lines and intervening spaces on which music notation is written (see Appendix C-III).

strophic—the form of a song in which all stanzas of the text are sung to the same music; the opposite of "through-composed."

subdominant—the fourth degree of a major or minor scale.

suite—a group of related compositions. (a) The *dance suite* is a group of contrasting dances. (b) The *ballet suite* is a concert rearrangement of music from a ballet. (c) The *programmatic suite* consists of separate compositions related to a single story or descriptive idea.

suspension—the effect achieved when a tone in the melody or one or more tones of a chord are held over as the harmony changes in the other parts.

syllabic—referring to a vocal melody in which each syllable of the text is given one note; the opposite of "melismatic."

symphonic poem—a one-movement, programmatic composition for orchestra (see program music).

symphony—a composition for full orchestra, usually in four movements: a "sonata" for orchestra.

synthesizer—an electronic apparatus that generates sounds used in electronic music.

ternary form—a basic musical form in three sections, each complete within itself, and the third a repeat of the first: A B A; also called *three-part song form.*

terraced dynamics—an immediate, marked change in strength of sound, often achieved by alternating a solo with group performance; a characteristic of baroque music.

tessitura—the general range of a voice part, not taking into account occasional extremes of high or low.

theme—a distinctive melody which is a basic factor in a large musical composition such as a sonata or fugue; also "subject."

three-part song form—see ternary form.

through-composed—a song in which the music is written throughout to conform as closely as possible to the meaning and feeling of the text. Many art songs are through-composed (see strophic).

tonality—the characteristic of musical composition that establishes one tone as a tonal center to which all other tones are related.

tone cluster—a group of pitches, very close together, sounded simultaneously.

transpose—to change a section of music to a new pitch level and key.

treble—the highest part in a choral composition, or an instrument or voice performing in a high range.

trio—a composition for three vocal or instrumental performers.

troubadour—an aristocratic poet or poet-musician in southern France during the middle ages.

two-part song form—see binary form.

unison—the relationship of tones having the same pitch. Different voices or instruments simultaneously playing or singing the same melody do so "in unison."

variation—a change or elaboration of an established melody or rhythm.

waltz—a dance in triple meter.

white noise—a sound utilizing every audible frequency at the same intensity.

Subject Index

Index of Songs, Poems, and Stories

Index of Instrumental Music
Used in Musical Examples

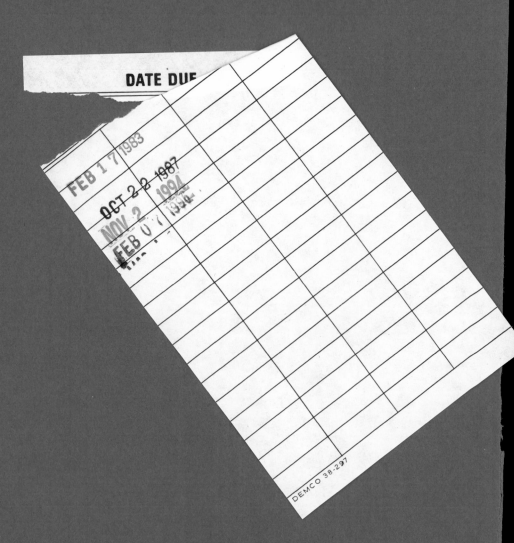